CAMBRIDGE GREEK

HOMER
ILIAD

BOOK XXII

EDITED BY

IRENE J. F. DE JONG

Professor of Ancient Greek
University of Amsterdam

CAMBRIDGE
UNIVERSITY PRESS

University Printing House, Cambridge CB2 8BS, United Kingdom

Published in the United States of America by Cambridge University Press, New York

Cambridge University Press is part of the University of Cambridge.

It furthers the University's mission by disseminating knowledge in the pursuit of education, learning and research at the highest international levels of excellence.

www.cambridge.org
Information on this title: www.cambridge.org/9780521709774

© Irene J. F. de Jong 2012

First published 2012
Reprinted 2013

Printed in the United Kingdom by Print on Demand, World Wide

A catalogue record for this publication is available from the British Library

Library of Congress Cataloguing in Publication data
Homer.
[Iliad. Book 22]
Iliad. Book XXII / Homer ; edited by Irene J. F. de Jong.
p.   cm. – (Cambridge Greek and Latin classics)
Text in Greek; introduction and commentary in English.
Includes bibliographical references and indexes.
ISBN 978-0-521-88332-0 (hardback) – ISBN 978-0-521-70977-4 (paperback)
1. Achilles (Greek mythology) – Poetry.   2. Trojan War – Poetry.   3. Homer. Iliad. Book 22.
I. Jong, Irene J. F. de.   II. Title.   III. Series.
PA4020.P22   2012
883′.01 – dc23   2011029431

ISBN 978-0-521-88332-0 Hardback
ISBN 978-0-521-70977-4 Paperback

CONTENTS

PREFACE

Some thirty years ago I applied for a grant to write a thesis that would consist of a commentary on *Iliad* 22. I was not awarded the grant and when a rumour started to spread that a team under the supervision of Geoffrey Kirk was preparing a commentary on the whole *Iliad* I turned my attention to another topic, the application of narratology to Homer. Given this history, it was with great joy that I accepted the invitation of the series editors Pat Easterling and Richard Hunter to write a 'Green and Yellow' on this very book.

I have focused on two aspects in this commentary: Homer's language (especially his oral syntax, the meaning of words, and the function of particles) and narrative style (for instance the structure of scenes, the relationship of narrator and characters, and the directing of the narratees' emotional response). Much important work has been done in the field of the language of the Homeric epics in the last decades. Thus, the invaluable *Lexikon des frühgriechischen Epos* was finally completed in 2010, and this treasure-trove of information deserves to be introduced more fully into English-speaking Homeric scholarship. I feel a special attachment to this formidable instrument because I spent a very pleasant and formative year as stipendiary in Hamburg, working on lemmata like θέλγω and ἰσόθεος. Our understanding of Greek particles has advanced greatly since the publication of Denniston's standard text, not least, if some chauvinism is allowed, thanks to the work of Dutch scholars on τε, περ, μήν, δή, and ἄρα. Finally, the insight has dawned that we should approach the oral syntax of Homer somewhat differently from that of later, written texts. It is a flow through time rather than a structure on the space of a page, and keeping this principle in mind can help us to appreciate and better understand the construction of his sentences.

Where the literary interpretation of Homer is concerned, a commentator finds herself in a land of plenty: the quantity of excellent scholarship is simply overwhelming. I have tried to summarise what I have read over the last thirty years as clearly and attractively as possible. Of course, I have profited considerably from the work of earlier commentators: Ameis-Hentze, Leaf, Richardson, and the recent Basler Kommentar (though not yet for book 22).

The introductory sections are geared to students and offer no more than a state-of-the-art summary of some central aspects of Homeric scholarship. Bibliographical references should lead the way to more in-depth discussions. Where the commentary is concerned I hope to facilitate and enrich students' reading of the Homeric text, while at the same time proposing new insights and springboards for new interpretations or research to professional classicists.

In writing this commentary I have been very fortunate in my readers and advisers. In the first place, Pat Easterling and Richard Hunter offered comments on yearly instalments of my draft quickly, cheerfully, and expertly. Where the minutiae of the Homeric language and metre were concerned, I was happy to be able to consult my former colleague Frits Waanders. Three colleagues and friends read the entire draft: Rutger Allan, Marietje van Erp Taalman Kip, and Sebastiaan van der Mije. They saved me from many errors, and their perceptive questions and constructive remarks helped me to rethink my text at innumerable places. I would also like to thank Elizabeth Upper for polishing my English. I take full responsibility for all remaining infelicities of expression. The cross-references were checked by David van Eijndhoven and (again) Marietje van Erp Taalman Kip. I also owe much gratitude to Dr. Andrew Dyck for his exemplary copy-editing. A grant of the Loeb Classical Library Foundation allowed me to finish the MS in a term without teaching obligations.

A special word of thanks is due to one of my readers. The thesis on *Iliad* 22 that I referred to earlier was designed as a two-person project for Sebastiaan van der Mije and myself. Although that project was never realised and we have never officially worked together, he has read and commented upon draft versions of much of my work in the past thirty years. I have no hesitation in claiming that his acute eye, literary sensibility, and unfailing generosity in sharing his time and ideas with me have greatly contributed to its quality. It is therefore with the greatest pleasure and gratitude that I dedicate this book to him.

Amsterdam   I. J. F. d. J.
August 2011

ABBREVIATIONS

BK	Bierl, A., Latacz, J., eds. *Homers Ilias Gesamtkommentar* (Basler Kommentar) Latacz, J., Nünlist, R., Stoevesandt, M. 2000. *Band 1. Erster Gesang*, München-Leipzig Brügger, C., Stoevesandt, M., Visser, E. 2003. *Band II. Zweiter Gesang*, München-Leipzig Krieter-Spiro, M. 2009. *Band III. Dritter Gesang*, Berlin-New York Stoevesandt, M. 2008. *Band IV. Sechster Gesang*, Berlin-New York Coray, M. 2009. *Band VI. Neunzehnter Gesang*, Berlin-New York Brügger, C. 2009. *Band VIII. Vierundzwanzigster Gesang*, Berlin-New York
DELG	Chantraine, P. 1968. *Dictionnaire étymologique de la langue Grecque*, Paris
GH	Chantraine, P. 1958–1963. *Grammaire Homérique*, I-II, 3rd edn, Paris
GP	Denniston, J. P. 1959. *The Greek Particles*, 2nd edn, Oxford
KG	Kühner, R., Gerth, B. 1898–1904. *Ausführliche Grammatik der griechischen Sprache. Zweiter Teil: Satzlehre*, I-II, 3rd edn, Hannover-Leipzig
LfgrE	1955–2010. *Lexikon des frühgriechischen Epos*, Göttingen
LIMC	Ackermann, H. C., Gisler, J. R., eds. 1981–1999. *Lexicon Iconographicum Mythologiae Classicae*, Zürich
scholia	Erbse, H. 1969–88. *Scholia Graeca in Homeri Iliadem*, Berlin, New York

The following editions of and commentaries on the *Iliad* or *Odyssey* are referred to by name of author(s) only

Ameis-Hentze	Ameis, K. F., Hentze, C. 1922. *Homers Ilias für den Schulgebrauch erklärt, Gesang 22–24*, 5th edn, Leipzig-Berlin
Edwards	Edwards, M. W. 1991. *The Iliad. A Commentary. Vol. V: Books 17–20*, Cambridge
Janko	Janko, R. 1992. *The Iliad. A Commentary, Vol. IV: Books 13–16*, Cambridge
de Jong	de Jong, I. J. F. 2001. *A Narratological Commentary on the Odyssey*, Cambridge
Kirk	Kirk, G. S. 1985. *The Iliad. A Commentary, Vol. I: Books 1–4*, Cambridge 1990. *The Iliad. A Commentary, Vol. II: Books 5–8*, Cambridge
Leaf	Leaf, W. 1900–1902. *The Iliad* I-II, 2nd edn, London
Macleod	Macleod, C. W. 1982. *Homer: Iliad Book xxiv*, Cambridge

Pulleyn   Pulleyn, S. 2000. *Homer, Iliad Book One*, Oxford
Richardson   Richardson, N. J. 1993. *The Iliad. A Commentary, Vol. VI: Books 21–24*, Cambridge
West   West, M. L. 1998, 2000. *Homerus Ilias*, 1–2, Stuttgart-Leipzig

INTRODUCTION

1. HOMER, THE HOMERIC EPICS,
AND LITERARY INTERPRETATION

(a) Homer

The life and times of the poet who created the Homeric epics are shrouded in mystery, as they have been since antiquity. He himself is partly to blame for this, in that he never mentions his name or gives any other personal information. The name Homer at some point in the seventh or sixth century BC came to be connected to the poems that are called *Iliad* and *Odyssey* (the titles are found for the first time we know of in Herodotus *Histories* 2.116), and more than one place in Ionia, most prominently Smyrna and Chios, claimed Homer as its native son. He was supposed to have lived at any time between the fall of Troy (traditionally placed in the twelfth century BC) and the seventh century. Some *Lives of Homer* are known from Roman imperial times, but they are worthless as historical sources because they are largely composed out of elements taken from the poems themselves (the boy Homer is taught by Phemius, a name suspiciously similar to that of the singer in Odysseus' palace, and travels together with someone called Mentes, recalling Odysseus' old friend and advisor of Telemachus, etc.).[1] More than once it has even been suggested that Homer never existed; a recent proponent of this view argues that he was the creation of a group of professional performers called 'the descendants of Homer (*Homeridai*)', who thus endowed themselves with a mythical forefather. The name Homer, not common in Greek, would be their reinterpretation of the designation ὁμηρίδαι, which originally referred to professionals singing at a *ὅμαρος, 'assembly of the people'.[2] Conversely, some think there may have been two 'Homers', one composing the *Iliad*, the other the *Odyssey*.[3]

Modern scholarship concurs with antiquity in placing Homer in Ionia, on account of the predominance of Ionian forms in his language;[4] however, his dates remain contested. Can archaeology perhaps be of help? Here we must distinguish between the world created by Homer in his poems and the world in which Homer himself lived. As for the first, modern opinions vary between considering the setting of the Homeric epics by and large Mycenaean (1600–1200 BC), 'dark age' (1200–900 BC), eighth- or early seventh-century, or an amalgam. The dating of Homer's own world would seem to be revealed by an awareness of

---

[1] For these biographies see Latacz (1996) 24–30; in general for ancient views on Homer see Graziosi (2002).

[2] West (1999).　　[3] For a summary of the discussion see e.g. Garvie (1994) 2–3.

[4] One of the few exceptions is West (1988) 166–72, who argues for Euboea, an island opposite the east coast of Attica and Boeotia, as the place of origin of the Homeric epics.

some particular material circumstances not found before the later eighth or early seventh century, including temples, cult statues, and a geography that includes the Black Sea and Sicily.[5] When we turn, finally, to linguistic criteria, the picture again is highly complicated, and features have been differently evaluated.[6] The conclusion must be fairly vague: Homer seems to have lived somewhere between 800 and 700 BC.

(b) The Homeric epics

More consensus than on the date of Homer seems to have been reached on the oral background of his poems. The important figures here are the Americans Milman Parry and Albert Lord. Parry wrote a dissertation in Paris in 1928 in which he argued that the *Iliad* and *Odyssey* were the product of a long tradition of oral-formulaic poetry. Both ideas, that the Homeric epics were oral and that they for a large part consisted of formulas, recurrent standard phrases employed at the same position in the verse ('swift-footed Achilles'), had been ventured before, but Parry laid bare the system for the first time in great detail. Moreover he went to Yugoslavia to look for comparative material among the still existing oral traditions there, an approach continued by his pupil Lord after his premature death.[7]

Parry's theory of the oral-formulaic nature of Homeric composition put an end to a debate that had divided Homerists ever since Friedrich August Wolf's publication of his *Prolegomena ad Homerum* in 1795.[8] In this treatise the German scholar argued that the poems were put together by a compiler living long after Homer, who himself had been a singer of short epic songs. Before Wolf the Italian philosopher Giambattista Vico (1668–1744) had already argued that the epics were the products not of an individual poet but rather of an entire people, while the 1769 *Essay on the Original Genius and Writings of Homer* by the British traveller and politician Robert Wood claimed that Homer had been illiterate and the epics had been transmitted orally. Wolf's ideas were worked out by the so-called Analysts, who broke each of the poems up into separate layers and attributed older ones to Homer himself and younger ones to later singers or editors. They used linguistic, historical-archaeological, and also aesthetic criteria to distinguish between different poets. Thus, they pointed to forms deriving from different phases of the Greek language and to incongruities in customs such as cremation

---

[5] For an overview of the positions in both debates see e.g. Crielaard (1995) or Osborne (2004).

[6] See e.g. Janko (1982), Horrocks (1997), and Ruijgh (1995).

[7] See Parry (1971) and Lord (1960), (1995). A still very readable introduction to the subject is Kirk (1962).

[8] For a translation with introduction see Grafton-Most-Zetzel (1985). For an overview of the debate see e.g. Dodds (1954), Heubeck (1974) 1–130, and Fowler (2004).

versus inhumation. Where aesthetic criteria were concerned, the rule of thumb employed was that good poetry derives from the original poet, bad poetry from a second-rate epigone or redactor. A particularly vexed question concerned the many repeated lines or sets of lines, which already had much occupied critics before them, including the ancient Alexandrian scholar Aristarchus. Attempts were made to determine which repeated lines were original and which were (clumsily) re-used.

Unfortunately, the Analysts could not agree on what was good or bad, and their criticism was often a subjective affair. It was this subjectivism that their opponents, the Unitarians, held against them. They stressed the carefully planned design, consistent artistic quality, and hence essential unity of the poems, which must be the work of one masterly poet. Some Unitarians made lasting contributions to our insight into Homeric artistry.[9] However, often the Unitarian responses to the analytic attacks made use of the same subjective aesthetic arguments: they simply proclaimed beautiful what their opponents had considered bad poetry. Moreover, they were as bothered by repetitions or loosely constructed scenes as the Analysts.

It was this debate between the Analysts and Unitarians which was relegated to the background by the theory of the oral-formulaic composition of the Homeric epics developed by Parry and countless other 'oralist' scholars in his wake. Briefly put, this theory sketches the picture of a singer who, forming part of a long tradition, composed, after long training and some form of premeditation, poems *while performing*. He was able to do so because he could use 'prefabricated' elements, such as the formula and the so called type-scene, a more or less standard combination of narrative elements describing recurrent events like preparing a ship, putting on armour, or receiving a guest.

Parry already suspected that the tradition was ancient, but only the decipherment of Linear B in 1952 enabled scholars to see how old it was: the Homeric epics turned out to preserve expressions current in Mycenaean times, e.g. ἄρουρα (a-ro-u-ra), δέπας (di-pa), φάσγανον (pa-ka-na), ἄναξ (wa-na-ka), etc. Prosodic irregularities likewise could be explained when reconstructing a Mycenaean original (the formula Διΐ μῆτιν ἀτάλαντος, with irregularly long -ι and -ιν, goes back to Διϝεὶ μῆτιν ʰατάλαντος). Linguistics therefore confirmed what archaeology had already shown for certain objects, places, and customs, i.e. that the Greek epic tradition must reach back at least to that era (and presumably to even older times; see the end of the next section). After the destruction of the palaces around 1100 BC it was transported by migrating Greeks from the Greek mainland, via Aeolia (the north coast of present-day Turkey) to Ionia (the middle and south coast). The contours of this movement can be traced on the basis of the various dialects that together form the Homeric *Kunstsprache* (see 4a).

---

[9] See e.g. Schadewaldt (1966) and Bassett (1938).

The oral-formulaic theory was able to explain the repetitions and inconsistencies that had so occupied the Analysts and Unitarians. The oral nature of the composition, the singer 'improvising' his song, accounts for the large role played by repetition, while the length of the tradition in combination with the adherence to stock formulas over time explains why old (linguistic, historical, or archaeological) features are found next to late ones. Yet not all problems have been solved, and new ones have arisen. One of the issues not yet settled is the context in which Homer's performance must be situated. Some have wanted to start from the singers depicted in the *Odyssey*, Phemius on Ithaca and Demodocus on Scheria. The latter in particular, the highly esteemed blind singer, has often been taken for Homer's alter ego, albeit an idealised one. If this comparison is valid, we could imagine Homer to be a singer who was based at an aristocratic court, sang epic lays after dinner, and was rewarded by a meal and general esteem. Were the exceptionally long Homeric epics commissioned in the eighth century BC by an Ionian aristocrat who wanted a last, nostalgic depiction of his lifestyle that was about to disappear?[10]

Almost the exact opposite view is that the Homeric epics were composed for one of the Panhellenic festivals that came into existence during the seventh century BC in Ionian places like Delos or Mycale. It was in these new festivals, drawing large audiences from all levels of society, that Homer found the incentive and the occasion to compose not the kind of two-hour lays produced by his predecessors, but long and complex poems.[11] Interestingly enough, this performance setting may likewise be 'illustrated' from the poems themselves, where we see Demodocus sing in the course of athletic games (*Od.* 8.250–369). What does single out the Homeric epics when compared with their fictional counterparts within the texts themselves is their length. More on this will be said in section 2a.

Another question that still is not settled concerns the *exact* origin of the text: how did his performance text become a written text? Did the master himself use writing, did he dictate his poems, did his pupils memorise his texts until they were written down (somewhere between the seventh and the end of the sixth century BC, when the Athenian tyrant Pisistratus instituted the Panathenaic festival where the Homeric epics were recited)? Or should we give up the idea of ever being able to reconstruct Homer's archetype and content ourselves with a multiform text, the final product of a long process of oral *and* textual transmission, attributed to Homer but actually shaped by generations of poets, and not really coming to an end until the classical or perhaps even Hellenistic period? This new 'Homeric question' is – again – a battlefield where scholars cross swords no less fiercely than did the Analysts and Unitarians.[12]

---

[10] Latacz (1995), (1996) 65–6.   [11] Taplin (1992).
[12] See e.g. Jensen (1980) 128–71, Kirk I 10–16, Nagy (1996), Janko (1998), West (2001). For a detailed overview of the debate see Reece (2005).

(c) The literary interpretation of an oral text

Another new problem was that, although the large body of work done since 1928 on formulaic aspects of the *Iliad* and *Odyssey* had much increased understanding of these works qua oral compositions, it seemed to have lessened appreciation of Homer's artistry; could one still speak of individual and conscious artistic intent? Parry's main object of investigation was the noun-epithet formula, 'swift-footed Achilles', 'much-enduring Odysseus', and the like. The choice between epithets, he argued, is determined by metrical factors. As a rule, there is one noun-epithet combination for each case of a name or noun, for each metrical slot in the verse and metrical condition. Thus for the name of Odysseus in the nominative we have six different formulas, for four different slots: διογενὴς Ὀδυσσεύς, πολύτλας δῖος Ὀδυσσεύς, πολύμητις Ὀδυσσεύς (or if a preceding syllable needed to be long: πτολίπορθος Ὀδυσσεύς), ἐσθλὸς Ὀδυσσεύς (or if a preceding syllable needed to be long: δῖος Ὀδυσσεύς). For Parry this implied that literary critics should not attach a specific, contextually determined significance to the epithet. Later critics, generalising this claim, decreed that the Homeric poems *as a whole* could no longer be interpreted according to normal literary standards but required a new oral poetics.

Unfortunately, such an oral poetics was not available. The only thing scholars could come up with was a wealth of negative prescriptions: there was a ban not only on contextually significant epithets but also on long-range cross-references, intentional repetition of lines and scenes, and the concept of an overarching structure. An oral poet could only think some lines ahead, an oral audience only remember some lines before. Thus, at the height of Parryism with its flux of technical studies, a sharp drop in literary studies was discernible.

Only gradually were strategies developed to find a way back to literary appreciation of the Homeric epics. One consists of largely ignoring the oral-formulaic background of the epics.[13] Another, very fruitful and widespread, demonstrates Homer's individual genius precisely in the subtle and effective use he makes of the traditional, oral style: it sees Homer as master, not slave of his tradition.[14] Yet another consists of looking at the texts as narratives: thinking in terms of a narrator telling a story to narratees (rather than a poet of flesh and blood speaking to an audience) makes the distinction between an oral or a written genesis less pertinent and opens the way to a full appreciation of Homer's artistry.[15] More will be said about this narrator and his narratees in section 3a.

Two other actual currents in Homeric literary interpretation deserve to be mentioned. The first is neo-analysis, which seeks to trace back elements in the

---

[13] An eloquent and influential proponent is Griffin (1980).
[14] The list of scholars who have adopted this approach is too long to be given here but see e.g. Edwards (1980), (1987), Martin (1989), and Taplin (1992).
[15] E.g. de Jong (2004), (2001), Richardson (1990), Scodel (2002), and Grethlein (2006) 160–310.

Homeric epics to other, earlier, putative poems within the oral tradition (for instance an *Aethiopis*, featuring the Ethiopian king Memnon, who comes to Troy as ally of the Trojans, kills Antilochus, close companion of Achilles, and is then killed himself by Achilles). Evidence for these poems is extracted and extrapolated mainly from the so-called Epic Cycle (a group of originally independent hexametric poems by different authors dealing with episodes of the Trojan war and its aftermath, which is known to us only in the form of a few fragments and summaries by a later scholar named Proclus) and painted images from pottery.[16] The poems of the Epic Cycle have traditionally been seen as post-Homeric, filling in the gaps left by the *Iliad* and *Odyssey*. Recently it has been argued that they may have developed *at the same time* as the Homeric poems, the Homeric and Cyclic traditions mutually influencing each other.[17] Though much must remain speculation in this field, neo-analysis has made clear that Homer was not only working in an *old* tradition (Parry's point) but also in a *broad* tradition, and that his audience would have been familiar with other versions and episodes.

Another important factor to bear in mind when interpreting the Homeric epics is that of their oriental and Indo-European 'roots'. The Greek epic tradition to which Homer belongs was certainly considerably influenced by poetic traditions from the East or, to put it more accurately, formed part of a common Mediterranean literary culture.[18] Shared features include not only motifs, such as the descent into the underworld or the loss of a dear comrade (both also encountered in the *Epic of Gilgamesh*), but also matters of literary technique, such as the epithet or comparison. Before starting to interact with eastern traditions Greek language and culture had formed part of an Indo-European world, including its poetic traditions, as 'Indo-European' formulas like ἱερὸν μένος or κλέος ἄφθι-τον witness.[19] This insight only increases the fascination of the Homeric epics: although they are traditionally seen as the first work of Western literature, they must now be understood to encapsulate centuries of Eastern and Indo-European story-telling.

2. BOOK 22 AND THE STRUCTURE OF THE *ILIAD*

(a) Length and pace

One of the hallmarks of the Homeric epics, which probably sets them apart from other epic texts (and certainly from their fictional counterparts, the songs of Demodocus in *Odyssey* 8), is their length and monumental scale. The *Iliad* counts some 15,700 lines, which take up twenty-five hours to perform, the *Odyssey* 12,000. The length is the result of a leisured style of narration: much of the story is told scenically, with the narrator meticulously recording all actions of his heroes and

---

[16] See e.g. Kullmann (1984), Danek (1998), and West (2003).
[17] Burgess (2001) and (2009).
[18] See e.g. Burkert (1992), West (1997), and Haubold (2002).   [19] See West (2007).

heroines (including such mundane and recurrent ones as dressing or eating) and quoting many of their speeches (in the *Iliad* no less than 45 per cent of the text is taken up by direct speech). Only at times, in the *Iliad* mainly at the beginning and end, does the Homeric narrator accelerate: the nine days of the plague wreaking havoc in the Greek camp are presented in one line (1.53), as are the nine days of lamentation for Hector (24.784). In between, four days packed with dramatic events take centre stage. Indeed, at moments of high tension the narrator may even further decrease his tempo. A famous example is found at the moment when Andromache faints at the sight of Hector dragged lifeless behind Achilles' chariot and the narrator describes in detail her headdress and recalls the glitter of her wedding (22.468–72).

Despite the length of his story the Homeric narrator has managed to give it a tight structure and build up tension, in short to 'enthral' his narratees, much as Odysseus does with his Phaeacian listeners (*Od.* 13.2). The repetition of words, the recurrence of themes and motifs, the parallelism of scenes, and prolepses (anticipations) of events to come or analepses (flashbacks) of events already told are important means of connecting episodes.[20] At the same time, he manages to include the Trojan War as a whole through recollections and anticipations of characters and through scenes which mirror events which must have taken place before and after the *Iliad*: the Catalogue of Ships recalls the departure from Aulis; the Teichoskopia evokes the beginning of the war; the duel between Paris and Menelaus calls to mind the origin of the Trojan war; Hector prophesies Achilles' death; Priam and Andromache foresee the fall of Troy.

Book 22 arguably is the climax of this whole structure, recounting the event to which much of the *Iliad* has been building up: the confrontation between Hector and Achilles, which brings both the revenge for Patroclus (which Achilles had been seeking from book 18 onwards) and the death of Hector (which Andromache had already feared in book 6). At the same time, the death of Achilles himself and the fall of Troy loom large in this book. Thus, although the *Iliad*, famously, covers only a segment of the Trojan War, book 22 is at the heart of both poem and war.

(b) The plot of the Iliad: *Zeus's will and Achilles' anger* [21]

The narrator announces as the subject of his song the anger (*mēnis*) of Achilles, which will lead to the death of many Greeks and Trojans, notably Patroclus and Hector, though their names are not mentioned. Book 1 recounts the origin of this anger: Agamemnon's refusal to give back the captive Chryseïs to her father

[20] For overviews of prolepses and analepses in the *Iliad* see Duckworth (1933) and Reichel (1994).

[21] On the plot see e.g. Schadewaldt (1966), Owen (1947), Mueller (1984) 28–76, and Latacz (1996) 71–133.

Chryses, the priest of Apollo; the plague sent by the god as punishment; and the quarrel between Achilles, who urges Agamemnon to heed the seer Calchas' interpretation of the plague and give back Chryseïs, and Agamemnon, who demands to be given another slave girl and takes Achilles' own captive Briseïs. A furious Achilles resigns from the war and asks his mother Thetis to implore Zeus temporarily to help the Trojans. Reluctantly Zeus accepts Thetis' request and from that point on Achilles' mortal anger has become part of Zeus's divine will (*Dios boulē*). The exact content of the god's plan is not revealed right away: its contours become clear only gradually, probably because the narrator wants to disclose it step by step to his narratees rather than because Zeus devises it slowly. Although not completely informed from the beginning, these narratees of course know more than the mortal characters. At this stage Zeus's plan consists of supporting the Trojans until the Greeks honour Achilles again (1.509–10).

Book 2 sees the start of the execution of his plan: Zeus manages to rouse the Greeks into action via a deceitful Dream. In typical Homeric manner the plot is almost immediately sidetracked (an instance of misdirection),[22] however, in that a duel between Paris and Menelaus threatens to end the war and hence abort Zeus's plan (book 3). When Paris is mysteriously whisked away from the battlefield by Aphrodite, the Greeks proclaim themselves the winners and a pre-ordained truce ensues. At the opening of book 4, the pro-Greek goddess Athena makes one of the Trojans break the truce and general fighting finally starts. But again the plot does not take its expected course, since it is one of the Greek generals, Diomedes, who is awarded an *aristeia* (a moment of excellence, of being the *aristos*) by the narrator, killing many Trojans (book 5). He is so destructive that Hector leaves the battlefield and goes back to Troy in order to ask his mother to bring a sacrifice to Athena, hoping to enlist this goddess's help (book 6). While in town he also meets Helen and his wife Andromache, and this episode, showing Hector as son, brother-in-law, and husband, brings him close to the narratees, who will thereby all the more come to see his death as tragic.

After some skirmishes and the building of a wall around the Greek camp, which will play a central role in ensuing battles (book 7), book 8 sees the start of the second of the four major days of battle in the *Iliad*, which will last until book 10 and finally bring the Trojans their military successes. Zeus not merely supports the Trojans, he actively protects and gives glory to Hector, who is thus clearly marked as the major instrument in executing his plan. But the dire consequences of this role are hinted at almost immediately, when Zeus reveals to the pro-Greek goddess Hera, who complains about the Greek losses, that Hector will only be stopped when Achilles returns to the battlefield to fight over the dead Patroclus (8.473–7). Although it is not yet spelled out, Hector's death is here adumbrated. Zeus's will also turns out to give an entirely new twist to Achilles' *mēnis*: it will come to an end not so much when the Greeks honour him again (Thetis' initial

---

[22] See Morrison (1992).

idea) but when he has to avenge his beloved friend Patroclus. The insight here provided to the narratees allows them to see the tragic nature of what will follow; the characters involved either never come to understand the true nature of things, or understand only when it is too late (see sections d and e).

The Trojans are very successful and, brimming with confidence, camp outside the city for the first time since the start of the war. Their superiority leads to panic in the Greek camp, and Agamemnon tries to persuade Achilles to join the action again (book 9). He sends an embassy and promises to give back Briseïs, offering many gifts as compensation. This looks like the moment Thetis had hoped for, when the Greeks would honour Achilles again, but Achilles does not accept Agamemnon's offer. He sticks to his decision to refrain from fighting, but makes one concession that contains the seed for later developments: he will return to action when Hector reaches his ships and sets them on fire.

Book 11 then launches the third major day of battle, which will last until the end of book 18. Hector is informed by the messenger of the gods Iris that Zeus supports him 'until he will reach the Greek ships and the sun sets' (11.208–9). As is shown by his subsequent behaviour, Hector primarily understands this to mean that he will reach his goal, i.e. to seize the Greek ships. However, the narratees may pay more attention to the ominous restriction (the 'until' will turn out to mean 'and no longer'), of which they will be reminded by the narrator at 15.596–602. Zeus's promise thus has the ambiguity of an oracle, which also predicts a negative truth while seeming to bring what its recipient desires. Things now rapidly go downhill for the Greeks, with three leading generals, Agamemnon, Diomedes, and Odysseus, being wounded and forced to leave the battlefield. Achilles, who is watching the Greek rout, sees Nestor bringing in another wounded Greek and sends Patroclus to find out who it is. The vital moment of Patroclus leaving his tent and hence starting his fatal role in Zeus's plan is awarded a memorable prolepsis by the narrator: 'that meant the beginning of his doom' (11.604). Nestor informs Patroclus about the plight of the Greeks and urges him to ask Achilles to allow him to fight in his armour.

While Patroclus returns the situation gets even worse for the Greeks. Hector is able to destroy part of the wall around the Greek camp, and the battle is now near (and about) the ships (book 12). The situation is completely reversed: it is not so much the Trojans whose city is beleaguered and who have to defend themselves but the Greeks who have to fight for their lives and their 'home'. The pro-Greek Poseidon does what he can to help the Greeks (book 13), but most effective is Hera's seduction of Zeus, which diverts his attention from the battle. The Trojans are rebuffed by the Greeks, and Hector even gets wounded (book 14).

But in book 15 Zeus awakes and, provoked by Hera's attempt to thwart his plan, sets it out once again, revealing new details: Hector will re-enter battle, Achilles will send out Patroclus, who will kill many Trojans (including Zeus's own son Sarpedon) but eventually be killed himself by Hector. Achilles will kill Hector, and the Greeks will capture Troy through the designs of Athena, probably a veiled reference to the Wooden Horse (15.59–77).[23] We may note how the divine plan again has absorbed mortal ideas, this time Nestor's suggestion that Patroclus act as Achilles' stand-in. By the end of the book Hector is at the height of his glory: he has broken Greek resistance near the ships and is about to set them on fire (the event marked earlier by Achilles as the moment of his return to battle: 9.651–3). In typical Homeric fashion, his zenith is counterpointed by the narrator, who once more recalls that Hector is soon to die at the hands of Achilles (15.612–14).

At the beginning of book 16 Patroclus finally returns to Achilles and begs him to allow him to lead the Myrmidons into battle, dressed in his (Achilles') armour. Achilles agrees but instructs him to return after he has driven the Trojans away from the ships and not to attack Troy itself, for fear that one of the gods, notably pro-Trojan Apollo, might come against him. Praying to Zeus he remarks that the god has granted his earlier request, a temporary setback for the Greeks, and now asks a new favour, the safe return of Patroclus. Zeus's reaction, only disclosed to the narratees, makes clear that Achilles' mortal plans and desires have definitely been superseded by divine intentions: Patroclus is *not* to come back. 'Zeus's mind is always stronger than the mind of men' (16.688) could well be the motto of the *Iliad*. Patroclus is highly successful and kills amongst others Sarpedon (as foretold by Zeus). However, buoyed by his own successes (and, at the same time, according to the principle of double determination,[24] led by Zeus) he does not heed Achilles' instructions and presses on towards Troy. Exactly as foreseen by Achilles, this arouses Apollo, who knocks the armour from Patroclus, allowing a minor Trojan to wound him and then Hector to kill him.

When Achilles is informed about Patroclus' death at the beginning of book 18, he decides to return to battle again in order to avenge himself on Hector, even if, as his mother Thetis informs him, this will entail his own death. For a brief moment he shows himself to the Trojans, who are frightened and retreat, leaving Patroclus' body to be rescued. Then Hera sends the sun down to end this long day of fighting. The Trojans, again camping outside the city, hold a council in which Polydamas advises Hector to return to the city. This would have been the moment for Hector to recall the restrictions of Zeus's support (until nightfall), but instead he fatally dismisses the prudent advice. Thetis goes to Hephaestus and in a celebrated passage, the model for countless later extended descriptions or *ekphraseis*, Achilles' new armour, especially his Shield, is described in detail while the divine smith is making it. The predominantly peaceful scenes which decorate it symbolise the life which Achilles is now renouncing in favour of avenging his friend.

Book 19 starts the fourth and final fighting day of the *Iliad*, which will end at the beginning of book 23. In an assembly Achilles formally renounces his *mēnis*,

---

[23] Aristarchus athetised 15.56–77; for a discussion see Janko ad loc.
[24] The classic discussion is Lesky (1961).

and Agamemnon offers the same gifts as book 9, now publicly acknowledging his mistake in taking away Briseïs from Achilles. He tries to save face by claiming to have been led by Zeus-sent delusion or *atē*, an analysis which is accepted by Achilles (19.270–4), for whom the whole issue after Patroclus' death has lost its importance, but which is not backed up by the narrator's version of events in book 1 (and is therefore best understood in terms of the common archaic Greek strategy of ascribing irrational human behaviour to the gods).[25]

Achilles' anger towards Agamemnon, which had led to passivity, is now replaced by his anger at Hector, which entails an active search for revenge. His revenge is postponed — and thereby, according to Homeric standards, magnified — through many retardations. When he starts massacring Trojans (book 20) he is nearly drowned by the river god Xanthus; he is saved only because Hephaestus forces the river to give up. Achilles' behaviour throughout these books does not bode much good for Hector, since he no longer accepts pleas for life, in sharp contrast to his previous conduct on the battlefield. By the end of book 21 Achilles has driven all Trojans in panic into the city, and book 22, finally, after many more delays, brings the confrontation of Achilles and Hector, ending with the latter's death. But even now Achilles' anger does not come to an end. He ties Hector's corpse behind his chariot, drags it towards the Greek camp, and then leaves it uncared for, face down in the dust but saved from real harm by the gods. Divine initiative in book 24 leads to the surprising denouement of the old king Priam going to the Greek camp, conversing with his enemy Achilles, and securing the body of his son. Though the proem had announced the non-burial of heroes as a result of Achilles' anger, the story actually closes with the burial of the hero who came closest to this fate. There is no epilogue to match the proem, but the closural motifs of burial and reconciliation, together with the ring-composition of a father coming to get back a child strongly create the sense of an ending.

(c) Parallels between books 6, 22, and 24

As the above analysis of the plot of the *Iliad* has shown, the different parts of the story are closely connected to each other so as to form a suspenseful and dramatic unity. Book 22 takes a prominent place in this whole, but it shows particularly close connections with books 6 and 24.[26]

One important binding factor is the figure of Andromache, who only in these three books plays a role (while we are briefly reminded of her at 8.186–90 and 17.207–8).[27] In book 6 she is introduced to the narratees, with a focus on her sad family history (her home town Thebes was sacked and her father and brothers

---

[25] The classic discussion is Dodds (1951) 1–27.

[26] See Schadewaldt (1959) 328–32 and Grethlein (2006) 245–53.

[27] See Lohmann (1988) and Reichel (1994) 272–8, with more literature; de Romilly (1995) 29–43 discusses Andromache in European literature, both ancient and modern.

killed), her child Astyanax, and her fear for the life of Hector. Book 22 brings echoes, contrasts, and complements. In book 6 Hector expected Andromache to be at home, but she actually had gone to the walls to watch the battle; in book 22 she is at home weaving, just as Hector had ordered her to do at 6.490–2, while all other Trojans are on the walls. Whereas in book 6 she lamented Hector though he was still alive (499–502), she is preparing a bath in book 22 although he is already dead (442–6). In book 6 she gave Hector martial advice (433–9), while at 22.440–1 she is weaving a peaceful design of flowers. When she hears shouting and has a foreboding of Hector's death, she uses words very similar to those she voiced before to Hector himself: 'I fear that Achilles has put an end to Hector's courage' (22.455–7) ≈ 'your own courage will destroy you' (6.407). In both books she runs towards the walls 'like a frenzied woman' (μαινομένηι ἐϊκυῖα: 6.389 ≈ μαινάδι ἴση: 22.460). Her sketch of their little son's (πάϊς . . . ἔτι νήπιος αὔτως: 22.484 ≈ παῖδά . . . νηπίαχον: 6.408) future life as an orphan at 22.484–506 contrasts with the hopes still entertained by Hector at 6.476–81 and fleshes out her own fears of 6.432. In her final speech in book 24 she goes even further: now she envisions Astyanax's death, after the fall of Troy (727–39). For herself she foresees the status of widow (χήρη(ν): 725, cf. 6.408; 22.484) and captive woman (731–2), of which Hector had earlier given a moving description (6.454–63).

There are more points of contact between books 22 and 6. At the beginning of book 22 Hector waits for Achilles at the Scaean gate (6), the same place where he had had his memorable conversation with Andromache in book 6 (393). In a monologue he toys with the idea of trying to strike a bargain with Achilles, but he rejects this, realising that Achilles is not in the mood for ὀαρίζειν (127), the very verb which had been used of his own intimate conversation with Andromache at 6.516. He also uses the same formulation about his 'feeling shame before the Trojan men and Trojan women' as he had voiced before vis-à-vis Andromache (22.105 = 6.442). Whereas at that time his shame was still of a general nature (a man should fight and a general should be with his men), here it has acquired a more specific reference: he has made a strategic mistake and now fears being reproached by his compatriots.

Book 22 is also closely connected to book 24, the later book both contrasting with and complementing the earlier one. The contrast concerns the fate of Hector's body. When Hector begs Achilles to return his corpse, promising that his parents will give a ransom (340–4), Achilles harshly says he will not, not even if Hector's parents were to give him a huge ransom or Priam offered his weight in gold (348–54). After these forceful words the actual denouement in book 24 (Achilles returning Hector's body to his father Priam for a ransom) comes as a surprise. When at 22.416–22 Priam announces that he wants to go to the ships of the Greeks alone and supplicate Achilles, appealing to the persons of Peleus and himself as old fathers bereft of their sons, he is held back by his fellow Trojans. But what at first looked like an absurd and impossible mission is carried out after all in book 24. By then Priam's grief-driven impulse has become Zeus's will, which is successfully accomplished with Hermes escorting the old king and Achilles being duly moved by the reference to Peleus.

Book 24 complements book 22 in that the three improvised and spontaneous laments of Priam, Hecuba, and Andromache there uttered from a distance and without the corpse of Hector, are now replaced by official ones, voiced by Andromache, Hecuba, and Helen, and with the corpse carefully laid out. While in book 22 the women spoke about the loss which Hector's death brings to his wife, son, mother, and city, in 24 they re-evoke his earlier gains as warrior and husband, gods' favourite and dear son, and kindly brother-in-law. These three women are the same ones whom Hector met in book 6, when they tried to make him stay in Troy. The tension there created as to whether Hector would come back safely to the inner circle of his family is resolved by the intensity and dignity of their last farewell in book 24.

It is characteristic of the Homeric narrator to allow women to have the last (sad) word in his story. Though belonging to heroic poetry, the Homeric epics do not share that genre's interest in bloodshed and male glory per se. The two elements are present, even to a large extent, but much attention is also paid to the other side of the coin: the high price paid for victory and the pursuit of glory. No less than three women mourn Hector, while Patroclus is grieved over by both a woman (Briseïs: 19.286–301) and a man (Achilles: 19.314–38). The many lesser heroes killed throughout the poem are for a brief moment lifted out of anonymity, when they are given a name, family, and brief personal touch in Homer's celebrated 'necrologies'.[28] The Trojan opponents are endowed with such fates and families to become dear to the Greek narratees. Indeed, Homer's exceptional sympathy for the Trojans has paved the way for their presence in Greek tragedy as the victims of war par excellence. Even the gods, impassive onlookers for the greater part of the story, at times react emotionally to the death of their favourite heroes or sons (15.113–18; 16.433–8; 22.168–76). But Homer's prime example is the figure of Achilles, the best of the Achaeans (and indeed of all warriors before Troy), yet the one who pays the highest price for his status: he loses his best friend and dies young. The *Iliad* shows human life for what it is, an alternation of good and bad things, the latter usually self-inflicted but at the same time part of divine machinations which often find their origin in personal whims of the gods, rather than principles of justice or morality.[29]

(d) The interrelated deaths of Sarpedon, Patroclus, and Hector[30]

If, as the preceding section has shown, book 22 has close ties with books 6 and 24, there is also a thread which binds it tightly to the rest of the *Iliad*: the

[28] See Griffin (1980) 103–43 and Stoevesandt (2004) 126–59.
[29] On gods and morality in the *Iliad*, see e.g. – the opposite views of – van Erp Taalman Kip (2000) and Allan (2006).
[30] See Leinieks (1973), Mueller (1978), and Rutherford (1982).

series of interrelated deaths of the three heroes Sarpedon, Patroclus, and Hector. These deaths are emphatically mentioned in one breath by Zeus when he sets out his plan to Hera at 15.65–8 (see section b). They are also linked in narrative reality, in that they come about according to the 'killing in succession' pattern so often observed in the *Iliad*: warrior X kills opponent Y and is then killed himself by a compatriot, friend, or family-member of Y, who avenges him. Patroclus kills Sarpedon (book 16); Hector kills Patroclus, initially setting out to avenge Sarpedon but after more skirmishes also having to avenge his charioteer Cebriones, killed by Patroclus too (book 16); and Achilles kills Hector to avenge Patroclus (book 22). These killings, because of their concatenation in Zeus's plan, acquire an ominous undertone: the death of each hero dooms his killer to die in turn.

The *Iliad* features hundreds of deaths, but these three clearly are the central ones, and their prominence is underlined by the many times they are anticipated. Thus the death of Sarpedon is foreshadowed by the narrator (5.662; 12.402–3; 16.460–1) and by characters (5.685–8; 15.67; 16.433–4, 451–2); the death of Patroclus by the narrator (11.604; 16.46–7, 252, 686–91, 692–3) and by characters, both in thought, focalisation (16.646–55), and in speech (8.476; 15.65–7); and that of Hector by the narrator (15.612–14; 16.800; 22.5) and by characters, in thought (6.501–2; 20.77–8) and speech (6.407–10; 8.358–9; 15.68; 16.852–4; 17.201–8; 18.132–3, 334–5; 21.296–7). Symbolic actions also prefigure the deaths of Patroclus (putting on Achilles' armour but not taking his spear, which only Achilles can handle: 16.140–4; yoking the mortal horse Pedasus in addition to the two immortal horses, Xanthus and Balius, to his chariot: 16.152–4) and Hector (putting on Patroclus' = Achilles' divine armour, which, as Zeus notes, does not befit him as a mortal: 17.194–208).

The narrator brings home the connectedness between these three central deaths through thematic repetition and verbal echoes: Patroclus and Hector receive warnings (Achilles urges Patroclus to return after he has driven the Trojans away from the ships and not to press on to Troy: 16.83–100; Polydamas advises Hector to return inside the city after Achilles has returned to battle: 18.254–83); Zeus contemplates saving Sarpedon and Hector (16.431–61; 22.166–87); Sarpedon, Patroclus, and Hector speak last words when fatally wounded (Sarpedon to his friend Glaucus: 16.492–501; Patroclus and Hector, more dramatically, to their victorious opponents, prophesying their deaths: 16.844–54; 22.356–60); and the moment of Patroclus' and Hector's deaths is described in the same memorable couplet (16.855–7 = 22.361–3).

An important parallel which connects the fates of Patroclus and Hector is the fatal pattern of optimism and hope, which, fed by apparent triumph, grows into overconfidence and delusion, and eventually leads to death. Patroclus starts chasing the Trojans away from the ships into the Trojan plain. When one of his Myrmidons is killed, he pursues the Trojans and Lycians and even kills the king of the Lycians, Sarpedon. Zeus considers having Patroclus killed at this point but decides to make him first wreak more havoc among the Trojans (16.646–55). 'Foolish' Patroclus (16.684–91) even heads for Troy, the very thing Achilles had forbidden him to do. It is only an intervention of Apollo that can stop him, the god informing him that he is not fated to take Troy. He keeps on killing Trojans, however, and Apollo once again intervenes, this time fatally. Patroclus dies with defiant words on his lips ('but for the gods overpowering me I would have killed even twenty men like you (Hector)': 16.847–50) and without any idea about his role in Zeus's plan.

Hector[31] displays a mixture of pessimism (6.447–65) and optimism (6.475–81) in his meeting with his wife Andromache. But then Iris' message that Zeus supports him (11.202–9) leads to an unprecedented offensive strategy, successes (he breaks through the wall around the Greek camp, sets fire to a Greek ship, and kills Patroclus), and a repeatedly voiced confidence (11.288–9; 12.235–6; 15.490–3, 719–25), which fatally continues even after the time limit of the god's help (nightfall) has come (18.293–4). This, in turn, makes him refuse to heed Polydamas' advice to return inside the city. In contrast to Patroclus, however, Hector also 'cools down'. When he awaits vengeful Achilles, who is heading for him, he is considerably less confident, although he still reckons he has a chance to be awarded victory by Zeus (22.130). He also realises that he has made a mistake in not heeding Polydamas' advice (22.103–4). Just prior to his death, noting that Athena has deceived him, he understands that his death has always been part of Zeus's plan (22.301–3). That he is awarded this moment of insight makes Hector's death even more memorable and tragic than that of Patroclus.

There are explicit indications that both heroes make mistakes. When Patroclus presses on the Trojans and Lycians his action is labelled *atē*, 'delusion', by the narrator (μέγ' ἀάσθη: 16.685). When the Trojans applaud Hector's offensive strategy rather than the more prudent one of Polydamas, the narrator speaks of Athena taking away their wits (18.311–13), and this obviously also pertains to Hector himself. Hector later disqualifies his own actions at that moment as *atasthaliē*, 'reckless behaviour' (ἀτασθαλίῃσιν ἐμῇσιν: 22.104). The errors of the two men are most plausibly seen in a tragic rather than a moralistic light: Homer's poem lays bare, time and again, the limitations of mortal insight. Human beings make plans, have aspirations, and initiate actions, but for the outcome they are always dependent on the power of the gods, who often have very different intentions. Thus, as we have seen, the deaths of Patroclus and Hector had been determined long before their fatal errors (15.65–8), and these errors are presented by the narrator in terms of double motivation: Athena taking away the Trojans' (and Hector's) wits (18.311–13) and Zeus urging on Patroclus (16.688–91).

---

[31] For studies on this figure see, e.g., Bassett (1923), Schadewaldt (1970), Redfield (1994) 136–59, Erbse (1978), Farron (1978), Metz (1990), and de Romilly (1997).

(e) Achilles

Achilles forms part of the concatenation of deaths that involves Sarpedon, Patroclus, and Hector, yet it will turn out that his life and manner of death evolve along somewhat different lines. For one, he knows right from the start that he is destined to die young (1.352, 416). This fact is, in typical Homeric manner, 'dramatised' in book 9 when he tells that he has a choice between a short and glorious life, if he stays in Troy, and a long and uneventful one, if he returns home (410–16), and then chooses to stay (650–5). When Achilles decides to avenge Patroclus after his death, his mother Thetis discloses that he will die soon after killing Hector (18.95–6), a fact that he embraces. More details about his own death are disclosed to him by his horse Xanthus (19.416–17) and Hector (22.358–60). Thus Achilles, unlike Patroclus and Hector, is fully aware of his own imminent death; as Schadewaldt puts it, Hector is 'the one who is in the grip of death unawares', while Achilles is 'the one who is knowingly ready for death'.[32]

Has Achilles somewhere made a tragic error, like Patroclus or Hector? Here opinions between scholars are widely divergent; indeed, Achilles is the most hotly disputed of Homeric characters.[33] Unlike Hector and Patroclus, he is nowhere explicitly connected with notions like *atē* or *atasthaliē*, either by one of the characters or by the narrator. But perhaps there are deeds of his that can be seen as a form of error *by implication*. Scholars have noted the following critical acts:

1) His quarrel with Agamemnon in book 1 and resulting prolonged *mēnis*.
2) His rejection of the embassy in book 9.
3) His acceptance of Patroclus' plea to fight in his place in book 16.
4) His extreme revenge (including the killing of countless Trojans and the treatment of Hector's body).

Regarding our evaluation of the quarrel we can be brief: it is Athena herself who identifies Agamemnon's behaviour as *hubris* (1.214) and thereby signals that Achilles' anger is justified. (We may compare her early disqualification of the suitors' behaviour in the *Odyssey* as *hubris* (1.227), thereby condoning Odysseus' bloody revenge at an early point.) His angry inactivity is the kind of heroic behaviour known from other heroes (Meleager: 9.524–99; Aeneas: 13.459–61). The crucial point is, of course, how long such anger should last, especially when it leads to so much harm to one's *philoi*.

---

[32] Schadewaldt (1959) 262 ('*der unwissend todbefangene*' versus '*der wissend todbereite*').

[33] Achilles makes one or more tragic errors: e.g., Bassett (1934a), Redfield (1994) 106–7, and passim, Rutherford (1982) 155–6, Effe (1988), Erbse (2001), Allan (2006) 9. Achilles is not to blame: e.g., Yamagata (1991) and Latacz (1995). Achilles creates his own heroic norms: e.g., Whitman (1958) 181–220 and Zanker (1994). For a discussion of the figure of Achilles before and in Homer see Burgess (2009), from Homer to the Middle Ages King (1987).

Here the scene of the embassy is crucial. When diplomatic Odysseus presents Agamemnon's offer and appeals to Achilles' desire to win glory (now he could kill Hector), old Phoenix tells an allegory (about Prayers, daughters of Zeus) and a paradigm (Meleager), and the sturdy warrior Ajax appeals to Achilles' solidarity towards his fellow warriors, Achilles does not give up his *mēnis*. Many scholars have seen this as a tragic mistake for which he is punished by the death of Patroclus. Just as Meleager only relented and re-entered battle when his wife Cleopatra asked him but did not get the promised reward, Achilles will give in to Patroclus (letting him go to war in his place) but when he himself re-enters battle take no pleasure in Agamemnon's conciliatory gifts. Just as the allegorical Prayers, *Litai*, when not treated with respect by a man, beg Zeus to visit that man with Folly 'so that he pays with his own hurt', so Achilles' rejection of the prayers of the ambassadors (cf. λίσσεσθαι: 9.698) will lead to the death of his best friend and eventually his own death.[34]

There are strong indications, however, that Agamemnon's gesture of reconciliation simply was not good enough: he should have come himself and publicly admitted his earlier error in taking away Achilles' prize Briseïs and hence dishonouring him. That this would have been the right course of action becomes clear from book 19, where we see Agamemnon doing exactly this. In book 9, however, he is not yet ready to apologise or restore Achilles' honour: instead of the sweet words prescribed by Nestor (9.113), he ends his 'conciliatory' speech with a harsh demand for Achilles to acknowledge his higher rank ('let him yield . . . and let him submit to me, in that I am the greater king': 9.158–61), words wisely suppressed by Odysseus when conveying the message. As regards the allegory and mythical paradigm, here it is important to distinguish between the function which these stories have for the characters and that for the narratees. Phoenix tells the Meleager story by way of dissuasive example: Achilles should *not* act like Meleager. Likewise, the allegory is held up as a model: a sensible man accepts prayers and prospers (an example to be followed by Achilles), while someone who does not heed them comes to harm (an example not to be followed). For the narratees, however, Phoenix's stories are not so much warnings as prolepses; they know from Zeus's announcement at 8.473–7 that Achilles will only re-enter battle because of Patroclus' death. They can 'read' these events in Phoenix's stories; the characters cannot.

Did Achilles make a mistake when he accepted Patroclus' plea to let him fight in his armour? According to some scholars he did, for he should have recalled Thetis' prophecy that 'the best of the Myrmidons would die while he (Achilles) was still alive' (18.9–11). Here it should be noted, however, that the narrator relates Thetis' prophecy only at the moment when Achilles worries about Patroclus (whom the narratees know is already dead), not when he accepts

---

[34] For discussions of the allegory and Meleager-story see esp. Rosner (1976), Yamagata (1991), and Alden (2000) 179–290, who also cites more literature.

his plea (16.49–100). This suggests that the narrator does not expect us to see Achilles' acceptance as a fatal — and reprehensible — neglect of a divine warning.

Finally, there is Achilles' bloody revenge. His rampage in books 20–2 is naturally criticised by the Trojan river god Scamander (21.213–21), but it is not condemned by the narrator, and the hero is duly saved from drowning in the river's streams by Poseidon and Athena. Many have taken the reference to Achilles' treatment of Hector's body as ἀεικέα... ἔργα (22.395) as a sign of criticism on the part of the narrator. But it should be realised that this means 'disfiguring deeds' and does not so much imply wrong deeds (for Achilles to commit) as shameful deeds (for Hector to suffer). Moreover, ἀεικέα... ἔργα forms part of *Achilles'* focalisation (μήδετο), who earlier had announced that he intended to let dogs maul his opponent ἀϊκῶς (22.335–6). Finally, the narrator indicates that it is *Zeus* who allows his enemies to disfigure (ἀεικίσσασθαι) Hector (22.403–4).

Hector's prophecy that Achilles' failure to take proper care of his body will lead to his own, divinely ordained death (22.358–60) is perhaps the closest we get to the idea that, in a way, Achilles himself 'earned' the death which fate had meted out for him, just as Patroclus and Hector did. When Achilles continues to mistreat Hector's body for twelve days, this leads to a condemnation by the pro-Trojan god Apollo, who calls Achilles 'wild' and 'lacking in respect and pity' and refers to the danger of *nemesis* on the part of the gods (24.39–54). But Zeus's decision that Achilles should give back Hector's body flows from a desire to honour him, rather than from a condemnation of his behaviour (24.65–76). And the way in which Achilles indeed releases Hector's body and allows it to be buried would seem to absolve him from all blame.

All in all, it would seem that Achilles stands out among Homeric heroes for his clear-sightedness: he knows — and chooses and accepts — that he is to die young. He makes important decisions himself or after a discussion with a god (e.g. Athena when deciding upon his *mēnis* and Thetis when deciding to kill Hector), while other characters are much more (mis)led by the gods. The death of Patroclus was the only thing Achilles did not foresee, but he takes full responsibility. He is therefore the right person to cap the *Iliad* with a memorable speech on the *condition humaine*, the fellowship of suffering which links friend and foe, Greek and Trojan (24.518–51).

3. NARRATIVE ART AND ORAL STYLE

(a) Narrator and narratees

The Homeric narrator,[35] the 'I' of 'Muse tell *me* about the man' (*Od.* 1.1), is a highly elusive entity: he does not mention his name, place of birth, time of

---

[35] See de Jong (2004) 3–28, 41–9, Richardson (1990), and Morrison (2007) 36–102. Though it is debated whether *Iliad* and *Odyssey* stem from the same poet (see section 1a), it is customary to speak of the Homeric narrator in both cases.

living, or any other item of personal information. We can deduce a few things, most importantly that he is a professional singer like Phemius and Demodocus in the *Odyssey*; these alone invoke the Muses, the 'patron' goddesses of their art, whereas 'amateurs', such as Achilles in the *Iliad* (9.186–91) or Odysseus in the *Odyssey* (books 9–12), do not. Another tiny scrap of information is that he, and, by implication his addressees, the narratees, belong to a later period than that of the story, since he contrasts his characters with 'men such as they are *now*' (e.g. *Il.* 5.302–4). This difference in time is also suggested by his use of the expression ἤματι κείνωι, 'on that remote day' (*Il.* 2.482 and 4.543), and his – single – reference to the heroes of his tale as ἡμιθέων γένος ἀνδρῶν, 'a race of semi-divine men' (*Il.* 12.23).

From the eighteenth century onwards, the near absence of the Homeric narrator in his own work led to the widely held view that the narrative style of the *Iliad* and *Odyssey* was distanced and objective, and that events told themselves. Closer scrutiny has revealed this view to be questionable: although largely invisible, the Homeric narrator qua narrator and focaliser (the one who 'sees' the events) is very active, rigorously controlling his narratees' beliefs, interests, and sympathies. To start, there are a handful of devices which show him *openly* stepping forward: Muse invocations, which mark decisive points in the narrative (e.g. 'Tell me now, Muses, who have your homes on Olympus, how fire was first thrown upon the Greek ships': *Il.* 16.112–13); apostrophes, when the narrator addresses one of his characters (e.g. 'Then whom did you kill first, whom last, Patroclus, when the gods called you to your death?': *Il.* 16.692–3); narratorial comments (e.g. concerning Andromache, 'Poor woman, she did not know that far away from any bath Athena had brought Hector down at the hands of Achilles': *Il.* 22.445–6); rhetorical questions (e.g. 'How could Hector have kept clear of the fates of death, if Apollo had not stood by him for the very last time?': *Il.* 22.202–4); and 'if not'-situations, which sketch what might have been (e.g. 'And now the Greeks would have taken Troy at the hands of Patroclus, if Apollo had not taken his stand on the battlements, intending death for Patroclus and helping the Trojans': *Il.* 16.698–701).

Much more numerous are the *implicit* ways in which the narrator steers his narratees' reception of the story and often stirs their empathy:[36] through the insertion of motifs such as 'death far from home' and 'bereaved parents' (e.g. 'he collapsed . . . far away from generous Larisa, and he could not repay his dear parents' care; he was short-lived, beaten down beneath the spear of high-hearted Ajax': *Il.* 17.300–3); the description of symbolic objects and places (e.g. Andromache's headdress given to her on the day of her marriage with Hector, which recalls her former happiness: *Il.* 22.468–72, and 'the washing-places where the Trojan women used to wash their shining clothes, in earlier times, in peace, before the Greeks came': *Il.* 22.154–6); and the use of pathetic comparisons

---

[36] See Griffin (1980) 103–43.

and similes (e.g., young Imbrius 'dropped like an ash-tree which is felled by the bronze . . . and brings its soft leaves down to the ground': *Il.* 13.178–80).

The Homeric narrator should not therefore be called objective, but there is a marked difference between his vocabulary and that of the characters: emotional or evaluative language is largely relegated to the speeches. Only (or mainly) characters use words like '*hubris*', 'unfortunate', 'most pitiable', 'dearest', 'reckless', etc. When such words occur outside speeches, they are usually found in passages of embedded focalisation, when the narrator represents the perceptions, thoughts, or feelings, of one of the characters, e.g. Andromache seeing Hector 'being dragged in front of the city; fast horses pulled him *without proper care* (ἀκηδέστως) away towards the hollow ships of the Greeks' (*Il.* 22.464–5). It is thus appropriate to speak of a distinct character-language in the Homeric epics.[37]

The addressees of the narrator are the narratees, who, like him, are hardly visible. The most *explicit* sign of their presence is an occasional 'you' (e.g. 'then you would not have seen godlike Agamemnon sleeping, or cowering in fear, or reluctant to fight, but he was in fact rushing towards the fight where men win glory': *Il.* 4.223–5). But their constant *implicit* existence is unmistakable and essential: the narratees are the active recipients of the devices of the narrator, the ones who pick up the pathos or feel the suspense he creates. It is for their benefit that the narrator inserts explanations (e.g. concerning the *ichor* which runs in the gods' veins, 'for they do not eat food, nor drink wine, and so are without blood': *Il.* 5.339–42), or to contradict their expectations or pique their curiosity that he uses negations (e.g. the fact that Patroclus did *not* take Achilles' spear with him at *Il.* 16.140–4 both counters an expectation based on other arming scenes and creates tension about its later use).

The Homeric narrator is omniscient, in that he reveals the outcome of events beforehand in numerous prolepses (e.g. 'this was the beginning of Patroclus' downfall': *Il.* 11.604), and in that he has access to the inner thoughts of his characters (e.g. 'the Dream left Agamemnon there with thoughts in his mind which were not fated to be fulfilled. For he thought that he would take Priam's city that day': *Il.* 2.35–7). He is also omnipresent: he recounts what happens among the gods on Mount Olympus and among the heroes on earth, in the Greek camp and in Troy, on Ithaca and on such remote places as the island of Calypso, regularly and effortlessly switching back and forth between the different locations.

Such an omniscient and omnipresent narrator is in fact the archetypical story-teller, but what singles out the Homeric narrator is that he accounts for his omniscience. In his proems (and in the *Iliad* also in the course of his narrative) the narrator invokes the Muses and asks them to 'tell' him (ἔννεπε/ἔσπετε) certain facts. Since the Muses are eyewitnesses of everything that happens in history

---

[37] See Griffin (1986) and de Jong (1988), (1992).

(*Il.* 2.485), it is they who feed his omniscience.[38] Far from considering the narrator a mere mouthpiece of the Muses, however, the collaboration between mortal and goddesses should be understood in terms of double motivation: they are both involved at the same time, just as the Ithacan singer Phemius claims that he is both 'self-taught' and that 'a god has implanted' songs in his mind (*Od.* 22.347–8).

The narrator's concern for explaining his omniscience is clearly related to what could be called the proto-historiographical function of his epics. Although offered as entertainment (whether on a more private or public scale, see section 1b), epic song has serious aspirations. Telling of the deeds of heroes from the – recent or more remote – past, it preserves their glory. Gaining such *kleos*, fame as 'doer of deeds and speaker of words' (*Il.* 9.443), is a central concern of Homeric heroes. They themselves can broadcast their feats, as we see Odysseus do among the Phaeacians, but professional singers offer a divinely authorised version of the κλέα ἀνδρῶν. By becoming part of his poetry, the narrator self-consciously suggests, their *kleos* will even become immortal (cf. *Il.* 9.413). Where physical remains of the war may disappear with time, as is graphically illustrated by the wall around the Greek camp (*Il.* 12.3–33), poetry is 'more durable than bronze', as Horace later will say. The idea that preserving the memory of the past is worthwhile will be taken up by historiography, with its founding father Herodotus acknowledging his debt to Homer by the prominent use of the key term *kleos* in his proem (μήτε ἔργα μεγάλα τε καὶ θωμαστά . . . ἀκλεᾶ γένηται).

(b) Comparisons and similes

One stock ingredient of epic poetry that Homer bequeathed to European literature is the simile.[39] While other epic texts[40] employ the same type of short comparisons, 'like a god', 'like a lion', it seems to have been Homer's invention to develop such comparisons into extended similes that take up several verses. This thesis is corroborated by the fact that the phrasing of the similes is much less formulaic, and that they contain many *hapax legomena* and late linguistic features.[41] Also, of the *c.* 200 similes in the *Iliad* only six are repeated verbatim (in the *Odyssey*, the figure is two out of forty).

Most extended similes take one of the following three forms:

1) X did Y, like a . . . ; thus X did Y:
    e.g., σευάμενος ὥς θ᾽ ἵππος . . . | ὅς ῥά τε . . . θέησι . . . | ὣς Ἀχιλεὺς λαιψηρὰ πόδας καὶ γούνατ᾽ ἐνώμα, 'Achilles was moving at full speed, like a horse which gallops . . . ; thus Achilles quickly moved his feet and knees' (22.22–4; 26–32 and 308–11 have the same structure).

---

[38] For the Homeric Muses see e.g. Murray (1981), de Jong (2004) 45–53, Finkelberg (1990), and Ford (1992) 57–89.
[39] An excellent brief introduction is Edwards 24–41.
[40] See Bowra (1952) 266–80 and West (1997) 217–19.
[41] Discussed in Shipp (1972) 3–222.

2) X did Y. As (when) a . . . ; thus X did Y:

e.g., ἀλλ' ὅ γε μίμν' . . . | ὡς δὲ δράκων . . . μένησιν . . . | ὡς Ἕκτωρ . . . οὐχ ὑπεχώρει, 'but Hector awaited Achilles. As a snake awaits a man . . . ; thus Hector did not recoil' (22.92–7; cf. 138–44).

3) As (when) a . . . ; thus X did Y:

e.g., ὡς δ' ὅτ' . . . περὶ τέρματα . . . ἵπποι | . . . τρωχῶσι . . . | ὡς τὼ . . . πόλιν πέρι δινηθήτην, 'As when horses run around turning-posts . . . ; thus the two (Hector and Achilles) circled around the city' (22.162–6; cf. 189–93, 199–201, 317–20).

Similes and comparisons draw their material (in technical terms, their vehicles) from the world of nature and the everyday, often humble, life of ordinary men and women. Thus, we hear about lions, stags, wolves, dogs, boars, donkeys, bulls, eagles, hawks, flies, wasps, locusts, bees, snakes, goats, an octopus and a dolphin; about poplars, oaks, and a poppy; about snowstorms, gales, tempestuous seas, and forest fires, as well as starry, windless nights; and about reapers, smiths, carpenters, threshers, fishermen, herdsmen, and hunters.[42]

Almost without exception the setting of the similes is not geographically spec-ified, its inhabitants are anonymous, and the action timeless or rather of all times (omnitemporal), as is linguistically marked by the use of presents, gnomic aorists, iterative subjunctives and epic τε. Whenever the narrator does refer to a specific place, it is located in Asia Minor (e.g. a water-meadow beside the river Caÿstrius: *Il.* 2.460–1; a woman making a cheek-piece for horses in Maeonia or Caria: *Il.* 4.141–7). Needless to say, some situations, although presented linguis-tically as omnitemporal, refer to a world which is not ours anymore (e.g. when people stretch and drench a bull's hide with fat: *Il.* 17.389–95, or when a woman stains ivory with crimson dye: *Il.* 4.141–7). But the majority of similes refer to phenomena we are still familar with, such as a bird of prey hovering in the air and then swooping down to catch its prey (*Il.* 13.62–5), waves roaring against a jutting cliff (*Il.* 2.394–7), or a dreamer's feeling of being unable to move properly (*Il.* 22.199–201).

In the *Iliad* the world of the similes, with their scenes from ordinary life and vignettes of nature, contrasts with the harsh reality of the battlefield. It should be noted, however, that most similes show mankind in a losing struggle with nature (storms, flooding rivers, and wild animals) or animals killing each other; only a handful provide more peaceful scenes, such as harvesting, fishing, and irrigating a garden. Just as heroes have their battles to fight, ordinary man is engaged in an unending struggle to survive in an often hostile natural world. In the *Odyssey* similes are fewer but often more closely linked to the narrative in their imagery: when Odysseus is tossed about by a storm on sea, we get wind similes (5.328–30); Penelope's joy at being reunited with Odysseus is compared

---

[42] For the subjects of similes see Fränkel (1921), Lee (1964) 65–73, and Scott (1974) 56–95.

to that of a shipwrecked man spotting land (23.233–40); when Odysseus weeps at hearing Demodocus sing about the sacking of Troy, he is likened to a woman weeping over the dead body of her husband who has died fighting for his city and people (8.523–31). The effectiveness of these Odyssean similes consists in their supplementing or reversing the main story (the victor Odysseus becoming a victim, Penelope a ship-wrecked sailor such as Odysseus).

Similes and comparisons illustrate an element of the main narrative: the movement of a person (Achilles quickly running back to Troy like a race horse: 22.22–4) or his appearance (the glitter of Achilles' armour resembling that of a star: *Il.* 22.25–32), sound (the Trojans marching with cries like those of cranes: *Il.* 3.2–7), space (Polypoetes out-throwing other discus-throwers by the distance a cowherd can reach with his throwing-stick: *Il.* 23.845–7), time (Charybdis spewing out Odysseus' mast and keel at the time of day when a judge rises from his seat in the marketplace and returns home for his meal: *Od.* 12.439–41), numbers (the mass of Greeks ready to attack the Trojans being like the great crowds of flies swarming around milk-pails: *Il.* 2.469–73), or an emotion (shipwrecked Odysseus being as joyful when he sees land as children when their father recovers from an illness: *Od.* 5.394–8). The point of comparison, or *tertium comparationis* or tenor, is often 'advertised' by the narrator in the form of a verbal echo: e.g., ὡς δὲ πατὴρ οὗ παιδὸς <u>ὀδύρεται</u>..., ὡς Ἀχιλεὺς ἑτάροιο <u>ὀδύρετο</u> (*Il.* 23.222–4).

Homeric similes are famous – or notorious – for their length, or as the French critic Charles Perrault called it in his *Parallèle des Anciens et des Modernes* (1688–92), their 'tail', by which he meant that they seem to detach themselves from their context and start to lead a life of their own. An example is *Il.* 5.87–94, when Diomedes fiercely attacking the ranks of the Trojans is compared to a river sweeping over a plain and bursting dykes. The river is not checked by the banks of thriving vineyards, and many farmers see it flatten the fruit of their labour. It is clear that the Trojans are to be compared with the dykes, banks, and farmers, but there is no exact correspondent in the story for the fruit of their labour. In most cases, however, details do make sense. For this we have to realise that similes, not only those with a tail, usually have more than a mere illustrating function, either in relation to the surrounding lines or to the wider context.[43]

A first, fairly common additional function is to create *pathos*: e.g. when Apollo kicks down the wall erected with so much effort by the Greeks around their ships 'most easily, like a child playing in the sand by the sea, who makes buildings in his childish play and then in sport destroys them with his feet and hand' (*Il.* 15.361–6). The juxtaposition of the Greeks' hard toil to build the wall and the divine ease in destroying it conveys something of the pathos that the narrator feels attached to human effort. The narrator may also choose to stress the point of view of one party (e.g. when he describes the glitter of Achilles running towards

---

[43] For the functions of similes see Fränkel (1921), Coffey (1957), Moulton (1977), Minchin (2001) 132–60, Danek (2006), and Scott (2009).

Troy through Priam's eyes, comparing the Greek hero to 'the star called Orion's Dog, a sign of evil, bringing much fever to poor mortals': *Il.* 22.27–31; or when Odysseus, 'terrible and disfigured by brine' looks like a lion who is 'rained and blown upon' to the frightened eyes of Nausicaa and her maids: *Od.* 6.130–6).[44]

A second function is that of the *anticipation* or prolepsis, as when Hector is compared to a boar or a lion that feels no fear when facing a mass of hunters and dogs but keeps on attacking, and the narrator ominously adds, 'it is his courage that kills him' (*Il.* 12.41–50). Next, there is the *symbolic* function, e.g. when warriors are compared to a star or fire, so as to underline their heroic stature (e.g. *Il.* 22.134–5).

The *characterising* function of similes is well illustrated by the series of 'parents-children' similes that are found in connection with Achilles, the 'parent', and Patroclus, 'the child' (9.323–7; 16.7–11; 17.4–6, 133–7; 18.318–23). Of these, the pathetic climax comes when Achilles is mourning as he burns Patroclus' bones, as a father mourns who burns the bones of his son who was recently married and whose dying has brought intense grief to his parents (23.222–5). Similes may also run through the poem or parts of the poem by way of a leitmotif and acquire a *thematic* function. An example is the series of similes dealing with a beleaguered city. The first is found at 18.219–21, when Achilles has just announced to the Trojans that he will return to battle. His shouting is compared to the sharp and clear sound of a trumpet blown when a city is surrounded by murderous enemies. The next time the theme occurs, the beleaguered city has already been taken and the gods are bringing its inhabitants hardship and loss, just as Achilles is doing, wreaking havoc among the Trojans (21.522–5). The climax of this series is then formed by the brief comparison of the Trojans wailing and lamenting over the dead Hector as if Troy itself was on fire and smouldering from top to bottom (22.410–11).

Finally, there is the *structuring* function of similes. From antiquity onwards similes have been said to achieve *poikilia* or variation; the long battle narratives in particular would seem to need them in order to avoid monotony. This idea hardly seems to do justice to this celebrated narrative device. To start with, similes produce a pause in the action and hence are well suited to mark an important point in the story. The moment need not necessarily be a turning point[45] or the start or end of an action,[46] but may just be something the narrator wants to dwell upon for some reason: the marching out of the Greeks, which has no fewer than six similes (*Il.* 2.455–83); the start of Achilles' pursuit of Hector, which has two comparisons and one simile (*Il.* 22.131–44;); the reunion of Penelope and Odysseus (*Od.* 23.233–40); but also a stalemate in the fighting between Greeks and Trojans (*Il.* 12.433–6). Often, similes come in pairs, one for each opponent (e.g. Paris versus Menelaus: *Il.* 3.21–37, and Hector versus Achilles: *Il.* 22.308–11, 317–19), or two for one and the same person (e.g. Ajax is first compared to a lion

---

[44] See de Jong (2004) 123–36.   [45] Bassett (1921).   [46] Martin (1997).

driven away by herdsmen and then to a donkey stubbornly ignoring the sticks of children: *Il.* 11.548–61).

The imagery of similes and comparisons is a particularly powerful means of establishing connections between different parts of the story (Andromache is compared to a frenzied woman both in book 6, when her fear is still unfounded, and in 22, when disaster has struck). It can also mark the stages in an action (e.g. when the Trojan Asius attacks the Greek wall, the stones of the defenders are compared to snowflakes: *Il.* 12.156–60; but when great warriors like Sarpedon and Glaucus attack, the stones volleyed from both sides are compared to a snowstorm: 12.278–89). Or it can point up a reversal of fortune (e.g., Diomedes is first compared to a swollen river: *Il.* 5.87–94, but later to a man who has to jump back in front of a turbulent river: 5.596–600).[47] In book 22 we may note how the imagery of the racehorse is briefly adumbrated when Achilles runs back to Troy in search of Hector (22–4) and fully worked out when his pursuit is in full swing (162–6); how the fleeing Trojans are compared to fawns at a moment when Hector still confronts Achilles (1), but this hero later finds himself in the position of a fawn, too, when fleeing from Achilles (189–98); and how Achilles is compared to a star both when Priam first spots him running towards Hector (26–32) and when he is about to kill him (317–19).

(c) Epithets

Another well known characteristic of the Homeric epics is the epithet. Persons, places, and objects are regularly accompanied by an attributive adjective (or substantive): 'swift-footed Achilles', 'leader of men Agamemnon', 'high-gated Ilion', and 'curved ships'. As was already noted in antiquity, epithets are occasionally also used in contexts where they are less apt, e.g. when 'swift-footed Achilles' is sitting idly near his ships (πόδας ὠκὺς Ἀχιλλεύς: *Il.* 1.488–9), or Nausicaa sets out to wash 'shining clothing' (ἐσθῆτα φαεινήν: *Od.* 6.74). The explanation of the ancient commentators is that the clothing is shining 'not then, but in general'. It would seem that epithets are not chosen with an eye on the specific context but are used in general, or, as Alexander Pope once phrased it, are 'a sort of attribute with which it was a matter of religion to salute them (heroes) on all occasions, and which it was an irreverence to omit. They were in the nature of Sir-names.'[48]

The question of the interpretation of the Homeric epithets was revolutionised with the advent of Parry's line of research (see section 1b above) in 1928. In his theory of the oral-formulaic nature of the Homeric epics, epithets play a central role;[49] indeed most of his formulas, 'expressions regularly used, under the same metrical conditions, to express a given essential idea', consist of a noun and epithet. He contends that epithets are chosen because of their metrical shape,

---

[47] See esp. Moulton (1977).   [48] Preface of *The Iliad of Homer* (1715–20).
[49] See Parry (1971).

not because of their meaning. When the poet needed to fill the metrical slot after a bucolic diaeresis, he used δῖος Ὀδυσσεύς (or after a consonant ἐσθλὸς Ὀδυσσεύς); after a hephthemimeral caesura, he used πολύμητις Ὀδυσσεύς; and after a penthemimeral caesura, he used πολύτλας δῖος Ὀδυσσεύς. The essential idea of all these three formulas remained the same, i.e. 'Odysseus'.

At a single stroke, Parry's theory solved the problem of unfitting epithets, such as the dirty 'shining' clothes, by suggesting that they were chosen for purely metrical reasons. But the baby seemed to be thrown out with the bath-water, since now *all* epithets were considered devoid of any contextual relevance. Thus Combellack in 1959 rejected an ironic interpretation of φυσίζοος αῖα at *Il.* 3.243, where Helen, standing on the walls of Troy, does not see her brothers, Castor and Polydeuces, after which the narrator remarks that 'the *life-generating* earth already held them under, in their native land Lacedaemon'. He wrote that 'such interpretations have lost any plausibility they once have had, because they require us to believe, not only that the formulary poet used his formulas every now and then in a nonformulary way, but also that his audience, thoroughly trained in the techniqe of listening to formulary verse, could be expected to know when an epithet was formulary and when it was not.'[50] In other words, Parry's theory appeared to have dealt a deathblow to the literary significance of epithets.

Epithets have not fared much better in the more recent theories on Homeric versification of Visser and Bakker,[51] which replace Parry's formula model with the nucleus-periphery model. It is unlikely that a singer would have thousands of noun-epithet formulas in his head; rather, he built his sentences like every other speaker, by starting with the nucleus (the verb, subject, and object) and then filling up the remaining periphery with epithets and conjunctions. Since the noun belongs to the nucleus and the epithet to the periphery, they no longer together form a noun-epithet formula. In this model epithets are not necessarily interchangeable, but their choice would still be determined by and large by metrical factors.

Of course, strategies have been developed to salvage as much as possible of the significance of the epithet. In the first place, there is what could be called the ad hoc strategy, which is followed e.g. by Kirk in connection with the passage just mentioned, φυσίζοος αῖα at *Il.* 3.243: 'It is unlikely, in view of the careful construction of Helen's whole speech and the pathetic tone of these verses in themselves . . . that "life-generating earth" is to be taken as just a standard formular phrase, used at this juncture without special significance . . . In general it is true that formular epithets are not specially selected for their appropriateness to a particular occasion; but nevertheless the singer does from time to time choose language, including formular language, that takes on special significance or irony in an individual context.' This strategy – or actually hardly a strategy but more a *cri de coeur* of a commentator who wants to give as rich as possible an exegesis of

---

[50] Combellack (1959) 198.   [51] Visser (1988) and Bakker (1997).

a beloved text – is familiar, sympathetic, and one to which most commentators are likely to resort from time to time.

But in many cases it is possible to back up one's interpretation by observable facts. For one thing, not all epithets are the same. Thus Parry himself suggests that we distinguish between *ornamental* epithets and *particularised* epithets, the latter having contextual relevance or, as Parry formulates it, pertaining 'directly to the action of the moment'. Acknowledging the subjectivity of this criterion he adds the following elaboration: 'It will be objected that opinions here will differ, and the objection has some force. But in practice, if we keep in mind the directness which is from every point of view the mark of Homeric style, and firmly exclude any interpretation which does not instantly and easily come to mind, we shall find that there is hardly a case where variety of opinion is possible'.[52] His rule of thumb, directness, is not watertight, but in practice he looks for particularised epithets amongst those epithets that are indeed likely to have a special meaning: (1) determinative epithets (e.g. χολωτοῖσιν ἐπέεσσιν, 'with angry words', as opposed to ἀγανοῖς ἐπέεσσιν, 'with gentle words'); (2) epithets with an identical metrical shape, which means that the singer had a choice (e.g. between διΐφιλος, 'dear to Zeus' and πελώριος, 'gigantic'); (3) epithets that are separated from their noun (e.g. παῖδα δ' ἐμοὶ λύσαιτε φίλην: *Il.* 1.20); and (4) epithets in runover position (e.g. μῆνιν ἄειδε, θεά, . . . | οὐλομένην: *Il.* 1.1–2). Parry also distinguishes between *generic* epithets, which are used of more than one person or entity (e.g. δῖος, 'glorious', said of more than twenty different persons), and *distinctive* epithets, which are found in combination with one person or entity only (e.g. πολύτλας, 'much-enduring', used only of Odysseus). It is obvious that distinctive epithets are more likely to be significant.

A third strategy for saving the literary value of epithets consists in enlarging the context. Thus Whallon has argued, for example, that Nestor's epithet ἱππότα, 'horseman' (22 x *Il.*), is not significant in every context in which it occurs, yet is relevant to the *Iliad* as a whole, because this character is clearly portrayed as a man who knows about horses, e.g. when he expertly instructs his son when he participates in the chariot-race: *Il.* 23.306–48.[53] Vivante, who has devoted a whole monograph to the poetic defence of the epithet, goes even further: epithets describe the quality that is intrinsic to a person or entity. A ship is called 'curved' by Homer since that is what it is, true to itself and not subjected to the particular requirement of the action at a certain point.[54] In effect, this position is close to that of Alexander Pope and even Parry, who claims that the ornamental epithet does not so much adorn a single line or even a single poem as the entirety of heroic song. At this point it is important to realise that the ornamental epithet is a hallmark of *all* heroic poetry throughout the world, both oral and written.[55] It seems likely that it found its origin not in metrical exigencies but in stylistic

52 Parry (1971) 155–6.   53 Whallon (1969).   54 Vivante (1982).
55 See Bowra (1952) 221–6 and West (1997) 169.

register: it served to add lustre to the people, the objects, in short, the world of heroic times. In an oral tradition like Homer's it could, precisely because of its recurrent nature, become an important element of versification.

A fourth strategy consists of analysing the context of *all* epithets of one noun to see whether there are significant patterns. The word 'hand', for example has five epithets, of which three (ἄαπτος, 'irresistible'; θρασύς, 'stout'; βαρύς, 'heavy') have emotional force, describing the hand as a harmful instrument, while two (παχύς, 'thick'; στιβαρός, 'strong') are merely descriptive.[56]

A fifth approach is to look at the distribution of an epithet over the text: is it found throughout or is it inserted at (a) particular point(s)? For instance, it seems significant that Odysseus is first given the epithet πτολίπορθος, 'sacker of cities', at the opening of book 8 of the *Odyssey*, because this book features Demodocus singing about the Greeks capturing Troy with the help of the Wooden Horse devised by Odysseus. Obviously, this approach is liable to subjectivity (again), as can be illustrated by the metrically equivalent pair Ἕκτορος ἱπποδάμοιο (5 x) versus Ἕκτορος ἀνδροφόνοιο (11 x). It has been suggested that ἱπποδάμοιο is used where Apollo plays a role, ἀνδροφόνοιο where Achilles does.[57] However, we actually find ἱπποδάμοιο when *Achilles* is Hector's direct opponent (*Il.* 22.161) and ἀνδροφόνοιο when *Andromache* comes home after her conversation with Hector (*Il.* 6.498).

A final parameter that seems relevant when interpreting epithets is their presentation: are they used by the narrator or by characters?[58] For one thing, epithets occur much more often in narrator-text than in speeches. But when we turn to emotional or subjective epithets, these are found more often in speeches or passages of embedded focalisation, not surprisingly considering the existence of a separate character-language in Homer (see section 3a): e.g. ὑπερφίαλος, 'overbearing', is found 22 times in speech, four times in embedded focalisation, and only once in narrator-text. The intuition that the epithet of night ὀλοήν, 'baneful', which is used by Achilles at 22.102 (νύχθ' ὕπο τήνδ' ὀλοήν) might be significant because it is separated from its noun, is fully confirmed when we realise that it only occurs in speech (here and *Od.* 11.19) and embedded focalisation (*Il.* 16.567).

All in all, there seems to be enough room for arguing for the literary value of (many) epithets, although the subjectivity of the interpreter, a factor which can never be totally excluded in literary criticism, is likely to play a larger role than usual. The reader should refer to the commentary for further examples.

---

[56] Eide (1986). An invaluable tool for carrying out this kind of research are the indices of epithets compiled by Dee (2000), (2001), (2002).

[57] Sacks (1987) 220–6, 163–75.

[58] This point is addressed by Austin (1975) 1–80, Vivante (1982) 27–33, Shive (1987), and de Jong (1988). For Achilles' use of (noun-epithet) formulas see Martin (1989) 146–205.

4. LANGUAGE, METRE, AND TEXT

(a) Language

The language of the Homeric epics is not the spoken dialect of any period or area but an artificial language. It is a composite of different dialects: primarily Ionian, with some elements of Aeolian (e.g. infinitive endings in -μεν, -μεναι) and 'Achaean', the language of the Mycenaeans known to us through the decipherment of Linear B (e.g. αὐτάρ, αἶσα). There are occasional Attic elements, which probably result from the regular performances of the Homeric poems in Athens at the Panathenaic festival (see section c below). This dialectal mixture is the result of the long tradition of Greek oral poetry before it culminated in the Homeric epics; it started in the Mycenaean centres; after their destruction, it was transported by migrating Greeks to Aeolia, and it ended in Ionia (see section 1b). Although singers would always modernise the language and adapt it to their own dialect, the formulaic nature of their medium encourages fossilisation and the creation of artificial forms.[59]

The following pages offer an overview of the most frequent characteristics of Homeric language, which are referred to in the commentary as '(L 1)', etc.

Phonology

1. Many forms are not yet contracted, e.g. ἀκέοντο (2), τείχεος, σάκεα (4).
2. Many forms have ου or ει, where Attic has ο or ε. This is in some cases the result of the disappearance of the digamma (ϝ, the Greek letter pronounced as *w*), which in Ionian (but not Attic) leads to lengthening of the preceding vowel, e.g. γούνατα (24) from *γόνϝατα (Attic: γόνατα). In other cases we are dealing with an artificial lengthening of a syllable for metrical reasons, e.g. Οὐλύμποιο (187) instead of Ὀλύμποιο (which would yield an unmetrical sequence of $\cup - - \cup$).
3. Words often show a single or a double consonant, depending on metrical convenience, e.g. τοσ(σ)όνδε, ἔσ(σ)ονται, Ἀχιλ(λ)εύς.
4. Contracted forms may be 'stretched' (metrical *diectasis*), so as to regain their former metrical shape, e.g. ἰδέειν ($\cup \cup -$) < ἰδεῖν ($\cup -$) < ἰδέεν ($\cup \cup -$) (47). Often the wrong vowel is restored: μητιάασθε ($- \cup \cup - \cup$) < μητιᾶσθε ($- \cup - \cup$) < μητιάεσθε ($- \cup \cup - \cup$) (174).

Morphology

5. The genitive singular of first declension words may end in -αο or -εω, e.g. Ἀΐδαο (52). Genitive plural of first declension words may end in -αων or -εων, e.g. ἁρμονιάων (255).

---

[59] The best grammar of Homeric Greek is still Chantraine (1958–63), referred to in the Commentary as *GH*, but for a shorter overview and update on many details one may fruitfully consult Wachter (2000).

6. The genitive singular of second declension words may end in -οιο, e.g. πεδίοιο (23).

7. The dative plural of first and second declension words may end in -ῃσι, -ῃις, -οισι, -αισι, e.g. καλῇσιν (3), ὀλοῇις (65), ὤμοισι (4).

8. Dative plural of third declension words may end in -εσσι, e.g. ταχέεσσι (8), λεχέεσσι (87).

9. The suffix -φι(ν) may be added to form the equivalent of genitives and datives, singular and plural, e.g. σὺν ὄχεσφιν (22), ἦφι βίηφι πιθήσας (107), διὰ στήθεσφιν (284).

10. The augment is optional: ἀπεψύχοντο, πίον, ἀκέοντο (2).

11. Infinitives may end in -μεν, -μεναι (athematic stems) or -εμεν, -εμεναι (thematic stems), e.g. δωσέμεν (117), ὀαριζέμεναι (127).

12. The addition of the suffix -σκ- may turn past verbs into iteratives, e.g. πλύνεσκον (155), 'they were in the habit of washing', ἀποτρέψασκε (197), 'every time he would head him back'.

13. The subjunctive of thematic stems may have athematic endings: ἐθέλωμι (*Od.* 21.348), πάθῃσθα (24.551), θέῃσι (23). In the third person an iota subscript has entered the texts at a later stage (ἐθέλητι > ἐθέλησι > ἐθέλῃσι, in analogy with ἐθέλῃ).

14. In the third person plural we find the endings -αται, -ατο, e.g. εἰρύατο = εἴρυντο (303). Likewise we find -ν (after a short vowel) next to -σαν (after a long vowel), e.g. ἄλεν = ἄλησαν (12), ἔσταν = ἔστησαν (473), ἔβησαν (8.343).

15. Originally, only thematic stems had a subjunctive with -η- and -ω-, while all other stems had -ε- and -ο-. The Homeric epics still contain many instances of this short-vowel subjunctive, e.g. εἴδομεν (130), σαώσομεν (175).

16. In Homeric Greek the dual, a separate form to indicate 'two things or persons', is found frequently:

Verbs

second person, present and past	-τον, -σθον
third person, present:	-τον, -σθον
third person, past:	-την, -σθην

e.g. προσαυδήτην (90), ἀρνύσθην (160).

Nouns

second declension	(nom./acc.) -ω, (gen./dat.) -οιιν
third declension	(nom./acc.) -ε, (gen./dat.) -οιιν

e.g. παῖδε (46), κρουνὼ . . . καλλιρρόω (147).

The dual is an inheritance from the Aeolic, but its use was continued by the Ionian-speaking singers, who had no dual in their daily dialect. Often it is no more than an expedient metrical variant of the plural, with which it may be combined in one verse. But there are also places where its original force is exploited, e.g. in a line like ὡς τώ γε κλαίοντε προσαυδήτην φίλον υἱόν (90), where the dual stresses the joint effort of Hector's parents in imploring him.

17. The forms of the later definite article ὁ, ἡ, τό in the Homeric epics still have demonstrative force. They are used as anaphoric pronouns, i.e. pronouns which refer *back* to somebody/something just mentioned, e.g. ὡς Ἀχιλεὺς ... ἐνώμα. | τὸν δ᾽... Πρίαμος... ἴδεν (24–5), 'Thus Achilles moved... And him Priam saw', θεοὶ ... ὁρῶντο· | τοῖσι δὲ... (166–7), 'the gods watched. And amidst them...' The person or thing need not literally have just been mentioned but may instead be foremost in the mind of the speaker or implied by the context, e.g. τοὺς δ᾽ ἐσάωσας (18), 'you have saved them', where τούς are the Trojans, mentioned last in 11.

The pronoun may also point *forward* to somebody/something about to be mentioned (the so-called cataphoric use), e.g. ὁ δέ οἱ σχεδὸν ἦλθεν Ἀχιλλεύς (131), 'and he came near to him, Achilles'.

Sometimes the pronoun and substantive follow immediately upon each other and we are close to the later article, e.g. ὁ γέρων Πρίαμος (25), 'he, the old man Priam' virtually amounts to 'the old man Priam'.

The anaphoric pronoun can be used as relative pronoun, e.g. δύο παῖδε..., | τούς... τέκετο (46–8), 'two sons..., whom X bore'. Often metrical factors are involved, e.g. σεῦ ἀποτεθνηῶτος; ὅ μοι νύκτάς τε καὶ ἦμαρ (432), where we find ὁ instead of ὅς in order to avoid the pronoun having to be scanned long.

There are some variant forms: τοῖο (= τοῦ), τοῖιν (= τοῖν), τοί (= οἱ), ταί (= αἱ), τάων (= τῶν), τοῖσι (= τοῖς), τῇσι, τῆις (= ταῖς). There is also a dual: (nom./acc.) τώ, (gen./dat.) τοῖν, τοῖιν.

18. Possessive pronouns:

τεός = σός	'your'
ἑός = ὅς	'his/her'
(reflexive like Latin *suus*)	
ἀμός = ἡμέτερος	'our'
ὑμός = ὑμέτερος	'your'
σφός = σφέτερος	'their'

19. Personal pronouns:
First person

ἐγώ(ν)	ἡμεῖς, ἄμμες
ἐμέο, ἐμεῖο, ἐμεῦ, ἐμέθεν (μευ)	ἡμέων, ἡμείων
ἐμοί (μοι)	ἡμῖν, ἄμμι
ἐμέ (με)	ἡμέας, ἄμμε
νῶϊ, νώ (dual nom./acc.)	
νῶϊν (dual gen./dat.)	

Second person

σύ, τύνη	ὑμεῖς, ὕμμες
σέο, σεῖο, σέθεν (σεο, σευ)	ὑμέων, ὑμείων, ὕμμεων
σοί (τοι, σοι)	ὑμῖν, ὕμμι
σέ (σε)	ὑμέας, ὕμμε
σφῶϊ, σφώ (dual nom./acc.)	
σφῶϊν (dual gen./dat.)	

Third person

ἑο, εὑ, ἕθεν, ἕο, εἷο, εὗ, ἕθεν	σφεων, σφείων, σφέων
οἱ, οἷ, ἑοῖ	σφισι(ν), σφι(ν), σφίσι(ν)
ἑ, μιν, ἕ, ἑέ	σφεας, σφέας, σφας
σφωε (dual nom./acc.)	
σφωϊν (dual gen./dat.)	

When the third person personal pronoun has an accent, it is reflexive, e.g. ἐπὶ οἷ μεμαῶτ' (326): Achilles hit Hector 'who was charging him'.

Syntax

20. Prepositions are used much more independently in Homer and often function as adverbs, e.g. πρὸς δ' ἐμὲ... ἐλέησον (59), 'and in addition pity me', ἐπὶ δὲ στενάχοντο πολῖται (429), 'and in response (to Priam's lament) the citizens mourned'.

    Likewise they often are not yet combined into a compound verb, e.g. ἀπό... ἔλθοι (43), ἀνὰ... ἕλκετο (77). Grammars refer to this phenomenon as *tmesis*, the 'cutting' of a compound verb, which is incorrect: the Homeric language has not severed an existing compound. Instead, the split form is the older, original one.

    Prepositions frequently follow the noun they govern, e.g. πόλιν πέρι (165), πύργωι ἔπι (97). In those cases the accent moves to the first syllable: ἔπι instead of the normal ἐπί.

21. The particle τε is a connector (standing after the word it connects), e.g. ἱδρῶ ἀπεψύχοντο πίον τ' ἀκέοντό τε δίψαν: 'they dried the sweat from their bodies and drank and slaked their thirst' (2). It may also be used in relative, less often conditional or temporal clauses, often as part of a simile. In those cases we are dealing with so-called *epic* τε: the particle signals that the action or event described is regularly recurring or exists in all times (hence linguists speak of omnitemporality). E.g. οἴμησεν... ὥς τ' αἰετὸς..., ὅς τ' εἶσιν πεδίονδε (308–9), 'he swooped like an eagle, which darts to a plain'; epic τε often occurs in conjunction with a gnomic aorist and in similes.

22. In Homer the possessive dative is used more widely than in Attic, where it is confined to the combination with εἶναι (type 'there is for me' = 'I have'); e.g. οἱ αὐγαί (27), 'its rays', οὐδ' Ἕκτορι θυμὸν ἔπειθεν (78), 'he did not persuade Hector's heart'. Linguists call this the 'sympathetic' dative.

23. Homeric style has a strong tendency towards parataxis (lit. 'setting along-side') instead of hypotaxis ('setting below'), that is to say towards coordination (the adding of independent clauses) instead of subordination (the combination of main clause and subordinate clause). E.g. ἂψ δ' Ἀχιλῆϊ δίδου, λάθε δ' Ἕκτορα (277), '(Athena) gave back the spear to Achilles *and* escaped the attention of Hector = *while* escaping the attention of Hector'.

(b) Metre

The metre of Homeric epic[60] is the dactylic hexameter, which consists of six metra or 'feet':

$$\underline{\overline{}}\ \underline{\smile\smile}\ |\ \overline{}\ \underline{\smile\smile}\ |\ \overline{}\ \underline{\smile\smile}\ |\ \overline{}\ \underline{\smile\smile}\ |\ \overline{}\ \underline{\smile\smile}\ |\ \underline{'}\ x.$$

In this notation – indicates a long syllable, ◡ a short one, while x (*anceps*) indicates that a syllable can be either long or short. The last syllable will be metrically treated as long because of the slight pause after each verse. One long and two short syllables form a *dactyl*, while two long syllables form a *spondee*. A spondee in the fifth foot is less common than in the first four (some instances in book 22 are lines 4, 6, 25, 101, 128, 146, 164, and 165), while a wholly spondaic verse is extremely rare.

Prosody

A syllable is *short* if it contains a short vowel (ε, ο, ᾰ, ῐ, ῠ), which is followed by no more than one consonant; this consonant in the syllabification belongs to the next syllable, e.g. αὐτὰρ Ἀχαιοί (au-ta-ra-chai-oi), – ◡ ◡ | – x (3).

A syllable is *long* (1) by nature if it contains a long vowel (η, ω, ᾱ, ῑ, ῡ) or a diphthong, or (2) by position if it contains a short vowel followed by more than one consonant; the first consonant in the syllabification belongs to this syllable, the other(s) to the next: e.g., ἄλεν, σύ (= a-len-su), ◡ | – ◡ (12).

The rough breathing (*spiritus asper*) does not count as a consonant. ζ = σδ; ξ = κς; ψ = πς.

Length by position is often due to the original presence of the digamma, e.g. πρῶτος (ϝ)ίδεν ὀφθαλμοῖσιν, – | – ◡◡ | – – | – x‖ (25), where the final syllable of πρῶτος is scanned long because it was originally followed by a consonant.

Words starting with λ-, μ-, ν-, ρ-, σ- may also cause lengthening when they originally started with two consonants, e.g. οὐδὲ κατὰ μοῖραν, – ◡◡ | – – | – (16.367), where the final syllable of κατά is scanned long because μοῖρα originally was *smorya. Even words which did not originally start with two consonants may make position in this way, through analogy, e.g. μηδὲ μέγα κῦδος ὀρέξῃις,

---

[60] For fuller treatments see e.g. West (1982) and Sicking (1993).

– | – ⌣⌣ | – ⌣⌣ | – – ‖ (57), where the final syllable of μηδέ is scanned long because of μέγα = μμέγα.

The combination of mutes (π, β, φ, κ, γ, χ, τ, δ, θ) and liquids or nasals (μ, λ, ν, ρ), both within words and between two words, occasionally does *not* make position, e.g. πτερόεντα προσηύδα, ⌣⌣|– ⌣⌣ | – x (215), where the final syllable of πτερόεντα is scanned short in spite of it being followed by two consonants (πρ).

Diphthongs are pronounced as one syllable. When two adjacent vowels belong to two syllables, this is indicated with a double dot (*diaeresis*) in modern editions, e.g. ῥηϊδίως, – ⌣⌣ | – (19), Ἀχιλῆϊ, ⌣⌣| – ⌣ (36).

Two or more vowels within a word are occasionally treated as one (long) vowel (*synizesis*), e.g. ἀλλ' ἄγε δή στέωμεν, – ⌣ ⌣ | – – | – (231), with -εω taken as one long syllable.

In the case of a series of three or more short syllables, one (usually the first) syllable is scanned long to fit the metre, e.g. Ζεὺς ἐθέληι τελέσαι ἠδ' ἀθάνατοι, – ⌣ ⌣ | – ⌣ ⌣ | – – | – ⌣ ⌣ | – (366), where the first syllable of ἀθάνατοι is scanned long. This licence is frequently taken with words which would otherwise not fit the hexametric metre. In the case of ε and ο, we find the lengthening reflected in the spelling, e.g. Οὐλύμποιο (187) instead of Ὀλύμποιο (see above L 2).

When a word ends with a short vowel and is followed by a word beginning with a vowel, there may be *elision* ('squeezing out'), which means that the first vowel is dropped and (largely) ignored in pronunciation. The elision is marked by an apostrophe, e.g. τ' ἀκέοντο (2), where the ε of τε is dropped; σάκε' ὤμοισι (4), where the final α of σάκεα is dropped; or παμφαίνονθ' ὥς (26), where the final α of παμφαίνοντα is dropped and the τ assimilated to θ under the influence of the following rough breathing. In Homer -αι of person endings and infinitives and -οι of dative singular of the personal pronouns may also be elided.

When a word ends with a long vowel or diphthong and is followed by a word beginning with a vowel, the first vowel or diphthong is scanned short (*epic correption*, 'tightening up'), e.g ἱδρῶ ἀπεψύχοντο, – ⌣ ⌣ | – – | – ⌣ (2), where -ω of ἱδρῶ is scanned short; ἤ νυ τοι οὔ, – ⌣ ⌣ | – (11), where τοι is scanned short (compare τοι scanned regularly long in οὔ τοι μόρσιμος: 13).

In Greek poetry *hiatus* ('gap'), i.e. the conjunction of a final vowel and an initial vowel in which both vowels retain their full pronunciation, is normally avoided. Regular exceptions are final υ and monosyllables ending in other letters than ε (e.g. τά, τό, τί, τι, πρό), which are never elided. In Homer there are many more instances of *hiatus*. It is often due to the loss of an initial digamma, e.g μυρία ἔδνα (472), where the -α of μυρία is not elided because ἔδνα originally started with ϝ. Another generator of *hiatus* is the use of the more recent form -ου instead of -οι(ο), e.g. ἢ πυρὸς αἰθομένου ἢ' ἠελίου ἀνιόντος, – ⌣ ⌣ | – ⌣ ⌣ | – – | – ⌣ ⌣ | – ⌣ ⌣ | – x (135), where the -ου of αἰθομένου and ἠελίου are scanned long although they are followed by a vowel (no epic correption) because the original form was ἢ πυρὸς αἰθομένοι᾽ ἢ᾽ ἠελίοι᾽ ἀνιόντος. Hiatus often occurs at caesurae and when two formulas are juxtaposed.

Caesurae

The internal articulation or rhythm of a verse is determined by the occurrence of word end at regular places: the main caesura occurs in the third foot, either after the first, long syllable (penthemimeral or masculine caesura) or between the two shorts (κατὰ τὸν τρίτον τροχαῖον or feminine caesura). There usually are additional word ends after the first foot (diaeresis) or the first, long syllable of the second foot (trithemimeral caesura), and also after the first long of the fourth foot (hepthemimeral caesura) or after the fourth foot (bucolic diaeresis).

Enclitics like με, τις, ποτε, τε, γε, particles like δέ, μέν, γάρ, ἄν, proclitics like καί, οὐ, μή, and monosyllabic prepositions cohere so closely with the preceding or following word that no caesura occurs between them.

The opposite of a caesura is a 'bridge' (*zeugma*), a place in the verse where word end is avoided. There is one significant bridge in the Homeric hexameter, detected by the German scholar Gottfried Hermann and consequently called Hermann's bridge: it refers to the fact that there is hardly ever word break after the first short of a fourth foot dactyl.

The caesurae contribute to the variety of Homeric versification. They allow the singer to avoid the monotony that would result from sequences of lines that have the same rhythm, all the more so since the melody of each line probably was the same. How far metrical rhythm also corresponds to sense is a matter of debate.[61] It is clear, however, that there is a close correspondence between formulas and the cola (lit. 'members', units) created by the caesurae, e.g.

αὐτὰρ Πηλείωνα προσηύδα / (bucolic diaeresis) **Φοῖβος Ἀπόλλων** (7)
τὸν δὲ μέγ᾽ ὀχθήσας προσέφη / (hephthemim.) **πόδας ὠκὺς Ἀχιλλεύς** (14)
ὣς ἄρα φωνήσας / (penthem.) εἰρύσσατο φάσγανον ὀξύ (306)
τὸν δ᾽ ἐπεὶ ἐξενάριξε / (feminine caesura) **ποδάρκης δῖος Ἀχιλλεύς** (376)

Cola also often correspond to syntactic units (which in our modern texts are regularly marked by punctuation), e.g.

ἔβλαψάς μ᾽, / (trithem.) ἑκάεργε, / (feminine caesura) θεῶν ὀλοώτατε πάντων (15)
λαμπρότατος μὲν ὅ γ᾽ ἐστί, / (feminine caesura) κακὸν δέ τε σῆμα τέτυκται (30)
τίλλων ἐκ κεφαλῆς· / (penthemim.) οὐδ᾽ Ἕκτορι θυμὸν ἔπειθεν (78)[62]

---

[61] See e.g. Macleod 54–6 and Kirk I 18–30.
[62] This approach has made much progress since the introduction of the modern linguistic concept of the intonation unit, which is the oral pendant of the sentence and clause of written grammar; see Bakker (1997).

Enjambement

We speak of enjambement when a sentence does not correspond to one verse but continues into the next one, e.g. σείων Πηλιάδα μελίην κατὰ δεξιὸν ὦμον ‖ δεινήν (133–4). We may distinguish between (at least) two different forms of enjambement in Homer:[63] (1) *adding* enjambement, when a sentence in principle is finished but receives additional information in the next line, as happens in the example just quoted, and (2) *necessary* or *periodic* enjambement, when a sentence or clause is not finished but needs (part of) an additional verse, e.g. ὧι μοι ἐγών, εἰ μέν κε πύλας καὶ τείχεα δύω, ‖ Πουλυδάμας μοι πρῶτος ἐλεγχείην ἀναθήσει (99–100), οὐδέ νύ πώ με ‖ ἔγνως ὡς θεός εἰμι (9–10).

Enjambement occurs quite often in Homer and it can therefore not be maintained that *every* word in runover position is emphatic, but in combination with other phenomena, e.g. the separation of noun and epithet, the device may acquire weight, e.g. μένεος δ᾽ ἐμπλήσατο θυμόν ‖ ἀγρίου (312–13). There is also a tendency for enjambement to occur in clusters, when we find a row of sentences where neither the beginning nor the end coincides with verse boundaries. A clear example is found at 451–6, as part of Andromache's anxious speech at the moment she hears the wailing of the Trojans: αἰδοίης ἑκυρῆς ὀπὸς ἔκλυον, ἐν δέ μοι αὐτῆι ‖ **στήθεσι** πάλλεται ἦτορ ἀνὰ στόμα, νέρθε δὲ γοῦνα ‖ **πήγνυται·** ἐγγὺς δή τι κακὸν Πριάμοιο τέκεσσιν.‖ αἶ γὰρ ἀπ᾽ οὔατος εἴη ἐμεῦ ἔπος· ἀλλὰ μάλ᾽ αἰνῶς ‖ **δείδω** μὴ δή μοι θρασὺν Ἕκτορα δῖος Ἀχιλλεύς ‖ **μοῦνον** ἀποτμήξας πόλιος πεδίονδε δίηται. Higbie speaks of *skewed verses* and argues that these are found at moments of heightened emotion.[64]

An Example

Here is the opening of book 22, with metrical annotation:

$\acute{-} - \mid \acute{-} / \cup \cup \mid \acute{-} \cup / \cup \mid \acute{-} \cup \cup \mid / \acute{-} \cup \cup \mid \acute{-} - \parallel$
ὣς οἱ μὲν κατὰ ἄστυ, πεφυζότες ἠΰτε νεβροί, (1)

$\acute{-} \cup \cup \mid \acute{-} - \mid \acute{-} \cup / \cup \mid \acute{-} \cup \cup \mid \acute{-} \cup \cup \mid \acute{-} - \parallel$
ἱδρῶ ἀπεψύχοντο πίον τ᾽ ἀκέοντό τε δίψαν,

$\acute{-} \cup \cup \mid \acute{-} / - \mid \acute{-} \cup / \cup \mid \acute{-} \cup \cup \mid / \acute{-} \cup \cup \mid \acute{-} - \parallel$
κεκλιμένοι καλῆισιν ἐπάλξεσιν· αὐτὰρ Ἀχαιοί

$\acute{-} \cup \cup \mid / \acute{-} \cup \cup \mid \acute{-} / \cup \cup \mid \acute{-} - \mid \acute{-} - \mid \acute{-} - \parallel$
τείχεος ἄσσον ἴσαν, σάκε᾽ ὤμοισι κλίναντες.

---

[63] See e.g. Parry (1971) 251–65, Kirk I 31–4, Higbie (1990), and Friedrich (2000).

[64] Higbie (1990) 90–151, esp. 112. Bakker (1997) 153–5 speaks of antimetry (a secondary rhythm is temporarily set up against the normal hexametric flow of sentences).

‾ ⌣ ⌣ | / ‾ – | ‾ ⌣ /⌣| ‾ – | / ‾ ⌣ ⌣ | ‾ – ‖
Ἕκτορα δ᾽ αὐτοῦ μεῖναι ὀλοιὴ μοῖρ᾽ ἐπέδησεν (5)

‾ – |‾ / ⌣ ⌣ | ‾ ⌣ /⌣ | ‾ – | ‾ –| ‾ – ‖
Ἰλίου προπάροιθε πυλάων τε Σκαιάων.

‾ – | / ‾ – | ‾ ⌣ / ⌣ | ‾ – |/ ‾ ⌣ ⌣ | ‾ – ‖
αὐτὰρ Πηλείωνα προσηύδα Φοῖβος Ἀπόλλων·

‾ ⌣ ⌣ |/ ‾ ⌣ ⌣|‾ ⌣/⌣|‾ /⌣ ⌣|‾ ⌣ ⌣| ‾ – ‖
"τίπτέ με, Πηλέος υἱέ, ποσὶν ταχέεσσι διώκεις,

‾ – | / ‾ ⌣ ⌣ |‾/ ⌣ ⌣ |‾ ⌣ ⌣ |/ ‾ ⌣ ⌣| ‾ – ‖
αὐτὸς θνητὸς ἐὼν θεὸν ἄμβροτον; οὐδέ νύ πώ με

‾ – |/ ‾ ⌣ ⌣ | ‾ ⌣/ ⌣ |‾ – | ‾ ⌣ ⌣ | ‾ – ‖
ἔγνως ὡς θεός εἰμι, σὺ δ᾽ ἀσπερχὲς μενεαίνεις. (10)

‾ ⌣ ⌣ |/‾ ⌣ ⌣ |‾ / – | ‾ ⌣ ⌣ |/ ‾ ⌣ ⌣| ‾ – ‖
ἦ νύ τοι οὔ τι μέλει Τρώων πόνος, οὓς ἐφόβησας,

‾ – | ‾ / – | ‾ ⌣/⌣|‾ / ⌣ ⌣ ⌣ |‾ ⌣ ⌣ | ‾ – ‖
οἳ δή τοι εἰς ἄστυ ἄλεν, σὺ δὲ δεῦρο λιάσθης.

‾ – | ‾ / ⌣ ⌣ |‾ / ⌣ ⌣| ‾ – |/ ‾ ⌣ ⌣ | ‾ – ‖
οὐ μέν με κτενέεις, ἐπεὶ οὔ τοι μόρσιμός εἰμι."

‾ ⌣ ⌣ |/ ‾ – | ‾ / ⌣ ⌣ |‾ / ⌣ ⌣ | ‾ ⌣ ⌣ | ‾ – ‖
τὸν δὲ μέγ᾽ ὀχθήσας προσέφη πόδας ὠκὺς Ἀχιλλεύς·

‾ – | ‾ ⌣ ⌣ |‾ ⌣ /⌣|‾ / ⌣ ⌣| ‾ ⌣ ⌣ | ‾ – ‖
"ἔβλαψάς μ᾽, ἑκάεργε, θεῶν ὀλοώτατε πάντων, (15)

Notable features:

Line 1: first caesura after μέν rather than οἱ because μέν is enclitic. There is
    hiatus between κατά and ἄστυ because it originally was ϝάστυ.
Line 2: epic correption of the ω of ἱδρῶ. There is only one caesura.
Line 3: the α of καλῇσιν is long because the form originally was καλϝός.
Line 4: has a spondaic fifth foot (which occurs in 5% of Homer's hexameters).
    There is no third caesura.
Line 5: epic correption of the αι of μεῖναι.
Line 6: the second iota of Ἰλίου must scan long. This is a linguistically modern
    version of an older (metrically regular) formula: Ἰλίοο προπάροιθε, ‾ ⌣ ⌣ ‾ ⌣
    ⌣ ‾ ⌣. Besides the older genitive ending -οιο a new ending -οο was created,
    which eventually contracted to -ου. The line has a spondaic fifth foot. There
    is no third caesura because τε is enclitic.

Line 7: the mute + liquid of προσηύδα fail to make position.

Line 10: there is no third caesura.

Line 11: epic correption of τοι. The first word break falls after τοι because τοι is enclitic and οὔ proclitic.

Line 12: there is hiatus between τοι and οὔ, since τοι is not shortened. (N.B. There can of course never be epic correption of the first long of a foot).

Line 13: epic correption of the ει of ἐπεί.

(c) Text

The history of the transmission of the Homeric text is long, complex, often obscure, and, especially where its first phases are concerned, the subject of fierce debate. What follows is a mere outline, which is needed to understand the critical apparatus.[65]

1. Writing down of the oral-performance text. How this was accomplished is a matter of debate (see the end of section 1b), but most scholars would agree that it took place somewhere between 800 and 500 BC.

2. Classical period. Variant texts started to circulate, which were the possession of individuals or cities. There were also public recitations of the Homeric texts by rhapsodes, who (probably) recited from memory. The most important were the recitations at the Athenian Panathenaic festival, instituted in the late sixth century BC by Pisistratus and his son Hipparchus. Scholars are divided over the question of how to evaluate the (fourth-century and Hellenistic) tradition of a 'Pisistratean recension': was the Homeric text then fixed in script, was it edited into monumental form (i.e. was a full set of the separate book-rolls which make up the whole being collected), or was one text chosen to become the official festival text? At any rate the Athenian phase in the transmission of the text has left its traces in linguistic and orthographic Atticisms and, probably, some interpolated Athenocentric passages (the most striking being the Attic entry in the Catalogue of Ships: 2.546–56).

   We can get an idea of how these texts looked from papyri of the third and second centuries BC, quotations by ancient authors, and ancient variants mentioned by the Alexandrians. In comparison to the later manuscripts these texts include many additional lines (so-called 'plus'-verses). The fourth-century quotations in authors like Plato and Aristotle show a high proportion of variant readings, but these are largely to be explained by the fact that those authors quoted from memory.

---

[65] A full and lucid overview, with older secondary literature, is Haslam (1997). Since then see West (2001) and Nagy (2004).

3. Alexandrians. In the third and second century BC the famous library of Alexandria hosted three scholars who made editions of Homer (and numerous other texts): Zenodotus of Ephesus, Aristophanes of Byzantium, and Aristarchus of Samothrace. Of these Aristarchus was the most important. One of his main concerns was to eliminate the numerous 'plus'-verses that had crept into the tradition. He did not remove lines that he suspected, but he 'athetised' them, i.e. marked them with an *obelos* or dash in the left-hand margin. The original works of these scholars are lost, but we do have excerpts, preserved as part of the scholia (from σχόλιον, 'comment', the explanatory glosses which were inserted in the margins of ancient manuscripts, from the fifth century BC until the eighth century AD).[66]

4. Roman and Byzantine times (150 BC–AD 600). The Homeric text at this stage of its transmission is known to us from over 600 manuscripts, quotations, and the scholia. In many places it presents a different reading from that known to have been preferred by Aristarchus. In this respect his influence seems to have been small. His determination of the number of lines and length of each book was more influential. From that time, the 'plus'-verses largely disappeared.

5. Middle Ages and Renaissance (AD 900–1550). There are some 200 manuscripts, of which the most famous is the Codex Venetus A from the tenth century. It is also an important source for our Homeric scholia.

   Scholars regularly use the term 'vulgate' (from Latin *vulgata*, 'common' or 'standard') to refer to the Homeric text in stages 4 and 5. Unlike the Bible, for which the 'vulgate' refers to the fourth-century Latin version by Jerome, this term does not designate one particular text. Instead, it is merely a form of shorthand that indicates that a reading is found in all or most of the manuscripts of this period.

6. *Editio princeps*. In 1488 Demetrius Chalcondyles printed the first text of the *Iliad* in Florence.

The text presented in this volume is my own but is essentially a 'collation' of the editions of Monro-Allen (1920), van Thiel (1996) and Martin West (2000). On the whole I have stayed closer to Monro-Allen, because scholars are still debating many of West's editorial principles and decisions, a discussion which lies outside the scope and aims of this commentary.[67] I have adopted punctuations of my own, not found in any of these editions, at 71–3, 271–2, 273, and 467–8 (see notes ad locc.). Parallels from other books are quoted from the OCT (for the *Iliad*) and von der Mühll (for the *Odyssey*).

[66] For the literary criticism by scholiasts see Nünlist (2009).
[67] For a detailed review see Führer and Schmidt (2001).

The selective apparatus criticus follows the example of that of Richard Rutherford in his edition of *Odyssey* 19–20 in this series (1992). I have not reported obvious scribal errors, variations of spelling, or minor variants. Nor have I given details of which manuscripts contain a given reading. The edition of Martin West presents a full overview, including some 15 medieval manuscripts not previously collated by Monro-Allen in the OCT edition, some 800 papyrus fragments, and ancient quotations from the classical period until the ninth century.

I present manuscript evidence in the form:

2 ἀπεψύχοντο : ἀνεψύχοντο

This indicates that both readings are found in the manuscript tradition; the reading preferred is given first. It is indicated whether a reading occurs only in a papyrus, is an ancient variant, a modern editor's conjecture, or a quotation in an ancient author.

ΙΛΙΑΔΟΣ Χ

ΙΛΙΑΔΟΣ Χ

ὣς οἱ μὲν κατὰ ἄστυ, πεφυζότες ἠΰτε νεβροί,
ἱδρῶ ἀπεψύχοντο πίον τ' ἀκέοντό τε δίψαν,
κεκλιμένοι καλῇσιν ἐπάλξεσιν· αὐτὰρ Ἀχαιοί
τείχεος ἆσσον ἴσαν, σάκε' ὤμοισι κλίναντες.
Ἕκτορα δ' αὐτοῦ μεῖναι ὀλοιὴ μοῖρ' ἐπέδησεν   5
Ἰλίου προπάροιθε πυλάων τε Σκαιάων.
    αὐτὰρ Πηλεΐωνα προσηύδα Φοῖβος Ἀπόλλων·
"τίπτε με, Πηλέος υἱέ, ποσὶν ταχέεσσι διώκεις,
αὐτὸς θνητὸς ἐὼν θεὸν ἄμβροτον; οὐδέ νύ πώ με
ἔγνως ὡς θεός εἰμι, σὺ δ' ἀσπερχὲς μενεαίνεις.   10
ἦ νύ τοι οὔ τι μέλει Τρώων πόνος, οὓς ἐφόβησας,
οἳ δή τοι εἰς ἄστυ ἄλεν, σὺ δὲ δεῦρο λιάσθης.
οὐ μέν με κτενέεις, ἐπεὶ οὔ τοι μόρσιμός εἰμι."
    τὸν δὲ μέγ' ὀχθήσας προσέφη πόδας ὠκὺς Ἀχιλλεύς·
"ἔβλαψάς μ', ἑκάεργε, θεῶν ὀλοώτατε πάντων,   15
ἐνθάδε νῦν τρέψας ἀπὸ τείχεος· ἦ κ' ἔτι πολλοί
γαῖαν ὀδὰξ εἷλον πρὶν Ἴλιον εἰσαφικέσθαι.
νῦν δ' ἐμὲ μὲν μέγα κῦδος ἀφείλεο, τοὺς δ' ἐσάωσας
ῥηϊδίως, ἐπεὶ οὔ τι τίσιν γ' ἔδδεισας ὀπίσσω.
ἦ σ' ἂν τεισαίμην, εἴ μοι δύναμίς γε παρείη."   20
    ὣς εἰπὼν προτὶ ἄστυ μέγα φρονέων ἐβεβήκει,
σευάμενος ὥς θ' ἵππος ἀεθλοφόρος σὺν ὄχεσφιν,
ὅς ῥά τε ῥεῖα θέῃσι τιταινόμενος πεδίοιο·
ὣς Ἀχιλεὺς λαιψηρὰ πόδας καὶ γούνατ' ἐνώμα.
    τὸν δ' ὁ γέρων Πρίαμος πρῶτος ἴδεν ὀφθαλμοῖσιν,   25
παμφαίνονθ' ὥς τ' ἀστέρ' ἐπεσσύμενον πεδίοιο,
ὅς ῥά τ' ὀπώρης εἶσιν, ἀρίζηλοι δέ οἱ αὐγαί
φαίνονται πολλοῖσι μετ' ἀστράσι νυκτὸς ἀμολγῷ,
ὅν τε κύν' Ὠρίωνος ἐπίκλησιν καλέουσιν.
λαμπρότατος μὲν ὅ γ' ἐστί, κακὸν δέ τε σῆμα τέτυκται,   30
καί τε φέρει πολλὸν πυρετὸν δειλοῖσι βροτοῖσιν·
ὣς τοῦ χαλκὸς ἔλαμπε περὶ στήθεσσι θέοντος.

2 ἀπεψύχοντο : ἀνεψύχοντο   10a Ἰλίου ἐξαλαπάξαι ἐϋκτίμενον πτολίεθρον (= 4.33)
added by one papyrus   12 δή τοι : δ' ἤτοι   15 ὀλοώτατε : δολοώτατε (ancient
variant)   18 δ' ἐσάωσας : δὲ σάωσας   20 τεισαίμην (Fick) : τισαίμην (MSS)   31
δειλοῖσι : μερόπεσσι (one papyrus) : παν]τ[εσ]σι ? (Philodemus)   32 περὶ : ἐπὶ : ἐνὶ

ὤιμωξεν δ' ὁ γέρων, κεφαλὴν δ' ὅ γε κόψατο χερσὶν
ὑψόσ' ἀνασχόμενος, μέγα δ' οἰμώξας ἐγεγώνει
λισσόμενος φίλον υἱόν· ὁ δὲ προπάροιθε πυλάων   35
ἑστήκει, ἄμοτον μεμαὼς Ἀχιλῆϊ μάχεσθαι.
   τὸν δ' ὁ γέρων ἐλεεινὰ προσηύδα χεῖρας ὀρεγνύς·
"Ἕκτορ, μή μοι μίμνε, φίλον τέκος, ἀνέρα τοῦτον
οἶος ἄνευθ' ἄλλων, ἵνα μὴ τάχα πότμον ἐπίσπηις
Πηλεΐωνι δαμείς, ἐπεὶ ἦ πολὺ φέρτερός ἐστιν,   40
σχέτλιος. αἴθε θεοῖσι φίλος τοσσόνδε γένοιτο
ὅσσον ἐμοί· τάχα κέν ἑ κύνες καὶ γῦπες ἔδοιεν
κείμενον· ἦ κέ μοι αἰνὸν ἀπὸ πραπίδων ἄχος ἔλθοι·
ὅς μ' υἱῶν πολλῶν τε καὶ ἐσθλῶν εὖνιν ἔθηκεν
κτείνων καὶ περνὰς νήσων ἔπι τηλεδαπάων.   45
καὶ γὰρ νῦν δύο παῖδε, Λυκάονα καὶ Πολύδωρον,
οὐ δύναμαι ἰδέειν Τρώων εἰς ἄστυ ἀλέντων,
τούς μοι Λαοθόη τέκετο κρείουσα γυναικῶν.
ἀλλ' εἰ μὲν ζώουσι μετὰ στρατῶι, ἦ τ' ἂν ἔπειτα
χαλκοῦ τε χρυσοῦ τ' ἀπολυσόμεθ'· ἔστι γὰρ ἔνδον·   50
πολλὰ γὰρ ὤπασε παιδὶ γέρων ὀνομάκλυτος Ἄλτης.
εἰ δ' ἤδη τεθνᾶσι καὶ εἰν Ἀΐδαο δόμοισιν,
ἄλγος ἐμῶι θυμῶι καὶ μητέρι, τοὶ τεκόμεσθα·
λαοῖσιν δ' ἄλλοισι μινυνθαδιώτερον ἄλγος
ἔσσεται, ἢν μὴ καὶ σὺ θάνηις Ἀχιλῆϊ δαμασθείς.   55
ἀλλ' εἰσέρχεο τεῖχος, ἐμὸν τέκος, ὄφρα σαώσηις
Τρῶας καὶ Τρωιάς, μηδὲ μέγα κῦδος ὀρέξηις
Πηλεΐδηι, αὐτὸς δὲ φίλης αἰῶνος ἀμερθῆις.
πρὸς δ' ἐμὲ τὸν δύστηνον ἔτι φρονέοντ' ἐλέησον,
δύσμορον, ὅν ῥα πατὴρ Κρονίδης ἐπὶ γήραος οὐδῶι   60
αἴσηι ἐν ἀργαλέηι φθείσει, κακὰ πόλλ' ἐπιδόντα,
υἷάς τ' ὀλλυμένους ἑλκηθείσας τε θύγατρας,
καὶ θαλάμους κεραϊζομένους, καὶ νήπια τέκνα
βαλλόμενα προτὶ γαίηι ἐν αἰνῆι δηϊοτῆτι,
ἑλκομένας τε νυοὺς ὀλοῆις ὑπὸ χερσὶν Ἀχαιῶν.   65
αὐτὸν δ' ἂν πύματόν με κύνες πρώτηισι θύρηισιν
ὠμησταὶ ἐρύουσιν, ἐπεί κέ τις ὀξέϊ χαλκῶι
τύψας ἠὲ βαλὼν ῥεθέων ἐκ θυμὸν ἕληται,

---

33 κόψατο : λάζετο   42 ἔδοιεν (Aristarchus) : ἔδονται (MSS)   45 τηλεδαπάων :
θηλυτεράων (ancient variant)   50 ἀπολυσόμεθ' : ἀπολύσομεν (ancient variant)   51
πολλὰ . . . παιδὶ : παιδὶ . . . πολλὰ (Aristophanes of Byzantium)   γέρων : φίληι   56
τέκος : θάλος (ancient variant, cf. 87)   59 φρονέοντ' : φρονέων   61 αἴσηι : νούσωι
(pseudo-Plutarch) : δύηι (Stobaeus)   φθείσει : φθίσει   68 ἕληται : ἕλοιτο

οὓς τρέφον ἐν μεγάροισι τραπεζῆας θυραωρούς·
οἵ κ' ἐμὸν αἷμα πιόντες ἀλύσσοντες περὶ θυμῶι 70
κείσοντ' ἐν προθύροισι. νέωι δέ τε πάντ' ἐπέοικεν,
ἀρηΐ κταμένωι δεδαϊγμένωι ὀξέϊ χαλκῶι
κεῖσθαι· πάντα δὲ καλὰ θανόντι περ, ὅττι φανήηι·
ἀλλ' ὅτε δὴ πολιόν τε κάρη πολιόν τε γένειον
αἰδῶ τ' αἰσχύνωσι κύνες κταμένοιο γέροντος, 75
τοῦτο δὴ οἴκτιστον πέλεται δειλοῖσι βροτοῖσιν."
ἦ ῥ' ὁ γέρων, πολιὰς δ' ἄρ' ἀνὰ τρίχας ἕλκετο χερσίν
τίλλων ἐκ κεφαλῆς· οὐδ' Ἕκτορι θυμὸν ἔπειθεν.
μήτηρ δ' αὖθ' ἑτέρωθεν ὀδύρετο δάκρυ χέουσα,
κόλπον ἀνιεμένη, ἑτέρηφι δὲ μαζὸν ἀνέσχεν· 80
καί μιν δάκρυ χέουσ' ἔπεα πτερόεντα προσηύδα·
"Ἕκτορ, τέκνον ἐμόν, τάδε τ' αἴδεο καί μ' ἐλέησον
αὐτήν, εἴ ποτέ τοι λαθικηδέα μαζὸν ἐπέσχον·
τῶν μνῆσαι, φίλε τέκνον, ἄμυνε δὲ δήϊον ἄνδρα
τείχεος ἐντὸς ἐών, μηδὲ πρόμος ἵστασο τούτωι, 85
σχέτλιος· εἴ περ γάρ σε κατακτάνηι, οὔ σ' ἔτ' ἐγώ γε
κλαύσομαι ἐν λεχέεσσι, φίλον θάλος, ὃν τέκον αὐτή,
οὐδ' ἄλοχος πολύδωρος· ἄνευθε δέ σε μέγα νῶϊν
Ἀργείων παρὰ νηυσὶ κύνες ταχέες κατέδονται."
ὣς τώ γε κλαίοντε προσαυδήτην φίλον υἱόν, 90
πολλὰ λισσομένω· οὐδ' Ἕκτορι θυμὸν ἔπειθον,
ἀλλ' ὅ γε μίμν' Ἀχιλῆα πελώριον ἆσσον ἰόντα.
ὡς δὲ δράκων ἐπὶ χειῆι ὀρέστερος ἄνδρα μένησιν
βεβρωκὼς κακὰ φάρμακ', ἔδυ δέ τέ μιν χόλος αἰνός,
σμερδαλέον δὲ δέδορκεν ἑλισσόμενος περὶ χειῆι, 95
ὣς Ἕκτωρ ἄσβεστον ἔχων μένος οὐχ ὑπεχώρει,
πύργωι ἔπι προὔχοντι φαεινὴν ἀσπίδ' ἐρείσας.
ὀχθήσας δ' ἄρα εἶπε πρὸς ὃν μεγαλήτορα θυμόν·
"ὤι μοι ἐγών, εἰ μέν κε πύλας καὶ τείχεα δύω,
Πουλυδάμας μοι πρῶτος ἐλεγχείην ἀναθήσει, 100
ὅς μ' ἐκέλευεν Τρωσὶ ποτὶ πτόλιν ἡγήσασθαι
νύχθ' ὕπο τήνδ' ὀλοήν, ὅτε τ' ὤρετο δῖος Ἀχιλλεύς.

69 θυραωρούς (Aristarchus and a papyrus) : πυλαωρούς   74–6 appear to have been
omitted by a Hellenistic papyrus   83 ἐπέσχον : ἀνέσχον   85 ἐών (Aristarchus and
some MSS) : ἰών   86 κατακτάνηι : κατακτείνει   ἐγώ γε (Bekker) : ἔγωγε   87
θάλος : τέκος   93 ὀρέστερος ἄνδρα μένησιν (Aristarchus and MSS) : ὀρέστερον ἄνδρα
δοκεύηι   99 ὤι : ὤ   99a λωβητός κεν πᾶσι μετὰ Τρώεσσι γενοίμην added by one
papyrus   102 νύχθ' ὕπο τήνδ' ὀλοήν : νυκτα ποτι δνοφερην (one papyrus)

ἀλλ' ἐγὼ οὐ πιθόμην· ἦ τ' ἂν πολὺ κέρδιον ἦεν.
νῦν δ' ἐπεὶ ὤλεσα λαὸν ἀτασθαλίηισιν ἐμῆισιν,
αἰδέομαι Τρῶας καὶ Τρωιάδας ἑλκεσιπέπλους,   105
μή ποτέ τις εἴπηισι κακώτερος ἄλλος ἐμεῖο·
"Εκτωρ ἦφι βίηφι πιθήσας ὤλεσε λαόν.'
ὡς ἐρέουσιν· ἐμοὶ δὲ τότ' ἂν πολὺ κέρδιον εἴη
ἄντην ἢ' Ἀχιλῆα κατακτείναντα νέεσθαι
ἠέ κεν αὐτῶι ὀλέσθαι ἐϋκλειῶς πρὸ πόληος.   110
εἰ δέ κεν ἀσπίδα μὲν καταθείομαι ὀμφαλόεσσαν
καὶ κόρυθα βριαρήν, δόρυ δὲ πρὸς τεῖχος ἐρείσας
αὐτὸς ἰὼν Ἀχιλῆος ἀμύμονος ἀντίος ἔλθω
καί οἱ ὑπόσχωμαι Ἑλένην καὶ κτήμαθ' ἅμ' αὐτῆι,
πάντα μάλ' ὅσσά τ' Ἀλέξανδρος κοίληις ἐνὶ νηυσίν   115
ἠγάγετο Τροίηνδ', ἥ τ' ἔπλετο νείκεος ἀρχή,
δωσέμεν Ἀτρεΐδηισιν ἄγειν, ἅμα δ' ἀμφὶς Ἀχαιοῖς
ἄλλ' ἀποδάσσεσθαι ὅσα τε πτόλις ἧδε κέκευθεν·
Τρωσὶν δ' αὖ μετόπισθε γερούσιον ὅρκον ἕλωμαι
μή τι κατακρύψειν, ἀλλ' ἄνδιχα πάντα δάσεσθαι,   120
κτῆσιν ὅσην πτολίεθρον ἐπήρατον ἐντὸς ἐέργει· –
ἀλλὰ τίη μοι ταῦτα φίλος διελέξατο θυμός;
μή μιν ἐγὼ μὲν ἵκωμαι ἰών, ὁ δέ μ' οὐκ ἐλεήσει
οὐδέ τί μ' αἰδέσεται, κτενέει δέ με γυμνὸν ἐόντα
αὔτως ὥς τε γυναῖκα, ἐπεί κ' ἀπὸ τεύχεα δύω.   125
οὐ μέν πως νῦν ἔστιν ἀπὸ δρυὸς οὐδ' ἀπὸ πέτρης
τῶι ὀαριζέμεναι, ἅ τε παρθένος ἠίθεός τε,
παρθένος ἠίθεός τ' ὀαρίζετον ἀλλήλοιιν.
βέλτερον αὖτ' ἔριδι ξυνελαυνέμεν ὅττι τάχιστα·
εἴδομεν ὁπποτέρωι κεν Ὀλύμπιος εὖχος ὀρέξηι."   130
    ὡς ὥρμαινε μένων· ὁ δέ οἱ σχεδὸν ἦλθεν Ἀχιλλεύς
ἶσος Ἐνυαλίωι κορυθάϊκι πτολεμιστῆι,
σείων Πηλιάδα μελίην κατὰ δεξιὸν ὦμον

103, 108 κέρδιον : κάλλιον (ancient variant)   109 ἢ' (Fick) : ἢ (MSS)   κατακτεί-
ναντα : κατακτείναντι (ancient variant)   110 η [αυ]τωι π[ρο πολ]ηος ευκλειω[ς]
απ[ολεσθαι (one papyrus)   113 ἀντίος : ἀντίον   115 ἐνὶ : ἐπὶ   118 ἀποδάσσ-
εσθαι (Aristarchus, papyri, and MSS) : ἀποδάσσασθαι (papyri and MSS)   ὅσα τε :
ὅσσα   119 ἔλωμαι : ὀμοῦμαι (ancient variant)   120 δάσεσθαι : δάσασθαι   121
this line, which is nearly identical with 18.512, is omitted in some papyri and MSS   122
τίη : τί δή (ancient variant)   125 ἐπεί κ' : επην (one papyrus)   126a]πολεμοιο
μεματα δακρυοεντος (added by one papyrus)   129–30 ὅττι τάχιστα· εἴδομεν : ὄφρα
τάχιστα εἴδομεν   130 κεν Ὀλύμπιος : Κρονιδης Ζευς (one papyrus)   131 ὥρμαινε :
ὅρμαινε   133–5 these lines are lacking in one papyrus (which has them as 316a-c instead)

δεινήν· ἀμφὶ δὲ χαλκὸς ἐλάμπετο εἴκελος αὐγῆι
ἢ πυρὸς αἰθομένου ἤ' ἠελίου ἀνιόντος.　　　　　　　　　135
Ἕκτορα δ', ὡς ἐνόησεν, ἕλε τρόμος· οὐδ' ἄρ' ἔτ' ἔτλη
αὖθι μένειν, ὀπίσω δὲ πύλας λίπε, βῆ δὲ φοβηθείς.
Πηλεΐδης δ' ἐπόρουσε ποσὶ κραιπνοῖσι πεποιθώς.
ἠΰτε κίρκος ὄρεσφιν, ἐλαφρότατος πετεηνῶν,
ῥηϊδίως οἴμησε μετὰ τρήρωνα πέλειαν,　　　　　　　140
ἡ δέ θ' ὕπαιθα φοβεῖται, ὁ δ' ἐγγύθεν ὀξὺ λεληκώς
ταρφέ' ἐπαΐσσει ἑλέειν τέ ἑ θυμὸς ἀνώγει,
ὣς ἄρ' ὅ γ' ἐμμεμαὼς ἰθὺς πέτετο, τρέσε δ' Ἕκτωρ
τεῖχος ὕπο Τρώων, λαιψηρὰ δὲ γούνατ' ἐνώμα.
οἱ δὲ παρὰ σκοπιὴν καὶ ἐρινεὸν ἠνεμόεντα　　　　145
τείχεος αἰὲν ὕπεκ κατ' ἀμαξιτὸν ἐσσεύοντο,
κρουνὼ δ' ἵκανον καλλιρρόω· ἔνθα δὲ πηγαί
δοιαὶ ἀναΐσσουσι Σκαμάνδρου δινήεντος.
ἡ μὲν γάρ θ' ὕδατι λιαρῶι ῥέει, ἀμφὶ δὲ καπνός
γίνεται ἐξ αὐτῆς ὡς εἰ πυρὸς αἰθομένοιο·　　　　150
ἡ δ' ἑτέρη θέρεϊ προρέει ἐϊκυῖα χαλάζηι
ἢ χιόνι ψυχρῆι ἤ' ἐξ ὕδατος κρυστάλλωι.
ἔνθα δ' ἐπ' αὐτάων πλυνοὶ εὐρέες ἐγγὺς ἔασιν
καλοὶ λαΐνεοι, ὅθι εἵματα σιγαλόεντα
πλύνεσκον Τρώων ἄλοχοι καλαί τε θύγατρες　　　155
τὸ πρὶν ἐπ' εἰρήνης, πρὶν ἐλθεῖν υἷας Ἀχαιῶν.
τῆι ῥα παραδραμέτην, φεύγων, ὁ δ' ὄπισθε διώκων·
πρόσθε μὲν ἐσθλὸς ἔφευγε, δίωκε δέ μιν μέγ' ἀμείνων,
καρπαλίμως, ἐπεὶ οὐχ ἱερήϊον οὐδὲ βοείην
ἀρνύσθην, ἅ τε ποσσὶν ἀέθλια γίγνεται ἀνδρῶν,　160
ἀλλὰ περὶ ψυχῆς θέον Ἕκτορος ἱπποδάμοιο.
ὡς δ' ὅτ' ἀεθλοφόροι περὶ τέρματα μώνυχες ἵπποι
ῥίμφα μάλα τρωχῶσι· τὸ δὲ μέγα κεῖται ἄεθλον,
ἢ τρίπος ἠὲ γυνή, ἀνδρὸς κατατεθνηῶτος·
ὣς τὼ τρὶς Πριάμοιο πόλιν πέρι δινηθήτην　　　165
καρπαλίμοισι πόδεσσι· θεοὶ δ' ἐς πάντες ὁρῶντο.
τοῖσι δὲ μύθων ἦρχε πατὴρ ἀνδρῶν τε θεῶν τε·

---

135 ἤ' (Fick) : ἢ (MSS)　　138 ποσὶ κραιπνοῖσι πεποιθώς : ποσιν ταχεεσσ[ι διώκων
? (one papyrus)　140 ῥηϊδίως οἴμησε : καρπαλιμ[ως] ωρμη[σε (one papyrus)　144
τεῖχος : τείχει　145 ἠνεμόεντα : ἠνεμόεσσαν　146 τείχεος : ἄστεος　148 ἀναΐσ-
σουσι : ἀναΐσχουσι : αναβλύσσουσ[ι (one papyrus)　150 γίνεται : γίγνεται　152
ἤ' (Fick) : ἢ (MSS)　158a φεῦγ' υἱὸς Πριάμοιο, δίωκε δὲ δῖος Ἀχιλλεύς (ancient addi-
tion)　162 τέρματα : τέρμασι : τέρματι　163 τὸ δὲ μέγα κεῖται : τὸ δὴ κεῖται μέγ'
166 δ' ἐς : δέ τε

"ὦ πόποι, ἦ φίλον ἄνδρα διωκόμενον περὶ τεῖχος
ὀφθαλμοῖσιν ὁρῶμαι· ἐμὸν δ' ὀλοφύρεται ἦτορ
Ἕκτορος, ὅς μοι πολλὰ βοῶν ἐπὶ μηρί' ἔκηεν   170
Ἴδης ἐν κορυφῇσι πολυπτύχου, ἄλλοτε δ' αὖτε
ἐν πόλει ἀκροτάτηι· νῦν αὖτέ ἑ δῖος Ἀχιλλεύς
ἄστυ πέρι Πριάμοιο ποσὶν ταχέεσσι διώκει.
ἀλλ' ἄγετε φράζεσθε, θεοί, καὶ μητιάασθε,
ἠέ μιν ἐκ θανάτοιο σαώσομεν, ἦέ μιν ἤδη   175
Πηλεΐδηι Ἀχιλῆϊ δαμάσσομεν ἐσθλὸν ἐόντα."
    τὸν δ' αὖτε προσέειπε θεὰ γλαυκῶπις Ἀθήνη·
"ὦ πάτερ ἀργικέραυνε κελαινεφές, οἷον ἔειπες·
ἄνδρα θνητὸν ἐόντα, πάλαι πεπρωμένον αἴσηι,
ἂψ ἐθέλεις θανάτοιο δυσηχέος ἐξαναλῦσαι;   180
ἔρδ'· ἀτὰρ οὔ τοι πάντες ἐπαινέομεν θεοὶ ἄλλοι."
    τὴν δ' ἀπαμειβόμενος προσέφη νεφεληγερέτα Ζεύς·
"θάρσει, Τριτογένεια, φίλον τέκος· οὔ νύ τι θυμῶι
πρόφρονι μυθέομαι, ἐθέλω δέ τοι ἤπιος εἶναι.
ἔρξον ὅπηι δή τοι νόος ἔπλετο, μηδ' ἔτ' ἐρώει."   185
    ὣς εἰπὼν ὤτρυνε πάρος μεμαυῖαν Ἀθήνην·
βῆ δὲ κατ' Οὐλύμποιο καρήνων ἀΐξασα.
Ἕκτορα δ' ἀσπερχὲς κλονέων ἔφεπ' ὠκὺς Ἀχιλλεύς.
ὡς δ' ὅτε νεβρὸν ὄρεσφι κύων ἐλάφοιο δίηται
ὄρσας ἐξ εὐνῆς διά τ' ἄγκεα καὶ διὰ βήσσας·   190
τὸν δ' εἴ πέρ τε λάθηισι καταπτήξας ὑπὸ θάμνωι,
ἀλλά τ' ἀνιχνεύων θέει ἔμπεδον, ὄφρα κεν εὕρηι·
ὣς Ἕκτωρ οὐ λῆθε ποδώκεα Πηλεΐωνα.
ὁσσάκι δ' ὁρμήσειε πυλάων Δαρδανιάων
ἀντίον ἀΐξασθαι ἐϋδμήτους ὑπὸ πύργους,   195
εἴ πως οἱ καθύπερθεν ἀλάλκοιεν βελέεσσιν,
τοσσάκι μιν προπάροιθεν ἀποτρέψασκε παραφθάς
πρὸς πεδίον· αὐτὸς δὲ ποτὶ πτόλιος πέτετ' αἰεί.
ὡς δ' ἐν ὀνείρωι οὐ δύναται φεύγοντα διώκειν –
οὔτ' ἄρ' ὁ τὸν δύναται ὑποφεύγειν, οὔθ' ὁ διώκειν –   200
ὣς ὁ τὸν οὐ δύνατο μάρψαι ποσίν, οὐδ' ὃς ἀλύξαι.
πῶς δέ κεν Ἕκτωρ κῆρας ὑπεξέφυγεν θανάτοιο,

---

168 ὦ : ὢ   τεῖχος : ἄστυ (Plato *Rep.* 388c)   171 κορυφῇσι : κνημοῖσι   185
μηδ' ἔτ' : μηδέ τ'   186 ὤτρυνε : ὄτρυνε   194 ὁρμήσειε : ὁρμήσαιτο   195
ἀντίον : ἀντίος   ἀΐξασθαι : ἀΐξεσθαι   ὑπὸ : ἐπὶ : ἀπὸ   197 ἀποτρέψασκε :
ἀποστρέψασκε : παρατρέψασκε (ancient variant)   παραφθάς : παραστάς : αχιλλευ[ς
(one papyrus)   199–201 athetised by Aristarchus   202–204 suspected by Nauck and
others   202 ὑπεξέφυγεν : ὑπεξέφερεν (papyrus and an ancient variant)

εἰ μή οἱ πύματόν τε καὶ ὕστατον ἤντετ᾽ Ἀπόλλων
ἐγγύθεν, ὅς οἱ ἐπῶρσε μένος λαιψηρά τε γοῦνα;
λαοῖσιν δ᾽ ἀνένευε καρήατι δῖος Ἀχιλλεύς,   205
οὐδ᾽ ἔα ἱέμεναι ἐπὶ Ἕκτορι πικρὰ βέλεμνα,
μή τις κῦδος ἄροιτο βαλών, ὁ δὲ δεύτερος ἔλθοι.
ἀλλ᾽ ὅτε δὴ τὸ τέταρτον ἐπὶ κρουνοὺς ἀφίκοντο,
καὶ τότε δὴ χρύσεια πατὴρ ἐτίταινε τάλαντα,
ἐν δ᾽ ἐτίθει δύο κῆρε τανηλεγέος θανάτοιο,   210
τὴν μὲν Ἀχιλλῆος, τὴν δ᾽ Ἕκτορος ἱπποδάμοιο,
ἕλκε δὲ μέσσα λαβών· ῥέπε δ᾽ Ἕκτορος αἴσιμον ἦμαρ,
ᾤχετο δ᾽ εἰς Ἀΐδαο, λίπεν δέ ἑ Φοῖβος Ἀπόλλων.
Πηλεΐωνα δ᾽ ἵκανε θεὰ γλαυκῶπις Ἀθήνη,
    ἀγχοῦ δ᾽ ἱσταμένη ἔπεα πτερόεντα προσηύδα·   215
"νῦν δὴ νῶϊ γ᾽ ἔολπα, διίφιλε φαίδιμ᾽ Ἀχιλλεῦ,
οἴσεσθαι μέγα κῦδος Ἀχαιοῖσι προτὶ νῆας,
Ἕκτορα δηιώσαντε μάχης ἄτόν περ ἐόντα.
οὔ οἱ νῦν ἔτι γ᾽ ἔστι πεφυγμένον ἄμμε γενέσθαι,
οὐδ᾽ εἴ κεν μάλα πολλὰ πάθοι ἑκάεργος Ἀπόλλων   220
προπροκυλινδόμενος πατρὸς Διὸς αἰγιόχοιο.
ἀλλὰ σὺ μὲν νῦν στῆθι καὶ ἄμπνυε, τόνδε δ᾽ ἐγώ τοι
οἰχομένη πεπιθήσω ἐναντίβιον μαχέσασθαι."
    ὣς φάτ᾽ Ἀθηναίη· ὁ δ᾽ ἐπείθετο, χαῖρε δὲ θυμῶι,
στῆ δ᾽ ἄρ᾽ ἐπὶ μελίης χαλκογλώχινος ἐρεισθείς.   225
ἡ δ᾽ ἄρα τὸν μὲν ἔλειπε, κιχήσατο δ᾽ Ἕκτορα δῖον,
Δηϊφόβωι εἴκυῖα δέμας καὶ ἀτειρέα φωνήν·
    ἀγχοῦ δ᾽ ἱσταμένη ἔπεα πτερόεντα προσηύδα·
"ἠθεῖ᾽, ἦ μάλα δή σε βιάζεται ὠκὺς Ἀχιλλεύς,
ἄστυ πέρι Πριάμοιο ποσὶν ταχέεσσι διώκων.   230
ἀλλ᾽ ἄγε δὴ στέωμεν καὶ ἀλεξώμεσθα μένοντες."
    τὴν δ᾽ αὖτε προσέειπε μέγας κορυθαίολος Ἕκτωρ·
"Δηΐφοβ᾽, ἦ μέν μοι τὸ πάρος πολὺ φίλτατος ἦσθα
γνωτῶν, οὓς Ἑκάβη ἠδὲ Πρίαμος τέκε παῖδας·
νῦν δ᾽ ἔτι καὶ μᾶλλον νοέω φρεσὶ τιμήσασθαι,   235
ὃς ἔτλης ἐμεῦ εἵνεκ᾽, ἐπεὶ ἴδες ὀφθαλμοῖσιν,
τείχεος ἐξελθεῖν, ἄλλοι δ᾽ ἔντοσθε μένουσιν."
    τὸν δ᾽ αὖτε προσέειπε θεὰ γλαυκῶπις Ἀθήνη·

---

205 λαοῖσιν : ἄλλοισιν   211 ἱπποδάμοιο : ἀνδροφόνοιο (Maximus of Tyre x 8)   212
μέσσα : ῥῦμα (ancient variant)   216 νῶϊ γ᾽ (Aristarchus, MSS) : νῶϊν (Zenodotus,
MSS) : νωϊ (Bentley)   218 ἄτόν : ἄατόν   219 ἄμμε : ἄμμι   228 ἔπεα πτερόεντα
προσηύδα : προσέφη γλαυκῶπις Ἀθήνη (one papyrus and one MS)   232 τὴν : τόν
(one MS)

"ἠθεῖ', ἦ μὲν πολλὰ πατὴρ καὶ πότνια μήτηρ
λίσσονθ' ἐξείης γουνούμενοι, ἀμφὶ δ' ἐταῖροι,   240
αὖθι μένειν· τοῖον γὰρ ὑποτρομέουσιν ἅπαντες·
ἀλλ' ἐμὸς ἔνδοθι θυμὸς ἐτείρετο πένθεϊ λυγρῶι.
νῦν δ' ἰθὺς μεμαῶτε μαχώμεθα, μηδέ τι δούρων
ἔστω φειδωλή, ἵνα εἴδομεν εἴ κεν Ἀχιλλεύς
νῶϊ κατακτείνας ἔναρα βροτόεντα φέρηται   245
νῆας ἔπι γλαφυράς, ἦ κεν σῶι δουρὶ δαμήηι."
ὣς φαμένη καὶ κερδοσύνηι ἡγήσατ' Ἀθήνη.
οἱ δ' ὅτε δὴ σχεδὸν ἦσαν ἐπ' ἀλλήλοισιν ἰόντες,
τὸν πρότερος προσέειπε μέγας κορυθαίολος Ἕκτωρ·
"οὔ σ' ἔτι, Πηλέος υἱέ, φοβήσομαι, ὡς τὸ πάρος περ   250
τρὶς περὶ ἄστυ μέγα Πριάμου δίον, οὐδέ ποτ' ἔτλην
μεῖναι ἐπερχόμενον· νῦν αὖτέ με θυμὸς ἀνῆκεν
στήμεναι ἀντία σεῖο· ἕλοιμί κεν, ἢ κεν ἁλοίην.
ἀλλ' ἄγε δεῦρο θεοὺς ἐπιδώμεθα· τοὶ γὰρ ἄριστοι
μάρτυροι ἔσσονται καὶ ἐπίσκοποι ἁρμονιάων.   255
οὐ γὰρ ἐγώ σ' ἔκπαγλον ἀεικίω, αἴ κεν ἐμοὶ Ζεύς
δώηι καμμονίην, σὴν δὲ ψυχὴν ἀφέλωμαι,
ἀλλ' ἐπεὶ ἄρ κέ σε συλήσω κλυτὰ τεύχε', Ἀχιλλεῦ,
νεκρὸν Ἀχαιοῖσιν δώσω πάλιν· ὣς δὲ σὺ ῥέζειν."
τὸν δ' ἄρ' ὑπόδρα ἰδὼν προσέφη πόδας ὠκὺς Ἀχιλλεύς·   260
"Ἕκτορ, μή μοι, ἄλαστε, συνημοσύνας ἀγόρευε.
ὡς οὐκ ἔστι λέουσι καὶ ἀνδράσιν ὅρκια πιστά,
οὐδὲ λύκοι τε καὶ ἄρνες ὁμόφρονα θυμὸν ἔχουσιν,
ἀλλὰ κακὰ φρονέουσι διαμπερὲς ἀλλήλοισιν,
ὣς οὐκ ἔστ' ἐμὲ καὶ σὲ φιλήμεναι, οὐδέ τι νῶϊν   265
ὅρκια ἔσσονται, πρίν ἢ' ἕτερόν γε πεσόντα
αἵματος ἆσαι Ἄρηα, ταλαύρινον πολεμιστήν.
παντοίης ἀρετῆς μιμνήσκεο· νῦν σε μάλα χρὴ
αἰχμητήν τ' ἔμεναι καὶ θαρσαλέον πολεμιστήν.
οὔ τοι ἔτ' ἔσθ' ὑπάλυξις, ἄφαρ δέ σε Παλλὰς Ἀθήνη   270
ἔγχει ἐμῶι δαμάαι. νῦν δ' ἀθρόα πάντ' ἀποτείσεις,
κήδε' ἐμῶν ἑτάρων, οὓς ἔκτανες ἔγχεϊ θυίων."
ἦ ῥα καὶ ἀμπεπαλὼν προΐει δολιχόσκιον ἔγχος.

243 μηδέ τι : μὴ δ' ἔτι   246 δαμήηι : δαμείη   251 δίον : δίες   252 ἀνῆκεν :
ανωγει (one papyrus)   254 ἐπιδώμεθα : ἐπιβώμεθα : ἐπιδωσόμεθ' οἳ   255 μάρ-
τυροι : μάρτυρες   256 ἀεικίω : ἀεικιῶ   259 a, b = 342–3 added by one papyrus
265 οὐδέ τι : οὔτε τι : οὔτε τε   266 πρίν : πρίν γ'   ἢ' (Fick) : ἦ (MSS)   271 νῦν
δ' : νῦν   ἀποτείσεις : ἀποτίσεις   272 θυίων : θύων

καὶ τὸ μὲν ἄντα ἰδὼν ἠλεύατο φαίδιμος Ἕκτωρ·
ἕζετο γὰρ προϊδών, τὸ δ᾽ ὑπέρπτατο χάλκεον ἔγχος,   275
ἐν γαίηι δ᾽ ἐπάγη. ἀνὰ δ᾽ ἥρπασε Παλλὰς Ἀθήνη,
ἂψ δ᾽ Ἀχιλῆϊ δίδου, λάθε δ᾽ Ἕκτορα ποιμένα λαῶν.
Ἕκτωρ δὲ προσέειπεν ἀμύμονα Πηλεΐωνα·
"ἤμβροτες, οὐδ᾽ ἄρα πώ τι, θεοῖς ἐπιείκελ᾽ Ἀχιλλεῦ,
ἐκ Διὸς ἠείδης τὸν ἐμὸν μόρον. ἤτοι ἔφης γε,   280
ἀλλά τις ἀρτιεπὴς καὶ ἐπίκλοπος ἔπλεο μύθων,
ὄφρά σ᾽ ὑποδδείσας μένεος ἀλκῆς τε λάθωμαι.
οὐ μέν μοι φεύγοντι μεταφρένωι ἐν δόρυ πήξεις,
ἀλλ᾽ ἰθὺς μεμαῶτι διὰ στήθεσφιν ἔλασσον,
εἴ τοι ἔδωκε θεός. νῦν αὖτ᾽ ἐμὸν ἔγχος ἄλευαι   285
χάλκεον. ὡς δή μιν σῶι ἐν χροῒ πᾶν κομίσαιο
καί κεν ἐλαφρότερος πόλεμος Τρώεσσι γένοιτο
σεῖο καταφθιμένοιο. σὺ γάρ σφισι πῆμα μέγιστον."
ἦ ῥα καὶ ἀμπεπαλὼν προΐει δολιχόσκιον ἔγχος,
καὶ βάλε Πηλεΐδαο μέσον σάκος, οὐδ᾽ ἀφάμαρτεν·   290
τῆλε δ᾽ ἀπεπλάγχθη σάκεος δόρυ. χώσατο δ᾽ Ἕκτωρ,
ὅττί ῥά οἱ βέλος ὠκὺ ἐτώσιον ἔκφυγε χειρός·
στῆ δὲ κατηφήσας, οὐδ᾽ ἄλλ᾽ ἔχε μείλινον ἔγχος.
Δηΐφοβον δ᾽ ἐκάλει λευκάσπιδα μακρὸν ἀΰσας·
ἤιτεέ μιν δόρυ μακρόν· ὁ δ᾽ οὔ τί οἱ ἐγγύθεν ἦεν.   295
Ἕκτωρ δ᾽ ἔγνω ἧισιν ἐνὶ φρεσὶ φώνησέν τε·
"ὢ πόποι, ἦ μάλα δή με θεοὶ θάνατόνδε κάλεσσαν.
Δηΐφοβον γὰρ ἐγώ γ᾽ ἐφάμην ἥρωα παρεῖναι,
ἀλλ᾽ ὁ μὲν ἐν τείχει, ἐμὲ δ᾽ ἐξαπάτησεν Ἀθήνη.
νῦν δὲ δὴ ἐγγύθι μοι θάνατος κακός, οὐδ᾽ ἔτ᾽ ἄνευθεν,   300
οὐδ᾽ ἀλέη. ἦ γάρ ῥα πάλαι τό γε φίλτερον ἦεν
Ζηνί τε καὶ Διὸς υἷι ἑκηβόλωι, οἵ με πάρος γε
πρόφρονες εἰρύατο· νῦν αὖτέ με μοῖρα κιχάνει.
μὴ μὰν ἀσπουδεί γε καὶ ἀκλειῶς ἀπολοίμην,
ἀλλὰ μέγα ῥέξας τι καὶ ἐσσομένοισι πυθέσθαι."   305
ὡς ἄρα φωνήσας εἰρύσσατο φάσγανον ὀξύ,
τό οἱ ὑπὸ λαπάρην τέτατο, μέγα τε στιβαρόν τε,

274 φαίδιμος Ἕκτωρ : χάλκεον ἔγχος   275 χάλκεον : μείλινον (ancient variant)   280
ἠείδης : ἠείδεις   281 μύθων : μύθοις (ancient variant)   282 ὑποδδείσας : ὑποδείσας
282 λάθωμαι : λαθοίμην   284 μεμαῶτι : μεμαῶτα   285 ἄλευαι : ἄλευε   287
κεν : σφιν (ancient variant)   ἐλαφρότερος : ἐλαφρότατος   294 ἐκάλει : ἐβόα   297
ὢ : ὣ   300 οὐδ᾽ ἔτ᾽ : οὐδέ τ᾽   301 πάλαι τό γε : πάλαι τότε : πάροιθέ γε   304
ἀσπουδεί : ἀσπουδί

οἴμησεν δὲ ἀλεὶς ὥς τ' αἰετὸς ὑψιπετήεις,
ὅς τ' εἶσιν πεδίονδε διὰ νεφέων ἐρεβεννῶν
ἁρπάξων ἢ ἄρν' ἀμαλὴν ἢ πτῶκα λαγωόν·   310
ὣς Ἕκτωρ οἴμησε τινάσσων φάσγανον ὀξύ.
ὡρμήθη δ' Ἀχιλεύς, μένεος δ' ἐμπλήσατο θυμόν
ἀγρίου· πρόσθεν δὲ σάκος στέρνοιο κάλυψεν
καλὸν δαιδάλεον, κόρυθι δ' ἐπένευε φαεινῆι
τετραφάλωι· καλαὶ δὲ περισσείοντο ἔθειραι   315
χρύσεαι, ἃς Ἥφαιστος ἵει λόφον ἀμφὶ θαμειάς.
οἷος δ' ἀστὴρ εἶσι μετ' ἀστράσι νυκτὸς ἀμολγῶι
ἕσπερος, ὃς κάλλιστος ἐν οὐρανῶι ἵσταται ἀστήρ,
ὣς αἰχμῆς ἀπέλαμπ' εὐήκεος, ἣν ἄρ' Ἀχιλεύς
πάλλεν δεξιτερῆι, φρονέων κακὸν Ἕκτορι δίωι,   320
εἰσορόων χρόα καλόν, ὅπηι εἴξειε μάλιστα.
τοῦ δὲ καὶ ἄλλο τόσον μὲν ἔχε χρόα χάλκεα τεύχεα
καλά, τὰ Πατρόκλοιο βίην ἐνάριξε κατακτάς,
φαίνετο δ' ἧι κληῖδες ἀπ' ὤμων αὐχέν' ἔχουσιν,
λαυκανίην, ἵνα τε ψυχῆς ὤκιστος ὄλεθρος.   325
τῆι ῥ' ἐπὶ οἷ μεμαῶτ' ἔλασ' ἔγχεϊ δῖος Ἀχιλλεύς,
ἀντικρὺ δ' ἁπαλοῖο δι' αὐχένος ἤλυθ' ἀκωκή.
οὐδ' ἄρ' ἀπ' ἀσφάραγον μελίη τάμε χαλκοβάρεια,
ὄφρά τί μιν προτιείποι ἀμειβόμενος ἐπέεσσιν.
ἤριπε δ' ἐν κονίηις. ὁ δ' ἐπεύξατο δῖος Ἀχιλλεύς·   330
"Ἕκτορ, ἀτάρ που ἔφης Πατροκλῆ' ἐξεναρίζων
σῶς ἔσσεσθ', ἐμὲ δ' οὐδὲν ὀπίζεο νόσφιν ἐόντα·
νήπιε, τοῖο δ' ἄνευθεν ἀοσσητὴρ μέγ' ἀμείνων
νηυσὶν ἔπι γλαφυρῆισιν ἐγὼ μετόπισθε λελείμμην,
ὅς τοι γούνατ' ἔλυσα. σὲ μὲν κύνες ἠδ' οἰωνοί   335
ἑλκήσουσ' ἀϊκῶς, τὸν δὲ κτεριοῦσιν Ἀχαιοί."
    τὸν δ' ὀλιγοδρανέων προσέφη κορυθαίολος Ἕκτωρ·
"λίσσομ' ὑπὲρ ψυχῆς καὶ γούνων σῶν τε τοκήων,
μή με ἔα παρὰ νηυσὶ κύνας καταδάψαι Ἀχαιῶν,
ἀλλὰ σὺ μὲν χαλκόν τε ἅλις χρυσόν τε δέδεξο,   340

---

309 διὰ : ἀπό (ancient variant)   310 ἁρπάξων : ἁρπάζων   ἀμαλὴν : ἁρπαλὴν
314 ἐπένευε : ἐπένευσε   315 καλαὶ : δειναὶ   316 = 19.383 omitted by some MSS
316 a–c = 133–5 inserted after 316 by one papyrus   324 φαίνετο : φαῖνεν (ancient
variant)   325 λαυκανίην : λαυκανίης (ancient variant)   326 μεμαῶτ' : μεμαὼς
ἔγχεϊ : Ἕκτορα   329 athetised by Aristarchus   330 ἐπεύξατο : ἐπεύχετο   331
ἀτάρ : ἄφαρ (ancient variant)   336 ἑλκήσουσ' ἀϊκῶς : ἑλκήσουσ' ἀεικῶς : ἑλκήσουσι
κακῶς (Antimachus) : ἑλκήσουσ' ἀικέως (West)   κτερίουσιν (Buttmann) : κτεριοῦσιν
340 χαλκόν... χρυσόν : χρυσόν... χαλκόν   δέδεξο : δέχεσθαι

δῶρα τά τοι δώσουσι πατὴρ καὶ πότνια μήτηρ,
σῶμα δὲ οἴκαδ' ἐμὸν δόμεναι πάλιν, ὄφρα πυρός με
Τρῶες καὶ Τρώων ἄλοχοι λελάχωσι θανόντα."
    τὸν δ' ἄρ' ὑπόδρα ἰδὼν προσέφη πόδας ὠκὺς Ἀχιλλεύς·
"μή με, κύον, γούνων γουνάζεο μηδὲ τοκήων.   345
αἲ γάρ πως αὐτόν με μένος καὶ θυμὸς ἀνείη
ὤμ' ἀποταμνόμενον κρέα ἔδμεναι, οἷά μ' ἔοργας,
ὡς οὐκ ἔσθ' ὃς σῆς γε κύνας κεφαλῆς ἀπαλάλκοι.
οὐδ' εἴ κεν δεκάκις τε καὶ εἰκοσινήριτ' ἄποινα
στήσωσ' ἐνθάδ' ἄγοντες, ὑπόσχωνται δὲ καὶ ἄλλα,   350
οὐδ' εἴ κέν σ' αὐτὸν χρυσῷ ἐρύσασθαι ἀνώγοι
Δαρδανίδης Πρίαμος, οὐδ' ὧς σέ γε πότνια μήτηρ
ἐνθεμένη λεχέεσσι γοήσεται, ὃν τέκεν αὐτή,
ἀλλὰ κύνες τε καὶ οἰωνοὶ κατὰ πάντα δάσονται."
    τὸν δὲ καταθνήισκων προσέφη κορυθαίολος Ἕκτωρ·   355
"ἦ σ' εὖ γιγνώσκων προτιόσσομαι, οὐδ' ἄρ' ἔμελλον
πείσειν· ἦ γὰρ σοί γε σιδήρεος ἐν φρεσὶ θυμός.
φράζεο νῦν, μή τοί τι θεῶν μήνιμα γένωμαι
ἤματι τῷ, ὅτε κέν σε Πάρις καὶ Φοῖβος Ἀπόλλων
ἐσθλὸν ἐόντ' ὀλέσωσιν ἐνὶ Σκαιῇσι πύληισιν."   360
    ὣς ἄρα μιν εἰπόντα τέλος θανάτοιο κάλυψεν,
ψυχὴ δ' ἐκ ῥεθέων πταμένη Ἄϊδόσδε βεβήκει
ὃν πότμον γοόωσα, λιποῦσ' ἀνδροτῆτα καὶ ἥβην.
    τὸν καὶ τεθνηῶτα προσηύδα δῖος Ἀχιλλεύς·
"τέθναθι· κῆρα δ' ἐγὼ τότε δέξομαι, ὁππότε κεν δὴ   365
Ζεὺς ἐθέληι τελέσαι ἠδ' ἀθάνατοι θεοὶ ἄλλοι."
    ἦ ῥα καὶ ἐκ νεκροῖο ἐρύσσατο χάλκεον ἔγχος,
καὶ τό γ' ἄνευθεν ἔθηχ', ὁ δ' ἀπ' ὤμων τεύχε' ἐσύλα
αἱματόεντ'. ἄλλοι δὲ περίδραμον υἷες Ἀχαιῶν,
οἳ καὶ θηήσαντο φυὴν καὶ εἶδος ἀγητόν   370
Ἕκτορος· οὐδ' ἄρα οἵ τις ἀνουτητεί γε παρέστη.
    ὧδε δέ τις εἴπεσκεν ἰδὼν ἐς πλησίον ἄλλον·
"ὢ πόποι, ἦ μάλα δὴ μαλακώτερος ἀμφαφάασθαι
Ἕκτωρ ἢ ὅτε νῆας ἐνέπρησεν πυρὶ κηλέωι."
    ὣς ἄρα τις εἴπεσκε καὶ οὐτήσασκε παραστάς.   375
τὸν δ' ἐπεὶ ἐξενάριξε ποδάρκης δῖος Ἀχιλλεύς,

---

341 δῶρα : πολλα τ[(one papyrus)   344 ἄρ' ὑπόδρα ἰδὼν : ἀπαμειβόμενος
(ancient variant)   347 οἷά : ὅσσα   357 ἐν φρεσὶ : ἔνδοθι   363 = 16.857 absent
in some papyri and MSS   ἀνδροτῆτα : ἀδροτῆτα (Plutarch De aud. poet. 17d)   371
ἀνουτητεί (Barnes) : ἀνουτητί (MSS)   373 ὤ : ὦ   374 ἐνέπρησεν : ἐνέπρηθεν

στὰς ἐν Ἀχαιοῖσιν ἔπεα πτερόεντ' ἀγόρευεν·
"ὦ φίλοι, Ἀργείων ἡγήτορες ἠδὲ μέδοντες,
ἐπεὶ δὴ τόνδ' ἄνδρα θεοὶ δαμάσασθαι ἔδωκαν,
ὃς κακὰ πόλλ' ἔρρεξεν, ὅσ' οὐ σύμπαντες οἱ ἄλλοι,   380
εἰ δ' ἄγετ' ἀμφὶ πόλιν σὺν τεύχεσι πειρηθέωμεν,
ὄφρά κ' ἔτι γνῶμεν Τρώων νόον, ὅν τιν' ἔχουσιν,
ἢ καταλείψουσιν πόλιν ἄκρην τοῦδε πεσόντος,
ἦε μένειν μεμάασι καὶ Ἕκτορος οὐκέτ' ἐόντος.
ἀλλὰ τίη μοι ταῦτα φίλος διελέξατο θυμός;   385
κεῖται πὰρ νήεσσι νέκυς ἄκλαυτος ἄθαπτος
Πάτροκλος· τοῦ δ' οὐκ ἐπιλήσομαι, ὄφρ' ἂν ἐγώ γε
ζωοῖσιν μετέω καί μοι φίλα γούνατ' ὀρώρῃ.
εἰ δὲ θανόντων περ καταλήθοντ' εἰν Ἀΐδαο,
αὐτὰρ ἐγὼ καὶ κεῖθι φίλου μεμνήσομ' ἑταίρου.   390
νῦν δ' ἄγ' ἀείδοντες παιήονα, κοῦροι Ἀχαιῶν,
νηυσὶν ἔπι γλαφυρῇσι νεώμεθα, τόνδε δ' ἄγωμεν.
ἠράμεθα μέγα κῦδος· ἐπέφνομεν Ἕκτορα δῖον,
ᾧ Τρῶες κατὰ ἄστυ θεῶι ὣς εὐχετόωντο."
ἦ ῥα καὶ Ἕκτορα δῖον ἀεικέα μήδετο ἔργα·   395
ἀμφοτέρων μετόπισθε ποδῶν τέτρηνε τένοντε
ἐς σφυρὸν ἐκ πτέρνης, βοέους δ' ἐξῆπτεν ἱμάντας,
ἐκ δίφροιο δ' ἔδησε, κάρη δ' ἕλκεσθαι ἔασεν.
ἐς δίφρον δ' ἀναβὰς ἀνά τε κλυτὰ τεύχε' ἀείρας
μάστιξέν ῥ' ἐλάαν, τὼ δ' οὐκ ἀέκοντε πετέσθην.   400
τοῦ δ' ἦν ἑλκομένοιο κονίσαλος, ἀμφὶ δὲ χαῖται
κυάνεαι πίτναντο, κάρη δ' ἅπαν ἐν κονίῃσιν
κεῖτο πάρος χαρίεν· τότε δὲ Ζεὺς δυσμενέεσσιν
δῶκεν ἀεικίσσασθαι ἑῇ ἐν πατρίδι γαίῃ.
ὣς τοῦ μὲν κεκόνιτο κάρη ἅπαν. ἡ δέ νυ μήτηρ   405
τίλλε κόμην, ἀπὸ δὲ λιπαρὴν ἔρριψε καλύπτρην
τηλόσε, κώκυσεν δὲ μάλα μέγα παῖδ' ἐσιδοῦσα·

377 πτερόεντ' ἀγόρευεν : πτερόεντα προσηύδα   378 ὦ φίλοι, Ἀργείων ἡγήτο-
ρες ἠδὲ μέδοντες : Ἀτρεΐδη τε καὶ ἄλλοι ἀριστῆες Παναχαιῶν (Zenodotus) : ὦ
φίλοι ἥρωες Δαναοί, θεράποντες Ἄρηος   380 ἔρρεξεν : ἔρδεσκεν   381 πειρηθέω-
μεν : πειρηθῶμεν   386 ἄκλαυτος : ἄκλαυστος   387 ἐγώ γε (Bekker): ἔγωγε
388 ζωὸς ἐν Ἀργείοισι φιλοπτολέμοισι μετείω (ancient variant)   392a καὶ τ]εθνηότα
περ τοσα γαρ κακ εμη[σατ Αχαιους (one papyrus)   393–4 athetised by Aristarchus
395 μήδετο : μήσατο   396 ἀμφοτέρων : ἀμφοτέρω   τένοντε : τένοντας : τένοντα
399 omitted by one papyrus   402 πίτναντο : πίλναντο (ancient variant) : πίδναντο :
πίμπλαντο (Dion. Halicarnassus De comp. verb. 18a)   403 δυσμενέεσσι : τερπικέραυνος
(ancient variant)

ὤιμωξεν δ' ἐλεεινὰ πατὴρ φίλος· ἀμφὶ δὲ λαοί
κωκυτῶι τ' εἴχοντο καὶ οἰμωγῆι κατὰ ἄστυ.
τῶι δὲ μάλιστ' ἄρ' ἔην ἐναλίγκιον, ὡς εἰ ἅπασα   410
Ἴλιος ὀφρυόεσσα πυρὶ σμύχοιτο κατ' ἄκρης.
λαοὶ μέν ῥα γέροντα μόγις ἔχον ἀσχαλόωντα,
ἐξελθεῖν μεμαῶτα πυλάων Δαρδανιάων.
πάντας δ' ἐλλιτάνευε κυλινδόμενος κατὰ κόπρον,
ἐξ ὀνομακλήδην ὀνομάζων ἄνδρα ἕκαστον·   415
"σχέσθε, φίλοι, καί μ' οἶον ἐάσατε κηδόμενοί περ
ἐξελθόντα πόληος ἱκέσθ' ἐπὶ νῆας Ἀχαιῶν·
λίσσωμ' ἀνέρα τοῦτον ἀτάσθαλον ὀβριμοεργόν,
ἤν πως ἡλικίην αἰδέσσεται ἠδ' ἐλεήσηι
γῆρας. καὶ δέ νυ τῶι γε πατὴρ τοιόσδε τέτυκται,   420
Πηλεύς, ὅς μιν ἔτικτε καὶ ἔτρεφε πῆμα γενέσθαι
Τρωσί· μάλιστα δ' ἐμοὶ περὶ πάντων ἄλγε' ἔθηκεν.
τόσσους γάρ μοι παῖδας ἀπέκτανε τηλεθάοντας.
τῶν πάντων οὐ τόσσον ὀδύρομαι ἀχνύμενός περ
ὡς ἑνός, οὗ μ' ἄχος ὀξὺ κατοίσεται Ἄϊδος εἴσω,   425
Ἕκτορος. ὡς ὄφελεν θανέειν ἐν χερσὶν ἐμῆισιν·
τώ κε κορεσσάμεθα κλαίοντέ τε μυρομένω τε
μήτηρ θ', ἥ μιν ἔτικτε δυσάμμορος, ἠδ' ἐγὼ αὐτός."
ὣς ἔφατο κλαίων, ἐπὶ δὲ στενάχοντο πολῖται.
Τρωῆισιν δ' Ἑκάβη ἀδινοῦ ἐξῆρχε γόοιο·   430
"τέκνον, ἐγὼ δειλή· τί νυ βείομαι αἰνὰ παθοῦσα
σεῦ ἀποτεθνηῶτος; ὅ μοι νύκτας τε καὶ ἦμαρ
εὐχωλὴ κατὰ ἄστυ πελέσκεο, πᾶσί τ' ὄνειαρ
Τρωσί τε καὶ Τρωῆισι κατὰ πτόλιν, οἵ σε θεὸν ὣς
δειδέχατ'· ἦ γὰρ καί σφι μάλα μέγα κῦδος ἔησθα   435
ζωὸς ἐών· νῦν αὖ θάνατος καὶ μοῖρα κιχάνει."
ὣς ἔφατο κλαίουσ', ἄλοχος δ' οὔ πώ τι πέπυστο
Ἕκτορος· οὐ γάρ οἵ τις ἐτήτυμος ἄγγελος ἐλθὼν
ἤγγειλ' ὅττί ῥά οἱ πόσις ἔκτοθι μίμνε πυλάων,
ἀλλ' ἥ γ' ἱστὸν ὕφαινε μυχῶι δόμου ὑψηλοῖο,   440
δίπλακα πορφυρέην, ἐν δὲ θρόνα ποικίλ' ἔπασσεν.

411 σμύχοιτο : σμήχοιτο   412 μόγις : μόλις   414 ἐλλιτάνευε : ἐλιτάνευε   416 κηδόμενοί : κηδόμενόν   418 λίσσωμ' : λίσσομαι   419 ἤν : εἰ   420 τῶι γε : τῶιδε   422 ἄλγε' ἔθηκεν : ἄλγεα θῆκεν   423 τόσσους : τοίους (one papyrus)   424 πάντων : πόλλων   427 τώ : τῶ   429 πολῖται : γέροντες (ancient variant) : γυναῖκες   431 βείομαι : βίομαι : βέομαι   παθοῦσα : τεκοῦσα (Aristarchus)   435 καί : κέ   436 rejected by West   441 πορφυρέην : μαρμαρέην   θρόνα : θρόα

κέκλετο δ' ἀμφιπόλοισιν ἐϋπλοκάμοις κατὰ δῶμα
ἀμφὶ πυρὶ στῆσαι τρίποδα μέγαν, ὄφρα πέλοιτο
Ἕκτορι θερμὰ λοετρὰ μάχης ἒκ νοστήσαντι.
νηπίη, οὐδ' ἐνόησεν ὅ μιν μάλα τῆλε λοετρῶν   445
χερσὶν Ἀχιλλῆος δάμασε γλαυκῶπις Ἀθήνη.
κωκυτοῦ δ' ἤκουσε καὶ οἰμωγῆς ἀπὸ πύργου·
τῆς δ' ἐλελίχθη γυῖα, χαμαὶ δέ οἱ ἔκπεσε κερκίς.
   ἡ δ' αὖτις δμωῇσιν ἐϋπλοκάμοισι μετηύδα·
"δεῦτε, δύω μοι ἕπεσθον, ἴδωμ' ὅτιν' ἔργα τέτυκται.   450
αἰδοίης ἑκυρῆς ὀπὸς ἔκλυον, ἐν δέ μοι αὐτῆι
στήθεσι πάλλεται ἦτορ ἀνὰ στόμα, νέρθε δὲ γοῦνα
πήγνυται· ἐγγὺς δή τι κακὸν Πριάμοιο τέκεσσιν.
αἲ γὰρ ἀπ' οὔατος εἴη ἐμεῦ ἔπος, ἀλλὰ μάλ' αἰνῶς
δείδω μὴ δή μοι θρασὺν Ἕκτορα δῖος Ἀχιλλεύς   455
μοῦνον ἀποτμήξας πόλιος πεδίονδε δίηται,
καὶ δή μιν καταπαύσηι ἀγηνορίης ἀλεγεινῆς,
ἥ μιν ἔχεσκ', ἐπεὶ οὔ ποτ' ἐνὶ πληθυῖ μένεν ἀνδρῶν,
ἀλλὰ πολὺ προθέεσκε, τὸ ὂν μένος οὐδενὶ εἴκων."
   ὡς φαμένη μεγάροιο διέσσυτο μαινάδι ἴση,   460
παλλομένη κραδίην· ἅμα δ' ἀμφίπολοι κίον αὐτῆι.
αὐτὰρ ἐπεὶ πύργον τε καὶ ἀνδρῶν ἷξεν ὅμιλον,
ἔστη παπτήνασ' ἐπὶ τείχεϊ· τὸν δὲ νόησεν
ἑλκόμενον πρόσθεν πόλιος· ταχέες δέ μιν ἵπποι
ἕλκον ἀκηδέστως κοίλας ἐπὶ νῆας Ἀχαιῶν.   465
τὴν δὲ κατ' ὀφθαλμῶν ἐρεβεννὴ νὺξ ἐκάλυψεν,
ἤριπε δ' ἐξοπίσω, ἀπὸ δὲ ψυχὴν ἐκάπυσσεν,
τῆλε δ' ἀπὸ κρατὸς βάλε δέσματα σιγαλόεντα,
ἄμπυκα κεκρύφαλόν τε ἰδὲ πλεκτὴν ἀναδέσμην
κρήδεμνόν θ', ὅ ῥά οἱ δῶκε χρυσῆ Ἀφροδίτη   470
ἤματι τῶι, ὅτε μιν κορυθαίολος ἠγάγεθ' Ἕκτωρ
ἐκ δόμου Ἠετίωνος, ἐπεὶ πόρε μυρία ἕδνα.
ἀμφὶ δέ μιν γαλόωι τε καὶ εἰνατέρες ἅλις ἔσταν,
αἵ ἑ μετὰ σφίσιν εἶχον ἀτυζομένην ἀπολέσθαι.

---

442 αι]ψα δ αρ αμφιπ[ολοισιν ευπλοκαμοισι κελευσεν (one papyrus)   446 χερσὶν :
χερσ] υπ (one papyrus)   450 ὅτιν' : ὅττι : ἄτιν'   451 ἐν δέ μοι : ἐν δ' ἐμοί   αὐτῆι :
αὐτῆς   452 γοῦνα : γυῖα   461 κραδίην : κραδίηι   462 αυταρ επει Σκαιας] τε
πυλ[ας και] πυργον ικανεν (one papyrus)   463 τείχεϊ : τειχ[εσι] (one papyrus)   467
ἀπὸ : ἀνὰ   468 βάλε : χέε   473 ἔσταν : ἦσαν

ἣ δ' ἐπεὶ οὖν ἄμπνυτο καὶ ἐς φρένα θυμὸς ἀγέρθη,   475
ἀμβλήδην γοόωσα μετὰ Τρωιῆισιν ἔειπεν·
"Ἕκτορ, ἐγὼ δύστηνος· ἰῆι ἄρα γεινόμεθ' αἴσηι
ἀμφότεροι, σὺ μὲν ἐν Τροίηι Πριάμου κατὰ δῶμα,
αὐτὰρ ἐγὼ Θήβηισιν ὑπὸ Πλάκωι ὑληέσσηι
ἐν δόμωι Ἠετίωνος, ὅ μ' ἔτρεφε τυτθὸν ἐοῦσαν,   480
δύσμορος αἰνόμορον· ὡς μὴ ὤφελλε τεκέσθαι.
νῦν δὲ σὺ μέν ῥ' Ἀΐδαο δόμους ὑπὸ κεύθεσι γαίης
ἔρχεαι, αὐτὰρ ἐμὲ στυγερῶι ἐνὶ πένθεϊ λείπεις
χήρην ἐν μεγάροισι. πάϊς δ' ἔτι νήπιος αὔτως,
ὃν τέκομεν σύ τ' ἐγώ τε δυσάμμοροι· οὔτε σὺ τούτωι   485
ἔσσεαι, Ἕκτορ, ὄνειαρ ἐπεὶ θάνες, οὔτε σοὶ οὗτος.
ἤν περ γὰρ πόλεμόν γε φύγηι πολύδακρυν Ἀχαιῶν,
αἰεί τοι τούτωι γε πόνος καὶ κήδε' ὀπίσσω
ἔσσοντ'· ἄλλοι γάρ οἱ ἀπουρήσουσιν ἀρούρας.
ἦμαρ δ' ὀρφανικὸν παναφήλικα παῖδα τίθησιν·   490
πάντα δ' ὑπεμνήμυκε, δεδάκρυνται δὲ παρειαί,
δευόμενος δέ τ' ἄνεισι πάϊς ἐς πατρὸς ἑταίρους,
ἄλλον μὲν χλαίνης ἐρύων, ἄλλον δὲ χιτῶνος·
τῶν δ' ἐλεησάντων κοτύλην τις τυτθὸν ἐπέσχεν·
χείλεα μέν τ' ἐδίην', ὑπερώιην δ' οὐκ ἐδίηνεν.   495
τὸν δὲ καὶ ἀμφιθαλὴς ἐκ δαιτύος ἐστυφέλιξεν,
χερσὶν πεπληγώς, καὶ ὀνειδείοισιν ἐνίσσων·
"ἔρρ' οὕτως· οὐ σός γε πατὴρ μεταδαίνυται ἡμῖν."
δακρυόεις δέ τ' ἄνεισι πάϊς ἐς μητέρα χήρην,
Ἀστυάναξ, ὃς πρὶν μὲν ἑοῦ ἐπὶ γούνασι πατρός   500
μυελὸν οἶον ἔδεσκε καὶ οἰῶν πίονα δημόν,
αὐτὰρ ὅθ' ὕπνος ἕλοι, παύσαιτό τε νηπιαχεύων,
εὕδεσκ' ἐν λέκτροισιν, ἐν ἀγκαλίδεσσι τιθήνης,
εὐνῆι ἔνι μαλακῆι, θαλέων ἐμπλησάμενος κῆρ.
νῦν δ' ἂν πολλὰ πάθησι, φίλου ἀπὸ πατρὸς ἁμαρτών,   505
Ἀστυάναξ, ὃν Τρῶες ἐπίκλησιν καλέουσιν·
οἷος γάρ σφιν ἔρυσο πύλας καὶ τείχεα μακρά.
νῦν δὲ σὲ μὲν παρὰ νηυσὶ κορωνίσι νόσφι τοκήων

475 ἄμπνυτο : ἔμπνυτο   476 Τρωιῆισιν : δμωηισιν   478 κατὰ δῶμα : ἐνὶ οἴκωι
(ancient variant)   482 μέν ῥ' : μὲν   487–99 athetised by Aristarchus   487–505
deleted by Lehrs, 487–507 by Düntzer   487 ἤν περ γὰρ : ἦν γὰρ δὴ   488 αἰεί
τοι : ἀλλ' ἤτοι (ancient variant)   489 ἀπουρήσουσιν : ἀπουρίσσουσιν (Aristarchus)
491 παρειαί : παρειά   497 ἐνίσσων : ἐνίσπων   498 οὕτως : οὕτω : οὗτος   500
γούνασι : γούνατα

αἰόλαι εὐλαὶ ἔδονται, ἐπεί κε κύνες κορέσωνται,
γυμνόν· ἀτάρ τοι εἵματ' ἐνὶ μεγάροισι κέονται   510
λεπτά τε καὶ χαρίεντα τετυγμένα χερσὶ γυναικῶν.
ἀλλ' ἦτοι τάδε πάντα καταφλέξω πυρὶ κηλέωι,
οὐδὲν σοί γ' ὄφελος, ἐπεὶ οὐκ ἐγκείσεαι αὐτοῖς,
ἀλλὰ πρὸς Τρώων καὶ Τρωϊάδων κλέος εἶναι."
  ὣς ἔφατο κλαίουσ', ἐπὶ δὲ στενάχοντο γυναῖκες.   515

509 κορέσωνται : κορέσονται   512 τάδε : τα γε (one papyrus)   515 ἔφατο : αρ
ε]φη (one papyrus)

COMMENTARY

1–24

In the preceding book the stage has been prepared for the final, climactic battle of the *Iliad*, the fight between Hector and Achilles: the gods, who had temporarily joined the fighting on earth, have returned to Olympus, and pro-Trojan Apollo has sidetracked Achilles from the city via the Trojan Agenor to allow the other Trojans to flee inside the safety of the walls. The dramatic nature of the encounter between the two heroes of the *Iliad* is increased by the presence of spectators: not only the divine audience of the gods, as always sitting in their Olympic 'sky-boxes', but also the old Trojan king Priam, Hecuba, and the other Trojans (but not Andromache! see 437–46n.), who are standing on the walls of Troy. We are virtually dealing with a *teichoskopia* as found in book 3 (146–244) and depicted on the Shield of Achilles (18.514–15). In the case of the duel between Paris and Menelaus in book 3, Priam does not 'dare to look with his own eyes on his dear son fighting' (3.306–7).

Before the confrontation between the two heroes can start, however, another scene has to be rounded off. The fight between Achilles and Agenor (21.544–98) at 21.599 had evolved into a 'god meets mortal' scene, when Apollo had taken the place (and shape) of Agenor. The opening of this book recounts the customary final part of such a meeting, the god revealing his divine identity. For 'god meets mortal' scenes see 226–47n.

1–4 ὡς οἱ μὲν . . . αὐτὰρ Ἀχαιοί: there is no scholarly consensus about who is responsible for the Homeric book-divisions: Homer himself, the rhapsodes, who recited the epics during the Panathenaic festival, or the Alexandrian scholars who edited the texts; for an overview of the positions see the special issue of *Symbolae Osloenses* 74 (1999) edited by Jensen, to which should now be added Edwards (2002) 39–47. Whoever was responsible clearly had a method in mind: books very often open with a sunrise (e.g. *Il.* 8, 11, 19) or a change of scene (here and cf. *Il.* 4, 7, 8, 9, 12, 13, 14, 15, 16, 18, 20, 23).

The change of scene is accomplished by a combination of a μέν-clause, which recounts the activities of one party (Trojans inside Troy), and a δέ/αὐτάρ-clause, in which the narrator turns to another party (Greeks and Hector outside the walls); see Richardson (1990) 115–17. The μέν-clause forms a recapitulation of what preceded: from 21.527 onwards the Trojans have been fleeing in panic inside the city, parched with thirst (cf. πεφυζότες at 21.528, 532, πεφοβημένοι at 21.606, and δίψηι at 21.541). The imperfects suggest that they continue to cool down and slake their thirst while the narrator turns to the action on the battlefield, effectively contrasting their respite with the martial and athletic exertions of Achilles and Hector.

59

1 ἄστυ: in Homer a metrical variant of πόλις; see 432–4n. πεφυζότες 'having fled in panic'; this form of the perfect exists alongside πεφευγότες (*Od.* 1.12). ἠΰτε: see 139n. νεβροί: deer/fawns typically symbolise the chased as opposed to chasing lions, dogs, or hunters; often there is an undertone of fear and helplessness. The imagery will be taken up in the form of a full simile at 188–98n. (see also Introduction 3b).

2 ἱδρῶ ἀπεψύχοντο: lit. 'they let their sweat cool down'; cf. 11.621; 21.561. The verb is probably related to both ψυχή, 'blowing', and ψυχρός, 'cold'; see *LfgrE* s.v. There is an ancient variant ἀνεψύχοντο, which is favoured by Aristarchus; this verb is however combined with φίλον ἦτορ (10.575; 13.84) rather than ἱδρῶ. ἀκέοντο . . . δίψαν: the meaning to 'heal' one's thirst occurs only here, but the verb is used metaphorically at other places (e.g. patching up a ship: *Od.* 14.383).

3 κεκλιμένοι καλῇσιν ἐπάλξεσιν 'leaning against the beautiful breastworks'; it seems most natural to take this posture as expressing their exhaustion, but there might also be a hint of their seeking the protection of the walls (so the scholia, and cf. e.g. Paris στήληι κεκλιμένος, when shooting an arrow at Diomedes: 11.371). ἔπαλξις, from ἐπαλέξω, 'to defend', is a breastwork on a wall to protect defenders (cf. 12.397–9). We hear about such breastworks repeatedly in connection with the wall around the Greek ships, but only here with the Trojan walls. The narrator typically zooms in on a detail of the scenery when his story asks for it; see 145–57n. This is the only instance where breastworks are given an epithet, the 'beautiful' perhaps reflecting the relief of the Trojans, who have been able to flee inside the city (cf. their being called ἀσπάσιοι 'glad', at 21.607, typically of those who have escaped from danger).

3–4 αὐτὰρ Ἀχαιοί: though the Greek forces at large are briefly mentioned here, the ensuing action will revolve mainly around Achilles and Hector; their presence is acknowledged again at 205–6 and 369–75, but their role is that of onlookers. ἆσσον 'nearer' (comparative of ἄγχι). West 1, xx prefers this accentuation to that of the vulgate (ἄσσον). ἴσαν = ἦισαν. σάκε' ὤμοισι κλίναντες: lit. 'leaning their shields on their shoulders'. The exact interpretation of this posture, which recurs only twice (11.593 and 13.488), is unclear, but 'it might indicate a shield held out almost horizontally, with the top resting on the shoulder' (Richardson). It would seem to be a defensive manoeuvre for protection against missiles thrown from the walls of Troy (cf. the Trojans who at 12.137–8 hold up their shields to protect themselves against stones thrown by the Greek defenders from the wall around the ships; at 196 the possibility of the Trojans pelting Achilles from the walls is mentioned).

5–6 The last time we saw Hector, he was snatched away and wrapped in mist by Apollo at the moment Achilles attacked him (20.443–4). When we meet him again, he is standing alone in front of the walls of Troy, i.e. fulfilling his quintessential role of its 'sole' defender (506–7n.). His moving to this place has been 'passed over in silence', according to the typical Homeric principle of κατὰ τὸ σιωπώμενον.

5 'Hector baneful fate shackled, so that he stayed on the spot'. αὐτοῦ μεῖναι: in Homer infinitives are often (syntactically) loosely attached to other verbs, having final or consecutive force (*GH* II 301–2). ὀλοιὴ μοῖρ' ἐπέδησεν: μοῖρα is one of many Homeric words for fate, cf. αἶσα (61, 477) and πότμος (39n.). Since it usually pregnantly means 'death-fate', it is often accompanied by negative epithets, such as 'forceful' (5.629), 'accursed' (12.116), and 'evil' (13.602). The force of the metaphor 'fate (or a god) *shackling* people' (4.517; *Od.* 3.269; 11.292; 18.155–6) nearly always is still felt: whereas the other Trojans 'did not dare to wait for each other outside the city and wall' (21.608–9), Hector has to stay, since he is doomed to die at Achilles' hands (see Introduction 2d). Soon we will see that Hector is forced to stay not only by an external force, fate (208–13n.), but also by an internal one, his own resolve.

6 Ἰλίου προπάροιθε: the preposition follows the word it governs (L 20). The form Ἰλίου occurs in all MSS and scans with an irregular long second iota; the original formula presumably was Ἰλίοο προπάροιθε (printed by West in his text). πυλάων . . . Σκαιάων: again, the narrator mentions a significant piece of scenery: the Scaean gate is the main gate of Troy, giving access to the plain where the battles are fought. It was at this gate that Hector had his memorable meeting with his wife Andromache and son Astyanax in book 6 (cf. 6.392–3), a scene which clearly forms the backdrop to this entire book (see Introduction 2c). It is also the gate at which Achilles will be killed (cf. 360) and where earlier the Trojan women prayed for Diomedes to be killed by Athena (6.307). Troy has many gates (cf. 2.809), presumably in order to make it resemble that other famous mythical city, seven-gated Thebes. At 194–5 we will hear about a Dardanian gate. For discussion of the Trojan gates, including possible archaeological identifications, see Mannsperger (1993).

7–13 With a second αὐτάρ (cf. 3) the narrator turns from the Greeks and Hector near Troy to Achilles and Apollo, who are running farther away on the plain, near the river Scamander (cf. 21.602–3). Because the god's goal of averting the danger to Troy and the Trojans (cf. 21.544) has been reached, Apollo can end his 'ruse' of luring Achilles away from the city. His tone is offensively mocking, which is in tune with his being a pro-Trojan god and hence Achilles' opponent. (He will kill him together with Paris, as Hector predicts at 359–60.) Contrast the sympathetic mockery of Athena towards Odysseus at *Od.* 13.287–310, who likewise 'chides' her mortal addressee for not recognising her but at the same time offers support and praise.

7 Πηλεΐωνα 'son of Peleus'. Besides a patronymic on -ίδης, Achilles has two other ones (on -ίων, acc. -ίωνα, and on -ιος).

8 τίπτε: forceful 'why' (either τί + syncopated ποτε or IE *kʷidpe>*titpe> τίπτε).

9–10 θνητός . . . θεόν: the juxtaposition underlines the gulf between the two; cf., e.g. 24.464. ἐών: Ionic participle of εἶναι. οὐδέ νύ πω 'not even now'; cf. 21.410, also mocking. οὐδέ in Homer often is adverbial (*GH* II 339). Enclitic νυ is a shortened form of νῦν; it may be temporal (as here) or indicate a conclusion. με | ἔγνως ὡς θεός εἰμι: με is a proleptic object, anticipating the subject of the dependent clause; see 191–2n. σὺ δ'... μενεαίνεις 'but you keep on striving' sc. to get me; cf. αἰεὶ ἔλποιτο (Ach.) κιχήσεσθαι ποσὶν οἷσιν (21.605). δέ marks a new action rather than a new subject; see 368–9n. ἀσπερχές 'without pause' (adverbial), here with connotation 'to no avail', since a god cannot be overtaken. One papyrus adds an extra line (Ἰλίου ἐξαλαπάξαι ἐϋκτίμενον πτολίεθρον) after 10, which at 4.33 also follows after ἀσπερχές μενεαίνεις, but here is less apt (Achilles is not desiring to destroy Troy, but pursuing a Trojan *away* from that city).

11–12 Apollo mockingly suggests that Achilles is *not* interested in killing the Trojans he had been routing. Of course, the Greek hero had been very much intent on doing this before he was sidetracked by the god (cf. 21.540–3). ἦ νύ 'for sure'; the use of the particle ἦ, which stresses an objective truth (40n.) and is reinforced by νυ, creates a mocking effect when used in connection with an unlikely suggestion. τοι = σοι (L 19). Τρώων πόνος, οὓς ἐφόβησας 'the fight with the Trojans, whom you put to flight'. Τρώων is objective genitive (scholia and Ameis-Hentze). πόνος often specifically means the toil and moil of fighting (e.g. 4.456). οἳ δή τοι εἰς ἄστυ ἄλεν, σὺ δὲ δεῦρο λιάσθης 'who were penned up inside the city thanks to you, and (i.e. while) you bent away here'; an instance of the Homeric paratactic style (L 23). This second relative clause, added without a coordinator but with a repetition of the relative pronoun, specifies the first; see *GH* II 243. ἄλεν = ἄλησαν (L 14), passive aor. from εἴλω; cf. πόλις δ' ἔμπλητο ἀλέντων (21.607). λιάσθης has the connotation 'you turned aside from your original course', which was the pursuit of the Trojans. δή: see 76n. δεῦρο: the liveliness and naturalness of Homeric speeches is due in part to the presence of deictic words; 'here' evokes the picture of Apollo pointing at the spot near the river Scamander where they find themselves.

13 μέν = μήν, as often in Homer. With the particle μήν, 'really', 'in truth', a speaker, as it were, personally guarantees the truth of his proposition, often because it is in contrast with what his addressee supposes or wishes; see Wakker (1997b) 213–14. τοι: a frozen form of the 'ethic' dative (38n.) of the second-person personal pronoun. It functions as a particle, which, if pressed into words, should mean 'you see', 'you know', or 'let me tell you', but which is often left untranslated. μόρσιμος '(someone) fated to die' = '(someone) who could be killed'. At the end of his speech Apollo returns to its beginning: mortals can not overtake immortals, nor can they kill them.

14–20 Apollo's mocking tone has struck home: Achilles reacts with an angry speech, in which he picks up Apollo's points in reverse order: 'you deceivingly turned me out here away from the wall' (cf. 12b and the echo of δεῦρο in ἐνθάδε); '(if this hadn't happened) I would have killed many more Trojans' (cf. 11–12a); 'if you were no god, I would take my revenge on you' (cf. 8–10). Though Achilles' speech is unusually offensive (the only parallels being Menelaus addressing Zeus at 3.365–8 and Helen addressing Aphrodite at 3.399–412), it is not out of the ordinary: as Jones (1996) has shown, Homeric heroes speak about the gods in terms of powerful human beings (rather than numinous and venerable beings). This attitude and, of course, the frivolous behaviour of the gods themselves, was a cause of great concern to later Greeks; see Feeney (1991) 5–56.

14 μέγ' ὀχθήσας '(having become) greatly vexed', 'deeply troubled'; the aorist is ingressive. Although the etymology of this verb is unclear (related to ἔχθος, 'a taking of offence'?), it is clear that it conveys an emotional release (of frustration, fear, anger) when one cannot react in the way one would like, cf. *LfgrE*, with references. πόδας ὠκύς: Achilles is called 'swift-footed' thirty-one times, an epithet which he shares with the messenger of the gods Iris (nine times). Achilles has three more epithets which stress his swiftness: ποδάρκης, ποδώκης, and (πόδας) ταχύς. The present book shows him living up to his reputation with the spectacular chase of Hector; see Whallon (1969) 14–17.

15–16 ἔβλαψάς μ'... τρέψας ἀπὸ τείχεος 'you have fooled me ... by turning me away from the wall'; a coincident use of the aorist participle, which means that the main verb and the participle describe the same action or different aspects of the same action. βλάπτω, 'disable', 'hinder', often has a figurative sense 'to harm someone's wits', i.e. 'fool', with the gods, *atē*, or wine as agent. In his anger Achilles uses stronger language than the narrator, who at 21.604 had said: δόλωι... ἔθελγεν Ἀπόλλων, lit. 'Apollo beguiled him with a trick', i.e. 'tricked'. ἑκάεργε 'working from afar'. The etymology and meaning of this word are disputed. It is usually explained by modern scholars as *Ϝεκα (cf. ἑκών) + ἔργον, 'working at will', but it is clearly related by the epic singers to ἑκάς (*σϝεκάς), 'far', as in ἑκηβόλος, which refers to Apollo as an archer-god. The word is used as an epithet with the name Apollo, but it also occurs as a substantive, as here. Its use as a form of address is found only twice more (1.34; 21.472), both times in speeches by gods. Achilles' informal address to this venerable god seems indicative of his anger and is well suited to his speech as a whole, in which he does not mince his words. More generally, outspokenness is a prime characteristic of Achilles (cf. 9.312–13). Apollo, though revealing his true divine nature, had not mentioned his name; contrast Hermes at 24.460–1 (ἐγὼ θεὸς ἄμβροτος εἰλήλουθα, | Ἑρμείας). Achilles nevertheless correctly identifies him, presumably on the basis of his awareness of Apollo's constant support of the Trojans. Thus at 16.94 he said, μάλα τούς γε (Trojans) φιλεῖ ἑκάεργος Ἀπόλλων.

16–20 Achilles' angry frustration first finds expression in a counterfactual (past indicative + κε), followed, as often in Greek, by a νῦν δέ-clause, 'but now' = 'in truth', 'in reality' (cf. 104, 482). He then adds a potential optative + ἄν which refers to something that is not possible yet is imaginable for a moment; see *GH* II 219. Both utterances are headed by ἦ, 'for sure' (40n.), mirroring (and countering) Apollo's ἦ (11).

16–17 κ'... γαῖαν ὀδὰξ εἷλον 'would have bitten the dust' (lit. 'would have taken ground with their teeth'). ὀδάξ is adverbial.

18 ἐμὲ... κῦδος ἀφείλεο: as is common with verbs of taking away, it takes two objects ('to take away x from y'). For κῦδος see 205–7n. τούς: anaphoric pronoun (L 17), here of persons (the Trojans) who are uppermost in Achilles' mind.

19 ῥηϊδίως: it is a commonplace in Homer that gods do things 'easily' (cf. e.g. 15.361–6, where Apollo 'easily' destroys the wall around the Greek ships, like a child knocking down a sandcastle on the beach); see Griffin (1980) 188–9. Here this 'fact of life' becomes a complaint on the lips of the victim. οὔ τι: τι modifies οὐ: 'not at all'. ἔδδεισας = ἔδεισας, from ἔδϝεισας. ὀπίσσω: adverb, with τίσιν, '(vengeance) in the future'.

20 σ'... τεισαίμην 'I would have taken vengeance on you'; from τίνω. The MSS generally give τισαίμην, here and elsewhere, but this is probably due to iotacism; see GH I 13 and West I, xxxv–vi. δύναμις: while κράτος and σθένος mean power, force per se, δύναμις derives its meaning from the context, here 'power to take revenge', but, e.g. at 13.786, 'power to fight'.

21 A divine intervention is usually concluded by a statement that the god went away to X (Olympus or some other place); see de Jong on 6.21–7. The absence of such a conclusion here prepares us for the fact that Apollo will soon intervene again (203). προτί = πρός. μέγα φρονέων 'high-spirited'; the expression refers to a mixture of fighting spirit and confidence. One may hesitate whether to take μέγα as adverb, 'with a high pitch of resolve' or as object (as in ἀγαθὰ/φιλὰ φρονέων), 'with high thoughts in his mind'. ἐβεβήκει: verbs of motion in Homer often are in the perfect tense; see GH II 198.

22–4 A comparison with a racehorse illustrates Achilles' speed and at the same time introduces the theme of a race, such as will soon take place between Hector and Achilles. Another comparison involving a horse race will be used in the course of that scene (162–6n.). Horse-racing in the Homeric epics always involves chariots, never a single horse with jockey; for a detailed scene of horse-racing see 23.262–652. σευάμενος ὥς θ'... ὅς... τε... ὥς: for the structure of Homeric similes see Introduction 3b. For epic τε, which is typical in this context, see L 21.

22 ἀεθλοφόρος 'prize-winning'. In Homer this epithet is only given to horses; later it will also be attributed to men, e.g. Cleobis and Biton in Herodotus Histories 1.31. σὺν ὄχεσφιν: the suffix -φιν is added to form the equivalent of a dative plural (L 9).

23 ῥα: see 98n. θέῃσι: thematic subjunctive with athematic ending (L 13). In Homer the iterative subjunctive is found both with and without ἄν (as here); GH II 279. τιταινόμενος 'stretching himself', 'running at full stride'. πεδίοιο 'over the plain'; the genitive of the space traversed (GH II 58).

24 λαιψηρά 'quickly' (adverb). γούνατ': the first vowel is lengthened because of the disappearance of the digamma, < *γόνϝατα (L 2).

25–91

Achilles is running at full speed towards the city, where the narratees know Hector is waiting. Finally the fatal confrontation between the two heroes seems about to take place. Anticipated for the first time by Zeus at 15.68 and announced by Achilles at 18.114–15, it had been postponed many times. First Achilles had to be provided with new armour (book 18); then he had to reconcile himself with Agamemnon and allow the other Greeks to eat (book 19); when he entered the battlefield, he looked for Hector (20.75–8) but actually fought an abortive duel with Aeneas; when Achilles later spotted him, he was saved by Apollo (20.423–54); Achilles went on killing many Trojans but was nearly overwhelmed by the pro-Trojan river Scamander (21.136–382); the river being checked again by Hephaestus, other gods joined the battle; in order to allow the Trojans to flee inside the city, Achilles was lured away from Troy by 'Agenor'/Apollo (see 1–24n.). The retardations increase the tension and underscore the importance of the event; see Bremer (1987) 33–7, Morrison (1992) 43–9, and Introduction 2b. They also allow the narratees to see Achilles in martial action for the first time in the *Iliad*; see Schadewaldt (1959) 285–94.

But even now, with Achilles on his way towards Hector (again), the narrator does not bring the two together right away. Effectively filling in the time needed by Achilles to get back to the city, he shows us Hector's parents begging their son to come inside before it is too late and Hector struggling with his fear of confronting Achilles. For the Homeric 'fill-in' technique see 166–87n.

25–89 A typical Homeric narrative pattern: action (Achilles running through the plain) – perception (Priam sees him running through the plain *towards* the city and Hector; note the significant change of σευάμενος (22) into ἐπεσσύμενον (26)) – reaction (Priam urges Hector not to await Achilles); see de Jong on 5.279–90. The pattern here, in accordance with the importance of the moment, is elaborated with a simile (25–32) and a doubling of the reaction (Hecuba also addresses Hector).

25–32 This star simile illustrates the glitter of Achilles' armour as he runs through the plain; the point of contact between simile and context is 'advertised' through verbal echos (παμφαίνονθ' ≈ φαίνονται, λαμπρότατος ≈ ἔλαμπε). Warriors and their armour are often compared to stars, with the gleam underlining their heroic stature; cf. 5.5–6; 11.62–5; 19.381–2, and esp. 22.317–19 (Achilles again). In the case of Achilles we may also recall the stars *on* his shield, which have been described in detail as part of the *ekphrasis* of his new armour (18.485–9). But the simile also conveys something of Priam's feelings of fear: for him the star/Achilles is 'a bad omen', which/who will bring fever/misery to 'wretched mortals'. See Fränkel (1921) 47–50 and de Jong (2004) 126. For the typical use of epic τε (26, 27, 29, 30, 31) see L 21.

25 τόν 'him'; the anaphoric pronoun refers back to Ἀχιλεύς at 24 (L 17). ὁ γέρων Πρίαμος: lit., 'he, the old man Priam', but the pronoun here is close to its later use as the article, 'the old man Priam' (L 17). πρῶτος ἴδεν ὀφθαλμοῖσιν: for the 'X saw/heard as (very) first' motif cf. 10.532; 23.450; *Od.* 1.113. Priam already at 21.526–7 stood on the tower of the Scaean gate and, then also noting Achilles, had ordered the gates to be opened to let the fleeing Trojans in.

26 παμφαίνονθ'... ἐπεσσύμενον 'rushing *while* glittering'; for the asyndetic combination of participles see 70n. ἐπεσσύμενον is middle perfect participle of ἐπισσεύω. πεδίοιο: see 23n.

27 ῥα: see 98n. ὀπώρης 'in late summer': genitive of time within which (*GH* II 59). εἶσιν 'rises'; for this use of εἶμι cf. ἦμος... ἑωσφόρος εἶσι, 'when the Lightbringer (= the Morning Star, the planet Venus) rises' (23.226). See also 29n. οἱ αὐγαί 'its rays'. οἱ is third person personal pronoun (L 20), used as a possessive dative (L 22). The relative construction is given up: 'a star, which rises . . . , and *its*' (instead of 'whose').

28 νυκτὸς ἀμολγῷ: a typical example of an expression of which the exact meaning was obscure even in antiquity. Originally it may have meant 'at the milking time of night', i.e., 'the moment (at the beginning of the night) when animals are milked', but it is clear that it is interpreted by the singers as 'at the dead of night'. It is the time when stars are most clear (here and 317), when lions attack herds (11.173; 15.324), and when people have dreams (*Od.* 4.841).

29 κύν' Ὠρίωνος ἐπίκλησιν καλέουσιν '(whom) they call "Orion's dog" by way of nickname' (ἐπίκλησιν is internal accusative). Both narrator and characters employ this type of formulation (7.138–9; 18.487; 22.506; *Od.* 5.273). In its full form the expression runs 'X, whom they call Y by way of nickname', but here (and 506) X is lacking. From Hesiod *Erga* 417–19, 517, and especially 609 (where Orion and Sirius are mentioned together), it is clear that 'the dog of Orion' must be Sirius: 'Its heliacal rising (19 July for Hesiod) marked the season of most intense heat and severe fevers, and these were ascribed to the star's being in the sky all day with the sun' (West (1978) on 417). For the mythical hunter Orion see *Od.* 11.572–5.

30 ὅ γ' 'he, sc. the aforementioned star': anaphoric pronoun (L17). For the redundancy of this combination see 33–4n. τέτυκται 'is (made)'; the perfect middle of τεύχω is often used as a metrically convenient variant of ἐστί. Here a stylistic factor, the avoidance of repeating ἐστί, may also have played a role.

31 πυρετόν 'heat' or 'fever' (as in later Greek). δειλοῖσι βροτοῖσιν: δειλός belongs to the character-language: it is used mainly by characters (thirty-eight times out of a total of forty occurrences). Its exceptional occurrence here in the narrator-text underscores the point that the simile also gives expression to the effect of Achilles on Priam (25–32n.), who will use the same formulaic expression in his ensuing speech (76).

32 τοῦ 'of him', the anaphoric pronoun (L 17) refers to Achilles, last mentioned at 25. χαλκός: sc. his bronze corslet, which at 18.610 was said to be φαεινότερον πυρὸς αὐγῆς.

33–91 A rare combination of two 'supplication' scenes; cf. *Od.* 22.310–80, where we even find three supplications in a row. The supplications by Hector's father and mother form a pair and are meant to reinforce each other, as the capping line at 90 with duals demonstrates.

Suppliants supplicate to save their life, to acquire something important, or to persuade a person to do something. A 'supplication' scene typically consists of (1) the approach of a suppliant; (2) gesture(s); (3) the supplication speech; (4) the reaction of the *supplicandus*. Other examples are Thetis' supplication of Zeus (1.495–530), Priam's supplication of Achilles (24.477–551), and Odysseus' supplication of Nausicaa (*Od.* 6.141–97) and Arete (7.142–71); for supplications on the battlefield see 337–54n. Supplication in Homer is discussed by Gould (1973), Pedrick (1982), Thornton (1984), Crotty (1994), and Naiden (2006).

Here the special situation of Priam and Hecuba standing on the wall above Hector effects some variations to the pattern of supplication. (1) There is no approach of the suppliant. (2) Instead of grasping the knee or touching the chin of the *supplicandus*, Priam and Hecuba make gestures of mourning (weeping, beating their heads, tearing out their hair) and emotional appeal (stretching out the hands and exposing the breasts). The body language of mourning underscores the message of their ensuing (3) supplication speeches, in which they argue that confronting Achilles means Hector's certain death and beg him to come inside. (4) The reaction of the *supplicandus* in both cases is negative.

The sequence of pleas by Priam and Hecuba, which can be seen as a sequel to Andromache's earlier plea to Hector to stay inside at 6.407–39, will be paralleled at the end of the book by the sequence of laments by Priam (414–29), Hecuba (430–7), and Andromache (476–515); the two sets of speeches form a ring-composition around the central scene of the duel between Hector and Achilles.

Throughout this scene Priam is referred to as 'the old man' (33, 37, 77), a circumlocution which highlights the central theme of his speech, the appeal to his old age (60–1 and 74–6). Hector is referred to as φίλον υἱόν (35, 90) and Hecuba as μήτηρ (79). Contrast the scene of the truce and duel in book 3, where Priam is referred to with Πρίαμος (261, 303), since he is there acting as king of Troy. For the technique of circumlocution (periphrastic denomination) in Homer see de Jong (1993).

33–7 Speech-introductions are among the most formulaic parts of the Homeric epics: since the singer had to mark his change of role from narrator to character, speeches are introduced and capped by tags. But variations are found even within this group of formulas; see Edwards (1970). Thus here we find a unique speech-introduction, which is one of the longest. They usually take up only one verse but there are other long instances at 8.492–6 and 12.265–8. The narrator introduces Priam's speech with no less than four verbs of speaking, each with its own significance: ᾤμωξεν/οἰμώξας, crying out (always by men) as a spontaneous reaction to physical or mental distress (407–9n.); ἐγεγώνει, shouting so as to make oneself heard (necessary because of the distance between Priam and

Hector); λισσόμενος, supplicating; and ἐλεεινὰ προσηύδα, speaking in a piteous way or perhaps in a wailing tone (*BK* on 2.314).

The narrator underlines the high emotionality of the moment by using three skewed sentences, i.e. sentences of which neither the beginning nor the end coincides with the verse boundaries (33–6); see Higbie (1990) 90–151, especially 112, and Introduction 4b (the section on enjambement).

33–4 ὤιμωξεν . . . οἰμώξας: taking up a main verb by a participle is a common characteristic of the paratactic style, which is found regularly in Homer, e.g. μείδησεν δὲ θεὰ . . . Ἥρη. μειδήσασα δὲ (1.595–6), but also in Herodotus, e.g. ὁ Κανδαύλης ἠράσθη τῆς ἑωυτοῦ γυναικός, ἐρασθεὶς δέ (*Histories* 1.8.1). See *GH* II 359 and Fehling (1969) 197–8. In the Homeric epics men display sadness and despair and shed tears as freely as women; cf. again 90 and 408. As van Wees shows (1998), gender differentiation where weeping is concerned evolved only after Homer. ὅ γε: the anaphoric pronoun is often redundant and γε unnecessary: there is no doubt that the narrator is (still) talking about Priam. The combination is found very often, however, and may have been of metrical use to the singer. κεφαλὴν . . . κόψατο χερσίν | ὑψόσ' ἀνασχόμενος 'he beat his head with his hands, raising them high', in order to beat all the more forcefully; cf. 3.362; *Od.* 14.425; 18.95.

35–6 The narrator repeats the information of 5–6, but now stresses Hector's own resolve. ἄμοτον μεμαὼς Ἀχιλῆϊ μάχεσθαι: part. of μέμονα, 'to feel the urge', 'be eager' combined with an adverbial accusative of uncertain etymology, 'intensely', 'forcefully' (the interpretation 'incessantly', 'indefatigably', already found in the scholia, is now generally abandoned). This is the omniscient narrator's reading of Hector's mind, who is still fully determined to face Achilles (and will only start to waver when he actually sees him approaching), rather than the focalisation of Priam and Hecuba ('in the eyes of those who look on, Hektor initially displays a stubborn determination to stand firm': Richardson on 98–130 and Petersmann (1974) 154–5), while the hero himself would already be in inner turmoil. See further 91–137n.

37 ἐλεεινά: an internal accusative functioning as an adverb. χειρὰς ὀρεγνύς: stretching out one's hands (horizontally or vertically, towards heaven) is a gesture of prayer (cf. 1.351; 15.371), which also suits a supplication.

38–76 Priam's speech consists of two parts: 'Do not await Achilles, for confronting him will mean your death, the merciless man. I wish he would die (*here he starts trailing off*), that man who has already killed so many of my sons and caused me grief. The grief of the Trojans will be less, if at least you remain alive. (*He resumes his main point.*) Come inside, in order that you save the Trojans and yourself. (*Instead of continuing with 'and save me', he paints a picture of what will happen to him when Troy falls.*) Have pity on me, who will have to see my family killed and whose body will be mutilated after death.'

38 μοι: a so-called 'ethic' dative, which gives expression to the speaker's involvement. It cannot be easily brought out in translation, but here its force is captured by 'please'. See *GH* II 72. μίμνε: the force of the present tense in combination with μή is 'stop waiting'. ἀνέρα τοῦτον: ἀνέρα is a variant of ἄνδρα; the first syllable has to be scanned long in order to avoid three short syllables in a row (see Introduction 4b). Achilles is not referred to by his own name but by a circumlocution; see 33–91n., and compare Hecuba's δήϊον ἄνδρα at 84. It shows that the singer was not obliged to use name-epithet formulas; Shive (1987) discusses the many ways in which 'Achilles' can be referred to. The scholiast aptly remarks that Priam is evoked through the use of the deictic pronoun as pointing out Achilles to his son ('that man there with you'). There may also be a touch of the pejorative in the choice of this deictic pronoun; see *GH* II 169 and cf. e.g. 5.761 (ἄφρονα τοῦτον), 831 (τοῦτον μαινόμενον).

39 οἷος: see 455–6n. πότμον ἐπίσπῃς 'meet/touch your death-fate'. πότμος is one of several words for 'fate' in Homer; see 5n. It belongs to the character-language (29 x speech; 3 x embedded focalisation, e.g. 363 = 16.857; 2 x narrator-text) and is used often in warnings or prophecies; cf. e.g. 21.588.Traditionally ἐφ-έπω is taken as 'drive (your horses) in pursuit', hence in the aorist 'reach (or meet) your goal', but a recent interpretation is 'touch', on the basis of an original force of ἔπω (from *sep-) as 'handle'; see Forssman (2006).

40 Πηλεΐωνι: see 7n. ἦ 'for sure'; through this particle a speaker marks his proposition as objectively true; cf. Wakker (1997a) 218–22. The narrator calls Achilles πολὺ φέρτατος of the Greeks (2.769), Poseidon calls him κρείσσων than Aeneas (20.334), and Achilles and others call him(self) ἄριστον Ἀχαιῶν (1.244; 16.271–2); the last qualification he shares with others (Agamemnon: 1.91; Diomedes: 5.103). Priam's repeated ἦ in this part of his speech (cf. 43, 49) shows how intent he is on persuading Hector of the validity of his words.

41 σχέτλιος 'the merciless man' (Achilles); most likely an exclamation triggered by the preceding ἐπεί-clause, rather than a vocative addressed to Hector. This word, obviously related to ἔχω/ἔσχον, literally means 'holding out', 'tough', and is sometimes used in affectionate remonstrances, 'foolhardy' (cf. Hecuba of Hector at 86), but more often in a negative sense, 'harsh', 'merciless'.

41–3 For a brief moment Priam allows himself to picture the death of Achilles: αἴθε (= εἴθε) + optative expressing a wish, followed by two potential clauses (κε + optative). The three clauses follow each other without any connector (asyndeton). This, together with the verses being skewed (33–7n.), gives expression to Priam's intense emotion. Priam not merely wishes Achilles dead but his body eaten by dogs and birds, and the important theme of the mutilation of the corpse is voiced for the first time in this book; see 337–54n. It will return later in Priam's speech, then in connection with himself (66–71).

41–2 The grim irony of the αἴθε-clause resides in τοσσόνδε: 'may he become *so very* dear to the gods as he is to me = *so little*'. This is better than understanding φίλος to imply its opposite, 'so dear' = 'so hated' (Richardson, following the scholiast). At *Od.* 14.440–1 we find a similar wish, there uttered sincerely (Odysseus to Eumaeus: 'may you become so beloved to the gods as you are to me').

ἑ = αὐτόν (L 19). ἔδοιεν: this is the reading of Aristarchus, while the MSS have the future indicative ἔδονται (as at 4.237; 16.836; 18.271). We do find κεν/ἄν + future indicative in Homer (see 49–50 n.), but the optative is better in view of the other optatives in this passage; Priam is only imagining Achilles' death.

43 κείμενον: often in the pregnant sense of 'lying dead/slain', cf. e.g. 73; 16.541; 18.20; here with the additional suggestion of lying unburied (cf. 386–7). μοι αἰνὸν ἀπὸ πραπίδων ἄχος ἔλθοι: in Homer people may have pain, sorrows, etc., but pain, sorrows, etc. may also have, seize, reach, enter, or (as here) leave persons; see Rijksbaron (1997). For ἄχος see 425n. μοι is either 'ethic' dative (38n.), 'grief would be gone *for me* from the heart', or possessive dative (L 22), 'grief would be gone from *my* heart'. πραπίδων (plural only) means '(physical) breast', hence (mental) 'mind'; for the many words for 'heart' or 'mind' in Homer see 78n.

44–5 Priam's sad loss of many valiant sons in the Trojan war is mentioned by many, Priam himself (here, 423–6; 24.255–9, 493–501, and 506), Hecuba (24.204–5), and even Achilles (24.520–1). He is the embodiment of the theme of the 'bereaved parent', which is prominent in many 'obituaries', e.g. after Diomedes slew Xanthus and Thoon 'to their father he left lamentation and bitter grief, since he did not receive them alive returning from battle' (5.156–8); see Fenik (1968) 12, Griffin (1980) 123–7, and Stoevesandt (2004) 128–34. ὅς . . . εὖνιν ἔθηκεν: best analysed as a loosely attached relative clause, which almost functions as an independent exclamation ('. . . ; that man who robbed me of many sons'). Others take it as a relative clause dependent on ἑ (42), with the intervening ἤ-clause as a parenthesis ('soon dogs would devour him – indeed, grief would be gone from my heart – who') or a main clause introduced by ὅς, which for metrical reasons takes the place of ὁ and functions as an anaphoric pronoun ('He robbed me'). τε καί 'and'; the combination is used instead of καί in cases where the two connected words form a close unity. εὖνιν ἔθηκεν 'made me bereaved of', an emotional variant of ἐστέρησε. The expression occurs only once more: *Od.* 9.524 (Odysseus wishes to rob the Cyclops of his dear life). περνάς: for Achilles selling Trojan princes, cf. 21.78–9 (Lycaon: με πέρασσας . . . Λῆμνον ἐς ἠγαθέην) and 24.751–3 (Hecuba: ἄλλους . . . παῖδας ἐμούς. . . . Ἀχιλλεὺς | πέρνασχ᾽ . . . | ἐς Σάμον ἔς τ᾽ Ἴμβρον καὶ Λῆμνον ἀμιχθαλόεσσαν). ἔπι: in postposition (L 20). τηλεδαπάων 'remote' (and hence making it difficult for relatives to arrange ransom) suits the pathetic tone of Priam's speech. In view of the fact that Priam's sons have actually been taken to Lemnos, Samos, and Imbros, islands not that far from the Troad, there may be some rhetorical exaggeration involved (but note πέρνασχ᾽ . . . πέρην ἁλὸς ἀτρυγέτοιο at 24.752, where the word-play suggests distance). There is an ancient variant (also at 21.454) θηλυτεράων, 'female', which would here have to mean 'fertile' or refer to the fact that Lemnos and Imbros were ruled by women.

46–53 In order to exemplify his general claim of 44–5 (Achilles has killed and sold *many* of my sons) Priam mentions two sons whom he does not see among the Trojans who have fled inside Troy and whom he imagines to have been either captured or killed: Lycaon and Polydorus. The narratees know that the second alternative is true: both have been killed by Achilles (Polydorus at 20.407–18 and Lycaon at 21.34–135). Priam's voicing of the first alternative therefore is an instance of 'pitiable' dramatic irony (scholion). The situation resembles that at 3.236–44, where Helen says that she is not able to see her brothers Castor and Polydeuces among the Greeks in the plain, and the narrator, after her speech, comments that they are dead.

Making Priam mention precisely these two sons at this point, and not e.g. Mestor and Troilus, whom he mentions at 24.257–8, is highly effective. The narratees know from 20.408–10 that 'Priam tried to keep Polydorus from fighting because he was the youngest son and best beloved among his children' and from 21.89–92 that Lycaon had linked his own death at the hands of Achilles to that of his brother Polydorus.

46 καὶ γὰρ νῦν 'for now too'. καὶ γάρ typically signals the introduction of an example which must back up a general claim; cf. 19.91–5 (Ἄτη, ἣ πάντας ἀᾶται... καὶ γὰρ δή νύ ποτε Ζεὺς ἄσατο); 24.601–2 (νῦν δὲ μνησώμεθα δόρπου. | καὶ γάρ... Νιόβη ἐμνήσατο σίτου). παῖδε: the dual (L 16) is still regularly used in Homer, while in later Greek it became rare. Sometimes the form is used merely for metrical convenience, but often it has its full force. Thus it here suggests a close tie between these two children of Priam, which indeed exists: they were born from the same mother, Laothoa (21.84–91).

47 ἰδέειν: metrical diectasis (L 4): ἰδέειν (◡ ◡ –) < ἰδεῖν (◡ –) < ἰδέεν (◡ ◡ –). Τρώων εἰς ἄστυ ἀλέντων 'among the Trojans who are penned up in the city'. ἀλέντων is passive aor. from εἴλω (cf. ἄλεν: 12). It seems preferable to take Τρώων as partitive genitive, with ἀλέντων an adnominal participle, rather than, as Ameis-Hentze do, to take the phrase as a genitive absolute, a construction which is very rare in Homer (see GH II 323–4).

48 τούς: in Homer the anaphoric pronoun is regularly used as relative pronoun (L 17). κρείουσα 'distinctive','famous' among women (because of her beauty). This feminine form of κρείων occurs only here. The meaning of κρείων is unclear: perhaps originally 'distinctive', it developed into 'ruling, lording', notably of Agamemnon; see LfgrE. The epithet suggests that Laothoa is not a concubine but an official wife of Priam, which is confirmed at 51 by the mention of her dowry. As appears from 8.303–5, 21.88, and 24.495–7, Priam has at least three wives, an orientalising trait. As Hall (1989) 43 aptly suggests, the monogamy of Hector and Paris is the exception, created by the Homeric narrator in order to focus full attention on these characters as husbands.

49–50 The topic of ransom, which is fleetingly raised here, will recur in full, dramatic force when Hector begs Achilles to let his parents ransom his body (340–3n.). μετὰ στρατῶι 'among the (Greek) army' (collective noun). ἤ τ(ε) 'for sure'. This combination occurs often in the apodosis after a conditional clause; τε underlines the close connection between protasis and apodosis but is left untranslated. See Ruijgh (1971) 795–83. ἄν... ἀπολυσόμεθ': two interpretations are possible: (1) as prospective subjunctive (with short vowel: L 15), which in

Homer is also found in main clauses; or (2) as modal future indicative, which is a peculiar feature of Homeric syntax. See *GH* II 225–6, which opts for the first interpretation. The ancient variant ἀπολύσομεν is obviously inferior, since the active is always used of the one *accepting* the ransom (cf. e.g. 1.20). The plural 'we' indicates Priam and Laothoa. χαλκοῦ . . . χρυσοῦ 'for bronze and gold' (genitive of price).

51 The issue as to whether parents gave their daughters a dowry or the husbands paid a bride-price in Homeric society has been hotly debated among historians. Both practices are mentioned (for dowry cf. e.g. 9.147–8; for bride-price 472 or *Od.* 18.279), and Morris (1986) 105–10 argues for a combination: first gifts are offered in both directions to establish good relations between the bride's kin and potential suitors, then there is the bidding of gifts by suitors and acceptance of the best offer by the bride's father. ὀνομάκλυτος: although Altes is called 'of famous name', he is only mentioned here and 21.85–6. Ἄλτης: king of the war-loving Leleges, who lives in steep Pedasus, by the river Satnioeis, i.e. in the southern Troad (21.85–7). The Leleges live up to their reputation in that they are among the many allies of the Trojans in the war (10.429; 20.96).

52–5 Priam returns to Hector in chiastic order: '(A) if Lycaon and Polydorus are *dead*, (B) this means *grief* for their mother and me; (B') but for the Trojans *grief* will be shorter, (A') if you will not *die* also'. It is significant that Priam had used εἰ + indicative (neutral conditional) when talking about the fates of Lycaon and Polydorus, but that he now, discussing the fate of his addressee Hector, turns to ἤν + subjunctive (futural conditional; showing that the speaker considers the realisation of his proposition very well possible); see Wakker (1994) 174–6.

52 καὶ εἰν Ἀΐδαο δόμοισιν: sc. εἰσίν; cf. *Od.* 4.834. Ἀΐδαο is a genitive (L 5).

53 τοί = οἱ; the anaphoric pronoun is used as relative (L 17). τεκόμεσθα = τεκόμεθα.

54 λαοῖσιν . . . ἄλλοισι: ἄλλος has its 'inclusive' sense here: 'the others, i.e. the people (of Troy)'; see KG I 275. For λαός see 104n.

55 ἔσσεται = ἔσται.

56–76 Priam resumes his argument from 38–40 and once more urges Hector to come inside; note the repeated vocative ἐμὸν τέκος (56) ≈ φίλον τέκος (38). Whereas in the first half of his speech he merely indicated that Hector was sure to be killed by Achilles, he now reiterates this point but adds that Hector will actually save the Trojans by coming inside. The underlying, unexpressed thought here is that Hector is the most important defender of Troy and hence that his death will seal Troy's fate (see 506–7n.). Priam then works out this idea of the fall of Troy in terms of his own death rather than the destruction of the city. In so doing he follows the strategy of Andromache, who at 6.407–32 had likewise painted a moving picture of her own fate after Hector's death in order to persuade him to stay inside. Contrast 9.591–6, where we hear how Cleopatra, the wife of

Meleager, managed to *rouse* her husband from his wrathful *inactivity* by summing up all the evils which the fall of a city entails for its inhabitants.

Troy's fall is, like Achilles' death (358–60n.), not recounted in the *Iliad*. It is referred to, however, all the time, both by the narrator (12.10–16) and by characters (2.299–332; 4.163–5 = 6.447–9; 15.69–71; 22.60–8; 24.728–38). It is also suggested by a series of thematically linked similes concerning beleaguered or destroyed cities (see Introduction 3b). The fate of Thebes, Andromache's native city, also prefigures that of Troy (477–84n.). As a result, 'the later events – the death of Achilles and the fall of the fated city – have impressed themselves upon the consciousness of the reader as vividly as if the poet had extended his epic to include them' (Duckworth (1933) 302). For a full discussion, including instances where Troy seems *not* to be taken and the Greeks seem to return home empty-handed, see de Jong (2009). The 'Ilioupersis' theme returns in the *Odyssey* (4.271–89; 8.499–520; 11.523–32) and will be reworked by poets throughout antiquity; for archaic and classical Greek examples see Anderson (1997), especially 28–36.

When we compare Priam's speech with 9.591–6, we note how he has changed what may be considered the stock elements of the description of a captured city (the victors kill the men, set the city on fire, and drag away the children and women) into a family version: his *sons* are killed, his *daughters* and *daughters-in-law* are dragged away, and their *bedrooms* ruined. His extended family and their bedrooms have been introduced at 6.242–50. Priam's anticipation of the fall of Troy in terms of the dissolution of his family of course serves his persuasive aim: the infant children being flung to the earth and the daughters-in-law being dragged away should make Hector think of Astyanax and Andromache and bring the warning closer home to him. Hector himself at 6.448–65 had anticipated what the sack of Troy would mean for his own family. Priam further increases the pathos by making himself the one who has to watch all this first (61) and then be killed 'last' (66); cf. Polyphemus' perverse guest-gift to Odysseus, the promise to eat him 'last' (*Od.* 9.369–70). Homer's cue is taken up powerfully by Virgil, who makes the death of Priam the climactic end of Aeneas' story of the capture of Troy (*Aeneid* 2.506–558).

Though Priam here evokes his own death in harrowing detail, he, of course, does not know the name of his killer and instead speaks of τις (67). Likewise Andromache at 24.734–5 foresees that Astyanax will be thrown from a tower by τις Ἀχαιῶν. Assuming that the stories later assembled in the Epic Cycle (or perhaps even the cyclic poems themselves) were already current alongside the Homeric epics, as has been argued e.g. by Burgess (2001), the narratees will have been able to fill in the names: Priam will be killed by Neoptolemus, Astyanax by Neoptolemus or Odysseus.

56 ἀλλ' marks the transition from arguments for action to a statement of the action required, 'come now'; *GP* 14.

57 κῦδος: one of several Homeric words for 'glory'; see 205–7n.

58 φίλης αἰῶνος: αἰών (m.) primarily means 'life force', then 'life span' (cf. Latin *aevum*); it is often used together with ψυχή, and hence is taken as feminine here. For φίλης see 388n.

59 πρὸς δ' 'and besides' (πρὸς adverbial: L 20). **ἐμὲ τὸν δύστηνον** 'me that miserable one'. The pronoun may convey an emotional tone; *GH* II 163–4. **ἔτι φρονέοντ'** 'while I still have my senses', an emphatic variant for 'while I am still alive', which is chosen with an eye to what will follow (Priam will have to watch how his family is murdered). At 24.244–6 Priam wishes to be dead before the city is destroyed. **ἐλέησον:** suppliants do not ask for pity as a rule; it is primarily the old (here and 82, 419–20; 24.357, 503), young and inexperienced (20.465; 21.74), and lesser heroes (*Od.* 22.312, 344) who do so. See Konstan (2001) 78–9 and Naiden (2006) 97 ('the appeal to pity is optional'). The idea is taken up at the very end of his speech in οἴκτιστον. For pity (in the *Iliad*) see Crotty (1994) 3–88, Kim (2000) 35–67, and Most (2003).

60–1 ῥα: see 98n. **πατὴρ Κρονίδης... | αἴσηι ἐν ἀργαλέηι φθείσει** '(whom) father Zeus will destroy with a cruel fate'. ἐν expresses the circumstances under which something happens; *GH* II 102. Zeus is 'the father of men and gods' (167), and cf. *Od.* 20.202, where it is said that Zeus 'begets men', and the vocative Ζεῦ πάτερ, which is used by gods and mortals alike. In some cases this is literally true (he is the father of e.g. Sarpedon and Athena), but most of the time it is metaphorical in the sense that he enjoys the natural authority of a father in a patriarchal society, who watches over and rules his family. For the gods and fate see 208–13n. **ἐπὶ γήραος οὐδῶι** 'at the threshold (between life and death), which is formed by old age' (defining genitive). This formulaic expression (1 x *Il.*, 3 x *Od.*) is an emotional (and metrically useful) variant of simple γήραϊ, 'at old age'. **φθείσει:** for this spelling, instead of the vulgate's φθίσει, see West I, xxxvi.

61–5 For a similar series of participles, cf. *Od.* 16.108–10, where Odysseus says, 'I would rather die than watch these shameful things, strangers being beaten about (στυφελιζομένους), serving women being molested (ῥυστάζοντας) shamefully, wine being drawn to waste (διαφυσσόμενον), and men eating food (ἔδοντας) without end'. The effect is graphic rather than 'monotonous' (Richardson).

62 ἑλκηθείσας: the 'dragging' of women primarily refers to their being led from their homes to the ships and homes of the enemy as captives, cf. 6.454–5 (ἄγηται), 465 (ἑλκηθμοῖο); 9.594 (ἄγουσι); and *Od.* 8.529 (εἰσανάγουσι). At *Od.* 11.580 the (active form of the) verb seems to have the more violent sense of 'to rape'. This is an easy extension, since captivity would have implied sexual subservience to the new master; cf. Chryseïs (1.112–15) and Briseïs (24.676).

64 ἐν αἰνῆι δηϊοτῆτι: the capture of the city of course involves further fighting inside its walls; cf. *Od.* 8.516–20 (especially αἰνότατον πόλεμον).

66–76 Again the theme of the mutilation of the body or lack of care after death is voiced; see 337–54n. Priam here increases the horror of the idea of dogs devouring a corpse by envisioning that it will be domestic ones that he had reared as tabledogs and watchdogs, not wild dogs. The paragon of such a domestic dog is of course Odysseus' dog Argos (*Od.* 17.291–327). For dogs in Homer see Lilja (1976) 13–36.

66–7 ἄν... ἐρύουσιν: ἐρύουσιν is a future; see *GH* I 452. Together with ἄν this creates a modal future indicative (49–50n.). πρώτῃσι θύρῃσιν 'at the first doors', i.e. the doors which open to the street (dative of place). The same location in the *Ilias Parva* (fr. 25, ed. West 2003), while in other versions Priam is killed after having taken refuge at the altar of Zeus. Is it because dogs are most likely to find themselves near the entrance? Or does Priam give himself a similar liminal position to that of his son?

68 τύψας ἠὲ βαλών 'having struck (from nearby with a sword) or hit (from a distance, with a spear)'. ῥεθέων ἐκ θυμὸν ἕληται: originally ῥέθεα meant 'face', but in Homer it is reinterpreted as 'limbs' (cf. μέλεα). The only other occurrences are 22.362 = 16.856. ἐκ... ἕληται is tmesis (L 20); cf. νοῦσος..., ἥ τε μάλιστα... μελέων ἐξείλετο θυμόν, 'illness which most of all tends to take the life out of limbs' (*Od.* 11.200–1).

69 θυραωρούς: this is the reading of Aristarchus, a papyrus, and some manuscripts, while the vulgate has πυλαωρούς. πυλαωρός recurs at 21.530 and 24.681, while θυραωρός is found only here. It is to be preferred because πύλη in Homer refers to the gate of a city and θυραωρός ties in with πρώτῃσι θύρῃσιν (66) and ἐν προθύροισι (71): while the dogs are supposed to guard the palace (cf. the golden watchdogs at the entrance of the palace of Alcinous: *Od.* 7.91–4), the madness of war turns them into the attackers of their own master.

70–1 οἵ: anaphoric pronoun. κ'... κείσοντ': modal future indicative (49–50n.). πιόντες ἀλύσσοντες: when two participles are combined asyndetically, one is usually logically subordinate to the other (KG II 103–4): 'maddened *because of having* drunk my blood'. ἀλύσσω occurs only here and is either a variant of ἀλύω, 'to be beside oneself', or derived from λύσσα, 'madness'. If λύσσα originally meant 'rabies' (see *LfgrE* s.v.), the blood-drunk behaviour of Priam's dogs would resemble that of rabid dogs. περὶ θυμῶι 'very much (adverbial) in their heart'.

71–6 Priam ends his speech with an argument *e contrario*: 'in a young man it looks well to lie dead on the battlefield, but when dogs defile the body of an old man, this is most pitiful'. There are many indications of the old man pulling out all rhetorical stops: he no longer refers to himself with 'me' but as it were objectifies his appeal by speaking about 'an old man' (75), turns to generalising moods and tenses, employs anaphora (repetition at close distance) of πολιόν at 74, and twice uses the interactional particle δή (74, 76).

These lines are also found, with minor variations, in Tyrtaeus (fr. 10.21–30, ed. West 1972); the context is a speaker urging young men to fight. Scholars have taken up three positions: (1) Tyrtaeus intertextually reworks Homer, e.g. Garner (1990) 8–12; (2) Tyrtaeus' text has been interpolated into Homer's text and the lines should be excised, e.g. Lohmann (1970) 168; and (3) both Homer and Tyrtaeus are independently making use of a passage belonging to the epic tradition, e.g. Richardson. Of these three positions, the third is always possible. The main argument brought forward in support of the second is that the lines would be less fitting in the Homeric context, where Priam is begging the young man (Hector) to *abstain* from fighting instead of urging him to fight. However, Priam is playing upon Hector's pity for him as an old man in this final part of his speech. He introduces the young man only in contrast, without meaning him to be connected specifically to Hector. The careful echo of πολιόν (74) in the narrator-text (πολιάς: 77) also presupposes the lines. Finally, it should be observed that Homeric speeches often end with a general saying or *gnōmē*, as will many a *rhēsis* in later drama; cf. e.g. *Il.* 1.218; *Od.* 6.182–5; and see Lardinois (1997). This makes the first position the most likely one.

71–3 'Everything looks well in a young man, to lie killed in war and torn by sharp bronze'. The infinitive clause is epexegetic, explaining πάντα, and the participles κταμένωι and δεδαϊγμένωι are predicative with κεῖσθαι; cf. Patroclus, ὅς μοι ἐνὶ κλισίηι δεδαϊγμένος ὀξέϊ χαλκῶι | κεῖται (19.211). It is therefore best to place a comma after ἐπέοικεν, not after χαλκῶι (as all editors do). For the participles being attracted to the dative of νέωι cf. εἴ πέρ μοι ... μοῖρα Διὸς πληγέντι κεραυνῶι | κεῖσθαι, 'if it is fated for me to lie down hit by Zeus' (15.117–18); see *GH* II 313–14. Priam's claim that a young man is beautiful even when dead is backed up by 370–1, where the Greeks gather around the dead body of Hector and admire it. The Homeric narrator, on the other hand, often stresses the pathos of beauty brought low, most intensely in connection with Hector; see 401–4n.

72 ἄρηϊ κταμένωι is found only here; but cf. ἄρηϊ φατος, 'killed in battle' (e.g. 19.31). Some editions print one word, which is then an adjective (ἀρηϊ-κταμένωι); in view of the predicative function of the participle, it is preferable to print it separately. For ἄρης, 'the fury of battle', and Ἄρης, the god, see Clarke (1999) 269–72. Richardson notes that 'the series of dative endings, repetition of the same idea, and heavy spondaic opening' of this line give it 'a dirge-like effect'.

73 'Everything of him is beautiful even though he is dead, whatever part of his body is visible.' πάντα ... ὅττι φανήηι: for a (distributive) singular relative in connection with a plural antecedent cf. 11.367 (τοὺς ἄλλους ..., ὅν κε κιχείω), and see KG I 56. θανόντι περ: the particle περ indicates the highest degree: e.g. ἀγαθός περ ἐών, 'being much the best' (1.275). It often has, with or without preceding καί, a concessive nuance, as here; cf. later καίπερ. See Bakker (1988).

74–5 The theme of the mutilation of the body (337–54n.) is intensified by Priam. Rather than describing dogs as tearing apart (and devouring) a human body, he zooms in on the details of them mutilating the head, beard, and genitals. αἰδῶ: only here and 2.262 in the sense of 'private parts' (αἰδοῖα). Homeric decorum in general avoids references to the private parts; cf. only 13.568 (a clinical description of a wound) and *Od.* 6.129 (Odysseus is keen to cover his μήδεα, facing

Nausicaa and her servants). In the present context the use of αἰδῶ also suggests the shamefulness of an old body being exposed naked and mutilated, as opposed to the 'seemliness' (ἐπέοικεν) of a dead young man. κταμένοιο: the middle of root and thematic aorists may still have passive meaning in Homer; see Allan (2003) 169.

76 δή: different proposals have been made about the etymology and meaning of this particle. The two most widely accepted interpretations are (1) that it expresses that what is said is evident to both speaker and addressee (an exaggerated translation would be: '*as you and I know only too well*') or (2) that it draws special attention to the importance and interest of a proposition; see Wakker (1997a) 238–47, for discussion and bibliography. In regular combinations such as ὅτε δή (74), its force is less distinct. πέλεται 'turns out to be', 'is'; see 116n. δειλοῖσι βροτοῖσιν: see 31n.

77 ἦ 'he spoke'; this is the only form of this verb found in Homer, and it always appears at the beginning of a verse. This short speech-capping formula is used when words are immediately followed by action, usually by the same subject; cf. 273, 289, 367, 395. Capping formulas usually do not have an explicit subject, but here the narrator does not miss the opportunity to repeat ὁ γέρων (cf. 33–91n.). ῥ': for this particle see 98n.; here it avoids hiatus. πολιάς: the narrator echoes a word of Priam's speech and thereby renders his words all the more pathetic. ἀνά... ἕλκετο: tmesis (L 20). τρίχας: see 401–2n. Tearing out one's hair is a common sign of mourning in Greek culture; it is depicted in art from the Mycenaean and Geometric periods onwards.

78 οὐδ' Ἕκτορι θυμὸν ἔπειθεν 'but he did not move Hector's heart'; Ἕκτορι is possessive dative (L 22). As usual, the reaction of the *supplicandus* is noted explicitly; cf. e.g. 6.51. It is the failure of Priam's appeal which will lead to a second supplication by Hecuba.

A number of words in Homer refer to 'heart' or 'mind': θυμός, φρήν/φρένες, ἦτορ, κῆρ, κραδίη, νόος, and πραπίδες. Scholars have tried to connect each of these with parts of the body (lungs, heart, midriff), but this position has been generally abandoned; only rarely is a physical organ at play. The body-soul opposition, so common to our modern thinking, may be less relevant to Homer. There remains the question as to whether the terms refer to separate mental functions (Darcus Sullivan (1995), Schmitt (1990) 174–228) or are interchangeable (Jahn (1987) and Clarke (1999)). The latter very often is the case, but sometimes differences are observable. Thus it would seem that there is a difference between θυμός and φρήν/φρένες in the context of πείθειν, in that πείθειν someone's θυμόν presupposes (as πείθειν someone's φρένα(ς) does not) an addressee who is emotionally 'occupied' and therefore not open to rational arguments; see van der Mije (2011b). For the relation between *thumos* and *psuchē* see 362–3n.

79–89 At 21.526–7 only Priam had been mentioned as standing on the walls, but it now turns out that, as in book 6, the urgency of the situation has brought the women there too (although not Andromache: see 437–46n.). In order to underscore the pathos of the situation and to prepare for the approach which Hecuba is to follow in her supplication speech, the narrator does not mention her name but refers to her as 'his mother'. Her speech is much shorter than Priam's but no less emotionally intense; like him, she is convinced that Hector will be defeated by Achilles. She strengthens her request to come inside with an argument which also occurs in prayers: the claim to favour on the basis of past service, here her nursing of Hector (83b-4a). The underlying thought is that his death would rob her of the θρέπτρα, 'repayment for the care of rearing', which Hector owes her; cf. 4.474–9 and 17.301–3, where this motif occurs in obituaries. Like Priam, she ends with a horrifying picture of what will happen in the future if Hector does not listen to her (86–9). The urgency of her appeal is conveyed by her use of three vocatives (82, 84, 87) and the thrice repeated σε (86, 88).

This is the first in a series of three speeches by Hecuba: here she merely uses the (body) language of lament in order to persuade Hector, but later she will both spontaneously and officially lament him; see 405–36n.

79 αὖθ' = αὖτε, 'in turn' (119n.). ἑτέρωθεν 'on the other side' (of the tower); apparently the Trojan men and women stand on the tower in separate groups (cf. 3.383–4).

80 κόλπον ἀνιεμένη 'loosening (and hence opening) the fold of her dress'. The κόλπος is the fold which is formed by the upper part of the *peplos* falling loosely down over the girdle; it is fastened with brooches or clasps (περόναι, cf. *Od.* 18.293–4), and it is presumably by unfastening those that Hecuba now loosens the fold of her dress. ἑτέρηφι: sc. χειρί; –φι functions as dative ending (L 9). Baring a breast is a unique supplication gesture in Homer. It inspired Attic dramatists; cf. Aeschylus *Choephoroi* 896-8 (Clytemnestra: τόνδε δ'αἴδεσαι, τέκνον, | μαστόν); and Euripides *Electra* 1206–7 and *Phoenissae* 1567–9. It supports Hecuba's ensuing claim to favour on the basis of past service, i.e. her nursing of Hector. Murnaghan (1992) 249–50 suggests that pointing at her breasts might also signal to Hector to remember his mortal vulnerability. At 24.56–62 the nursing of Hector and Achilles by mortal and immortal mothers respectively is contrasted, and Hector seems to have 'taken in mortality itself along with his mother's milk'. It should be noted, however, that what is at issue there is not so much mortality versus immortality (Achilles is not immortal after all) but status: as the son of an immortal mother, Achilles may claim higher honour.

81 ἔπεα πτερόεντα: see 215n.

82–3 τάδε τ' αἴδεο καί μ' ἐλέησον | αὐτήν: suppliants are protected by Zeus and supposed to be treated with 'respect' (αἰδώς, see 105–6n.); cf. the Greeks who want to respect the priest Chryses at 1.22–3. Suppliants may, as here, explicitly urge their addressees to show such respect: 21.74; 24.503; *Od.* 22.312, 344; and cf. 22.123–4, 419, 24.207–8. In all these places, the suppliants also ask for pity (since they are young, old, or less valiant; see 59n.). εἴ ποτε... ἐπέσχον: conditionals may not so much indicate a condition as a fact (the so-called 'obviously realised conditional'; see Wakker (1994) 190–1): 'if ever I offered you' (almost '*since* I offered you'). τοι = σοι (L 19). λαθικηδέα 'bringing forgetfulness of cares', 'soothing'; only here in Homer.

84 τῶν: anaphoric pronoun (L 17): 'those things', i.e. the (repeated) breast-feeding as described in the εἰ-clause. δήϊον ἄνδρα: δήϊος means 'destructive' (often of fire or war), but also came to be used as a word for 'hostile', 'enemy'. Here its original force is still felt: 'the destructive man' = Achilles; for the effective circumlocutions for Achilles see 38n.

85 τείχεος ἐντὸς ἐών: the MSS hesitate between ἐών and ἰών (for the latter cf. 12.374: τείχεος ἐντὸς ἰόντες), and both readings are possible. μηδὲ πρόμος ἵστασο τούτωι 'and do not take up the position of frontline-fighter against that man', i.e. do not fight with Achilles. πρόμος = πρόμαχος. For single fights see 248–305n.

86–9 While Priam foresaw the mutilation of his own body, Hecuba foresees that of Hector's; see 337–54n.

86 σχέτλιος: see 41n. It seems most effective to take it as a vocative addressed to Hector. In principle it could also, as in 41, be taken as an exclamation and connected with Achilles, the subject of the ensuing clause. εἴ περ... κατακτάνηι: in Homer the prospective subjunctive can also occur without ἄν or κε. It expresses something the speaker expects to happen; everybody agrees that Achilles is the best fighter before Troy (40n.). The more urgent subjunctive is to be preferred to the neutral variant reading κατακτείνει. The particle περ here seems no more than a metrical filler. ἐγώ γε: this form instead of the Attic ἔγωγε of the MSS has been restored by Bekker; see West 1, xviii.

87 θάλος: literally 'young shoot', metaphorically 'offspring', always with affective connotation and focalised by parents: *Od.* 6.157; *Homeric Hymn to Demeter* 66, 187; *Homeric Hymn to Aphrodite* 278. Closely comparable is ἔρνος, 'sapling', to which beautiful and much loved youths are compared: 17.53; 18.56, 437; *Od.* 6.163, 14.175.

88 ἄλοχος πολύδωρος: this expression occurs only once more in the *Iliad* (6.394), again about Andromache. It refers to a woman bringing with her a dowry and/or eliciting a bride-price from suitors; see 51n. Hecuba hopes to increase the emotional force of her appeal by including Andromache in her plea. For the narratees she cues Andromache's appearance later in this book (437–515). ἄνευθε... μέγα νῶϊν 'at a very great distance from the two of us'. νῶϊν is genitive of the dual of the personal pronoun (L 19).

89 κατέδονται: the middle of the verb ἔδω is used as future, which can be explained as a reinterpretation of originally prospective subjunctive forms with short vowel, as ἔδω was originally athematic (cf. infinitive ἔδμεναι).

90–1 τώ γε κλαίοντε προσαυδήτην... λισσομένω: capping the double sup-plication scene with dual forms, the narrator stresses that the parents work together and increases the effect of Hector *not* heeding their combined plea. πολλά: adverbial, 'intensively'.

91–137

Having looked at Hector from his own omniscient standpoint (5–6, 35–6) and from the walls of Troy, via the eyes of his parents (37–91), the narrator now 'descends' to the position of the hero himself. His feelings are revealed to us in a monologue, which effectively 'fills in' the time Achilles needs to get near to him (see 25–91n.): at 92 Hector has spotted 'gigantic' Achilles, too (cf. Priam at 25), and fear starts to mingle with his heroic resolve. Nevertheless, he decides to make a stand. When his opponent has come close at hand (131), however, he panics and flees after all. Similar psychologically realistic and dramatically effective swings in Hector's mood will follow at 248–305. Hector's behaviour is movingly generalised by Cavafy in his poem 'Trojans': 'Our efforts are like those of the Trojans. We think we'll change our luck | by being resolute and daring, | so we move outside ready to fight. | But when the great crisis comes, | our boldness and resolution vanish; | our spirit falters, paralyzed, | and we scurry around the wall | trying to save ourselves by running away' (trans. E. Keeley and P. Sherrard).

The scene is an instance of the 'lone fighter' type-scene, which we also find at 11.401–20 (Odysseus); 17.89–113 (Menelaus); and 21.550–80 (Agenor). Such scenes typically consist of (1) a fighter finding himself alone facing a multitude of enemies or a superior opponent, (2) a monologue in which the alternatives of retreat or resistance are weighed and which leads to a decision for a course of action, (3) a simile illustrating the decision, and (4) the course of action. Odysseus deliberates in terms of honour and shame and decides to resist, is compared to a boar holding hounds at bay, and fights; Menelaus deliberates in similar terms as Odysseus but decides not to fight, is compared to a lion chased from a farmstead by men and dogs, and retreats; Agenor considers ways to escape Achilles but decides to make a stand, is compared to a leopard at his den holding out before hunters and dogs, and confronts Achilles.

Hector's monologue is the longest and most important of the four; it is the dramatic finale to which they build. It displays some significant variations on the pattern. Hector's argument mainly revolves around the question of how to escape, like Agenor, but he reaches his decision in terms of shame and honour, like Odysseus and Menelaus. His is the only case where the action does *not* match what the lone fighter has resolved to do. Because his quick change of mind after the monologue leaves no time for a simile, the simile *precedes* the monologue. The most dramatic difference is that all other lone fighters are saved in the end, while Hector dies. The monologue in a way provides an answer to the supplications of Hector's parents: it makes clear to the narratees why he does not heed their emotional appeals. The fact that he does not answer his parents but instead converses with himself underscores his loneliness.

The literary form of a person speaking to his own heart in a monologue also occurs in Near Eastern literature (see West (1997) 199). Homer's varied and complex use of it foreshadows that of the tragedians. The passages show how

Homeric characters are neither puppets controlled by the gods nor unthinking adherents to a heroic code, but human beings of flesh and blood who are capable of making their own decisions. For discussions of this scene see Petersmann (1974) 154–7, Fenik (1978) 81–5, and Burnett (1991) 283–7; for monologues and decision making, Gaskin (1990) and Gill (1996) 81–92; for Homeric monologues in general, de Jong on 5.299–312.

91–2 The narrator repeats the refrain 'but they did not move Hector's heart' from 78, but this time switches to Hector himself. πελώριον 'gigantic' (from πέλωρ, which is used of the Cyclops, *Od.* 9.428, and Scylla, *Od.* 12.87). It belongs to the character-language: 17 x speech; 3 x embedded focalisation (cf. 21.527); 5 x narrator-text. This detail signals that Hector spots Achilles and also sets the tone for what is to follow: Hector feels overpowered by his opponent. ἆσσον 'nearer by' (see 3–4n.).

93–7 At 3.33–7 Paris' frightened reaction to the sight of Menelaus stepping forward to fight him had been compared to a man suddenly spotting a snake. Here the perspective is reversed: Hector is compared to a snake coiling at its hole, determined to defend it against a man. The main point of the comparison is 'advertised' (μίμν' Ἀχιλῆα ≈ ἄνδρα μένησιν, and cf. οὐχ ὑπεχώρει), but there are two more points of contact: both man and animal are filled with 'adrenalin'/venom (μένος ≈ χόλος) and find themselves in front of their city/hole. Perhaps the choice of a snake low on the ground versus a man towering above also conveys something of the way Hector pictures himself in comparison to gigantic Achilles and thereby prepares for his frightened monologue.

As often in Homer, the animal of the simile is endowed with human traits (see Lonsdale (1990), Clarke (1995), and Heath (2005) 39–51): the snake, which apparently has been disturbed by the chance arrival of a man at his territory, awaits that man, like a warrior awaiting the enemy (cf. e.g. ὡς Δαναοὶ Τρῶας μένον ἔμπεδον: 5.527). It may seem unlikely that a snake would wait rather than hide in its hole in such circumstances, but this behaviour does suit the Homeric snake which 'does not forget its fighting spirit' even when held in the claws of an eagle (12.200–7). The snake is filled with *cholos* (usually of human anger or bile; see 94n.), and it has a menacing look (this fits both snake, δράκων, to be connected with δέρκομαι, (aor.) ἔδρακον, and man, cf. Paris and Menelaus, who start their duel δεινὸν δερκόμενοι: 3.342). For discussion and literature see van der Mije (2011a).

93 ἐπὶ χειῆι 'at its hole'. Snakes have holes to which they return year after year to hibernate or shelter from the heat of summer. ὀρέστερος: the MSS hesitate between ὀρέστερος and ὀρέστερον, but it clearly makes more sense to describe an animal as 'of the mountains'/'mountainbred' (cf. λύκοι... ὀρέστεροι ἠδὲ λέοντες: *Od.* 10.212) than a man. The specification of the locale, the same as that of the other snake simile (οὔρεος ἐν βήσσηις: 3.34), is meaningful: mountains in Homer have the connotation of danger; see 139n. μένησιν: third person thematic subjunctive with athematic ending (L 13); iterative subjunctive without ἄν (23n.). As usual in extended similes the subjunctive will be abandoned in favour of indicatives after the first clause (ἔδυ, δέδορκεν); see *GH* II 355–6.

94 βεβρωκώς: perfect participle from βιβρώσκω 'eat'; cf. Virgil *Aeneid* 2.471, who speaks of a *coluber mala gramina pastus* leaving his lair after hibernation and darting with his three-forked tongue (i.e. being ready to bite). **ἔδυ δέ τέ μιν χόλος αἰνός** 'and as a result terrible venom enters him'; gnomic aorist and epic τε (L 21). The ancients seem to have thought that snakes got their poison from the food they ate, see e.g. Aelian *De Natura Animalium* 6.4. χόλος is a psychological force, anger, as well as a substance in the body, bile, which is produced by the organs known as χολάδες (4.526 = 21.181); see Clarke (1999) 92–7. Here it is uniquely used to refer to the poison of a snake, and the translation 'venom' captures both aspects well. **μιν:** personal pronoun, 'him' (L 19).

95 σμερδαλέον 'dauntingly', accusative neuter used as an adverb; cf. the δράκων . . . σμερδαλέος of the omen at Aulis (2.308–9). **δέδορκεν** 'he glares out'; intensive perfect. See Rijksbaron (2002) 38. **ἑλισσόμενος περὶ χειῆι** 'coiling round in his hole'; the choice of περί rather than ἐπί (as at 93) is either determined by the circular movement implied by ἑλισσόμενος or the result of formulaic association (cf. ἑλισσομένη περὶ καπνῶι, '(fatty savour) twirling around the smoke': 1.317).

96 ἄσβεστον . . . μένος: μένος, related to μέμονα, μεμαώς (36), is a multifaceted concept, referring to a liquid substance which ebbs and flows in the *phrenes* and *thumos* (e.g. 312), the force of natural elements (e.g. 5.524), and the 'adrenalin' to move and fight, often given by gods to man (here and e.g. 204). See Redfield (1994) 171–3, Jahn (1987) 39–45, and Clarke (1999) 110–12.

97 πύργωι: a bulwark attached to the wall. The bulwark in the *Iliad* always is that at the Scaean gate; it offers a platform for viewers from the wall (cf. 447; 3.153; 6.373). **ἔπι:** the preposition stands after its substantive and hence the accent has moved backward (L 20). **προὔχοντι:** προέχοντι, from προέχω, 'protruding', 'jutting out'. An instance of crasis (lit. 'mingling'): the contraction of vowels across the boundary between words or, as here, parts of compounds, which is marked by a coronis (identical in appearance to a smooth breathing) over the contracted vowel. **φαεινὴν ἀσπίδ᾿ ἐρείσας:** Hector's gesture of leaning his shield against the bastion is purely pragmatic (the shield is heavy and Hector has to wait for some time; cf. Lycaon, who throws down his shield, helmet, and spear in exhaustion at 21.50–2). At 111–12, when he is considering surrender, this gesture will acquire symbolic significance. Two types of shield are mentioned in Homer: the long body shield, ἀσπίς, and the (nearly) round shield, σάκος (see Kirk on 6.117–18). Hector carries the heavy body shield here and elsewhere.

98 This verse invariably introduces monologues. **ὀχθήσας:** see 14n. **ἄρα:** this particle in Homer is found in several more forms: ἄρ᾿, ἄρ, ῥα, ῥ᾿, and ῥ. There is no consensus about its etymology; for a discussion see Ruijgh (1971) 433–5. Its basic meaning seems to be to express 'a lively feeling of interest', often for a surprising fact; *GP* 32–3. Here it marks the fact that furious Hector turns out to be troubled inside, but it is hardly to be captured in translation. The particle is very frequent in Homer, and this has weakened its force; the shortened forms in particular often are no more than an expedient metrical filler or a means to avoid hiatus. εἶπε πρὸς ὃν μεγαλήτορα θυμόν: Homeric monologues take the form of a dialogue with one's *thumos*; see also 122n. ὅν is possessive pronoun, 'his' (L 18). μεγαλήτωρ, lit. 'great-hearted', 'valorous', is a generic epithet of heroes. In combination with θυμόν (16 x), its etymology (μεγαλ + ἦτορ) seems forgotten; cf. 263n.

99–130 Hector's monologue, like the other ones by lone fighters (91–137n.), is deliberative: alternative courses of action are weighed until a decision is made in the end. Hector twice considers retreat and twice decides to fight: (A) if I flee inside the city, (B) I will be criticised by my fellow Trojans for having led so many to their deaths, (C) so it is better to face Achilles; (A') if I approach Achilles unarmed and offer him a truce, (B') he will kill me, (C') so it is better to fight with him.

The very structure of his speech suggests that Hector's decision to fight is fragile; he is nervous and feels outclassed by his superior opponent. Thus we need not be surprised at his flight immediately afterwards. Although Hector is realistic about his own chances against Achilles and the latter's implacable mood, he still does consider help from the gods a possibility (130). His moment of insight that the gods have deserted him will come only at 297–305.

99–110 Hector first considers the possibility that was also suggested to him by his parents: going inside the city (cf. 56 and 85). This option is precluded, however, not so much by the principle of *noblesse oblige*, i.e. leaders having always to fight in the front lines (his father had offered him a way out, by suggesting that, in his particular case, coming inside and not fighting would actually save the Trojans: 56–7), as by his own behaviour in the past (his failure to heed Polydamas' advice to lead the army back into the city): 'What bars his way to the city is he himself' (Schadewaldt (1959) 301, my translation).

It is part of the greatness of Homeric characters that they look back at and reflect on their own behaviour: Hector now sees that it would have been 'better' to have listened to Polydamas, just as Odysseus, while recounting the Cyclops adventure to the Phaeacians, admits that it would have been 'better' if he had not stayed to ask the monster for guest-gifts (*Od.* 9.228–9). With such reflective heroes, Homer anticipates historiography (Cambyses admits his mistake in killing his brother Smerdis: Herodotus *Histories* 3.65) and drama (Pentheus admits his mistake in not acknowledging Dionysus: Euripides *Bacchae* 1120–1).

It is one thing for Hector to admit his fatal mistake to himself, but he cannot live with (and hence is prepared to die for) the idea that others would confront him about it. This was a key passage in Dodds' (1951) famous qualification of Homeric society as a shame-culture (as opposed to a guilt-culture): it knew nothing of guilt or the sanction of guilt; rather, the fear of losing face (to equals or inferiors) impelled its heroes to take certain actions and restrained them from taking others. This qualification has been modified, e.g. by van Wees (1992) 61–165, Cairns (1993), and Williams (1993).

99 ὦι μοι: this spelling (instead of ὦ μοι) is considered the right one in ancient sources and is still found in many medieval MSS; see West I, xxxvii. ἐγών = ἐγώ; the ν is not a movable *nu* but an unexplained suffix which the pronoun gets in Homeric Greek, Lesbian and Dorian (see *DELG* s.v.). δύω: aorist subjunctive, from δύω, 'enter'.

100–3 The figure of Polydamas belongs to the type of the hero's companion (and often alter ego); cf. Roland and Olivier in the *Chanson de Roland*. He also anticipates the 'warner' we know from later Greek literature (Solon in Herodotus' *Histories* or Tiresias in Sophocles' *Oedipus Tyrannus*). His role as Hector's foil is clearly indicated by the narrator at 18.251–2 ('he was a companion of Hector, the two of them born in the same night, but he (Polydamas) was much better with words, the other (Hector) with the spear'). It is reinforced by the fact that he figures in the *Iliad* only during the third day of battle, the day of Hector's greatest successes and demise (see Introduction 2b). We see him occasionally participate in the fighting (e.g. 14.449–57), but his main activity consists in offering Hector cautious strategic advice (12.61–79, 211–29; 13.726–47; 18.254–83) that Hector twice follows (12.80–7; 13.748–53) and twice rejects (12.230–50; 18.284–309).

Here, Hector recalls the last (and longest) debate with Polydamas. Achilles had just made a brief appearance (the first after his protracted inactivity), which allowed the Greeks to save the body of Patroclus. However, nightfall and a lack of armour had prevented him from starting battle (18.202–42). Then Polydamas had advised the Trojans to withdraw inside the city and fight from the walls (18.254–83). Hector had scornfully rejected the advice and confidently announced that he would face Achilles (284–309). This time the debate was public, not private (unlike the previous three times), and the Trojans chose Hector's side en masse (18.310–13). The result was the massacre Achilles caused on the next day (books 20–21).

Polydamas' advice in 18 had been based on common sense (Achilles' absence made the Greeks easier to fight; his return would wreak havoc among the Trojans). The narratees know it to be sound advice because Iris had told Hector that Zeus would support him until nightfall (11.207–9), and night had just fallen (18.239–42). Moreover, the narrator 'plugs' the speaker and his advice both before and after Polydamas' speech. The debates with Polydamas make both Hector's error and his greatness as a hero clear. For Polydamas see Reinhardt (1961) 272–7, Redfield (1994) 143–53, and Schofield (1986) 18–22.

100 ἐλεγχείην ἀναθήσει 'will lay (heap) reproach upon'; the verb is found only here in Homer. Cf. 23.408, where we hear of ἐλεγχείην being 'poured down over' somebody.

101 ἐκέλευεν: at first sight it may seem surprising that Hector uses the imperfect rather than the aorist when referring back to the one particular moment of Polydamas' warning him on the night of Achilles' return. However, verbs indicating 'ordering' (κελεύω, ἐπιτέλλω) or 'sending on an errand' (πέμπω) are commonly used in the imperfect in Homer, since they 'imply an effort or are the start of a new development' (*GH* II 192). ποτί = πρός.

102 νύχθ' ὕπο τήνδε..., ὅτε 'during this... night, when'. For this rare temporal use of ὑπό cf. πάνθ' ὑπὸ μηνιθμόν, 'all the time during my wrath' (16.202). The temporal marker is to be taken with ποτὶ πτόλιν ἡγήσασθαι; cf. Polydamas at 18.274: 'let us keep the forces for the night (νύκτα) in the marketplace'. We are dealing with a unique variant of the 'ἤματι τῶι, ὅτε' motif (359n). τήνδε expresses emotional intensity: 'this night which I remember only too well'; see KG II 644. νύχθ'... ὀλοήν: νύξ is given an epithet in 62 of its 134 occurrences. Of the 20 different epithets, characters tend to use the more emotional ones, such as δυσκηδής, 'bringing discomfort', κακή, οἰζυρή, 'wretched', ἄυπνος, 'sleepless', and ὀλοή, 'baneful' (here and *Od.* 11.19); see de Jong (1998) 130–3. ὅτε τ' ὤρετο: an irregular use of epic τε, which normally occurs in omnitemporal contexts, here in connection with one specific event. It is inserted to prevent elision (which would result in the unmetrical sequence ὀλοήν, ὅτ' ὤρετο, ∪ ∪ – ∪ – ∪ ∪). ὤρετο is a (thematic) aorist of (athematic) ὄρνυμαι, 'rouse oneself'; an expressive verb for the crucial moment of Achilles (finally) shaking off his wrathful inactivity. δῖος Ἀχιλλεύς: this formula occurs 55 times in the *Iliad*. δῖος is a generic epithet, used of many heroes; cf. e.g. Ἕκτορα δῖον (226, 393n.). It is uncertain whether the word derives directly from the IE root *dei-* 'shine' or from Mycenaean *di-u-jo, di-wi-jo,* 'belonging to/descending from Zeus' (cf. Ζεύς, gen. Διός). In Homer it has weakened to 'godlike'or 'noble'. Characters regularly make use of the same stock epithets as the narrator, even if this implies speaking in positive terms about opponents, as here. One might ask whether this is a sign of heroic chivalry (the best example being the meeting between Glaucus and Diomedes at 6.119–236) or metrical convenience.

103 ἦ τ' 'and yet'; see Ruijgh (1971) 795–800. κέρδιον 'better'; comparative neuter, cf. κέρδος, 'profit', 'advantage (for oneself)'. There is an ancient variant κάλλιον (again at 108, and cf. 15.197, 226), which would fit 108, but not this line. Moreover, κέρδιον also occurs in the identical line *Od.* 9.228, in a very similar context of a character ruing earlier behaviour (99–110n.). ἦεν = ἦν.

104 νῦν δ' 'but now (in reality)'; see 16–20n. ὤλεσα 'I have caused the death of/destroyed'; cf. Agamemnon at 9.22 (πολὺν ὤλεσα λαόν) and Achilles at 18.82 (τόν, sc. Patroclus, ἀπώλεσα). λαόν: the Homeric λαός (more commonly, the plural λαοί) is the 'people' of a society: the men and women that come together during battle, assemblies, games, or funerals. It is typically dependent on a leader, who is called 'the shepherd of the people' and whose main task is to protect them. Failing this task and instead destroying one's people is therefore a justified reason for (self-)accusation; see Haubold (2000), esp. 14–46 and (for Hector) 83–95. ἀτασθαλίηισιν ἐμῆισιν 'my reckless behaviour'. This word belongs to the character-language (28 x speech, 1 x embedded focalisation, 1 x narrator-text).

It indicates behaviour which breaks social or religious rules and which people pursue despite warnings. A good example is Odysseus' crew in the *Odyssey*, who do not heed Odysseus' warnings and slaughter the cattle of the god Helios; see de Jong on 1.32–43, with further bibliography. Its use here is highly apt, in that Hector had been – twice – warned by Polydamas, who moreover had pointed at an omen to back up his warning at 12.211–29. This is Hector's moment of insight into his *own* error; at 301–3 he will realise how he has been part of Zeus's plan from the beginning. See also Introduction 2b and 2d.

105–6 'I feel shame before the Trojan men and women, lest somebody (sc. of them) will say'. The μή-clause is loosely added in the typical paratactical style; see *GH* II 208. Line 105 repeats 6.442, where Hector used it to justify his decision to return to the battlefield rather than follow Andromache's advice to stay inside. Though verbatim repetitions are part and parcel of Homeric oral technique, the many other echoes of book 6 in book 22 (see Introduction 2c) point to a deliberate effect: the same force which sent Hector into battle now prevents him from returning home. The expression later became proverbial, as witness e.g. Cicero *Letters to Atticus* 7.1.4 (and elsewhere): 'I fear not Pompey only but the Trojan men and women' (i.e. Atticus himself). **αἰδέομαι:** αἰδώς is a central concept in Homeric society. It indicates a sensitivity to what another is entitled to ('respect') or what another may say or think about oneself ('shame'). It is an emotion that is quintessentially bound up with the Homeric preoccupation with 'face' and honour, yet it is clearly fed by internal as well as external factors. Hector not only (prospectively) fears criticism from the Trojans, but also (retrospectively) condemns his own behaviour as ἀτασθαλίη. See Redfield (1994) 115–21 and especially Cairns (1993) 48–163 (for Hector: 79–83). **ἑλκεσιπέπλους:** usually taken to mean 'of the trailing robe', but perhaps 'drawing up the robe (at the ankles)'; see *LfgrE* s.v.

106–8 τις . . . κακώτερος ἄλλος ἐμεῖο: the structure of the line, with the first half also occurring elsewhere (23.575), suggests taking κακώτερος ἄλλος ἐμεῖο together as an apposition to τις: 'lest somebody will say, different and lesser than I'. An alternative is to take ἄλλος with τις and κακώτερος ἐμεῖο as an apposition: 'lest somebody else, lesser than I, will say'. κακός in Homer is not a moral term ('bad'), but it refers to a cowardly, socially inferior, or harmful person. Fear for the words of a κακώτερος ἄλλος is also expressed by the Phaeacian princess Nausicaa (*Od.* 6.275) and one of the Ithacan aristocratic suitors (*Od.* 21.324). **ἐμεῖο = ἐμοῦ** (L 19). **εἴπησι:** third person thematic subjunctive with athematic ending (L 13). **ᾗφι** 'his'. The ending –φι is equivalent to a dative (L 9); for the possessive pronoun ὅς see L 18. **πιθήσας:** intransitive aorist of πείθομαι, 'trusting'. **ἐρέουσιν:** future of εἴρω, 'speak', 'say' (cf. ῥῆσις, ῥητήρ).

Hector spells out the criticism that he fears in the form of a 'potential *tis*'-speech: an imaginary, future speech put in the mouth of an anonymous person, here, significantly, a Trojan man or woman of lower social standing than Hector himself (or, for that matter, Polydamas); see de Jong (1987b). It is clear that, as always, the speech of the anonymous person in fact externalises the inner thoughts of the speaker himself: thus the *tis* virtually repeats what Hector had earlier said himself ("Εκτωρ... ὤλεσε λαόν ≈ ὤλεσα λαόν), replacing 'through his reckless behaviour' by 'trusting in his own strength'. Of the eight 'potential *tis*'-speeches in the *Iliad*, five derive from Hector (as opposed to one each by Agamemnon, Sarpedon, and Menelaus): 6.459–62, 479; 7.89–90, 300–302. They contain (self-)praise or (self-)blame. They can be considered a characterising trait, marking Hector as a man who, as the single most important leader on the Trojan side, knows he has the eyes of the world on him; see Martin (1989) 136–8.

108–10 Hector decides to stay and kill or be killed; for this heroic idea see 13.326–7, 486; 15.511–13; 18.307–8; 20.172–3 (of a lion); 21.226; 22.244–6, 253. τότ' 'in that case', i.e. having to be spoken to in that way; cf. 4.182 = 8.150. ἄντην 'in a face to face meeting'. This crucial word (countering his first option of going inside) is put before the two alternative outcomes of such a confrontation. ἤ': the MSS have ἤ, but in cases where this word occurs before a vowel without corruption it probably represented elided ἠέ, and this form is restored by West in his text. κατακτείναντα: this reading of the vulgate is to be preferred to the ancient variant κατακτείναντι. It is characteristic of oral syntax that a speaker gives up the correct construction (κατακτείναντι in accordance with ἐμοί) and adopts an easier one (κατακτείναντα: the accusative is the most frequent case of participles); see Slings (2002) 53–4, who coined the term 'downslip'. νέεσθαι 'return', often with the connotation 'to escape safely'. κεν: the particle seems a mere repetition of ἄν (108), rather than turning ὀλέσθαι into a modal infinitive, of which construction there is only one sure instance (9.684); see *GH* II 311. The variant line found in one papyrus may have been an attempt to get rid of the particle. αὐτῶι ὀλέσθαι 'or die myself'; predicative αὐτός (dative after ἐμοί) marks the contrast with Ἀχιλῆα. ἐϋκλειῶς 'with good reputation', 'in a manner which will earn one glory'; for *kleos* see 304–5n. -ει- is metrical lengthening, to avoid a sequence ∪ – ∪ – (L 2). πρὸ πόληος: the literal meaning, 'in front of' (cf. 6), and figurative one, 'in defence of' (cf. 8.57), coincide.

The sentiment that it is glorious to die on the battlefield is also voiced by Hector at 15.496–7: οὔ... ἀεικὲς ἀμυνομένωι περὶ πάτρης | τεθνάμεν and 22.304–5. However, as Renehan (1987) observed, the way that the narrator presents heroic death differs considerably from the theory voiced by his characters in their speeches: Homeric heroes show fear in the face of death, and the narrator invariably stresses the sorrow their death causes to friends and family rather than the glory it brings. Hector himself will provide a prime example of this phenomenon. Its human, all-too-human, outlook is of course one of the main reasons for the *Iliad*'s eternal appeal. This realistic interpretation of heroic death in Homer is more convincing than Vernant's (1991) idealised claim that Homeric heroes *choose* early death as a means to avoid the ugliness of old age and to win eternal glory. The sentiment that it is *dulce et decorum* to die for one's fatherland (Horace *Ode* 3.2.13), though modelled after Hector's words in book 15, only becomes prominent after Homer; cf. Callinus 1.6–8; Tyrtaeus 10.1–2, 13–14; 12.23–4 (ed. M. West 1972). See Müller (1989).

111–30 Hector's second alternative is to approach Achilles unarmed and try to strike a bargain. This is virtually a supplication (cf. the key words ἵκωμαι, ἐλεήσει, αἰδέσεται), with the suppliant Hector, as general of Troy, offering a peace settlement instead of the customary private belongings. The conditional protasis is spun out and even turns into an independent main clause at 119–21, with Hector heaping detail upon detail and clinging to the possibility of a settlement and hence escape from death. He abruptly cuts off his own train of thought and rejects his second alternative on the basis of a realistic assessment of Achilles' present state of mind: he is not in the mood for talking (again Hector briefly trails off, lingering on the idea of intimate talk between men and women) and will kill him. Thus Hector had seen Achilles kill his brother Polydorus just before (20.419–21).

The narratees know even better that Hector is right: Achilles killed two other Trojans, Tros and Lycaon, although they had supplicated him (20.463–72; 21.34–119), and the narrator commented that he 'was no sweet-minded man, no gentle heart, but a man in full fury' (20.467–8).

111–13 καταθείομαι: subjunctive with short vowel (L 15); -ει- is due to metrical lengthening (L 2) to avoid a sequence of four short elements. ὀμφαλόεσσαν, βριαρήν 'bossed', 'heavy', are both stock epithets of shields and helmets, respectively; their use here by Hector adds to the lingering style of his speech, his clinging to life and all that belongs to it. The circumstance that Hector had already leaned his shield against the wall at 97 is here passed over: what he is considering is a symbolic disarmament to accompany his peace offer, such as we also find at 3.113–15. αὐτὸς ἰών 'going on my own, just like that', i.e. without armour. The idea will later be picked up by the graphic γυμνόν (124). Ἀχιλῆος ἀμύμονος: again (cf. 102) Hector uses a positive epithet in connection with his opponent. ἀμύμων is a frequently used generic epithet of heroes (116 x Il. and Od.). It is conventionally translated as 'blameless', but this is based on a questionable etymology (alpha privative + -μυμ-, to be derived from μῶμος, 'blame'). Amory Parry (1973) proposes 'beautiful (because possessing a strong, well-shaped, well-coordinated body)'. Heubeck (1987) suggests another etymology: ἀμυ- (from the verb ἀμεύομαι, 'to surpass', which is found in Pindar) + suffix -μων (which we also find in e.g. νοήμων, δαήμων); this would yield the meaning 'excellent'. ἀντίος ἔλθω: suggestive of a supplication, cf. e.g. 20.463.

114–21 Hector envisions offering Achilles a peace settlement. There have been three earlier talks about a peaceful solution to the war: one belonging to the time before the *Iliad* (11.125) and two in an early phase of the *Iliad*, the duels between Paris and Menelaus (3.284–7, cf. 70, 91) and Hector and Ajax (7.389–93, cf. 350–1, 362–4). When we compare what the Trojans' offer comprised on those occasions (book 11: Helen; book 3: Helen, Paris' booty, and additional recompense for the sons of Atreus; book 7: Paris' booty and additional recompense), we see how

Hector here surpasses those earlier offers in his desperation, adding half of the wealth of Troy (a common way to end a siege, cf. 18.510–12).

Hector starts rehearsing what he will say to Achilles in indirect speech ('I will promise him to give . . . '), but he seems to talk more to himself from 119 onwards ('I will later make the Trojans take an oath'). For a brief moment he is carried away by his own idea and starts daydreaming about returning to Troy. In a comparable way, Agenor dreams about escaping in his monologue: he might flee to the Trojan plain, to the spurs of Ida, and return in the evening to the city again after washing himself in the river and drying his sweat (21.558–61).

114–17 ὑπόσχωμαι Ἑλένην καὶ κτήμαθ᾽. . . | δωσέμεν Ἀτρεΐδηισιν ἄγειν: typical oral syntax, in that the accusatives Ἑλένην καὶ κτήμαθ᾽ are first taken by a hearer as object of ὑπόσχωμαι, ('I will promise Helen') and then, when hearing δωσέμεν . . . ἄγειν, are reinterpreted as object of these verbs ('I will promise to give Helen to the sons of Atreus to take away with them').

114 οἱ: personal pronoun (L 19).

115 ὅσσα τ᾽: τε mainly is inserted to avoid hiatus; for a possible linguistic explanation of its use here see Ruijgh (1971) 563–4. Ἀλέξανδρος: an alternative name for Πάρις; cf. Astyanax and Skamandrios (6.402–3). In the latter case the doubling of the name is explained, Skamandrios being the name given by Hector, Astyanax his nickname given by the people (506–7n.). In the case of Paris/Alexandros no such explanation is given. For a discussion of the provenance of the two names see Kirk on 3.16. He suggests that 'there is no difference in the nuance of the two names' and that they are merely useful 'metrical alternatives'. There has been an attempt to find a nuance: Paris is mainly used when a Trojan speaks or focalises, or more generally in a 'Trojan' context, while the international name Alexandros is reserved for the gods, the Greeks, the narrator, or Trojans addressing Greeks (as here); see de Jong (1987a). This thesis has been challenged by Lloyd (1989). κοίληις ἐνὶ νηυσίν: the typical epithet of ships when they transport goods; see 465n.

116 Τροίηνδ᾽ 'to Troy'. ἥ τ᾽: the relative is attracted to the gender of ἀρχή; it refers to all that preceded, i.e. Paris taking with him Helen and capturing goods. Here, as at 115 and 118, epic τε is illogically used in connection with a single event from the past, rather than having its normal omnitemporal force (L 21). ἔπλετο 'became', 'turned out to be'. The verb πέλομαι is often used as a metrically expedient variant of γίγνομαι or εἰμί but has a distinct semantic force of its own, related to its Indo-European root *k^wel-, 'to turn'; see Waanders (2000). νείκεος ἀρχή: Paris' role as the one who started the conflict is mentioned by friend and foe alike: Menelaus (3.100, and cf. 351), Helen (6.356), Hector (here and 3.87), and even the narrator (5.63–4), who characteristically stresses the misery which Paris' expedition brought the whole Trojan population: νῆας (sc. of Paris) . . . | ἀρχεκάκους, αἳ πᾶσι κακὸν Τρώεσσι γένοντο. For Hera and Athena, Paris' misbehaviour 'began' even earlier, when, on the occasion of his Judgement, he chose Aphrodite rather than them (24.28–30). The question 'who began?' was important in Greek warfare, as in modern; see *BK* on 3.100. An illustrative example is the start of Herodotus' *Histories* (1.1–5), where he goes to great lengths to recount the various opinions as to who started hostilities between Greeks and barbarians (even though he will reject all of them in the end); Paris features in that passage, too, although he is not the first to act but is part of a longer chain of retaliations.

The fact that Paris not only abducted Helen but also took with him, i.e. looted, many of Menelaus' possessions is important for understanding why the Trojan War started. Paris' expedition was a demonstration of his courage, of which Hector furiously reminds his brother at 3.46–9: 'Is this the man you were when you gathered your trusted companions and sailed out over the sea . . . mixed with strangers and brought back on board a beautiful wife?' By that same token the expedition brought a double disgrace to Menelaus, which needed to be avenged. For all aspects of Homeric society, in which status and prestige were of paramount importance, see van Wees (1992), especially 172–3 on Paris' expedition.

117–18 δωσέμεν = δώσειν (L 11). ἅμα δ' ἀμφὶς Ἀχαιοῖς | ἀλλ' ἀποδάσσεσθαι 'and at the same time apart from that (sc. what is given to the sons of Atreus) to give the Greeks other things as their share'. Aristarchus' reading ἀποδάσσεσθαι is to be preferred to the vulgate's ἀποδάσσασθαι, since the infinitive stands on a par with δωσέμεν. κέκευθεν 'holds', 'contains'.

119 Τρωσὶν 'among the Trojans' (local dative). αὖ: the basic meaning of αὖ or αὖτε is 'on the other hand' (cf. Latin *aut, autem*), which may have the nuances of an adversative 'on the contrary' or additive 'again'. Here it marks that Hector is mentally turning from Achilles and his promise to him, to the Trojans and what he will ask them. μετόπισθε 'later'. γερούσιον ὅρκον: an oath pledged by the Trojan elders in the name of the entire population. The *gerontes* of a Homeric community (city or army) deliberate in a *boulē*. These leaders are not necessarily old; cf. Latin *senator*, from *senex*. ἕλωμαι 'I will exact'; cf. *Od.* 4.746 ἐμεῦ δ' ἕλετο μέγαν ὅρκον. The subjunctive (with or without ἄν, κέν) in Homer is often used in a main clause, here as an emphatic future, with a clear undertone of the subject of the verb wanting to do something; see *GH* II 206–10.

120 δάσεσθαι: the future is to be preferred to δάσασθαι, which seems to have entered the text here from 18.511 (where it stands on a par with διαπραθέειν).

121 Some papyri and MSS omit this line, which may have entered the tradition from 18.512, and most editors want to remove it from the text as an unnecessary repetition of 118 (Ameis-Hentze, Leaf, West). If one retains the line, it is best to place a comma at the end of 120 to make clear that κτῆσιν . . . is an apposition to πάντα. It may be defended as forming part of the text of the oath which Hector draws up in his head; the official oath of the Trojan elders echoes his own. πτολίεθρον ἐπήρατον: πτολίεθρον is in principle a useful metrical variant of π(τ)όλις, but it is used less and seems to have a more solemn flavour about it. The word has many epithets (see *LfgrE* s.v.), but ἐπήρατος, 'lovely', is found only here and at 18.512. We are gradually prepared for the pathos of 153–6, the moving reference to the 'beautiful' Trojan scenery in peacetime. ἔργει: the original Ϝ has already disappeared (ἐϜέργει) but the two vowels have not yet been contracted.

122 This line occurs in the four 'lone fighter' monologues (11.407; 17.97; 21.562) and once in a dialogical speech (385). It is typically used to break off a train of thought abruptly and drastically. τίη = τί, 'why'. μοι: possessive dative (L 22). φίλος 'my dear'; see 388n. θυμός: for the *thumos* as seat of intellectual activity see *LfgrE* s.v. 6.

123–4 μή μιν ἐγὼ μὲν ἵκωμαι, ὁ δέ . . . οὐκ ἐλεήσει: an example of parataxis (L 23). In a translation we have to make some adaptations: 'I fear that *if* I will come up to him as a suppliant, he will not pity me'. For a prospective subjunctive in a main clause see 119n. ἵκωμαι here is specifically 'come as a ἱκέτης, suppliant, to someone' (cf. 417). οὐκ ἐλεήσει | οὐδέ . . . αἰδέσεται: the fact that Hector talks not merely about 'respect' but also about 'pity' makes clear that he feels weaker than Achilles (see 59n.) and leads up to his 'like a woman' in the next line. Apollo likewise concludes that Achilles has lost his sense of respect and pity at 24.44–5. For Achilles' anger after the death of Patroclus see Introduction 2b. οὐδέ τί 'and not a bit'. γυμνόν 'naked' in the sense of not wearing armour; cf. 17.122, 693; 18.21; and cf. Herodotus *Histories* 9.63.

125 αὔτως ὥς τε γυναῖκα 'exactly like a woman'; see *LfgrE* s.v. αὔτως 1a. Others take αὔτως to mean 'just as I am', but this results in the awkward sequence 'he will kill me naked, just as I am, like a woman'. The comparison with a woman here indicates defencelessness because of the lack of weapons. More often the comparison of a man with a woman is used tauntingly to suggest cowardice, e.g. 2.235, 289–90; 8.163. ἀπό . . . δύω: tmesis (L 20). The verb is used regularly for putting on or taking off clothes or armour.

126–8 οὐ μέν πως: a forceful denial, 'for sure, not by any means' (μέν = μήν, see 13n.). ἔστιν 'it is possible'. ἀπὸ δρυὸς . . . ἀπὸ πέτρης: although the precise meaning of the obviously proverbial 'from oak or from rock', which occurs once more (*Od.* 19.163) is lost (for a discussion see West (1966) on Hesiod *Theogony* 35), it here means something like '(to talk about) irrelevant, fanciful, things'. A scholion glosses περιττολογεῖν, 'speak superfluous things'. τῶι 'with him', sc. Achilles, who is constantly in Hector's mind. ὀαριζέμεναι, ἅ τε παρθένος ἠΐθεός τε, | παρθένος ἠΐθεός τ᾽ ὀαρίζετον ἀλλήλοιιν: the construction changes in the course of the sentence: 'to talk, (*apposition*) as girl and boy (do), (as) girl and boy (*predicate inserted*) talk with each other'. Perhaps under the influence of 'like a woman' of 125, Hector lets his thoughts trail and envisions the possibility of a friendly and leisured talk with his enemy, albeit in negated form. The verb ὀαρίζειν, 'to converse intimately' (from ὄαρ, 'wife'), only occurs once more, in the conversation between Hector and Andromache (6.516); it is one more significant reference to that earlier scene (see Introduction 2c). It also nostalgically evokes happier, peaceful times at the moment of the grimmest martial truth for Hector (cf. 156n.). Finally, this is an instance of the common Homeric tendency to speak about war in erotic terms, cf. ὀαριστύς, which is both lovers' talk (14.216) and the dalliance of fighters (13.291;17.228), and see Monsacré (1984) 63–77.

ἅ τε παρθένος ἠΐθεός τε | παρθένος ἠΐθεός τε is an instance of epanalepsis, the repetition of a word or word group at the beginning of the next verse. In Homer we find two types: epanalepsis of proper names (2.671–3, 837–8, 849–50, 870–1; 6.153–4, 395–6; 7.137–8; 12.95–6, 21.85–6, 157–8; *Od.* 1.23) and word groups (here; 20.371–2; 23.641–2). Two of the three longer instances of epanalepsis occur in speeches by Hector and concern Achilles. The phenomenon is nowadays seen as a figure to create emphasis or pathos (see Fehling (1969) 183–5 and the Byzantine commentator Eustathius, who suggests that it gives expression to Hector's fear and nervousness), but originally was a mere product of oral syntax. It was later taken up e.g. by Virgil *Aeneid* 4.25–6 ('may Jupiter hurl me' *ad umbras,* | *pallentes umbras Erebi*).

129–30 For the second time, Hector decides to confront Achilles, comforting himself with the thought that it is after all Zeus who decides who will win; for this idea cf. 5.33, 225; 8.141, 11.318–19, etc. Hector had uttered a similar sentiment (victory lies 'on the knees of the gods') at 20.434–7, during his first confrontation with Achilles. βέλτερον: the etymology of this word is unclear, but it means 'better' and is often found, as here, at a moment of decision-taking. αὖτ': see 119n.; it here underlines the idea that to fight is an alternative to the earlier option of trying to talk with Achilles. ἔριδι ξυνελαυνέμεν ὅττι τάχιστα· | εἴδομεν 'to engage in combat as soon as possible. (*asyndeton*) Let us find out'. This seems to be more forceful than the variant reading ὄφρα τάχιστα εἴδομεν, for which cf. 13.326–7. εἴδομεν is a subjunctive with short vowel (L 15). Ὀλύμπιος: 'the Olympian' in the singular in Homer always refers to Zeus; cf. the variant found in one papyrus. εὖχος: lit. 'a reason to boast', hence 'glory'; for the different words for glory see 205–7n.

131–5 Whereas at 92 Hector had merely spotted 'gigantic' Achilles from afar, Achilles is now σχεδόν, 'close at hand', and Hector is able to discern details. It is thus attractive to take the description of Achilles' armour at 133–5 as focalised by Hector (cf. ὡς ἐνόησεν at 136).

131 ὁ δέ . . . Ἀχιλλεύς 'and he . . . , Achilles', kataphoric use of the demonstrative pronoun (L 17).

132 As befits the moment of dramatic climax Achilles is awarded a unique four-word verse. Mortals are regularly compared to gods in Homer, warriors of course mainly to Ares; see Amory Parry (1973) 218–23. ἶσος Ἐνυαλίωι: in Homer Enyalios virtually is another name for Ares. In Mycenaean times, however, there existed a god Enyalios (the name is found on a clay tablet from Knossos), and this, taken together with the fact that the name Enyalios is most frequently associated with the Cretan Meriones (2.651; 7.166; 8.264; 17.259), suggests that he originally was a local Cretan god. For later Greeks the two are clearly identical: thus one may compare Homeric ξυνὸς Ἐνυάλιος (18.309) with Archilochus' ἐτήτυμον γὰρ ξυνὸς ἀνθρώποις Ἄρης (fr. 110 West 1972). ἶσος originally implies size ('as big as'), but the sense has weakened to a mere 'like'. κορυθάϊκι 'with quivering helmet', a Homeric *hapax*; cf. κορυθαίολος, once used of Ares (232n.). At other places Ares is called a ταλαύρινον πολεμιστήν, 'shield-bearing warrior' (266–7n.), but here the narrator draws attention to his helmet, perhaps to prepare for Achilles' helmet, which will be prominently mentioned later on during the fight (314–16).

133–4 σείων Πηλιάδα μελίην... | δεινήν: Achilles' spear is called 'Pelian' because the centaur Chiron made it of wood from Mt. Pelion in Thessaly and gave it to Peleus at the occasion of his marriage to Thetis, just as the gods gave him armour (16.143–4 = 19.390–1; 17.194–6; 18.84–5). The event was, according to a scholion on *Iliad* 16.140, recounted in more detail in the *Cypria*; see p. 85 of West's edition. For possible special qualities of this spear and armour see 322n. Warriors regularly brandish a spear by way of threatening gesture (cf. 311n.); Achilles doing so here creates suspense, since this weapon has been carefully introduced in preceding books. The spear is 'huge, heavy, massive', like Athena's spear (16.141 = 19.388; cf. *Od.* 1.100); no other Achaean can wield it except Achilles (16.141–2 = 19.388–9); and Chiron ominously gave it to Peleus 'to be death for heroes' (16.144 = 19.391). When Patroclus dons Achilles' armour it is explicitly said that he does *not* take his friend's Pelian spear (16.140–1), which therefore does *not* fall in the hands of Hector but remains available for Achilles to use; see Bannert (1984). Indeed, arming himself with his new armour, he pulls 'his father's spear out of its casing' (19.387). He kills many Trojans with it on his way to Hector, and the narrator takes care not to lose this important prop: when the spear is stuck in the earth after shooting through Aeneas' shield, Poseidon returns it to Achilles (20.279–81, 322–4); when it misses Asteropaeus and instead becomes stuck in the bank of the river Scamander, it is carefully pulled out by Achilles (21.169–72, 200). All of this leads up to the moment when Achilles, after a false start (he misses Hector, but Athena returns his spear to him: 22.275–7), will finally put his spear to its most important use: killing Hector (317–27).

Chiron once giving Peleus the spear that Achilles is now wielding is all Homer has to say about this famous centaur. However, Hesiod (*Catalogue of Women* fr. 155, 87–9, ed. Most), seventh century art (*LIMC*, s.v. Achilleus, pl. 21), and many later texts portray him as rearing Achilles. Instead, Homer makes Phoenix the educator of Achilles (9.438–46, 485–95), probably an ad hoc invention in order to make this aged retainer one of the ambassadors who try to make Achilles re-enter war.

134–5 Once again (cf. 26–32) the glittering of Achilles' corslet is mentioned, but this time it is compared not to the gleam of a star but to the brightness of the sun and fire. Achilles had also been compared to the sun after he had put on his new armour (19.398 ≈ 6.513, there of Paris). The comparison with fire has a thematic significance: the combination fire-Achilles constitutes a leitmotif in the final books of the *Iliad* from the moment when he returns to battle until his revenge on Hector is accomplished (cf. 18.205–14, 610; 19.17, 375–80; 21.522–5). The fire gives expression to Achilles' martial spirit (cf. e.g. 5.1–8, where the fire coming from Diomedes' head and shoulders represents the energy and courage which Athena has just given him), but also, more specifically, connotes destructiveness (cf. e.g. 11.155–7). It thus prepares for the climactic moment when the death of Hector is compared to Troy burning (410–11). See Whitman (1958) 132–44. ἀμφί 'around him' (adverbial).

136–7 The dramatic moment of Hector panicking and abandoning the decision to confront Achilles, which he had reached only seconds before, is presented emphatically: 'he no longer dared to stay (contrast μίμνε: 92 and μένων: 131), left the gates behind (which at 99 he had still contemplated entering), and fled'. Hector's reaction is understandable if we recall that Achilles' own Myrmidons reacted in a comparable way to their leader's new armour: Μυρμιδόνας δ' ἄρα πάντας ἕλε τρόμος, οὐδέ τις ἔτλη | ἄντην εἰσιδέειν, ἀλλ' ἔτρεσαν (19.14–15). The skewed verses (33–7n.) are suggestive of his panicky emotions. αὖθι: shortened form of αὐτόθι, 'on the spot'. βῆ ... φοβηθείς: lit. 'he set off in flight'. In Homer the verb φοβέω/φοβέομαι means 'to put to flight' (act.)/'flee' (middle and passive), with the connotation of fear; later this connotation will predominate and the verb will mean 'to frighten'/'be afraid' (perhaps already at 21.575).

138–207

Achilles' prolonged chase of Hector means yet another postponement of their final, fatal confrontation (see 25–91n.). It is, as Bassett (1938) 108 noted, 'the longest account of important action, unrelieved by speeches, in either poem'; this absence of speech will soon be fully compensated for by the actual fight, which, on the contrary, contains the longest battlefield conversation. The effect of an almost interminable pursuit is heightened by numerous devices that slow down the narration: four similes, a uniquely elaborate description of scenery, and an Olympic scene. Thus the speed of narration slows down where the action is at its fastest, which is always a sign of importance and emotional intensity in Homer. The unique episode of the chase seems to have been a celebrated one in antiquity: Aristotle *Poetics* mentions it as an example of the greater scope for 'the marvellous' which epic has as compared to drama (see also 205–7n.), and in Plato's *Ion* 535 B Socrates mentions it as one of Homer's most 'thrilling' scenes.

Normally warriors only flee when confronted with a greater number of opponents (5.571–2) or a god (e.g. 16.656–8), or when wounded (e.g. 11.397–400). At 18.305–9 Hector had declared emphatically that he would not flee before Achilles. Homer nevertheless manages to turn Hector's flight before Achilles into a heroic and pathetic high point. The fact that Hector manages to outrun the fastest runner of all for so long is a token of his qualities. The sight of Hector running past the wash-places of the Trojan women, symbols of the former peace of his city, creates pathos. But the surest way in which the narrator prevents us from seeing Hector's flight as an ignoble affair is by having the gods intensely follow it. Thus no contradiction will be felt when Hecuba later claims that 'it was no coward that Achilles killed, but he was standing in defence of the men and women of Troy, with no thought of flight or shelter' (24.214–16).

138–44 The first of four similes that illustrate Achilles' chase of Hector; see 162–6,188–98, and 199–201nn. Birds often figure in comparisons to make clear the speed of warriors (308–11; 16.582–5; 21.252–4), ships (*Od.* 13.86–8), and horses (2.764; 13.819). Here Achilles, 'trusting in his speedy feet', is compared to a hawk, 'fastest of birds'. But there are many more points of contact: Achilles/the hawk going after Hector/the dove (ἐπόρουσε, ἰθὺς πέτετο ≈ οἴμησε, ἐπαΐσσει); Hector/the dove trying to escape (τρέσε . . . τεῖχος ὕπο Τρώων ≈ ὕπαιθα φοβεῖται); and the eagerness of Achilles/the hawk to catch his prey (ἐμμεμαώς ≈ ἐλέειν . . . ἑ θυμὸς ἀνώγει). Since the hawk and the dove are natural enemies, we are prepared for Achilles' implacable words at 262–5. The Homeric narrator much more often compares Greeks to predators than Trojans; see Stoevesandt (2004) 253–66.

138 πεποιθώς 'trusting completely'; intensive perfect (95n.).

139 ἠΰτε: introduces comparisons in Homer, either short ones (ἠΰτε + substantive, e.g. 'like fawns': 1) or, as here, a longer one (ἠΰτε + finite verb: 'as a hawk swoops'), which is picked up in a 'so'-clause (143). For the form of Homeric similes see Introduction 3b. ὄρεσφιν 'in the mountains'; for -φιν as equivalent to a dative plural ending see L 9. Mountains are associated with danger in Homer: this is the place where wild animals live, fire rages, trees are felled, storms rage, and herdsmen fight a continuous battle against predators; see Elliger (1975) 89.

140 οἴμησε 'swoops'; a gnomic aorist, as often in similes. τρήρωνα: either an adjective 'timid' or a specifying substantive together with πέλειαν ('the timid one, a dove') of the type also found e.g. in σῦς κάπρος.

141–2 ὕπαιθα 'out from under'; the word is found twice more in the context of a living being escaping from the onrush of water (Achilles: Scamander, at 21.255) or an overpowering opponent (Hera: Artemis, at 21.493). φοβεῖται 'she flees' (see 136–7n.). ὀξὺ λεληκώς 'with a shrill cry' (unique expression); intensive perfect (95n.), with adverbial neuter accusative. ταρφέ(α) 'repeatedly' (adverbial use of accusative neuter). ἐλέειν: metrical diectasis (L 4): ἐλέειν (⌣ ⌣ –) < ἐλεῖν (⌣ –) < ἐλέεν (⌣ ⌣ –). ἑ: αὐτόν (L 19).

143 ἄρ': see 98n. ὁ γ': an anaphoric pronoun (L 17) which picks up Πηλεΐδης at 138. πέτετο: this verb is regularly used of horses and people moving quickly. Its metaphorical force is still felt here and e.g. at 16.149, but elsewhere is no longer discernible. τρέσε: the verb τρέω in Homer primarily means 'fear' (cf. Πηλεΐδη, μήτ' ἄρ τι λίην τρέε μήτε τι τάρβει: 21.288), but also, as here, 'flee' or 'retreat' (11.546).

144 τεῖχος ὕπο 'under the wall', i.e. at the foot of the walls, which provide Hector with (hypothetical) shelter, in the form of the Trojans on top who might shoot at Achilles; cf. 194–6. ὕπο in postposition (L 20). λαιψηρά . . . γούνατ': see 24n.

145–57 Marked off by ring-composition (παρὰ... ἐσσεύοντο ≈ παρα-
δραμέτην), this passage offers a description of the Trojan plain. Whereas the
Odyssey has quite a number of scenery descriptions (see de Jong on 5.63–75), the
only instances in the *Iliad* are this place and the descriptions of Priam's palace
(6.243–50) and Achilles' hut (24.449–56). We usually only get stray references
to single landmarks, which have a thematic or symbolic meaning. The present
description combines five of these props: a look-out place, the fig tree, a wagon
track, a miraculous pair of springs, and the Scamander.

As often in Homer, the description entails a slowing down of the speed of
narration but no complete pause: at 147 the heroes arrive at the springs, which
are then described, and at 157 they have passed them. Indeed, the series of
geographical references suggests the movement of the characters, as at 11.166–71
(Agamemnon pursues the Trojans, who flee past the mound of Ilus and the fig
tree, until they reach the Scaean gate and the oak). The slowing down effects
emphasis and suspense; see 138–207n. The way the narrator dwells on the wash-
places of the Trojan women, where they used to wash before the Greeks came,
is an effective flashback. It turns the scenery into a contrastive backdrop to the
deadly chase taking place before it: 'the beauty of the place, the prosperity and joy
it once brought when there was still peace, makes the present horror all the more
clear' (Schadewaldt (1959) 308; my translation). Finally, these quintessentially
Trojan landmarks touch on a theme that will soon become prominent: the
pathos of Hector fighting for his own land and being killed and mutilated in it
(see 401–4n.). Thus the whole passage is a prime example of the typically Homeric
technique of implicitly building up pathos by the description of an object; see
Griffin (1980) 21–2.

Though few would deny that the site of Hissarlik is Troy (for a spirited and
detailed defence see Latacz (2003)), it is more debatable whether the Homeric
landmarks here listed are discernible in the landscape around that site (an ardent
believer is Luce (1998), who even provides photographs). For literary discussions
of the scenery around Troy see Elliger (1975) 58–9, Thornton (1984) 150–63,
Scully (1990) 10–14, and Trachsel (2007) 79–98.

145 σκοπιήν: this look-out place is mentioned only here (for another one
see 2.793). ἐρινεόν: this fig tree is mentioned twice more (6.433–9 and 11.167);
it is positioned near the place where the wall of Troy is weakest. Its extended
description by Andromache in book 6 is one of many points of contact between
these two books (see Introduction 2c). Only here is the fig tree called 'windy', an
epithet usually reserved for Troy itself.

146 τείχεος... ὕπεκ 'a little way out from the wall'; the preposition in post-
position (L 20). West 1, xviii–xix follows ancient grammarians in accentuating
ὕπεκ rather than ὑπέκ. ἀμαξιτόν: this landmark, a wagon track, is mentioned
nowhere else. Ameis-Hentze suggest that the narrator inserts this detail here
in order to provide his 'athletes' with a smooth terrain. One might add that
the word suggests human activity and thus prepares for the theme worked out

more fully in connection with the springs which offer water for the Trojan women.

147–56 The landmark of the two springs only occurs here. Its description is organised as a list (ἔνθα, ἡ μέν, ἡ δ' ἑτέρη, ἔνθα). The verbs are in the present tense, except for the imperfect πλύνεσκον. The women 'used to wash' there (but since the war no longer do so); see 156n. Perhaps the imperfect is also a sign that we are dealing with Hector's (implicit) focalisation, who recalls the springs' use in former times while running past them. Cf. the description of the natural scenery around Calypso's cave (*Od.* 5.63–75), where the imperfects suggest that it is looked at through Hermes' admiring eyes; see de Jong ad loc.

Springs are typically situated just outside cities and are a liminal point of transition between culture and nature (cf. *Od.* 6.291–4; 10.103–8; 17.205–11). It is therefore symbolic that Hector, the main defender of the Trojan city, will eventually be killed at this very place (cf. 208) by the temporarily 'wild' Achilles (see 262–6n.). His death will mean the end of Troy and the end of the Trojan women's use of these springs; instead they will have to labour at Greek springs as slaves (cf. 6.456–8).

147–8 κρουνώ... πηγαὶ δοιαί: Greece being a country full of springs, we come across different words for 'spring' in Homer: κρουνός (big spring), κρήνη (spring with numinous association or fountain), πηγή (big spring), and πῖδαξ (small spring). Here the πηγαί of the Scamander must mean its 'sources'. κρουνώ... καλλιρόω: though the dual (L 16) is often inserted for metrical convenience, it here has its full force: the wondrous nature of this landmark consists in the two different springs (one hot, one cold) springing up as a pair, i.e. at the same time and at the same place. Springs are regularly said to be 'lovely-flowing' (cf. καλλιρέεθρον: *Od.* 10.107; καλλίροον: *Od.* 17.206), but here the epithet sets the tone for the peaceful scene, featuring καλοί wash-places and καλαί daughters, at 153–7. δοιαί: often is a mere metrical variant for δύω but occasionally has a special, stronger force, 'of two sorts'; cf. the δοιοί... πίθοι of Zeus (24.527–8) or the δοιαὶ... πύλαι of dreams (*Od.* 19.562–3). Σκαμάνδρου δινήεντος: together with the Simoeis, the Scamander is the main river near Troy; the two rivers, which are brothers (21.308), form the left and right boundaries to the battlefield. Of them, the Scamander plays a greater role in the story. Indeed, it is this personified river which, as natural defender of Troy, tries to kill Achilles at 21.136–384; and it is in connection with this river that Hector calls his son Astyanax Scamandrius (6.402). For the epithets and the formulaic system of the Scamander, see Richardson on 21.1–2. At 12.19–21 it is said that the Scamander (like many other Trojans rivers) streams from Mt. Ida to the sea, whereas here its sources are located near Troy. This contradiction had already been noted in antiquity, and various solutions had been offered (the springs are fed by Scamander underground or are near the river). It is more likely that either Homer 'was nodding' at this place or, preferably, sacrificed consistency to poetic effectiveness in order to bring in the prop of the Scamander in his evocation of the Trojan plain.

149 θ': epic τε (L 21). ὕδατι λιαρῶι (runs) 'with warm water'; comitative dative (describing the circumstances); see *GH* II 75. ἀμφί: adverbial, 'round it'.

150 ὡς εἰ 'as if' (from burning fire). A fossilised combination; see KG II 492.

151–2 θέρεϊ ' in summer'. ἐϊκυῖα: the perfect ἔοικα has two participles: ἐοικώς and εἰκώς. The verb normally describes a resemblance in outward appearance, but it here refers to likeness in temperature. χαλάζηι | ἢ χιόνι ψυχρῆι ἠ' ἐξ ὕδατος κρυστάλλωι: the three dative clauses form an instance of the 'Gesetz der wachsenden Glieder' or tricolon crescendo: each is longer than the previous. This ancient device of Indo-European rhetoric is also frequent in Latin and later literature (cf. Shakespeare's 'Friends, Romans, countrymen').

153 The proximity of the wash-places to the springs is indicated no less than three times: 'there beside these (springs) nearby are . . . ' The accumulation of adjectives describing them, 'broad', 'lovely', 'stone', has the effect of a close-up. ἔασιν = εἰσίν.

154 εἵματα σιγαλόεντα: the epithet is of uncertain etymology (see *DELG* s.v.) but is commonly taken as 'shining' (cf. Hesychius: λαμπρά, ποικίλα, καὶ τὰ ὅμοια); it is used of clothing (e.g. Andromache's headdress: 468), reins, a throne, and a chamber. In the case of clothes, the shine may result from metal objects being attached to them or their being treated with oil (for this latter procedure, known from Mycenaean times, see 18.595–6; *Od.* 7.107; and Marinatos (1967) 4–7). Elliger (1975) 96 has drawn attention to the fact that light and dark are more important than colour in Homer: thus forty-six per cent of the instances refer to light/shining, forty per cent darkness, eight per cent to red, six per cent to yellow, and only a handful to blue or green.

156 Throughout the *Iliad* we find references to (τὸ) πρίν, the time before the Greeks came, when Troy was at peace and still fabulously rich (9.401–3; 18.288–9; 24.543–6) and Priam still had many sons (24.495–7, 546). Together with other nostalgic moments (127–8, 440–1, 500–4), they form the backdrop against which the gruesome events of the war stand in pathetic contrast. In a similar way the *Odyssey* abounds with evocations of life on Ithaca at the time of Odysseus' departure for Troy (his son had just been born: 11.448–9; his wife was still a young bride: 11.447; his dog Argus was still vigorous: 17.314); there the evocations serve to make clear the length of Odysseus' absence. υἶας Ἀχαιῶν: this formula occurs 86 times in the Homeric epics. There is a variant formula to follow words ending with a vowel: κοῦροι Ἀχαιῶν (9 times). See Parry (1971) 100–1. This type of expression seems to be due to Near Eastern influence; see West (1997) 226, who compares Hebrew 'sons of the Levites' = 'Levites'. When the battle cry of the Greeks at Salamis sounds ὦ παῖδες Ἑλ-λήνων at Aeschylus *Persai* 402, this is a heroisation of this battle through Homeric language.

157–76 An instance of the 'action'–'perception'–'reaction' pattern; see 25–89n. Achilles pursues Hector – this is seen by the gods and – Zeus reacts with a speech, in which he first verbalises his perception (διωκόμενον . . . διώκει ≈

διώκων . . . δίωκε; περὶ τεῖχος . . . ἄστυ πέρι Πριάμοιο ≈ Πριάμοιο πόλιν πέρι)
and then comes up with a suggestion for counter action. See further 166–87n.

157–66 Wedged in between two aorists (παραδραμέτην . . . δινηθήτην), a
series of imperfects (ἔφευγε, δίωκε, ἀρνύσθην, θέον) scenically paint the footrace.
For the 'scenic' use of the imperfect in Greek see Rijksbaron (2002) 11–14.

At first sight, the combination of 'it was no sacrificial beast or ox-hide, typical
prizes of athletes, they were competing for' and 'they ran quickly like prize-
competing horses' seems odd. In fact, however, the juxtaposition is effective:
first we get the human focalisation of the narrator, who stresses that it was not
an ordinary contest but a race for life and death, and then we get the divine
focalisation of the gods, for whom the race is a spectacle, albeit a moving one.
The passage therefore forms the transition to the divine scene 167–87. See de Jong
(2004) 130–1. Somewhat different interpretations are given by Moulton (1974) 396,
who suggests that the narrator, wanting to bring home both the gravity of the
race and its swiftness, had no other method available than 'linear progression';
and Griffin (1980) 139, who merges the two pictures: 'It almost was an athletic
spectacle of the conventional sort – except that the gods were the audience and
the stake was the life of Hector.'

157–9 Throughout the protracted scene of the chase, we are reminded of the
situation: Hector is fleeing in front, while Achilles is chasing him (cf. 143–4; 172–3,
188–93, 199–201).

157 τῇ 'there'; dative singular of the feminine anaphoric pronoun (L 17).
ῥα: see 98n. παραδραμέτην, φεύγων, ὃ δ᾽ . . . διώκων 'the two ran past, the
one . . . , the other . . . ' The dual (L 16) is significant in that it stresses the fatal
connectedness between the two men locked in a race of life and death; cf. again
the duals at 160 (ἀρνύσθην) and 165 (δινηθήτην). Instead of ὃ μέν . . . ὃ δέ, we
only find ὃ δέ, although the two participles clearly stand in balance to each other;
cf. e.g. 9.415 and Aristophanes *Clouds* 1462: πονηρά γ᾽, ὦ Νεφέλαι, δίκαια δέ. See
GP 165.

158–9 ἐσθλὸς . . . μέγ᾽ ἀμείνων: characters and narrator agree that Achilles is
the best fighter before Troy (40n.), but by choosing this formulation the narrator
manages to add lustre to Hector's flight. πρόσθε μὲν . . . δίωκε δέ: while we
are used to μέν – δέ being symmetrically arranged, i.e. for the words standing
immediately before them to be the corresponding elements, there is much more
variation in the order in Homer (and poetry in general); cf. 226 and see *GP* 371–
2. μιν 'him', personal pronoun (L 19). καρπαλίμως: the adverb should be taken
with both ἔφευγε and δίωκε. It will be explained in the ensuing ἐπεί-clause: they
were running so quickly *because* this was no normal race but a race for life and
death.

159–61 These verses contain a priamel, the rhetorical device which consists in
listing a series of alternatives which serve as a foil to the true, climactic point: they
were not competing for a sacrificial animal, nor for a shield, but they ran for the
life of Hector. Cf. e.g. *Od.* 14.222–6: (the 'Cretan'/Odysseus speaking) 'Farming

was never to my taste, nor the care of the house. My love is ships and battles and spears and arrows.' A detailed discussion of Homeric priamels is found in Race (1982).

159–60 οὐχ . . . | ἀρνύσθην 'they were not trying to win', i.e. competing for. ἱερήϊον 'a sacrificial animal'. Oxen are used as prizes in the funeral games for Patroclus (23.260), notably as second prize during the footrace (750). βοείην: sc. ῥινόν (f.), 'an ox-hide', which could be used to make straps (22.397; 23.324) or shields (17.492), or for sitting (*Od.* 1.108) or lying on (*Od.* 20.2). ποσσίν 'for the feet', i.e. in a footrace.

161 περὶ ψυχῆς: originally the combination περί + genitive is used to indicate the prize 'around' which the combatants gather to compete (cf. e.g. 11.700–1). By an easy extension we find this combination in connection with what is 'at stake' during a contest, fight, or encounter, e.g. a dead man's body (17.120) or a person's *psuchē* (here and *Od.* 9.423; 22.245). See *GH* II 128. For the concept of ψυχή in Homer see 362–3n. It here virtually amounts to '(they ran) for Hector's life or death'. Ἕκτορος ἱπποδάμοιο: this noun-epithet formula is used five times of Hector, out of a total of 21 instances. There exists a metrically equivalent combination Ἕκτορος ἀνδροφόνοιο (used 11 times of Hector, out of a total of 12 instances). The existence of a pair of equivalent formulas suggests that they are meaningful and that they were chosen for contextual reasons. The presence of ἵπποι at 162 may have led to ἱπποδάμοιο by association, and the narrator, knowing that Hector's own death is at hand, would perhaps be reluctant to call him 'man-killing'. Sacks (1987) 163–75, 220–6 suggests that ἱπποδάμοιο is used in contexts where Apollo plays a role, but ἀνδροφόνοιο where Achilles plays a role. This observation fits ἱπποδάμοιο at 211 (where Apollo is mentioned at 203, 213), but not this place, where Achilles is Hector's direct opponent. Parry (1971) 185–6 can detect no significant distribution, while Janko (1981) suggests that the clustering of formulas may be a relevant factor.

162–6 The second of four similes in the context of the chase; see 138–44n. The simile of the horse race, adumbrated at 22–4, illustrates the speed (ῥίμφα μάλα τρωχῶσι ≈ καρπαλίμοισι πόδεσσι) and the circling movement (περὶ τέρματα ≈ Πριάμοιο πόλιν πέρι) of the two runners. It is perhaps not far-fetched to read the fact that the race in the simile forms part of funeral games as an ominous sign and to take it as an anticipation of Hector's death. This seems preferable to the rather prosaic note of the scholia that Homer only knows horse-racing in the context of funeral games.

162 ὡς δ' ὅτ': Homeric extended similes may be introduced by simple ὡς, '*as* X does Y' (e.g. 93) or longer ὡς ὅτε, '*as when* X does Y' (here) without any difference; see Ruijgh (1971) 627–8. ἀεθλοφόροι: see 22n. περὶ τέρματα 'round the turning posts'; for a graphic description of such turning posts and the technique for rounding them see 23.306–48. μώνυχες ἵπποι 'one-nailed horses', i.e. 'with unified hoof' (as opposed to cloven-hoofed animals like deer, sheep, and goats). This verse-end formula is found 36 times; the corresponding formula after consonants is ὠκέες ἵπποι. If a longer formula is needed there is, amongst others, κρατερώνυχας ἵππους, 'strong-hoofed horses' (3 times). Horses in Homer have no less than 38 epithets, describing their speed, manes, hoofs, and necks. See Parry (1971) 113–14 and Vivante (1982) 72–4, who notes that 300 of the *ca.* 450 occurrences of the word 'horse' are without an epithet, thus drawing attention to the important fact that nouns do not automatically get an epithet. This is often forgotten in view of the abundant presence of noun-epithet formulas in Homer.

163–4 τρωχῶσι: this verb occurs elsewhere only at *Od.* 6.318, in connection with mules drawing a cart (and cf. the clearly related τροχόωντα at *Od.* 15.451, there of a toddler). Both places make it difficult to take the verb to mean 'run' (cf. τρέχω). In *DELG* it is suggested that it is related to τροχός, 'wheel', and means 'go round'. τὸ δὲ μέγα κεῖται ἄεθλον | ... ἀνδρὸς κατατεθνηῶτος 'and it, a big prize, ... is set out for (i.e. in honour of) a man who has died'. For κεῖται cf. 23.262–73: 'First Achilles set out the prizes (ἄεθλα θῆκε) for the charioteers. Then he said: "These prizes are set out (τάδ' ἄεθλα ... κεῖτ') to await the charioteers ... "' Next to the regular perfect forms κατατεθνηότος and κατατεθνεῶτος, we find κατατεθνηῶτος for metrical reasons. For the genitive with ἄεθλον cf. παῖδες δὲ θέσαν βασιλῆος ἄεθλα, 'his sons set out prizes for the (dead) king' (23.631). ἢ τρίπος ἠέ γυνή: for a tripod or (slave) woman as prize see 23.262–5, where they are the first prize in a chariot-race.

165–6 A split variant of the 'three times X, three times Y, but the fourth time Z' motif: here we find the 'three times X' part, while only at 208–9 do we find the 'but the fourth time Z' part. This motif, which occurs eight times in the *Iliad* and *Odyssey*, usually marks a turning point in the story: e.g. 16.784–7 (Patroclus attacks the Trojans three times but is killed by Apollo the fourth time). The narratees would have expected a turning point to follow after hearing 'three times they ran', but, as so often in this book, the climax of the confrontation is postponed. See Bannert (1988) 40–57. πόλιν πέρι: the preposition stands in postposition (L 20). πόδεσσι = ποσί.

166–87 An Olympian scene interrupts the narration of the chase. The interruption does not create a pause; rather, it fills the time Hector and Achilles need to run around the city three times. In the same way the conversation between Glaucus and Diomedes at 6.119–236 fills the time Hector needs to move from the battlefield to Troy; for the 'fill-in' technique see de Jong (2003) xiv and (for this place) Schadewaldt (1959) 309. At the same time the Olympian scene is one more instance of retardation (see 25–91n.) and adds to the suspense: when is the fatal confrontation finally to take place?

The *Iliad* abounds in Olympian scenes, which provide a divine perspective on mortal events on earth and (often) are the start of interventions into those events by gods. They underline significant moments in the story and increase their dramatic effect. Clear examples are 4.1–72, where the continuation of the Trojan War is decided upon; *Od.* 1.26–95, where the return of Odysseus is initiated; and

Od. 12.374–90, where the time needed for Odysseus to get back to his ship is filled by a divine scene in which the destruction of his last ship and men is decreed. See Kullmann (1956), Griffin (1980) 179–204, and Taplin (1992) 128–43.

Zeus expresses pity for Hector and ponders saving him for the time being or letting him be killed now by Achilles. Athena rebukes him for trying to save a man who has long been fated to die, and Zeus quickly assures her that he was not serious and gives her permission 'to do as she likes' (which will turn out to be to help Achilles defeat Hector). Similar divine interruptions in the context of battle scenes are found at 16.431–61 (gods debate about Sarpedon) and 20.288–320 (gods debate about Aeneas), and cf. 16.647–55 (Zeus deliberates with himself, in embedded focalisation, whether to make Hector kill Patroclus now or later). While the debate about Aeneas leads to this hero's rescue by Poseidon, the situation around Sarpedon is very similar to the present one: when Zeus considers saving his son Sarpedon, Hera reacts angrily and says that Sarpedon has long been destined to die (16.440–3 = 22.178–81) but also suggests an intervention to secure Sarpedon's burial in his homeland. The correspondence between the scenes is one signal that the deaths of Sarpedon, Patroclus, and Hector form an interlocked chain; see Introduction 2d. On the other hand, there are also differences: Zeus's intervention in the case of Sarpedon does not lead to the hero's escape but at least to his honourable burial; his intervention in the case of Hector, activating Athena as it does, only precipitates Hector's death, while the topic of the hero's burial is not raised at all (yet).

At first sight this scene might suggest a somewhat cynical view of the gods: they watch the deadly chase just as spectators watch athletic games, discussing its outcome (as do the Greek spectators of the chariot race at 23.448–98). Also, Zeus suggests saving Hector but, being snubbed by Athena, reveals that he had not been serious. Upon reflection, however, scenes like these add to the grandeur and tragic nature of the *Iliad*. The continuous presence of a 'divine audience' 'both exalts and humbles human action. It is exalted by being made the subject of passionate concern to the gods, and at the same time it is shown to be trivial in the sublime perspective of heaven' (Griffin (1980) 201). The fact that we see Zeus wrestling with Hector's fate, grieving over it but eventually adhering to it, calls attention to its tragic nature: 'is that which causes Zeus grief not the most terrible truth?' (Reinhardt (1961) 458, my translation). For gods and fate see 208–13n.

A divine assembly in the highest god's palace was most probably a literary motif taken over by the Greeks from the Near East; see West (1997) 177–81. Religious reality in Greece consisted of local cults, a situation which is occasionally mirrored in the epics themselves (cf. Poseidon in Aegae: 13.20–2, Aphrodite on Paphos: *Od.* 8.363, Athena in Athens: *Od.* 7.81, and Achilles praying to Zeus of Dodona: 16.233). Homer showing gods living together in one place *and* having their individual haunts is one indication that his gods are both the metaphysical forces of everyday religion and humanised characters in a story. See Kearns (2004).

166 The change of scene from the plain around Troy to Zeus's palace on Mt. Olympus is effected midverse by following a line of perception: the gods see Hector being pursued, and this brings us to them. For this technique see Richardson (1990) 110–14 . **δ' ἐς:** this reading is preferable to δέ τε, since omnitemporal epic τε is out of place in a specific context. **ἐς. . . ὁρῶντο:** tmesis (L 20). The middle instead of the active form of the verb for 'seeing' is used (again at 169), because the perception strongly affects the viewer; cf. Zeus's own words at 168–72, where φίλον ἄνδρα and ὀλοφύρεται explicitly give expression to this emotional involvement. See Allan (2003) 100–1.

167 A formulaic speech-introduction (8 x *Il.*, 6 x *Od.*). For Zeus as father of men and gods see 60–1n. **τοῖσι** 'amongst them'; anaphoric pronoun (L 17), picking up θεοὶ. . . πάντες.

168–76 Zeus's speech almost completely consists of skewed verses (see 33–7n. and Introduction 4b), which evoke his emotional state of mind.

168 ὦ πόποι: gives expression to (often negative) surprise (29 x *Il.*, 22 x *Od.*), always at the opening of a speech. West opts for the ὤ of Herodian, instead of the ὦ of most of the MSS. ἦ 'for sure' (40n.). φίλον ἄνδρα 'a dear man'. In tune with his high-pitched emotions Zeus refers to Hector not by his name but by an expressive – and unique – circumlocution (33–91n.). Cf. 24.67, where Zeus even calls Hector φίλτατος. . . θεοῖσι βροτῶν οἳ ἐν Ἰλίωι εἰσίν. The idea that a hero is loved by the gods derives from the Near East, where it takes the form of the god protecting him against his enemies. In the Homeric epics the love of gods, except that of Athena for Odysseus, is a trickier affair: 'the love of Zeus . . . seems to be as dangerous to men and even to cities as it was to heroines like Semele and Callisto' (Griffin (1987) 90). Hector, Achilles, Sarpedon, and Troy, who are all loved, sometimes exceedingly, by Zeus, do not survive.

169–70 ὀλοφύρεται. . . |Ἕκτορος: the verb means 'lament', 'weep' (e.g. 5.871: ὀλοφυρόμενος ἔπεα πτερόεντα προσηύδα), hence 'feel pity for' (+ genitive) (here and e.g. 8.202; 17.648). Zeus's interventions often are triggered by pity: e.g. 15.12; 16.431; 17.441, 648; 24.332. ἦτορ: one of many Homeric words for 'heart' or 'mind'; see 78n.

170–2 Sacrifices play an important role in the *do ut des*-structure of Greek religion: gods feel obliged to help mortals in return for their sacrifices (4.46–9; 20.297–8; 24.33–4, 68–70; *Od.* 1.66–7), while mortals refer to sacrifices they have offered in their prayers for help (1.40–1; 8.238–41; *Od.* 4.763–4; 17.240–2).

170 μοι 'for me', dative of interest. ἐπὶ. . . ἔκηεν 'burnt (on an altar)'; aorist from καίω (for this form see *GH* I 385). The combination ἐπὶ. . . καίειν (also at *Od.* 3.9; 17.241) derives from fuller versions of the expression, e.g. πολλὰ δὲ μηρί' ἔκηε θεῶν ἱεροῖσ' ἐπὶ βωμοῖς (*Od.* 3.273).

171 Ἴδης. . . πολυπτύχου: Ida is a mountain range in the south of the Troad; it includes several peaks, of which Gargarus (modern Kaz Dagh) is the highest and the favourite haunt of Zeus (e.g. 14.292), 'where his precinct and altar are' (8.48). Ida is 'rich in springs', 'covered with wood', and (here) 'rugged' (an epithet it shares with Olympus). For Minoan-Mycenaean peak sanctuaries see Burkert (1985) 26–8. ἄλλοτε δ' αὖτε 'at other times' (without preceding ἄλλοτε μέν).

172 ἐν πόλει ἀκροτάτηι 'on the upper part of the city', i.e. on the acropolis (cf. *Od.* 8.494, 504, where we hear about the ἀκρόπολις of Troy). Troy's acropolis is also called Πέργαμος (e.g. 4.508; 24.700). The temples of Athena (6.88), Apollo (5.446), and we may assume Zeus (cf. 6.257) are located there. νῦν αὖτε 'now however': Zeus emphasises the contrast between Hector's pious behaviour in the past and his present plight. ἑ: personal pronoun (L 19). δῖος Ἀχιλλεύς: see 102n.

173 ἄστυ πέρι: the preposition stands in postposition (L 20).

174 ἀλλ' ἄγετε φράζεσθε 'but come consider'. ἄγε and ἄγετε, originally imperatives, occur usually in fixed combinations like ἀλλ' ἄγετε, εἰ δ' ἄγετε, and νῦν δ' ἄγετε and are used as exhortatory particles. θεοί: Zeus's use of a vocative and the rare vocative θεοί at that (cf. 8.5, 18; 24.33, 39, 62) underscores the urgency of his request; in the comparable debates on Sarpedon and Aeneas (see 166–87n.) no vocatives are found. μητιάασθε: metrical diectasis (L 4): μητιάασθε (– ⏑ ⏑ – ⏑) < μητιάσθε (– ⏑ – ⏑) < μητιάεσθε (– ⏑ ⏑ – ⏑).

175–6 σαώσομεν . . . δαμάσσομεν: deliberative aorist subjunctives with short vowel (L 15). μιν . . . Ἀχιλῆϊ δαμάσσομεν 'we will bring him low via Achilles', i.e. 'have him killed by Achilles'. This use of δαμάζω/δάμνημι with divine subject and mortal agent recurs at 270–1, 446; and cf. 3.352; 6.368; 16.543. ἐσθλὸν ἐόντα 'even though he is a brave fighter'; the upcoming defeat of Hector is presented as honourably as possible (cf. 138–207n.).

As ἤδη makes clear, the gods can only *temporarily* save a hero from death. They cannot exempt him from death altogether; cf. Athena telling Telemachus that 'even the gods cannot keep death away from a beloved man, when the cruel fate of death's long sorrow takes him' (*Od.* 3.236–8). Human mortality belongs to the cosmic order of the world, which the gods are keen to uphold.

177 προσέειπε: ἔειπε < ἔϝειπε, an older aorist form next to εἶπε. θεὰ γλαυκῶπις Ἀθήνη: verse-end formula (19 x *Il.*, 32 x *Od.*). The epithet is only given to Athena, as is βοῶπις to Hera. Its meaning is most probably 'bright-eyed'; see Pulleyn on 1.206. Although Zeus addressed all the gods, it is Athena who answers on their behalf (181).

178–81 Athena's speech closely mirrors that of Hera at 16.440–3; see 166–87n. The main difference lies in the way the two female goddesses address Zeus: Hera's αἰνότατε Κρονίδη, 'dread son of Cronus' is aggressive, while Athena's vocatives are more deferential.

178 πάτερ: this form of address is used both of literal fathers (as here, cf. Zeus's address of Athena as τέκος at 183) and of elderly or venerable people. The case of Zeus is special, since he is 'father of gods and men' (60–1n.). ἀργικέραυνε: probably 'with bright lightning'; the word recurs at 19.121; 20.16 (both times in speeches by gods). κελαινεφές '(god) of dark clouds', standard epithet of Zeus (11 x). For Zeus as weather god see 182n. οἷον ἔειπες: exclamatory, 'what a thing to say'.

179 πάλαι πεπρωμένον αἴσηι 'long ago destined by fate', sc. to die. The verb ἔπορον, 'give', 'bestow', in the perfect passive has the special sense of 'to be given by fate' = 'to be destined'; cf. e.g. ἄμφω γὰρ πέπρωται ὁμοίην γαῖαν ἐρεῦσαι, 'for it is fated that we both (Achilles and Patroclus) colour the same ground red' (18.329). Since πάλαι may refer to any moment in the past preceding the present of the speaker (cf. Eurycleia at *Od.* 23.29 telling Penelope that Telemachus πάλαι knew that Odysseus had returned, although the return had taken place only a couple of days earlier), it is not clear whether we are to understand that the deaths of Hector (and Sarpedon: 16.441) had been fated from their birth onwards (see 208–13n.) or only for one or two days (from the moment that Zeus authoritatively announced them: 15.67–8). Cf. Hector realising that his death πάλαι was dear to Zeus (301).

180 ἄψ 'away', 'back' (related to ἀπό). It conveys that what was settled (Hector's death) is being annulled; cf. Achilles who ἄψ . . . ἀπέλυσε the mother of Andromache, whom he had taken captive (6.427). θανάτοιο δυσηχέος: the exact meaning of this epithet has been disputed since antiquity: it is to be connected either with ἠχή, 'ill-sounding', or ἄχος, 'causing much misery'; see *LfgrE* s.v. The noun-epithet formula recurs twice (16.442; 18.464); all three times gods are speaking. Otherwise the epithet occurs with πόλεμος (7 x). ἐξαναλῦσαι 'deliver from'. For this metaphor cf. *Od.* 5.397 (θεοὶ κακότητος ἔλυσαν); 10.286; 16.364. It is to be related to the idea of death or bad fate shackling (5n.) or binding a person or a person getting entangled in the ropes of fate; see *BK* on 6.143.

181 This line is also found at 4.24 and 16.443. ἔρδε 'go ahead', lit. 'do (it)'. ἀτάρ: though etymologically distinct from αὐτάρ, it is used indiscriminately as a metrical variant, both words having an adversative ('but') and progressive ('and') meaning. See Ruijgh (1971) 714–18. τοι = σοι.

182 A common speech-introduction formula for Zeus (8 x *Il.*, 6 x *Od.*). νεφελ-ηγερέτα 'cloud-gatherer'. This nominative in -α is probably a secondary use of what originally was a vocative; see *GH* I 199. In the division of power between Zeus, Poseidon, and Hades (referred to at 15.189–93), Zeus was apportioned the sky, so nine of his sixty-one Homeric epithets are related to aspects of weather; see Dee (2001) s.v. Ζεύς. He was originally an Indo-European sky god, but as weather god, he also shows some resemblance to Near Eastern gods of storms; see West (1997) 114–16. He sends rain, thunderbolts, lightning, hail, and snow.

183–4 The same lines occur at 8.39–40, where Zeus has forbidden the gods to interfere in the battle and then, after Athena protests, speaks conciliatory words. For an interpretation of Zeus's words here see 166–87n. Τριτογένεια: a title of Athena which occurs 3 x *Il.*, 1 x *Od.* The meaning is unclear, 'born at the river Triton' (in Boeotia or Thessaly)? For discussion and literature see *LfgrE* s.v. οὔ νύ τι 'not at all'. Both νυ (see 9–10n.) and τι (see LSJ, A II c) intensify οὔ. θυμῶι | πρόφρονι 'with a sincere mind'. For πρόφρων see 302–3n. In the combination with θυμός its etymology (-φρων from φρήν) seems forgotten; see 263n. ἤπιος 'soothing' (of medicinal herbs), 'friendly', here 'I am willing to do you a favour', i.e. accept your protest.

185 ἔρξον ὅπηι δή τοι νόος ἔπλετο 'act in the way in which your mind is set': Zeus repeats a word of his interlocutor Athena (ἔρξον : ἔρδε); an instance of the 'catchword'-technique (see de Jong xii). For the alternation of the present imperative and aorist imperative cf. 4.29 + 37. For πέλομαι see 116n. The use of the past tense seems idiomatic in this type of expression, cf. ἔρξον ὅπως ἐθέλεις καὶ τοι φίλον ἔπλετο θυμῶι (*Od.* 13.145). μηδ' ἔτ' ἐρώει: urging Athena not to hold back 'any longer', Zeus alludes to the fact that Athena is the destined executor of Hector's death at Achilles' hands (cf. 15.613–14).

186 ὣς εἰπὼν ὤτρυνε 'by speaking such words he encouraged'; coincident use of the aorist participle (15–16n.). πάρος μεμαυῖαν Ἀθήνην: the same expression occurs at 4.73; 19.349; *Od.* 24.487; each time Athena is given an order by Zeus that she is only too eager to execute.

187 Οὐλύμποιο: instead of Ὀλύμποιο because of metrical lengthening (L 2). Olympus is a mountain ridge with several high peaks (the highest one approximately 2,900 m) in Thessaly. The Olympian gods are supposed to have their palaces there around the highest palace of the supreme god Zeus, just like a royal family that lives together on a citadel (e.g. the Trojan royal family: 6.242–50): cf. e.g. 1.606–8 and the expression Ὀλύμπια δώματ' ἔχοντες. Sometimes, however, we hear that the gods live in the sky (e.g. 1.194–5: ἦλθε δ' Ἀθήνη | οὐρανόθεν). This dual conception – which much occupied the ancient scholiasts, especially Aristarchus (see Schmidt (1976) 81–7) – may be explained by assuming that (1) the peaks are so high as to be virtually in the sky; (2) the sky is used by way of abbreviation for Olympus, since the main inhabitant of Mt. Olympus, Zeus, is a sky god, and (3) the two locations derive from the conflation of the Indo-European conception of a sky-god and the Near Eastern conception of gods living together on a mountain. For literature see *LfgrE* s.v. βῆ . . . ἀΐξασα 'she went darting'; coincident aorist participle (15–16n.).

188–207 Unusually, the narrator does not follow in the footsteps of Athena and arrive with her at the scene of action (cf. e.g. *Od.* 1.96–112). Instead, he paints another picture of the chase before reporting Athena's arrival at the place where Achilles finds himself (at 214). Having first indicated the speed of the runners and the deadly nature of the chase (136–66), he now describes a stalemate: Achilles is unable to overtake Hector and Hector is unable to find shelter near the Trojan walls. The two passages 136–66 and 188–207 *together* evoke the three 'rounds' of the chase (cf. 165–6), rather than subsequent stages in it. The scene contains two similes that by slowing down the narration emphasise the dramatic nature of what is going on. The elaboration of the stalemate prepares for the dramatic denouement, the tipping of the scales followed by Athena's intervention, starting at 208.

188–98 The simile describes how a hound/Achilles pursues a fawn/Hector incessantly (ἀσπερχές ≈ ἔμπεδον), how the fawn/Hector hides under a thicket/tries to move towards the Dardanian gate and under the wall (ὑπὸ θάμνωι ≈ ὑπὸ πύργους), but cannot escape the attention of the hound/Achilles (λάθησι ≈ οὐ λῆθε), who finds the hidden fawn/blocks Hector's way and heads him back towards the plain again. The incessant nature of the pursuit is linguistically expressed by the correlatives ὁσσάκι... τοσσάκι, the iterative optative ὁρμήσειε, and the iterative ἀποτρέψασκε (L 12). Deer in Iliadic comparisons/similes are typically symbols of helplessness, often fear (e.g. 11.113–21). Most 'deer' similes concern the Trojans; cf. 138–44n. At the same time, however, the simile seems to build up sympathy for Hector, casting him in the role of a young animal that is startled away from its lair. At the opening of this book the Trojans, having fled inside the city, were compared to fawns (22.1). Hector, who alone remained outside, stood in contrast to his compatriots at that stage; now he shares in their role of pursued prey. It has been a long time since Hector himself acted as the hunter (cf. the simile at 18.318–23). It is entirely appropriate to this stage of the story that the simile is inconclusive, with the outcome of the confrontation between hound and deer being omitted.

188 κλονέων 'putting to (panicked or confused) flight'; usually of masses, only here of a single person.

189 ὡς δ' ὅτε: see 162n. ὄρεσφι 'in the mountains'. –φι functions as dative ending (L 9). For the connotation of mountains see 139n. δίηται: this form can be the subjunctive of the thematic aorist διόμην or of the athematic present δίεμαι; see *LfgrE* s.v. δίημι, δίω.

191–2 τὸν δ' εἴ πέρ τε λάθησι: an instance of (grammatical) prolepsis; an element of the subordinate clause is put 'in advance' into the main clause. Instead of 'even if it (fawn) manages to hide from him', we have 'him, even if it manages to hide from (him)'; see *GH* II 234–5. For an analysis in terms of oral syntax (the accusative τὸν δ' is a *frame* within which other units are uttered) see Bakker (1997) 100–8. εἴ πέρ τε... | ἀλλά τ' 'even though... still'. The use of epic τε (L 21) in both subordinate and main clause strengthens the close connection between the actions expressed in them. For the concessive use of εἴ περ, which only occurs in Homeric Greek, see Wakker (1994) 315–19. After a conditional subordinate clause we may find apodotic ἀλλά in the main clause, which indicates the contrast between the two clauses; see *GP* 11. ὄφρα κεν εὕρηι 'until he finds it'; the temporal conjunction with κεν has a final undertone.

193 ποδώκεα: one of Achilles' four epithets indicating his swiftness, here used in a contextually relevant way; see 14n. Πηλεΐωνα: a patronymic (7n.).

194–5 'Whenever he set about to make a dash straight for the Dardanian gate (to get) under (the protection of) its well-built towers'. πυλάων Δαρδανιάων: the Dardanian gate is mentioned twice elsewhere (5.789, 22.413). Aristarchus identified it with the Scaean gate. Originally it may have been a separate gate leading to the city of Dardaniē (cf. 20.216). For the gates of Troy see 6n. ἀΐξασθαι: there is a variant ἀΐξεσθαι, but the close parallel 21.265–9 favours the aorist. The verb ὁρμάω is usually followed by a present infinitive (e.g. 13.64; 21.572).

ἐϋδμήτους ὑπὸ πύργους: since the bulwarks are places on which people find themselves (see 97n.), it is logical that Hector, seeking shelter, tries to reach them. Bulwarks are typically called 'well-built' (here, 12.154; 16.700), but here the epithet brings home the sense of security which Hector hopes to gain by getting near them.

196 'hoping that they (i.e. those standing on the bulwarks) might defend him with their missiles from above'. εἴ πώς: in Homeric Greek, conditional clauses with the optative (or subjunctive) may have a final nuance. The difference from regular final clauses is that the subject *hopes* or *tries* to achieve something; see Wakker (1994) 365–79. οἱ 'him' (personal pronoun, see L 19). ἀλάλκοιεν: a reduplicated aorist optative from ἀλέξω, 'defend'.

197–8 '(Each time Hector would dash for the walls), Achilles would be there before him and would turn him back towards the plain.'

197 προπάροιθεν: this word is used both with local ('before', 'in front') and temporal ('sooner', 'earlier') senses, the first being much more frequent than the second. Most commentators have opted here for the second meaning, following the scholiast, but the *LfgrE* suggests that we may be dealing with a combined local-temporal meaning: Achilles was *at the spot* Hector was heading for *before* he could reach it. ἀποτρέψασκε: this reading seems preferable to ἀποστρέψασκε in that τρέπω is more suggestive of Achilles *forcing* Hector from his course than στρέφω, which lays more stress on the *movement* of turning. There is also an ancient variant παρατρέψασκε, which is, however, precluded by the direct collocation with παραφθάς. παραφθάς: the same ambiguity is noticeable in this verb as in προπάροιθεν; the three times it occurs (all in a context of 'racing') it means 'getting ahead of' someone, both in time and place (cf. 10.346; 23.515).

198 ποτὶ πτόλιος 'on the city side'; this is an exceptional use of ποτί + genitive, which *GH* II 133–4 explains as an extension of the genitive of origin, Fr. 'du côté de'. While Hector runs along the wagon track (146), Achilles runs nearer to the city and hence debars him from reaching the walls and gate. ποτί is the Aeolic form of Ionian-Attic πρός. πτόλιος = πόλιος; the variant is chosen for metrical reasons (to lengthen the -ι of ποτί). πέτετ': see 143n.

199–201 Aristarchus athetised these lines as being 'shabby' (εὐτελεῖς), both as regards their content and their style: the simile, which indicates that the race does not progress, would contradict the simile of the racehorses at 162–6, and line 200 seems a mere repetition of 199. Here we may be grateful that Aristarchus merely obelised verses (putting an *obelos* or dagger in the margin) rather than removing them, because they are among the most haunting in the Homeric epics (and imitated to great effect by Virgil at *Aeneid* 12.908–14). Similes may illustrate different aspects of one and the same action: 162–6 the speed of the runners, 188–93 the impossibility for Hector to escape Achilles' attention, and 199–201 the equality of speed. As far as the style of this simile is concerned, 15.416–18 offers a parallel: οὐδὲ δύναντο | οὔθ' ὁ τὸν ἐξελάσαι ... | οὔθ' ὁ τὸν ἂψ ὤσασθαι.

This is the only Homeric simile to refer to dreaming. Dreams occur regularly in the Homeric epics and take one of two forms: most revolve around a *visit* by a dream figure (e.g. the misleading Dream which visits Agamemnon: 2.6–41), occasionally they involve a symbolic *episode* (e.g. Penelope dreaming how her geese are killed by an eagle, who turns out to be Odysseus: *Od.* 19.536–53). For dreams in Homer see Harris (2009), with more literature. This simile features the second, episodic type of dream. Placing himself in the position of both Achilles and Hector, the narrator makes their feelings clear: both men feel that they are hardly moving although they are running at full speed, since the one cannot overtake the other and the other cannot escape. We may all recognise this type of dream in which movements do not seem to yield results.

199 δύναται: sc. τις.

201 ὅς: the relative pronoun is here used as anaphoric pronoun (see L 17) for metrical reasons (because the next word begins with a vowel).

202–4 At this climactic point of his story the narrator gives up his usual reticence for once and steps forward qua narrator by inserting a rhetorical question. While rhetorical questions are posed regularly by characters (e.g. 431–2: 'Why would I go on living, now that you are dead?'), the narrator only uses them twice more, at 17.260–1 and *Od.* 22.12–14 (at a similarly climactic point of his story: the suitors are feasting, not expecting any harm: 'for who would think that one man, alone against many, though very strong, could ever inflict death and dark doom upon him?').

The present instance takes the form of an 'if not'-situation, a special type of counterfactual that describes a moment of high tension, e.g. 3.373–5: 'And now he (Menelaus) would have dragged him (Paris) back and throttling him would have won limitless glory, if Zeus's daughter Aphrodite had not watched sharply and saved Paris' life by breaking the strap around his neck'. Here, instead of 'and Hector would not have escaped death if he had not been helped by Apollo', we find 'how could Hector have escaped if he had not been helped?'. See Reinhardt (1961) 107–20, de Jong (2004) 68–81, Lang (1989), Nesselrath (1992) 5–38, Morrison (1992) 51–71, and Louden (1993).

The effect of this rhetorical question is complex: in the first place it answers a question which by now must have intrigued the narratees: how is it possible that Achilles, the fastest runner of all, cannot overtake Hector? Secondly, it adds to the pathos of the situation: whereas normally heroes in situations like these are saved, here Hector is assisted by a god only temporarily, as the ominous 'for the last and final time' reveals. Finally, Apollo's assistance of Hector adds, in the usual archaic way of thinking, to his glory: the gods only help those who deserve to be helped. The mention of Apollo, whom we had last seen conversing with Achilles in the opening scene of this book, also prepares for his dramatic exit at 213. All in all, there seems to be no reason to suspect these lines, as e.g. Leaf (see his appendix K) has done.

202 κῆρας . . . θανάτοιο 'the spirits of death'; 'these *kēres* of death are given little description, but it emerges, almost against the poet's will, that there are thousands of them, haunting human life, and in the end no man can escape them; those who die are "carried off" by them' (Griffin (1980) 43). Cf. e.g. 2.302; 18.535–8. At times κήρ seems no more than another word for death-fate; cf. e.g. 365.

203 οἱ: personal pronoun (L 19). **πύματον τε καὶ ὕστατον** 'for the very last time', lit. 'for the last and final time'. An instance of synonymous doubling such as we often find in Homer; see O'Nolan (1978). This emphatic expression, both in singular and plural, belongs to the character-language: it occurs in direct speech (*Od.* 4.685; 20.116) and embedded focalisation (20.13). Its unique use by the narrator shows his emotions at this high point of his story. **ἤντετ᾽** 'encountered', of an intended rather than a chance meeting; here virtually 'stood by'. The same verb occurs at 16.788–9, where Apollo 'meets' Patroclus in order to strike his first deathblow. **Ἀπόλλων:** Apollo in Homer belongs to the pro-Trojan gods (cf. his intervention to save the Trojans: 1–24n.), and particularly assists Hector: at 15.236–70 he encourages him and gives him renewed energy after he has been wounded by Ajax; at 20.443–4 he saves him from Achilles. After Hector's death he will continue to take care of his body (23.188–91 and 24.31–54). For possible reasons why Apollo supports the Trojans see Erbse (1986) 188–90.

204 ἐγγύθεν: originally 'from close at hand' but in Homer also simply 'close by'; cf. ἐγγύθι, ἄνευθεν (300). **ἐπῶρσε μένος λαιψηρά τε γοῦνα** 'he stirred up his energy and quick knees', i.e. 'made his knees move quickly'. Gods may stir up (cf. 20.93), give, send, throw, breathe into, or fill (heroes) with *menos*. For *menos* see 96n.

205–7 λαοῖσιν: see 104n. **ἀνένευε καρήατι:** it seems best to connect this verb closely with οὐδ᾽ ἔα ἱέμεναι: 'he nodded with his head and did (thereby indicate that he did) not allow the men to throw'. The raising of the chin as an emphatic 'no' is perhaps 'the best-known ancient and modern ethnogest . . . in symbolic communication' (Lateiner (1995) 78). **δῖος Ἀχιλλεύς:** see 102n. **ἱέμεναι:** infinitive (L 11). **πικρὰ βέλεμνα** 'sharp missiles' (arrows or spears). **κῦδος:** a kind of lustre or *mana*, specifically the glory of victory. It is objective glory that is often given by a god, is strictly personal, and belongs only to the living; εὖχος is the subjective glory a victorious warrior claims for himself directly after victory (cf. Achilles at 330); and κλέος is the objective fame which remains even after death and which may be won also for others (304–5n.). See Redfield (1994) 31–4. **ὁ δέ** 'while he'; anaphoric pronoun, referring back to δῖος Ἀχιλλεύς. It is perhaps surprising to find this pronoun as part of Achilles' own thoughts, but it is needed to make clear the opposition between the τις and Achilles himself. **δεύτερος ἔλθοι:** this expression, which recurs at 10.368, combines a literal and figurative meaning: coming second, because another acts first, and thereby becoming less honoured.

This passage was discussed by Aristotle in his *Poetics*, chs. 24 (1460a11–17) and 25 (1460b22–6): he argues that epic has greater scope for the 'marvellous' or 'illogical' in that it is not seen: 'The circumstances of the pursuit of Hector would be patently absurd, with the men standing and refraining from pursuit, and Achilles nodding his head, but in epic the effect is not noticed.' Somewhat later he adds that when such 'impossible things' increase the emotional impact, the poet may be forgiven this technical error. Coming to Homer's defence we might note that (1) (potential) interfering onlookers, namely Trojans standing on the walls and throwing missiles at Achilles, had been mentioned before (195–6) and hence the present passage might be seen as their necessary Greek counterpart; (2) the mention of the Greek onlookers, who must have come closer and closer to the city-walls since line three, adds to the pathos of the situation: virtually all players in the Iliadic drama are present as actors or spectators (see 1–24n.); and (3) the essential point of these lines is to portray Achilles' heroic temperament, which does not leave him even in these exceptional circumstances. His fear of being diminished in glory when killing Hector while coming second resembles his fear of being 'less honoured' if Patroclus should take Troy (16.87–90). We may also think of Patroclus' dying jeer at Hector (16.850) that the latter only killed him 'coming third' (after Apollo and Euphorbus). By implication, Achilles' concern for the glory attached to killing Hector adds to the glory of the Trojans. Cf. Achilles' words at 393–4: 'We have won great glory (*kudos*): we have killed glorious Hector, whom the Trojans venerated like a god in their city.'

208–47

The deadlock of the chase is ended, in the customary Homeric way, by a divine intervention. It happens in two stages: first, Zeus weighs the fates of the running heroes and Hector's fate sinks; then, the divine champion of the Trojans, Apollo, leaves and the pro-Greek Athena arrives at the scene. Although Homer's narratees are used to the idea that gods interfere in mortal life (see 166–87n.), the present intervention by Athena finds little sympathy because, as the narrator explicitly notes, she uses deceit (κερδοσύνηι: 247) to persuade Hector to make a stand (and die). Thus the scholia consider what Athena does here 'inappropriate' (ἄτοπον), and Erbse (1986) 149 thinks that 'Athena breaks all rules of chivalrous behaviour'. Her role remains unsympathetic in the ensuing duel, when she gives Achilles his spear back after it has missed Hector (276–7).

In order to evaluate Athena's behaviour fairly, we may recall Apollo's role in the fight between Hector and Patroclus (16.777–867): Apollo, who was invisible to Patroclus, struck him on the back, knocked off his armour, and broke his spear. Athena's use of deceit rather than force is in keeping with her famous wiliness (cf. *Od.* 13.298–9). It has even been suggested by Erbse (1986) 150 that Athena's use of deceit when killing the main defender of Troy mirrors her ruse to bring about the fall of Troy itself (the Wooden Horse). More generally, it should be noted that Homeric gods do not shun deception: for example, Zeus sends a Dream to Agamemnon that promises victory for the Greeks but in fact sets them back

(2.1–40). Their duplicity was one of the reasons why they were criticized in later Greek society; cf. 14–20n.

As always, the divine assistance does not detract from the glory of the mortal actor Achilles. On the contrary, the narratees would see it as a mark of respect, since the gods only help those who deserve to be honoured: 'The poet . . . prefers to use the gods, when it is some really great and famous action' (Willcock (1970) 4).

208–13 The climactic moment to which much of the *Iliad* has been leading and which many prolepses have announced, the death of Hector, is marked by a *kērostasia*, Zeus weighing the heroes' (death-)fates on his golden scales. The use of imperfects in this passage, framed by aorists (ἀφίκοντο . . . λίπεν), creates a scenic effect; see 157–66n.

Although the weighing suggests that the future is still open, Zeus's act only graphically and symbolically illustrates what had already been decided in the preceding Olympic scene. Even divine assistance can no longer postpone Hector's death, as Apollo's departure from the stage immediately after the weighing shows. See Erbse (1986) 289–90. Some scholars, e.g. Morrison (1997) 292, suggest that the weighing scene demonstrates Zeus's reluctance to implement Hector's fate: in this view he would be torn between the larger design of a Greek victory (including the sack of Troy) and his individual pity for one hero, and he would leave it to the objective weighing of the scales to decide between them. This is not plausible in view of the 'green light' that Zeus had already given Athena at 185.

A similar scene of weighing, that of the fates of the Trojan and Greek armies (i.e. their success in battle), is found at 8.69–72. Reichel (1994) 158 suggests that the two scenes mark the beginning and end of Hector's short period of success, which runs parallel with Zeus's plan to give defeat temporarily to the Greeks; see Introduction 2b. Zeus's scales are mentioned more briefly at 16.658 (Hector 'knew the holy scales of Zeus', i.e., that the Trojans' chances in the war were low) and 19.223–4 (Odysseus said that many men die in war, 'when Zeus, who holds the issue of men's fighting, inclines his scales'). At 12.432–6 an evenly balanced battle is compared to a woman weighing spun wool.

The image of weighing may go back to Mycenaean times and have an oriental background (it is often depicted in Egyptian art); see West (1997) 393–4. It perhaps also appeared in the *Aethiopis*, at the moment of the duel between Achilles and Memnon. The scholia and Plutarch suggest that Aeschylus was inspired by the Iliadic passage when writing his (now lost) *Psychostasia*, the weighing of the *souls* of Achilles and Memnon after their deaths, but the *Aethiopis* and vase paintings seem more likely sources; see Taplin (1977) 431–2.

Fate is one of the forces that propel the action in the Homeric epics, together with the gods and the heroes. There is a sense that important events in a man's life (e.g. the year of Odysseus' return: 1.16–18) or the moment of his death (5n.) are determined by fate, sometimes at the moment of birth (e.g. 1.414–18 or 20.127–8). But still there is room for the heroes to make their own decisions, if only because usually they do not know their own fate (Hector) or are confronted with different options (Achilles: 9.410–16). Zeus and the other gods accept fate (cf. 166–87) because they (ultimately) consider it beneficial to uphold the cosmic order, not because they are subordinate to it; they are often seen executing it (as here). Whether it is fate or the gods which are invoked largely depends on the context: 'if stress is placed on the inevitability of an event, its importance in a character's life-story or the need to endure it, fate is invoked; if the emphasis falls on an action's power or strangeness, then it tends to be the work of a god' (Janko 6). Scholars are divided as to whether fate in Homer is primarily a poetic device ('what happened' because of the demands of the tale or of tradition) or whether it represents a genuine religious concept. For discussions of fate in Homer see e.g. Eberhard (1923), Erbse (1986) 273–93, Janko 5–7, Jones (1996) 114–16, and Allan (2006) 7–8. For the interrelation of fate, gods, and hero in the case of Hector see Introduction 2d.

208–9 ἀλλ' ὅτε δὴ τὸ τέταρτον... | καὶ τότε δή: καὶ τότε δή marks significant moments in the story; cf. 1.92; 13.206. Often it is used as the main clause (*apodosis*) after a temporal subordinate clause; cf. 1.493–4. The incisive force of the 'but when..., then' is strengthened here by taking the form of 'but when *for the fourth time* (cf. 5.438; 16.705, 786; 20.447), then'. Only now do we have the 'but the fourth time Z' part, after the much earlier 'three times X' part; see 165–6n. ἐπὶ κρουνούς: for the landmark of the springs see 147–56n. πατήρ: an abbreviated form of πατὴρ ἀνδρῶν τε θεῶν τε (cf. 167) = Zeus. ἐτίταινε τάλαντα 'he stretched out the scales', apparently a technical term for setting up the balance (pans hanging from the ends of a horizontal pole supported by a vertical pole), which perhaps was folded up when not in use.

210–13 The weighing is described in a series of symmetrical half-line clauses: τὴν μέν... τὴν δ'... ἕλκε δέ... ῥέπε δ'... ᾤχετο δ'... λίπεν δέ. The staccato rhythm suggests speed: after all the retardation and building up of suspense, the actual sealing of Hector's fate takes only a few seconds. Whereas in the weighing scene of book 8 we hear of the fates of the Greeks settling on earth and those of the Trojans being lifted up into heaven, here all stress falls on Hector's doomed sinking fate.

210 'And in them, sc. the pans of the scales, he placed the two death-fates'. κῆρε τανηλεγέος θανάτοιο: for κῆρε θανάτοιο see 202n. The combination τανηλεγέος θανάτοιο occurs only in the genitive, always at the end of the verse, in combination with κήρ or μοῖρα (2 x *Il.*, 6 x *Od.*). The meaning of the epithet is debated, 'woeful' (from τανυ-, 'long', and ἄλγος, 'pain', 'sorrow') being most probable; see *LfgrE* s.v.

211 Ἕκτορος ἱπποδάμοιο: see 161n.

212 ἕλκε δὲ μέσσα λαβών 'he took (the scales) in the middle and raised them'; ἕλκω means not only 'draw', 'drag' (horizontally), but also 'draw up or down'. ῥέπε δ' Ἕκτορος αἴσιμον ἦμαρ: instead of saying 'Hector's death-fate' sank, the narrator turns to a much weightier expression 'Hector's day of doom' sank.

There are a number of such periphrases, including 'day of freedom' (ἐλεύθερον ἦ.), 'day of slavery' (δούλιον ἦ.), 'day of return' (νόστιμον ἦ.), and 'day of orphanage' (ἦ. ὀρφανικόν: 490). They belong to the character-language: of a total of forty-four occurrences, thirty-six are in direct speech; of the eight instances in narrator-text, four occur in special contexts (an 'if not'-situation: 17.615; a simile: *Od.* 8.525; a proem: *Od.* 1.9; a prolepsis: 15.613). The rare use by the narrator here (and 8.72) might betray emotion on his part. The older ἦμαρ is used much more in Homer than the younger but metrically difficult form ἡμέρη.

213 ὤιχετο δ᾽ εἰς Ἀΐδαο 'and tipped in the direction of (the house of) Hades'. The narrator uses a more dramatic expression than in the similar situation at 8.73–4, where the fates of the Greeks 'settled on the nourishing earth', in accordance with the fact that Hector will not merely be defeated (like the Greeks) but killed. λίπεν: the verb λείπω primarily means 'to leave a person behind while one departs' (e.g. 1.428: Thetis leaves Achilles after their conversation), but at times it may have the more pregnant meaning 'leave to one's fate', 'abandon' (e.g. 15.218–19: Poseidon leaves the Greeks after Zeus orders him to stop helping them, and they long for him). ἑ: personal pronoun (L 19). Φοῖβος Ἀπόλλων: standard verse-end formula (32 x *Il.*, 2 x *Od.*). The meaning of the epithet is unclear ('bright', 'pure'?); for literature see *LfgrE*.

214–25 The narrator, highly effectively, now resumes his narration of Athena's journey from Olympus to the Trojan plain (see 188–207n.) and thus is able to present the goddess's arrival in direct juxtaposition to the departure of Apollo. For Apollo and Athena as directly opposing forces cf. 4.507–16 and 7.17–27. Athena's intervention is a special variant of a 'god meets mortal' scene (see 226–47n.), in that she assumes no mortal disguise. Achilles is one of the few mortals who is directly approached by a god (again at 1.194–222). The others are Diomedes (5.793–835), Hector (15.236–70), and Odysseus (*Od.* 13.288–440; 16.155–77; 20.30–55). As the narrator states at *Od.* 16.161, 'the gods do not openly appear to all'.

214 Πηλεΐωνα: a patronymic of Achilles (7n.). γλαυκῶπις: see 177n.

215 ἀγχοῦ . . . ἱσταμένη: the speech-introduction that features speakers who are 'standing near' their addressee introduces intimate, secretive, or (feigned) affectionate words, cf. de Jong on 10.377. Athena's tone here is secretive, at 228 feigned affectionate. ἔπεα πτερόεντα: a common and celebrated Homeric formula (61 x *Il.* and *Od.*). Its exact meaning is, however, disputed: are we dealing with 'winged words', like birds, or 'feathered words', like arrows? In favour of the first, πτερόν normally means 'wing' rather than 'arrow'; in favour of the second, birds are called πετεηνός rather than πτερόεις, while arrows are called πτερόεις (4.117; 5.171; 16.773; 20.68). Whatever the exact metaphor, the expression refers to the spoken word, which swiftly and irrevocably finds its way from the mouth of the speaker to the ear of the addressee. According to Martin (1989) 30–7, speech-introductions with 'winged words' always introduce directive speeches, which are aimed at making the addressee do something; this suits Athena's speech well. For literature see Pulleyn on 1.201, to which Latacz (1968) should be added.

216–23 Athena's speech is an instance of a *parainesis* or exhortation to battle: friendly address ('splendid Achilles, dear to Zeus') – argument ('the moment to kill Hector has come and not even Apollo can prevent it') – call to action ('you stay here and I will exhort Hector to fight against you'). Indeed, many of the 'god meets mortal' scenes in the *Iliad* naturally concern divine *paraineseis*; cf. 4.507–14; 5.461–70, 784–92; 13.43–65, 89–125, 215–39; 14.135–52; 17.553–9, 582–92.

The stress on 'we', both plural (ἄμμε) and, even more emphatic, dual (νῶϊ, δηιώσαντε), is distinctive to Athena's speech. Although exhorting gods occasionally employ the 'we' form (5.469; 13.52, 115, 236, 238), Athena's repeated stress that she and Achilles would defeat Hector together stands out. Rather than referring to fate or Zeus's weighing of the scales Athena speaks about the upcoming death of Hector in martial terms, very much like the war-goddess she is (cf. her bloodthirsty words spoken to Odysseus at *Od.* 13.393–5: 'I will certainly be at your side and will not forget you, when we go to this work', i.e., the revenge on the suitors, 'and I am sure that endless ground will be spattered by blood and brains'). Also, if Achilles is taking revenge on his archenemy Hector, Athena seems to enjoy *her* moment of triumph over pro-Trojan Apollo (cf. also 221n.).

The thrice repeated νῦν (216, 219, 222, and cf. 235, 243, 252, 268, 300, 303) marks – to Achilles and narratees alike – that the moment of revenge has *now* come after all the delays and retardations.

216 νῶϊ 'the two of us' (dual of the first person personal pronoun: L 19). ἔολπα 'I am confident'; intensive perfect (95n.). δίφιλε φαίδιμ' Ἀχιλλεῦ: the default name-epithet formula for Achilles at this place in the verse is θεοῖς ἐπιείκελ' Ἀχιλλεῦ (279n.), but perhaps a divine speaker like Athena is not likely to use the epithet 'godlike', and, moreover, the notion that Achilles is 'dear to Zeus' is apt in view of the immediately preceding scene. The epithets δίφιλος and φαίδιμος are generic, i.e. are used of different heroes (δίφιλος : 5 x Achilles, 4 x Hector, 3 x Odysseus; φαίδιμος: 29 x Hector, 6 x Ajax). It may be significant that Hector is only called δίφιλος as long as he is granted victory by Zeus in the context of the *Dios boulē* (6.318; 8.493; 10.49; 13.674). The epithet is differently printed in our texts: δίφιλε or Διΐ φίλε; for the second option see West 1, xxviii. δίΐ- (with long second iota) is a replacement of the old dative in –ει; cf. Mycenaean di-we (Διϝεί).

217 '(I am confident) that we will bring great glory for the Achaeans to the ships.' οἴσεσθαι μέγα κῦδος: see 205–7n. κῦδος is normally connected with ἄρνυσθαι, '(trying to) win' (e.g. 207, 393). The combination here with φέρεσθαι may be due either to Athena's thinking of Hector's armour, cf. εἴ κεν . . . ἔναρα βροτόεντα φέρηται | νῆας ἔπι γλαφυράς, '(we will know) whether he will carry away our bloody armour to the hollow ships' (244–6), or to the closely similar κεν . . . φέροιτο μέγα κράτος, 'he would win a great victory' (13.486). Ἀχαιοῖσι: best taken as dative of interest ('for the Achaeans'), which is rhetorically forceful and apt in view of Achilles' later words to the Greeks, '*we* have won great glory' (393). Others take it as a dative of reference: '(great glory) in the eyes of the Achaeans'. προτί = πρός.

218 δηιώσαντε: dual of the aor. participle (L 16). μάχης ἀτόν περ ἐόντα 'even though he is most insatiate in fighting'. ἀτος < ἄατος < ἄ-σατος (privative *alpha* and ἄ-σαι, aorist infinitive, 'satisfy', cf. Lat. *satis*). Texts hesitate between the uncontracted older and contracted younger form. For περ see 73n.

219 'It now no longer is possible for him to escape the two of us.' οἱ . . . ἔστι πεφυγμένον ἄμμε γενέσθαι: ἔστι = ἔξεστι. ἄμμε is accusative plural of the first-person personal pronoun (L 19). The periphrastic construction 'become escaped' instead of simple φεύγειν adds a note of finality: Hector's chances to escape are over, once and for all. See Rijksbaron (2002) 128–9. In Homeric and later Greek we regularly find a shift from dative (οἱ) to accusative (πεφυγμένον) after impersonal verbs.

220–1 'Not even if Apollo would be prepared to suffer very much, grovelling before Zeus.' An instance of the '(not) even + hyperbole' motif, which also occurs, e.g., at 349–54; see de Jong on 4.595–8.

220 ἑκάεργος: see 15–16n.

221 προπροκυλινδόμενος: this verb only recurs at *Od.* 17.525, in a slightly different sense (Eumaeus: 'the beggar'/Odysseus has come to Ithaca, rolling, i.e., wandering, on and on). Here the image is that of Apollo supplicating Zeus to spare Hector; cf. Priam, who κυλινδόμενος κατὰ κόπρον, 'rolling in the dung', supplicates the Trojans to let him go to the Greek camp (414). The idea of Apollo supplicating Zeus in itself is already somewhat far-fetched (the only god we witness supplicating is Thetis at 1.500–30), but Athena paints an even stronger picture of Apollo actually humbling himself. We may compare 8.371, where Athena looks back on Thetis' supplication of Zeus with the exaggerated 'she kissed his knees'. The exaggeration expresses Athena's winning mood and at the same time is intended to encourage Achilles, who has been thwarted by Apollo in his attempts to take revenge on Hector twice before (20.443–4 and 22.7–20). αἰγίοχοιο: the epithet is usually interpreted as 'who has/holds the aegis' (from αἰγίς and ἔχω). The aegis is a kind of shield, originally from goatskin (cf. αἴξ, αἰγός, 'goat'), although we hear that the *bronzesmith* Hephaestus made it for Zeus at 15.309–10. When shaken it can produce a storm (e.g. 17.593–5) or put an enemy to flight (e.g. 15.229–30). The interpretation may be etymologically incorrect (an alternative is suggested by West (1966) 366–8: 'riding on a goat'), but this seems to be the way the singers saw it, as witness the expression αἰγίδ' ἔχων/-ουσα (15.361; 2.447). The epithet is used of Zeus only, although Athena (5.738–44) and Apollo (15.307–11) too wield the aegis.

222 ἄμπνυε 'you get your breath'; aorist imperative of ἀναπνέω (with apocope of ἀνα >ἀν, followed by assimilation ἀνπ > ἀμπ). Here we should recall that even before his protracted chase of Hector, Achilles had been running in pursuit of Agenor/Apollo for a long time. τόνδε: referring to Hector with this proximal deictic pronoun Athena suggests that he is nearby and hence reinforces her earlier claim that the Trojan hero no longer can escape them. τοι = σοι; the dative depends on ἐναντίβιον (μαχέσασθαι).

223 πεπιθήσω: reduplicated future of πείθω, 'I will persuade him to'. The reduplicated aorist πεπιθ- is found frequently, but the future derived from it occurs only here. According to *GH* I 203, the form may be no more than a metrically expedient variant of πείσω, but Latacz (1966) 58–6 argues that reduplicated futures and aorists have causative force ('will make him obey').

224 χαῖρε: Achilles' joy suggests that he recognises Athena; joy, next to awe, is a regular reaction to divine manifestations, such as omens (10.274–7; *Od.* 2.35) and interventions (*Od.* 24.504, 545 = *Il.* 22.224). Compare also his later words to Hector: 'there is no escape for you any longer, but soon *Pallas Athena* will beat you down under my spear' (270–1). In other meetings between mortals and undisguised gods, the recognition is noted explicitly with a form of the verb γιγνώσκω (1.199–200; 5.815; *Od.* 13.312–13).

225 As usual, the Homeric narrator reports the execution of an order: Achilles stands still (στῆ ≈ στῆθι), leaning on his spear (and, we may suppose, regaining his breath). Even though he is relaxing for a moment, the narratees are reminded of his famous ash spear (cf. 133–4n.) with which he will soon kill Hector. In other situations wounded warriors lean on their spears for support (14.38; 19.49), speakers to underscore their authority (8.493–6; cf. 2.109, there of a sceptre). χαλκογλώχινος 'bronze barbed' is a *hapax*.

226–47 Both the *Iliad* and *Odyssey* abound in 'god meets mortal' scenes: a god talks to a mortal, usually assuming a mortal disguise, and then either reveals his/her divine identity through words or a supernatural departure (epiphany) or is recognised by the mortal. The 'masks' put on by the gods are carefully chosen (that of a person holding authority for or being dear to the mortal). A clear Iliadic example is the meeting between Hermes, disguised as a Myrmidon, and Priam, where the god reveals that he is a god at the end of the conversation (24.347–469); cf. also e.g. 3.121–40, 389–424; 13.43–82, 215–39; 16.715–26; 21.599–22.20. See Kullmann (1956) 83–111, Smith (1988), Janko on 13.10–38, de Jong on 1.96–304.

Here Athena adopts – effectively but all the more cruelly in light of her deceitful purposes – the disguise of Hector's brother Deïphobus. In divine interventions the god usually gives advice or an order, occasionally strength or courage, and then leaves again; here Athena/'Deïphobus' stays and leads Hector towards his fatal duel with Achilles (247). Hector will only recognise her true identity at 294–9, when it is too late.

Deïphobus is the son of Priam and Hecuba (234) and hence Hector's full brother; contrast Lycaon and Polydorus (46–8), who are sons of Priam and Laothoa and hence Hector's half-brothers. He is one of the Trojan commanders during the raid on the Greek wall (12.94); at 13.156–64, he positions himself in the front line but retreats when Meriones strikes his shield with a spear; at 13.402–69, he attacks Idomeneus, misses him and hits Hypsenor instead, and rejects Idomeneus' challenge of a direct fight; at 13.516–37, he again attacks Idomeneus when the latter leaves the fight exhausted, misses again, is wounded in the arm by Meriones, and leaves the battlefield. His track record makes him a likely ally of Hector against Achilles, though the prime reason why Athena chooses this mask is Hector's affection for him (cf. 233). Thus, the Homeric narrator here effectively combines two motifs: (1) two heroes joining forces against a stronger opponent (5.217–96; 8.99–123; 11.310–27) and (2) two brothers fighting together (e.g., 5.9–29, 159–65, 541–61).

226 ἄρα: see 98n. τὸν μὲν ... κιχήσατο δ᾽: for the asymmetrical use of μέν-δέ see 158–9n. κιχάνω normally means 'meet', 'reach'; here 'caught up' aptly captures the goddess's movement (from Achilles to Hector). Ἕκτορα δῖον: for the epithet δῖος see 102n.

227 δέμας καὶ ἀτειρέα φωνήν '(resembling Deïphobus) as regards build and tireless voice'. When a god assumes a mortal disguise, details of the resemblance may be specified: build and/or voice (here and 2.791; 13.45, 216; 17.555; 20.81; 21.285) or a summarising 'everything' (21.600). According to Homeric belief, the voices of gods (ὀμφή) and men (φωνή) differ; see Clay (1974). For δέμας see 370n.

228 For this speech-introduction see 215n.

229 ἠθεῖ(ε) 'dear/trusted one' (from ἦθος, 'what one is used to'?). This is an affectionate and respectful appellative for an elder brother or friend that belongs to the character-language: it only appears in direct speech (7 x). Its repeated use by one speaker in one scene (cf. 239) is unique and underscores Athena's rhetoric (vis-à-vis Hector) and deceptiveness (as noted only by the narratees). ἦ μάλα δή: lit. 'indeed very much'. A common combination of particles, which belongs to the character-language (27 x Il. and Od; only in direct speech). It presents what is said as an objective truth (ἦ, cf. 40n.), shared by speaker and addressee alike (δή, cf. 76n.). Thus it is well suited to contexts in which a speaker expresses his sympathy for his addressee, as here, or reads his mind; cf. e.g. Hecuba asking Hector, who has returned from the battlefield: 'Why did you return to the city? The Greeks must be very much wearing you down, and therefore your heart has moved you to come here' (6.254–7). βιάζεται 'is pressing you hard'. ὠκὺς Ἀχιλλεύς: the use of this stock formula for Achilles (6 x Il., e.g. 188) here is contextually apt and leads up to the next line.

230 ≈ 173.

231 ἀλλ᾽ ἄγε δή 'come then', a common formula of exhortation. For ἄγε see 174n. στέωμεν: the two vowels -εω- are scanned as one long one (synizesis).

232 τήν: although Athena has assumed a male personality, the narrator continues to refer to her as a female to avoid confusing his narratees. This is common Homeric practice (cf. e.g. Od. 1.113, 213, 230), but it is not recognised by one MS, which has τόν. προσέειπε: see 177n. μέγας κορυθαίολος Ἕκτωρ: μέγας is a generic epithet of heroes, κορυθαίολος a distinctive epithet of Hector (49 x, once of Ares: 20.38). The combination μέγας κορυθαίολος Ἕκτωρ occurs 12 x Il., the shorter formula κορυθαίολος Ἕκτωρ 37 x Il. Despite the ubiquity of κορυθαίολος, its use at this phase of the story (again 249, 337, 355) calls attention to Hector's most distinctive piece of armour one last time just before he is stripped of it (368–9), leaving his unprotected head and hair to sweep through the dust (401–3). The exact etymology and meaning of the epithet are disputed: 'with glittering helmet' or 'helmet-shaking'. For details and literature see *LfgrE* s.v. It would seem that the singers thought of both aspects when using the epithet: at 13.805 we hear about Hector's shining helmet shaking around his temples and at 6.469–70 about Astyanax being frightened by its glitter and moving plume.

233–7 Hector's speech consists of one long clause only: '*already before* you were my *most* beloved brother, but *now* I see I have to honour you *even more*, since . . .'.

233 ἦ μέν 'truly': ἦ expresses objective certainty (40n.) and is here reinforced by μέν = μήν (13n.). τὸ πάρος: in Greek we find both πάρος and τὸ πάρος (νῦν and τὸ νῦν/τὰ νῦν, etc.), whereby the simple form is the indefinite one ('in the past'), the longer form the definite one ('in the entire past up until now'); see *LfgrE* s.v. πάρος and Rijksbaron (2006).

234 γνωτῶν means 'relatives' in general (3.174), but its meaning here (and elsewhere) is narrowed down to 'brothers', as becomes clear in the following relative clause ('whom Hecuba and Priam begot *as their children*'). Ἑκάβη ἠδὲ Πρίαμος τέκε: the number of the predicate is in accordance with the last of the two subjects (and hence singular instead of plural); cf. e.g. 17.398–9; 18.398 and see *GH* II 18–19.

235 νοέω φρεσὶ τιμήσασθαι 'I am minded/intend to honour' sc. you. The middle τιμήσασθαι is used instead of the active for metrical reasons. For the combination νοέω φρεσί cf. 9.600.

236 ἴδες ὀφθαλμοῖσιν: sc. με, derived from ἐμεῦ.

237 ἄλλοι δ' . . . μένουσιν '*while* the others stay inside' (parataxis: L 23).

239–46 Athena's answer consists of two parts: first she picks up on Hector's remark about Deïphobus daring to leave Troy (ἦ μέν: 239 = 233; μένειν ≈ μένουσιν) and then she reiterates and expands her own earlier exhortation to fight. 'Deïphobus' fictional account of his parents and companions begging him to stay will sound all the more plausible to Hector, who has just been supplicated by Priam and Hecuba, too (33–91).

240 λίσσονθ': imperfect. ἑξείης 'one after the other'. ἀμφὶ δ' ἑταῖροι 'and my friends around me', sc. begged me; ἀμφί is adverbial (L 20).

241 αὖθι 'on the spot', 'there', sc. inside the walls of Troy. τοῖον . . . ὑποτρομέουσιν ἅπαντες 'such is the fear of them all'. For this adverbial use of τοῖον cf. *Od.* 3.496; 13.115; 24.62. The element ὑπο- in ὑποτρομέουσιν indicates that their fear has a particular cause, sc. Achilles. The same verb is used in a fuller expression at 20.28: μιν . . . ὑποτρομέεσκον ὁρῶντες, 'they (Trojans) used to tremble at the sight of him' and cf. 282 σ' ὑποδδείσας.

242 ἐτείρετο πένθεϊ λυγρῶι '(my heart) was distressed by painful sorrow' sc. for you. This expression recurs once, at *Od.* 2.70–1 (when Telemachus speaks about the presence of the suitors in his palace).

243–6 The second half of Athena's speech consists of four skewed verses in a row, which suggests heightened excitement; see 33–7n.

243–4 ἰθὺς μεμαῶτε 'charging straight on'. This expression occurs regularly, e.g. again at 284.

μηδέ τι δούρων | ἔστω φειδωλή 'let there be no sparing of spears at all'. A unique expression (φειδωλή occurs only here in Homer). The combination of an abstract noun and third person imperative has a formal ring and resembles the equally formal μνημοσύνη τις... πυρὸς δηΐοιο γενέσθω, 'let there be considerable thought of destructive fire' (8.181).

244–6 εἴδομεν εἴ κεν... | ... φέρηται... | ... ἤ κεν... δαμήηι: εἴδομεν is a subjunctive with short vowel (L 15), δαμήηι an uncontracted subjunctive (L 1). For the pairing of alternatives in subjunctive clauses cf. e.g. φράσσομεθ' ἤ κε νεώμεθ'... ἤ κε μένωμεν, 'let us consider whether we will go home or whether we will stay' (9.619). The subjunctive + κε is prospective, here as part of an indirect question. Most MSS have δαμείη, and the alternation of subjunctive and optative in dependent clauses occurs quite regularly in Homer; cf. e.g. ἀλλὰ μάλ' ἄντην | στήσομαι, ἤ κε φέρησι μέγα κράτος, ἤ κε φεροίμην, 'I will position myself against him, to see whether he will win a great victory or I win it' (18.307–8). According to *GH* II 211–12, 295, the (potential) optative presents a less likely or more modest alternative. This pleads against δαμείη (adopted by West), since this would mean that 'Deïphobus'/Athena would undermine the rhetoric of her intervention by presenting Hector's victory as less plausible than Achilles'. It would also spoil the subtle effect of her claim that defeat would involve them both (νῶϊ) but victory would be the work of Hector alone (σῶι δουρί), as noted by the scholia.

245 νῶϊ 'the two of us'; accusative of the dual personal pronoun (L 19).

246 νῆας ἔπι γλαφυράς: this is one of the most common epithets of ships (cf. 392, 334), which seems no more than a metrical variant of κοίλας ἐπὶ νῆας. For epithets of ships see 465n.

247 The καί in this sentence has been variously analysed: (1) a scholion suggests 'thus Athena led him, speaking and with guile'; this analysis has the disadvantage of breaking up a speech-capping formula (ὣς φαμένη). (2) *GP* 308 takes καί as apodotic, the protasis uniquely taking the form of a participle: 'after having spoken thus, she led him with guile'. (3) Perhaps the singer, wanting to add κερδοσύνηι to two formulas (ὣς φαμένη and Παλλὰς Ἀθήνη (3x *Od.*)) and needing one more syllable, added a meaningless καί. ὣς φαμένη: although a present participle, φαμένη in this formula (4 x *Il.*, 5 x *Od.*) often has a past meaning (e.g. *Od.* 18.206, where it would be strange if Penelope came down her staircase *while* speaking rather intimate words to her servants) and is a metrical variant for the far more common ὣς εἴπουσα/ὣς ἄρα φωνήσασα. κερδοσύνηι 'in her cunning', almost adverbially 'cunningly'; it is, not surprisingly, found only with Athena (here) and Odysseus (*Od.* 4.251; 14.31). The abstract noun is derived from κέρδος, which means 'advantage (for oneself)', 'profit', pl. 'tricks', and refers to behaviour which is aimed at misleading another and thereby benefiting oneself. The word may have been chosen because Athena is not merely deceiving Hector (cf. 299) but at the same time preparing victory for herself and Achilles (cf. 216–17).

ἡγήσατ(ο): underscores Athena's active role in setting up the fight; she walks in front and leads the way, as generals lead their troops (cf. 12.251 = 13.833; 14.374) or Odysseus a delegation (9.192). It is a typical Homeric sleight-of-hand to let 'Deïphobus' disappear after this line (cf. 'Dymas' daughter'/Athena, who is not heard of again after she emphatically announces that she will accompany Nausicaa on her trip to the beach: *Od.* 6.31–2), and have only Hector and Achilles face each other (although Athena resurfaces suddenly and briefly at 276–7).

248–305

Finally, the fight between Hector and Achilles starts. The *Iliad* displays two kinds of single fights or *monomachiai*. There are (1) two ceremonial duels, when two heroes, representing the two armies, fight according to preagreed conditions while the rest of the army stops fighting to watch (Paris versus Menelaus at 3.67–382, and Hector versus Ajax at 7.37–312) and (2) numerous single fights which take place simultaneously between warriors in the frontline of each army (the *promachoi*) while the multitude (*plēthos*) keeps its distance. As van Wees (1994) 6 notes, 'the apparent isolation of individual "champions" is . . . to some extent an optical illusion, produced by the poet's habit of focusing on the actions of a few famous heroes amidst the general melée'. The fight between Hector and Achilles is a special, hybrid case: it is not really a ceremonial duel, since no terms are agreed upon beforehand, yet the rest of the armies do not fight but watch passively. For Homeric single fights see Latacz (1977) 81–4, 129–39, van Wees (1994, 1997), and Hellmann (2000) 122–34.

In its fullest form a single fight consists of the following elements: exchange of verbal challenges, exchange of missiles, hand-to-hand fight, death of one of the warriors, vaunt by victor, and stripping of armour. Most meetings between warriors in the *Iliad*, however, involve only one or two elements and are relatively brief ('hit-and-run attack(s)': van Wees (1997) 688). The longest fights are those between Patroclus and Sarpedon (16.419–507: 88 lines), Hector and Patroclus (16.777–867: 90 lines), and Hector and Achilles (22.248–369: 121 lines). As always, length indicates importance. These are the three most important single fights of the *Iliad*, which are causally related to each other: Patroclus kills Sarpedon, but is himself killed in turn by Hector, who is later killed by Achilles. Of these, the Patroclus-Hector and Hector-Achilles duels are crucially linked in that Achilles kills Hector to avenge Patroclus; the link is signalled both implicitly by verbal echoes (326–66n.) and explicitly by an analepsis or flashback (323n.). See also Introduction 2d.

The climactic meeting between the two main champions of the Greeks and Trojans consists of all of the standard stages: an exchange of verbal challenges (248–72); an exchange of missiles, expanded by two speeches by Hector and a divine intervention (273–305); hand-to-hand fighting (306–25); a protracted death scene which incorporates a vaunt by victorious Achilles while Hector is still alive and four more speeches (326–66); and a much expanded stripping of the armour (367–75).

248–72 After coming within reach of each other (σχεδόν) and hence within speaking distance, the warriors commence the customary exchange of challenges. These challenges mainly serve to pump up adrenalin, by insulting one's opponent and/or extolling oneself, only rarely to identify one's opponent. Most heroes – conventionally rather than realistically – simply know each other, see de Jong (2005) 15–17. A typical example is the exchange between Aeneas and Achilles at 20.176–258 (Achilles: 'Aeneas, why do you want to fight me? . . . Go back and do not oppose me, before you come to harm.' Aeneas: 'Achilles, do not think you will frighten me with words as if I were a child. I too know insulting words . . . So quickly now, let us try each other with our spears'); cf. 5.630–55; 6.121–211; 7.225–44; 21.148–61. For challenges see Létoublon (1983) and Stoevesandt (2004) 305–6, 424–7.

Achilles' challenge, bursting with self-confidence (and vindictive anger), is typical, but Hector's opening is untypically timid: instead of a confident announcement of imminent victory, there are (1) an admission of his earlier fear, (2) a hesitant potential 'I might kill you or be killed', and (3) a pacifying proposal concerning the treatment of the body of the vanquished. The exchange prefigures the supplication at 337–54, where Hector, by then mortally wounded, again asks for his body to be given back, only to be rebuffed by Achilles.

248–9 οἱ δ᾽ . . . , | τὸν . . . Ἕκτωρ: a pendant nominative (or frame), which is split up, literally 'and they, when they approached each other, him Hector addressed'. This is a fairly common phenomenon in the Homeric epics (*GH* II 15–16), a clear manifestation of their oral syntax (see 191–2n.).

248 This formulaic line typically introduces martial duels (10 x), once an athletic contest (23.816) and the approach of two armies (3.15).

249 This formulaic speech-introduction (10 x *Il.*, 1 x *Od.*) is used in situations where there is no prescribed rule as to who should talk first. πρότερος: suggests a speaker taking the initiative, either by way of apology (Paris at 6.517), in irritation (Apollo at 7.23), or as a challenge (here; 5.276; 6.122; 20.177; 21.149). προσέειπε: see 177n. μέγας κορυθαίολος Ἕκτωρ: see 232n.

250–3 The three consecutive skewed verses (33–7n.) are expressive of Hector's nervousness; cf. again 256–7. Hector's focalisation of his own behaviour mirrors that of the narrator: οὐ . . . φοβήσομαι ≈ βῆ . . . φοβηθείς (137); τρὶς περὶ ἄστυ . . . Πριάμου ≈ τρὶς Πριάμοιο πόλιν πέρι (165); οὐδέ . . . ἔτλην μεῖναι ≈ οὐδ᾽ . . . ἔτλη . . . μένειν (136–7). Whereas the narrator had added that Hector's fated moment of death had arrived as he circled the city a fourth time (208–13), the hero himself of course lacks this vital information.

250–1 'I will no longer run from you the way I fled three times before.' The verb δίω means 'to be afraid' (cf. δείδω), only here 'flee in fear'. The variant reading δίες, found in some MSS and papyri, is a rare active form of δίεμαι, 'pursue'; cf. ἐνδίεσαν (18.584). This would lead to a different syntactic analysis and punctuation of these lines: 'I will no longer run from you the way I did just before: (*explicative asyndeton*) for you pursued me three times.' σ' . . . φοβήσομαι: this verb (for which see 136–7n.) is only here construed with an object. ὡς τὸ πάρος περ: for τὸ πάρος see 233n. περ (73n.) is best taken with ὡς, like later ὥσπερ.

252 ἐπερχόμενον: sc. σε (from σ': 250). νῦν αὖτε: literally 'now conversely', αὖτε indicating that the 'now' contrasts with 'before'; see 119n. The combination occurs 12 x *Il.* and *Od.* (cf. 303), always in direct speech. For the prominence of 'now' at this crucial stage of the narrative see 216–23n. θυμὸς ἀνῆκεν: Hector does not refer to 'Deïphobus'/Athena's intervention, which actually had made him abandon his flight and take a stand. Indeed, her presence seems forgotten by narrator and heroes alike until 276. It is typically Homeric to say 'my *thumos* has incited me to do X' rather than 'I have decided to do X'.

253 στήμεναι: infinitive (L 11). ἀντία: neuter plural of ἀντίος, used adverbially (with genitive). ἕλοιμί κεν, ἤ κεν ἀλοίην: potential optatives, which sketch two alternatives both deemed (equally) possible by the speaker; cf. τὰ δέ κεν θεὸς ἤ τελέσειεν, ἤ κ' ἀτέλεστ' εἴη (*Od.* 8.570–1). For the sentiment 'to kill or be killed' see 108–10n. The aorist εἷλον in Homer is one of the many (*ca.* 20) verbs of killing; cf. ἔνθ' ἕλε Θερσίλοχον . . . καί νύ κ' ἔτι πλέονας κτάνε (*Il.* 21.209–11). For an overview see Visser (1987) 58–65.

254 ἀλλ' ἄγε δεῦρο 'but come'. δεῦρο is an adverb ('hither') which is also used as an exhortative particle, like ἄγε, ἄγετε (174n.), with which it is often combined. As usual the main verb follows asyndetically. θεοὺς ἐπιδώμεθα 'let us give each other the gods (as witnesses) to (what we agree)'; the expression virtually amounts to 'let us swear'. In the duels of books 3 and 7, too, an oath (3.276–91) and solemn declaration (7.76–91) are found, both accompanied by invocations of the gods. The middle ἐπιδίδομαι only occurs here and, as a variant adopted by Aristarchus, at 10.463. There the majority of MSS have ἐπιβωσόμεθα, 'we shall call upon', which is here found as a variant (ἐπιβώμεθα), and cf. *Od.* 1.378 = 2.143. τοί: anaphoric pronoun (L 17).

255 μάρτυροι . . . ἐπίσκοποι: the gods are witnesses (μάρτυροι) of the making of an agreement *now* and guardians (ἐπίσκοποι) of mortals adhering to it *in the future*. The same idea is expressed at 3.280 as 'you (gods) are witnesses (μάρτυροι) and watch over (φυλάσσετε) all oaths', and cf. 7.76 'may Zeus be our ἐπιμάρτυρος'. It is an ancient and universal function of gods to see everything and, if necessary, intervene to punish evil-doers, including oath-breakers. Whether the Homeric gods always live up to this ideal is debated; see Yamagata (1994), van Erp Taalman Kip (2000), and Allan (2006). The MSS regularly hesitate between μάρτυροι (from μάρτυρος, adjective used as substantive) and μάρτυρες (from μάρτυς, substantive). ἁρμονιάων: this word is used here figuratively, 'agreement', but elsewhere concretely, 'joints' (to connect the wooden beams of Odysseus' raft: *Od.* 5.248). The word will be picked up in Achilles' reaction by συνημοσύνας and ὅρκια. The preponderance of these types of words gives a legalistic ring to the exchange.

256–9 On the occasion of an earlier duel, too, Hector suggested that he and his opponent treat each other's bodies decently after death (7.77–91); see Thornton (1984) 68 and Kirk on 7.79–80. Hector's preoccupation with this topic from early on in the narrative adds to the suspense and pathos around the theme of the mutilation of his body (337–54n.). However, it should be noted Hector has no qualms about considering mistreating Patroclus' corpse (cf. 16.836; 17.125–7; 18.175–7).

256 γάρ: this is the typical γάρ 'after an expression denoting the giving or receiving of information, or conveying a summons to attention' (*GP* 59). It introduces the 'text' of the oath/agreement that Hector proposes. ἐγώ: the emphatic use of the personal pronoun prepares for σύ; the two pronouns together underline the reciprocity of the agreement. ἔκπαγλον: adverb from *ἔκπλαγλος (cf. ἐκπλήσσω, ἐκπλαγῆναι), which means 'striking', both in a positive ('wonderful') and, more often, in a negative sense ('vehement'). It is usually combined with ἐπεύξατο, 'he boasted in an excessive way', and only here with ἀεικίω: 'I will not defile your body outrageously (= which would be outrageous)'. ἀεικίω: future of ἀεικίζω, 'to mutilate', either by leaving a body for dogs and birds or by cutting off parts of it. As a result, the mutilated body becomes ἀεικής, 'unseemly'. See also 395n. MSS hesitate between ἀεικίω and ἀεικιῶ. *GH* I 451 defends the older form ἀεικίω < ἀεικίσω, which is also adopted by West in his text.

257 δώηι καμμονίην 'will give me endurance', i.e. the power to stay and hold out against you (cf. μένω); the same expression recurs at 23.661 at the same place in the verse, but in the context of an athletic rather than martial confrontation. The use of this rare expression, instead of the more usual 'will give me victory' (e.g. 7.292), may have been triggered here by the preceding οὐδέ ποτ' ἔτλην | μεῖναι. σὴν . . . ψυχὴν ἀφέλωμαι: one of the innumerable expressions for 'kill' in Homer (253n.). This is a – perhaps more expressive – variant of the common θυμὸν ἀφέλωμαι (5.852, 17.17; *Od.* 14.405), which recurs once with slight variation (24.754: ἐξέλετο ψυχήν).

258 κλυτὰ τεύχε': this formulaic expression occurs 16 x in the *Il.*, 2 x in the *Od.*; of these 18 instances, six concern Achilles' old armour, five his new (here; 18.144, 147; 19.10; 22.399), which we 'saw' Hephaestus making in book 18. κλυτός means 'famous', but lexica tend to weaken its meaning to 'glorious' or 'beautiful' in cases like the present, where, strictly speaking, the armour has just been made and can hardly be said to be famous. The word may, however, be metapoetical or self-referential: Achilles' armour instantly is famous because it forms part of a famous narrative. For Homer's self-confidence regarding his own poems see de Jong (2006). Ἀχιλλεῦ: the renewed insertion of a vocative (cf. 250) underscores the urgency of Hector's appeal.

259 νεκρὸν . . . δώσω πάλιν: during his earlier duel with Ajax, Hector had worked out this idea more fully: 'I will give back the body, so the Greeks may embalm it and heap a mound over it' (7.84–91). Normal practice is that the comrades of a fallen warrior fight to recover his body, preferably including his armour. In the case of (quasi-)ceremonial duels, where no such comrades are around, it makes sense to make arrangements of the type proposed by Hector. ῥέζειν: the infinitive is used as imperative, a common phenomenon in Homer; see 342–3n. Hector here uses it to imply that in light of the proposed agreement (ἁρμονιάων), Achilles is obliged to reciprocate his offer. After this verse one papyrus reads lines 342–3, which are, however, redundant after ὡς δὲ σὺ ῥέζειν.

260 ὑπόδρα ἰδών: lit. 'looking from under gathered and lowered brows'; <*ὑπό-δρακ, from ὑπό and the aorist ἔδρακον (δέρκομαι). This recurrent speech-introduction (17 x *Il.*, 9 x *Od.*), discussed by Holoka (1983) and Cairns (2003) 42–3, immediately bodes ill for Hector: it indicates irritation and anger with an element of threat, which is provoked when the speaker's *timē* is offended by rude or inconsiderate words, usually spoken by an inferior. Here and at 344 the expression 'prefaces speeches which express implacable hatred, desire for vengeance, and determination utterly to extinguish the prestige that Hector has won in killing Patroclus . . . the speech thus introduced gives off a strong flavour of contempt' (Cairns (2003) 43).

261–72 Achilles answers Hector in the usual reverse order: (Hector) '(A) I will no longer flee but make a stand, (B) but let us agree to give back the body of the vanquished' – (Achilles) '(B') There can be no agreements or friendship between you and me, so (A') now you will have to prove yourself a warrior, and there is no escape'.

261 μή μοι . . . ἀγόρευε: the force of the present tense is '*stop* talking to me about agreements'; cf. 38n. μοι is best taken with ἀγόρευε; cf. τῶι πάντ' ἀγορευέμεν, 'tell him everything' (9.369). An alternative interpretation would be to take it as an 'ethic' dative (38n.). ἄλαστε: the etymology and mean-ing of this adjective, usually found with πένθος (3 x) or ἄχος (1 x), only here in connection with a person, have been disputed from antiquity. Chantraine in his *DELG*, with some hesitation, opts for the connection with λανθάνω, 'forget'. An interpretation 'doer of unforgettable deeds' (following the scho-lion ad loc.) would suit the context, since Achilles will soon come to speak of Hector killing Patroclus (272). Others opt for 'fierce' (*LfgrE*) or 'accursed' (Richardson). συνημοσύνας 'agreements' (*hapax*), from συνίημι, 'come to terms' (13.381).

262–6 ὡς οὐκ ἔστι . . . ὣς οὐκ ἔστ' 'just as there exist no agreements between lions and men, and wolves and lambs have no mutual sympathy, in that way we cannot be friends or have oaths'. Similes and comparisons occur much less frequently in speeches than in narrator-text: the figures for the *Iliad* are 46 of a total of 346. Achilles utters not only the greatest number (8, as against Hector 5), but also the longest (9.323–7, 385, 648 = 16.59; 16.7–11; 18.109–10; 21.282–3; 22.262–6). His fondness for similes has been qualified as a characterising trait by scholars; see Moulton (1977) 100–116, Friedrich, Redfield (1978) 273, and Griffin (1986) 53.

The comparison, with the lions/wolves obviously standing for Achilles and the men/lambs for Hector, has a double significance: intended by Achilles to convey his absolute implacability and superiority in the upcoming confrontation with Hector, to the narratees it signals his present 'wildness', his animal-like lack of pity and respect after the death of Patroclus, which will only stop after his meeting with Priam. Thus at 18.318–22 and 20.164–75 he is compared to a lion; at 21.314 the river Scamandrius calls him ἄγριος; at 22.346–7 Achilles says that he would like to eat Hector's flesh raw; and at 24.39–45 Apollo says that Achilles behaves like a lion (cf. especially λέων δ' ὣς ἄγρια οἶδεν: 41). See Moulton (1977) 113–14, Clarke (1995) 144–7, and Kim (2000) 141. For Achilles' behaviour see also Introduction 2e.

262 οὐκ ἔστι . . . ὅρκια πιστά 'there do not exist reliable agreements, sanctified by oaths'.

263 A simile at 16.352–5 graphically paints a murderous confrontation between wolves and lambs, the latter being 'snatched from under their mothers' and 'torn apart' by the former. τε καί: this combination is used (instead of simple καί) in the case of natural pairs. It suggests that wolves and lambs are a proverbial pair of natural enemies; indeed, we may be dealing here with (a Greek echo of) 'a cliché of oriental rhetoric' (West (1997) 394–5, with examples). ὁμόφρονα θυμόν: the adjective occurs only here in Homer, but cf. ὁμοφρονέω (2 x) and ὁμοφροσύνη (2 x) in the Od. It literally means 'having one (ὁμός) mind (φρήν)', which amounts to 'harmonious', 'with mutual sympathy'. In combination with *thumos* the etymology seems forgotten; cf. μεγαλήτορα θυμόν (98) and θυμῶι πρόφρονι (183–4) .

265–6 ἔστ' 'it is possible'. φιλήμεναι = φιλεῖν. οὐδέ τι . . . ἔσσονται 'and there will be no . . . at all' (τι adverbial). νῶϊν 'for the two of us' (dual personal pronoun of the first person: L 19).

266–7 '(and there will be no agreements between us) before one of us at least (γε), fallen, has satiated Ares with his blood'. Achilles' formulation amounts to a strong denial: there will only be an agreement when one of the two is dead (and is no longer able to make agreements at all) = there will *never* be an agreement. The same type of expression occurs at 1.29–31; 8.164–6; 16.628–9; 18.282–3; and 24.550–1. πρίν ἤ': this combination effectively means the same as simple πρίν; it occurs only here and at 5.288 but is common in Ionic prose (e.g. Herodotus *Histories* 1.79). Originally an adverb, πρίν also functions as a conjunction, in Homer mainly with the (aorist) infinitive (cf. 156) but occasionally with other moods. The MSS hesitate between πρίν ἤ' and πρίν γ' ἤ', the first being slightly preferable (see Leaf on 5.288); the ι of πρίν was originally long by nature. For ἤ' instead of ἤ see 108–10n. ταλαύρινον 'carrying a leather shield' (*ταλάϝρινος, from ϝρινός, 'ox-hide', 'shield', and ταλάσσαι/τλῆναι, 'to bear'). This is a particularised epithet of Ares: cf. 5.289; 20.78.

268–71 Challenging Hector to fight, Achilles turns to asyndeton, which conveys urgency and perhaps impatience: 'Call to mind . . . Now is the time . . . There is no escape any longer.'

268 παντοίης ἀρετῆς μιμνήσκεο 'call to mind your various fighting abilities'. The combination παντοί- ἀρετ- occurs twice more, at the same place in the verse, and refers to different abilities in warfare (15.642: running, fighting, intelligence) or in general (*Od.* 18.205). Here it might refer to the various forms of fighting (with spear, sword, stones) which belong to a single fight. In Homer, the verb μιμνήσκομαι (related to the root *men-, found in μέμονα and Latin *memini*) primarily means 'muster and direct one's thoughts and energy at' (e.g. νόστου μιμνήσκεσθαι, 'to think of return': *Od.* 3.142), only at times specifically 'remember' (e.g. καὶ κεῖθι φίλου μεμνήσομ' ἑταίρου: 390), the common meaning in later Greek. See *LfgrE* s.v. Only here the verb is connected with ἀρετῆς, the usual combination being μιμνήσκεσθαι ἀλκῆς, 'to think of courage'. For the opposite, 'to forget courage', see 282n. Martin (1989) 84 suggests that, since this type of expression is usually employed by a commander urging on his own troops, its use here by Achilles against Hector may be insulting.

270–1 οὔ . . . ἔτ': Achilles ominously echoes Hector's οὔ . . . ἔτι (250): 'I will *no longer* flee you' becomes 'there will *no longer* be an escape for you'. τοι = σοι. ὑπάλυξις 'escape' (a *hapax*). Παλλὰς Ἀθήνη | ἔγχει ἐμῶι δαμάαι: for this use of δάμνημι + instrumental dative see 175–6n. δαμάαι is future of δάμνημι. The form is created by diectasis (L 4): δαμάαι (⌣ ⌣ –) < δαμᾶι (⌣ –) < δαμάει (⌣ ⌣ –). Achilles is using the information here that he got from Athena at 216–21. How exactly she will kill Hector will become clear at 276–7 and 326–7: she gives Achilles his spear back after an ineffective throw, and his second thrust, from close range, is successful and mortal.

271–2 'but now you will pay for everything in one go, my sorrows because of my comrades, whom you killed raging with your spear'. Cf. νῦν δ' ἀθρόα πάντ' ἀπέτεισε (*Od.* 1.43) and νῦν μὲν δὴ . . . ἦ μάλα τείσεις | γνωτὸν ἐμόν, τὸν ἔπεφνες (17.34–5). ἀθρόα: scholars are divided as to whether it should be ἀθρόα or ἀθρόα; for discussion see *LfgrE* s.v. ἀποτείσεις: future of ἀποτίνω. For the variation in MSS between ἀποτείσεις and ἀποτίσεις see 20n. κήδε' ἐμῶν ἑτάρων is in apposition to πάντ'; it is therefore best to place a comma after ἀποτείσεις. ἐμῶν ἑτάρων is objective genitive; Achilles is of course thinking primarily of Patroclus (cf. 321–3). He had first announced his intention to make Hector pay for his friend's death at 18.91–3: (I do not want to live) αἴ κε μὴ Ἕκτωρ . . . ἀπὸ θυμὸν ὀλέσσηι, Πατρόκλοιο δ' ἕλωρα . . . ἀποτείσηι, 'unless Hector dies and pays the price for his taking of Patroclus'; cf. also 21.133–4. ἔγχεϊ θυίων: the expression is typically used of warriors wreaking havoc amongst their opponents; cf. 11.180; 16.699; 20.493. According to West 1, xxxi, the best MSS have θυίων rather than θύων.

273–363 The usual Homeric pattern of two warriors fighting together is: (1) A throws at B and misses; (2) B strikes A's shield or body armour but fails to pierce it; (3) A kills B; see Fenik (1968) 6. This pattern is expanded here in accordance with the special occasion: (1) Achilles throws at Hector and misses (but is given back his spear by Athena); (2) Hector strikes Achilles' shield but fails to pierce it (he asks 'Deiphobus' for another spear, finds out that he has gone, and then attacks with his sword.); (3) Achilles slays him.

273 The fight begins routinely, the narrator employing a line which occurs 6 x more in the *Il.* (e.g. 289). ἦ ῥα καί: for ἦ see 77n. καί indicates that a speaker suits the action to the word; it therefore seems best not to print a comma after ἦ ῥα as most editors do. ἀμπεπαλών: aorist participle of ἀναπάλλω (with apocope ἀνα > ἀν, assimilation > ἀμ, and reduplication), 'swinging up to and to and fro' (before casting the spear). For this gesture cf. Αἴας πῆλ' . . . ἐν χειρὶ κόλον δόρυ (16.117), and see 311n. δολιχόσκιον ἔγχος: most probably 'casting a long shadow' (from δολιχός, 'long' and σκιά, 'shadow'); for other analyses see *LfgrE* s.v. This is one of many epithets for 'spear'; see Dee (2002) 204–9. It occurs 21 x *Il.*, 5 x *Od.*

274–5 'and Hector avoided it (sc. Achilles' ἔγχος): for he crouched down, and it flew over him, the bronze spear'. A typical specimen of oral syntax: at the end of the sentence, the singer feels the need to make clear (again) what τό refers to. Warriors often manage to dodge spears thrown at them. Thus line 274 recurs in almost identical form 6 x *Il.*, and 275b recurs at 13.408. The spear either hits another warrior instead (2 x) or, as here, gets stuck in the ground. ἄντα ἰδών 'looking straight ahead' (and thus anticipating the direction of the cast). φαίδιμος Ἕκτωρ: φαίδιμος is a generic epithet which is found with Hector (29 x), Ajax (6 x), and Achilles (4 x). It is studied in detail by Sacks (1987) 105–51, who suggests – not entirely convincingly – that it is used in contexts where Hector is 'retreating, deluded, defeated, and finally, essentially, dead' and hence would implicitly convey Homer's rejection of the 'shining' norms of heroism.

275–7 The series of six half-line clauses suggests speed; cf. 210–13n. There are more instances of gods returning a spear (20.322–4; a whip at 23.382–90), warding off blows (4.128–33; 8.311; 20.438–41), or breaking a spear/string of a bow (13.562–5; 15.461–5). Athena returning Achilles' spear may be a rationalised version of the folktale motif of a spear returning magically to its owner; see 322n. The detail that Athena's intervention is not seen by Hector heightens the tension and prepares for the tragic delusion of Hector claiming that Achilles was wrong in announcing his death (279–82). Athena's act forms part of a sustained deceitful intervention on behalf of Achilles; see 208–47n.

276 Παλλὰς Ἀθήνη: verse-end formula (23 x *Il.*, 18 x *Od.*). The etymology and meaning of the epithet are unclear: 'mistress', 'maiden'? It is used only in literature, not in cultic texts. For secondary literature see *LfgrE* s.v. Παλλάς.

277 Ἀχιλῆϊ δίδου, λάθε δ' Ἕκτορα: an example of parataxis (L 23): Athena gave back the spear and escaped = *while* escaping the notice of Hector. ποιμένα λαῶν 'shepherd of men'. This verse-end formula occurs frequently in connection with kings (44 x *Il.*, 18 x *Od.*). The metaphor is common in oriental texts, from which it might be derived (West (1997) 226–7), and is worked out in comparisons at 3.196–8 and 13.491–5. For a full discussion see Haubold (2000) 17–24.

278 προσέειπεν: see 177n. ἀμύμονα: see 111–13n.

279–88 Hector's speech is a variant of the motif of the 'premature boast': cf. 5.101–5, 283–5; 11.380–3. He can boast only that Achilles has not wounded him, whereas it would be normal for a warrior to vaunt that he had (mortally) wounded his opponent. He goes on to claim that he will not flee but instead attack Achilles. As in his first challenging speech (250–9), he does not sound convinced. As Stoevesandt (2004) 326–7 remarks, his words are less a provocation than a self-exhortation, a sign of the continuous struggle with the fear of dying that we have seen him engaged in since 92.

279–82 'It turns out (ἄρα) that you did not in any way (οὐδ'... πω) know at all (τι) my fate from Zeus (i.e. for sure). You *said* you did, but you lied, in order to frighten me'. ἤτοι (this spelling is to be preferred to ἦ τοι: *GP* 553) has the same force as preparatory μέν; see Ruijgh (1981). While limitative γε indicates that ἔφης contrasts with preceding οὐδ'... ἠείδης, ἤτοι indicates that another contrast is about to follow (ἀλλά). Others (Leaf, Richardson) take ἤτοι as adversative and put a semi-colon after γε ('You did not know my death for sure; yet you thought you did'). Cf. 16.60–3; *Od.* 11.430–4.

For the sentiment cf. Aeneas and Hector to Achilles at 20.200–2 = 431–3 ('Do not think you will frighten me with words as if I were a child').

279 ἤμβροτες: aorist of ἁμαρτάνω. θεοῖς ἐπιείκελ' Ἀχιλλεῦ: a regular vocative formula for Achilles after the feminine caesura (5 x *Il.*, 1 x *Od.*). Shive (1987) 111–14 suggests that the formula is not used automatically but only when effective, as e.g. at 9.494–5, when Phoenix says ἀλλά σὲ παῖδα, θεοῖς ἐπιείκελ' Ἀχιλλεῦ, | ποιεύμην, which virtually amounts to 'I made you the godlike man you are'. Here it could be argued that Hector is using the epithet in effective contrast to οὐδ'... ἐκ Διὸς ἠείδης: 'although you are godlike, your present claim about my fate has no divine origin'.

280 ἐκ Διὸς ἠείδης: ἠείδης is the pluperfect of (ϝ)οἶδα, with an augment η- instead of ε-, which is found before roots starting with ϝ; see *GH* I 479. For the combination 'to know from the gods' cf. θεῶν ἄπο μήδεα εἰδώς (*Od.* 6.12). ἔφης: φήμι means 'to think', 'imagine', 'declare', i.e., it introduces a subjective or illusory claim; see Fournier (1946) 3–39. In speech-capping formulas like ὡς ἄρ' ἔφη it has weakened to the neutral 'say'. Hector refers to Achilles' claim that Hector would surely die by his and Athena's hands (270–1).

281 ἀρτιεπής '(someone) who can fit together (ἀραρίσκω) words (ἔπος)', with the connotation of being so good at this that one can even sell lies as truth ('glib'). Thus at *Od.* 11.364–6 Alcinous talks about an ἐπίκλοπος man, of the type that puts together lies (ψεύδεα ἀρτύνοντας); at Hesiod *Theogony* 29 the Muses, who themselves admit that they also tell ψεύδεα (27), are called ἀρτιέπειαι. ἐπίκλοπος... μύθων 'cunning or skillful in words', cf. ἐπίκλοπος τόξων, 'skilful with the bow'. Since ἐπίκλοπος contains the root κλοπ- from κλέπτω, 'steal', it has a connotation of deceit, like ἀρτιεπής. ἔπλεο 'you turned out to be'; see 116n.

282 ὑποδδείσας: see 19n. μένεος ἀλκῆς τε λάθωμαι 'I would forget my energy and valour'. The combination ἀλκῆς λανθάνω is common (6 x *Il.*), but the combination μένεος ἀλκῆς τε occurs only here, but cf. (with a different construction) μή μ' ἀπογυιώσηις μένεος, ἀλκῆς τε λάθωμαι (6.265). Hector picks up Achilles' παντοίης ἀρετῆς μιμνήσκεο (268); an instance of the 'catchword' technique (185n.).

283–4 'me you will surely not while I am fleeing fix a spear in the back, but while I am charging straight on, drive it through my chest'. Hector emphatically uses a polar expression: οὐ . . . φεύγοντι corresponds to ἰθὺς μεμαῶτι, and μεταφρένωι to διὰ στήθεσφιν. μέν = μήν (13n.). μοι: dative of person involved, on which both participles depend. στήθεσφιν: the suffix -φιν forms the equivalent to a genitive plural (L 9). ἔλασσον: sc. δόρυ, 'drive a spear'; aorist imperative of ἐλάω, with metrical doubling of the -σ- (L 3).

285–6 εἴ τοι ἔδωκε θεός 'if a god really granted you this', sc. to hit me. The aorist in this context is common, cf. e.g. νῦν ἡμῖν πάντων Ζεὺς ἄξιον ἦμαρ ἔδωκε, 'now Zeus gave us a day that repays us for all' (15.719). For the gods 'giving' mortals things see 403–4n. The use of εἰ + indicative expresses a certain scepticism on the part of the speaker; see Rijksbaron (2002) 68, note 2. With this afterthought Hector returns to 279–80 and once more tries to play down Achilles' reference to Athena's support at 270–1. νῦν αὖτ' ἐμὸν ἔγχος ἄλευαι '(You missed.) Now in turn avoid *my* spear'; cf. τὸ μὲν . . . ἠλεύατο (274). ἄλευαι is aorist imperative of ἀλέ(ϝ)ομαι.

286 ὥς . . . κομίσαιο 'would that you took it home fully in your flesh'. The optative expressing a wish in Homer is generally introduced by εἰ γάρ, εἴθε, occasionally by ὥς, as here and 18.107; *Od.* 1.47; 14.503. κομίζω means 'take care of', 'take home'; here (and at 14.456) it is used metaphorically, by way of grisly sarcasm. Such sarcastic metaphors are common in the context of challenges and vaunts, cf. e.g. Patroclus about Cebriones, who has just fallen dead from his chariot: 'Oh this is really an agile man, a ready acrobat' (16.745) and 373n.

287–8 καί at the opening of a main clause has consecutive force, 'and as a result'. ἐλαφρότερος: the step from 'light in weight' to figuratively 'easy to bear' is easy to make, just as in the case of βαρύς, 'heavy' = 'hard to bear'. This metaphorical use occurs only here in Homer. σεῖο καταφθιμένοιο: the genitive absolute (which in Homer is still relatively rare) repeats the idea of 286. σφισι 'for them', personal pronoun of the third person plural (L 19). πῆμα: often of persons who bring disaster, calamity to other people; cf. 3.160; 10.453; 11.347; and see also 421–2n.

289–95 This passage nicely shows the variety in formulas which singers had at their disposal: δολιχόσκιον ἔγχος – δόρυ – βέλος ὠκύ – μείλινον ἔγχος – δόρυ μακρόν. It is hard to attach contextual significance to the different epithets.

289 See 273n.

290–1 The polar expression 'he hit and did not miss' is also found at 11.350; 13.160; and 21.591 (and cf. the closely similar 11.376). However, hitting is no guarantee of effectively wounding someone, since in all these cases the missile rebounds from the armour or breaks off at the socket. The narrator might have explained that Hector's spear did not pierce Achilles' shield because it was divinely made (as he did at 20.259–72 and 21.594). Taplin (1992) 242 suggests that his suppressing this detail 'makes Hector's failure seem horribly perfunctory'. μέσον σάκος '(hit) the shield at the centre' (μέσον predicatively).

291–2 χώσατο . . . | . . . χειρός = 14.406–7 (again of Hector). The aorist χώσατο is ingressive: 'he was angered'. The ὅττι-clause gives us Hector's focalisation, as the possessive dative οἱ (L 22) with βέλος, 'his spear' also suggests. We find a similar reaction at 13.165–6, where Meriones 'was terribly angered (χώσατο) on two accounts, because of the victory (which was denied to him) and his spear, which had broken'. ἐτώσιον 'ineffectively', 'fruitlessly'; the etymology of this word, which is used often in connection with missiles being thrown, is unknown.

293 στῆ . . . κατηφήσας, οὐδ' . . . ἔχε 'he stood there downcast, and (= for) he did not have'; an instance of parataxis (L 23). The combination of the participle and στῆ suggests that Hector was in a *state* of shock for some time; cf. the closely similar στῆ . . . ταφών, 'he stood there dazed' at 16.806 (when Patroclus has been stripped of his armour by Apollo) and 24.360 (when Priam has spotted 'the young Myrmidon'/Hermes in the dark). The etymology of the root κατηφ- is unclear, but it conveys a mixture of grief and shame. The expression, which occurs only here, therefore nicely suits the modulations of Hector's emotions: he shifts from being angry to downcast (when he realises that he has no other spear), and then resigned (when he realises that he has been abandoned by the gods). Though Hector usually carries two spears (cf. 5.495; 6.104, etc.), it is dramatically apt that the narrator here has endowed him with only one, like his opponent Achilles (and as in the ceremonial single fights: 3.338, 340–60; 7.244–54).

294–5 ἐκάλει . . . | ἤιτεε: the scholia perceptively note that the urgent asyndeton triggers our pity here. They are less correct in taking the two verbs to be a repetition: ἐκάλει means that Hector calls Deïphobus' name to attract his attention (hence the addition of μακρὸν ἀΰσας), while ἤιτεε indicates that he asks him for something. We may imagine him to shout (repeatedly): 'Deïphobus, your spear!'

294 λευκάσπιδα: a unique epithet; 'it is as if Hektor were looking all around the battlefield for this conspicuous sign of his brother's presence . . . only to find emptiness and silence' (Richardson). Deïphobus' shield had played a prominent role in book 13 (he advances under cover of it, and his opponent breaks his spear on it: 156–66), and it may be supposed to be a characteristic piece of his armour, although the visual detail of its whiteness is reserved for this place. The white may be due to painting, or to an alloy of gold and silver. White shields are the stock attribute of the Argives in Greek tragedy; see e.g. Euripides *Phoenissae*

1099 and Mastronarde (1994) ad loc. μακρὸν ἀΰσας 'shouting loudly'; ἀΰσας is a coincident aorist participle (15–16n.).This expression usually occurs in contexts where warriors have to raise their voice because of the noise of the battle; here it may suggest Hector's panic.

295 ὁ δ' οὔ τί οἱ ἐγγύθεν ἦεν 'but he was by no means near to him'. In ἐγγύθεν the original force of -θεν, 'from where', has weakened, and the form is a metrical variant of simple ἐγγύς. The half verse is likely to represent Hector's focalisation.

296–305 Plato called Homer 'the first of the tragedians' (*Republic* 607A), and this is one of the places that support this qualification. It presents the moment of insight (what Aristotle calls *anagnōrisis*; cf. ἔγνω), when a hero suddenly sees his true predicament. Actually, Hector had already acknowledged his own error (in not listening to Polydamas) at 101–7, but now he realises a much more profound truth: the divine support which had enabled his spectacular recent successes was temporary, it had not been given for his own sake, and it was part of a larger plan which had entailed his own death almost from the start. In other words, only now does he realise his true role in the *Dios boulē*, which the narratees have known about for a long time; see Introduction 2b and 2d. Hector's insight also has much to tell us about the divine in Homer: 'the *Iliad* is concerned with the relation of men and gods; and its plot . . . shows the divine as deceitful, leading men into disaster and to the insight, too late, that events have all the time been guided in a direction quite different from that which they imagined' (Griffin (1990) 355).

To be awarded this moment of insight just prior to his death confirms Hector's role as one of the main figures of the *Iliad* and the Homeric narrator's profound interest in and sympathy for the Trojans. We may note that Patroclus, whose death in many respects resembles that of Hector (see 326–66n.), is not given such insight: at 16.844–50 he speaks about the gods destroying him but does not reflect on his own error (made at 685–91) or show awareness of being part of the *Dios boulē* (cf. 15.64–8).

Hector's insight is complete: he understands that he has been deceived by Athena, concludes that Zeus and Apollo no longer protect him, and realises that his moment of death has come (earlier he had still believed he could win). From now on he will no longer fight for his life but for a heroic death.

296 The same line occurs almost verbatim at 1.333 = 8.446, in less dramatic situations (a character understands why other characters are silent). ἔγνω: absolute, 'he understood' (the situation he was in). ᾗσιν: possessive pronoun (L 18).

297 ὢ πόποι: see 168n. ἦ μάλα δή: see 229n. At first sight it may seem odd to find interactional particles in a monologue, because they presuppose an addressee, but Homeric monologues are in fact *Selbstgespräche*, dialogues between a speaker and his *thumos* (cf. 98n.). με θεοὶ θανατόνδε κάλεσσαν 'the gods called me to death', a sinister variant of calling someone to one's house for dinner (*Od.* 11.410: οἶκόνδε καλέσσας), to be put on a par with 'my (death-)fate has reached me' (303), rather than, as Ameis-Hentze suggest, taken as a reference to Athena literally summoning him to make a stand at 231, 243. The narrator had used the same words at 16.693, apostrophising Patroclus: 'whom did you kill, Patroclus', ὅτε δή σε θεοὶ θάνατόνδε κάλεσσαν; the repetition is one of the many points of contact between the deaths of these two heroes (326–66n.). At the same time there is a marked difference in that here the words are spoken by Hector, who is given exceptional insight into his own role in the machinations of the gods. See Griffin (1980) 42 and Rutherford (1982) 157.

298 Δηΐφοβον... ἥρωα: personal names in Homer are regularly accompanied by the qualification 'hero' in both narrator-text and speeches; this is the only instance in which the two words are separated. The etymology of ἥρως is unclear. In Mycenaean Greek it presumably referred to a special rank ('lord', 'master'), but it had become a general qualification of persons belonging to the leading class of heroic society by the time of the Homeric epics. ἐφάμην: for this verb see 28on. According to Fournier (1946) 34, there is no semantic difference between the active and middle forms of this verb, which are merely used as metrical alternatives. This position is defended, in the context of a discussion of a larger group of synonymous active and middle verbs, by Allan (2003) 207–8.

299 ἐξαπάτησεν: the verb means deceiving by picturing a false reality, here Athena pretending to be Deïphobus and on Hector's side. Cf. Odysseus inwardly laughing that his false name 'Nobody' ἐξαπάτησεν the Cyclops (Od. 9.414). Ἀθήνη: Homeric heroes do not always identify the specific god of an intervention (instead, they tend to speak in general terms of *theoi* or *daimon*, e.g 15.468), but at this crucial moment Hector is endowed with infallible insight.

300 The idea that 'death is near (ἐγγύθι, ἐγγύθεν, ἄγχι)' is also expressed elsewhere (at 16.853 and 18.133 in connection with Hector's death; at 19.409 and 24.132 with Achilles' death). Voiced here by Hector about himself, the expression is given extra force in two ways: it is turned into a polar expression ('death is near and not far any longer') and it contrasts with 295 (Deïphobus is *not* near, but death is). νῦν δὲ δή 'and now clearly'. See 216–23n. for the significant preponderance of νῦν at this stage of the story. ἐγγύθι: the original force of -θι, indicating the place where, has largely disappeared and the form, like ἐγγύθεν, is a metrical variant for simple ἐγγύς. θάνατος κακός: this combination recurs six times. It belongs to the character-language: 3 x direct speech (here; 3.173; Od. 24.153), 2 x embedded focalisation (21.66; Od. 22.14), and once in an obviously emotional comment of the narrator (16.47). For an overview of the epithets of θάνατος see Dee (2002) 255–6. ἄνευθεν: an adverb formed from (adverbial) ἄνευ, 'away from', with the ending -θεν, which originally indicates the place from where, but which, as in ἐγγύθεν (295), here has lost its specific force.

301 οὐδ' ἀλέη 'and (there is) no escape'; the word occurs only here in Homer. Hector echoes Achilles' earlier οὔ τοι ἔτ' ἔσθ' ὑπάλυξις (270). ἦ: Hector confirms (to himself) the objective truth of what he says; see 40n. ῥα... ἦεν: although the particle ἄρα is used so widely in Homer that it often lacks significance

(98n.), here, in combination with the imperfect, it has its well known force of 'surprise attendant upon disillusionment': 'the reality of a past event is presented as apprehended . . . at the moment of speaking' (see *GP* 36–7 and Ruijgh (1971) 434–8). πάλαι: see 179n. τό 'that', sc. my death.

302–3 Zeus and Apollo have indeed supported and even saved Hector many times during the past days of battle, e.g. (Zeus) 8.216; 11.163–4; 12.252–5, 436–8; 13.347–8; 15.461–4, 596–9; (Apollo) 15.260–2, 326–7; 20.443–4; 22.203–4; see Reichel (1994) 157–75. ἑκηβόλωι: as in the case of ἑκάεργος (15–16n.), the meaning may be either 'hitting from afar' or 'hitting at will'. πρόφρονες: literally 'with forward mind', i.e. 'energetic', 'sincere'. Cf. Hector earlier: 'I know that Zeus πρόφρων has granted me victory and great glory' (8.175–6). εἰρύατο: pluperfect (with imperfect force) of ἔρυμαι, 'they used to protect me'. For the ending -ατο see L 14. νῦν αὖτε 'now in turn'; αὖτε marks the change in situation, from rescue to death (see 119n.). με μοῖρα κιχάνει: although the expression 'death and fate (have) reached X' is common (cf. 436 = 17.478 = 17.672), it here has extra force. At 16.852–4 Hector's death had been prophesied to him by Patroclus (cf. esp. τοι ἤδη | ἄγχι παρέστηκεν θάνατος καὶ μοῖρα κραταιή); he shrugged it off then but now realises that fate, which he had so far been able to escape, has finally 'overtaken' him. For this meaning of κιχάνω cf. e.g. 21.602–6 (Achilles is pursuing Agenor, all the time hoping to overtake him).

304–5 μὴ μὰν ἀσπουδεί γε: the same half-verse occurs at 8.512; 15.476, but Hector adds καὶ ἀκλειῶς. The idea is then repeated in positive form in the next line to form a polar expression: μὴ . . . ἀσπουδεί ≈ μέγα ῥέξας τι, (μὴ) ἀκλειῶς ≈ καὶ ἐσσομένοισι πυθέσθαι. The particle μάν (aeolic for μήν) adds an asseverative force to his wish (*GP* 332). The MSS hesitate between ἀσπουδεί (adopted by West 1, xxx) and ἀσπουδί; -εί is probably originally a locative ending. The adverb belongs to a group of similar expressions: οὐδ᾽ ἀναιμωτεί γε, 'not without blood' (17.363); οὐ . . . ἀνιδρωτεί γε, 'not without sweat' (15.228); οὐ . . . ἀνουτητεί γε (371), 'not without stabbing'. In all cases the effect is one of litotes: 'not without a struggle' = 'after much resistance'. ἀκλειῶς: recurs at *Od.* 1.241 = 14.371, and cf. ἀκλεές at 7.100; ἀκλεέες at 12.318.

κλέος is an extremely important concept in Homeric society. Basically it can mean two things: (1) an oral report on an event (e.g. 11.21–2: the Cypriot king Kinyres gave Agamemnon a corslet, 'since he had heard the great *kleos* that the Greeks were to sail a fleet against Troy'); and (2) fame, which a hero or heroine acquires as a result of being the subject of such reports, preferably (but not exclusively) in their most sophisticated form, that of heroic song (e.g. *Od.* 24.196–8: Penelope's *kleos* will never die because the gods make a song about her). Since songs can survive their subjects, *kleos* implies eternal fame (as opposed to the more ephemeral forms of glory κῦδος or εὖχος, for which see 205–7n.), an idea occasionally made explicit (ἄσβεστον κλέος: *Od.* 4.584; κλέος ἄφθιτον: 9.413). See Maehler (1963) 10–13, 26–7, Redfield (1994) 31–5, Goldhill (1991) 96–166, and Olson (1995) 1–23, 224–7. μέγα ῥέξας τι: a unique phrase, but the notion of doing 'a big work' (μέγα ἔργον) is regularly found in connection with fighting (11.734; 12.416; 16.208), chasing the Greeks from Troy (13.366), or killing Hector (19.150). The big work Hector is thinking of here is to confront Achilles. καὶ ἐσσομένοισι πυθέσθαι '(something big) also for people of the future to hear about'; final-consecutive use of the infinitive (5n.). The expression recurs at *Od.* 3.204; 11.76; (in connection with *negative* things) 2.119; *Od.* 21.255; and 24.433. It is conceivable that the Homeric narrator is here subtly referring to his own poem, which indeed ensures Hector's *kleos* among later generations, just as he makes other heroines and heroes 'predict' the *Iliad* (Helen at 6.357–8; Achilles at 9.412–13); see de Jong (2006).

306–25

The fighting continues, now with sword (Hector) versus spear (Achilles); see 273–363n. For a warrior to attack first with his spear and then with his sword is not unusual (cf. e.g. 3.355–62), but what is of course special – indeed unique – in the present situation is that Achilles still has his spear (which was given back to him by Athena at 276–7, without Hector knowing this). This will give him the chance to hit Hector first while he is still, sword in hand, storming at him (326). Prior to Achilles' fatal hit (326) the narrator slows down his narrative speed (and increases suspense) with symmetrical descriptions of the opponents' armour (306b-7, 313–16), similes (308–11, 317–19), a close-up of Hector's (armoured) body (321–6), and analepses (316, 323).

306 ὣς ἄρα φωνήσας: a common and neutral speech-capping formula (35 x *Il.*, 27 x *Od.*). φάσγανον ὀξύ: the Homeric epics have three words for 'sword', which are conveniently used as metrical variants: φάσγανον, ξίφος, and ἄορ (the first two words are already found in Mycenaean Greek). When used in battle, as here, they receive epithets like 'sharp' or 'big'; when they are looked at as presents, their material, e.g. 'bronze', is indicated.

307 τό: the anaphoric pronoun is used as a relative pronoun (L 17). It irregularly counts as long, presumably under the influence of the following οἱ, to which is attributed the original metrical shape of reflexive (ϝϝ)οἷ (<*swoi). οἱ: personal pronoun (L 19), possessive dative (L 22). τέτατο: intransitive pluperfect of τείνω, 'to stretch', 'pull'. At 3.372 and 14.404 we hear of a strap (of a helmet) or baldrick (of a shield and sword) which is 'fastened'; here, in connection with a sword, we either have to assume an ad hoc meaning, such as 'hanging' or 'being extended', or adhere to the common 'fastened' and assume that the singer had the baldrick of the sword in mind. ὑπὸ λαπάρην: the λαπάρη is the soft part between the ribs and hip. The word is found elsewhere in the context of wounding, here to indicate the place where the sword is hanging. μέγα τε στιβαρόν τε: a common expression, elsewhere used of shields and spears. In accordance with the abundant descriptive style employed at this stage of the story, Hector's sword is put in the limelight, although it will soon prove ineffective.

308–11 The comparison with an eagle that darts down to the earth in order to snatch away a lamb or hare illustrates the speed of Hector's 'swooping' attack (cf. 138–44n. and note that the root οἰμ-, which is here used of Hector, at 140 and 21.252 is used of the bird of the simile) but above all his aggressive spirit; cf. 15.690–4, when he was also compared to an eagle pouncing upon a flock of geese, cranes, or swans at the moment he successfully attacked the Greek ships. The simile stresses the heroic and martial nature of Hector for the final time; soon this picture will be 'eclipsed' by that of the 'star' Achilles (317–19).

308–9 ἀλείς: part. aorist pass. from εἴλομαι, which here means 'drawing himself together' to increase the force of his attack (cf. *Od.* 24.538; and cf. a lion at 20.168; Agenor at 21.571). ὥς τ(ε) . . . , ὅς τ(ε): epic τε (L 21). ὑψιπετήεις 'high-flying'; a metrical variant (2 x) for ὑψιπέτης, a stock epithet of eagles (3 x *Il.*, 1 x *Od.*). νεφέων ἐρεβεννῶν: this combination is found only here and as a variant reading at 5.864, but clouds are often called 'dark' when they are employed by the gods to hide somebody or are a metaphor for death or unconsciousness. Against this background, the blackness of the cloud here (and cf. the κυάνεον Τρώων νέφος at 16.66) may be interpreted as having a menacing connotation.

310 ἀμαλήν 'tender, feeble'; the only other occurrence of this word is also in connection with young animals in a simile (*Od.* 20.14, of puppies). Some MSS read the much more common ἀπαλήν, 'soft', which is however normally used of parts of the human body (e.g. 'a soft neck': 327). πτῶκα 'cowering'. This adjective is also used as a substantive, 'the cowering one' = 'a hare' (e.g. 17.676).

311 τινάσσων φάσγανον ὀξύ: normally warriors brandish a *spear* before attacking to frighten (273) or challenge their opponent (3.19), or to encourage their own men (5.495). Here Hector makes the same movement with his sword (since he lacks a spear).

312–13 μένεος . . . ἐμπλήσατο θυμόν | ἀγρίου 'he filled his heart with savage *menos*'. It is more common to say that 'his *thumos/phrenes* filled itself/themselves with *menos*' (cf. e.g. 1.103–4), but cf. 17.499 'he filled his *phrenes* with courage and strength'. *menos* combines the notion of adrenalin and fury; see 96n. Only here is it called ἄγριος, the adjective thrown into relief by the enjambement. Ever since the death of Patroclus Achilles has been ἄγριος (cf. 21.314; 24.41, and see 262–6n.). This mood, contrasting with the beauty and glitter of his armour, bodes ill for Hector.

313–23 The word καλός is used six times within ten lines, an 'extraordinary concentration' (Griffin (1990) 365). Of these instances only two concern Hector (321, 323), and the narrator has opted at this stage to dwell on the beauty of victory rather than the pathos of death. The whole passage, with its stress on the beauty and glitter of Achilles' armour (including the comparison with a star and the successive mentions of his shield, helmet, and spear) recalls, partly verbatim, the scene of Achilles putting on his new armour for the first time (19.364–98). The recollection of this earlier scene brings the story full circle: the episode that started with Achilles arming himself to take his revenge on Hector is now about to come to its end.

313–14 πρόσθεν... σάκος στέρνοιο κάλυψεν 'he protectingly held his shield before his breast'; cf. πρόσθε... οἱ πέπλοιο... πτύγμ' ἐκάλυψεν, 'she held the fold of her robe as a covering in front of him' (5.315). καλὸν δαιδάλεον: the same combination had been used of Achilles' shield at 19.380 and the root δαιδαλ- occurs three times in the description of the making of Achilles' Shield: 18.479, 482, 612.

314–15 κόρυθι δ' ἐπένευε φαεινῆι | τετραφάλωι: shaking the helmet plume, like brandishing a spear (311n.), serves to intimidate the opponent; cf. 20.162, where the gesture is preceded by ἀπειλήσας ἐβεβήκει, 'he stepped forward threateningly'. It is the shaking of Hector's famous plume when reaching out for his son which frightens Astyanax at 6.468. The meaning of φάλος in τετραφάλωι: 'with four *phaloi*', has been disputed since antiquity; we are possibly dealing with metal sheets that were attached to a leather helmet either at the temples (ἀμφίφαλος) or on all four sides (τετράφαλος). Others think that the *phaloi* are bosses or horns. See Lebessi (1992).

315–16 'The beautiful golden (horse) hairs waved around it (the helmet), which Hephaestus let hang thick from both sides of the crest'. The same words (minus καλαί) occurred at 19.382–3, in the context of Achilles arming himself. Line 316 is omitted by some MSS (followed by West). It may be seen, however, as an effective analepsis of Hephaestus making Achilles' armour (18.478–613): we are reminded of its divine nature. A papyrus inserts lines 133–5 after 316. These plus verses may be due to a rhapsode wanting to slow down the narrative pace even more at this climactic moment (cf. 306–25n.), but they create an unattractive doubling with 318–20 (σείων ≈ πάλλεν, ἐλάμπετο ≈ ἀπέλαμπε). καλαί: the variant δειναί was known in antiquity, but the sustained stress on beauty of καλαί suits the context much better (313–23n.). ἔθειραι: in Homer this word is always in the plural, of a horse's mane (cf. 8.42) or a horsehair crest (here; cf. ἱππόκομον πήληκα: 16.797); in later Greek it is used in the singular of human hair. ἵει: cf. ἐπὶ... χρύσεον λόφον ἧκε, 'Hephaestus made a golden crest on it (the helmet)' (18.612). λόφον ἀμφί: the preposition is placed after the substantive it governs (L 20), but in the case of this preposition the accent does not move backwards.

317–19 οἷος... ὥς 'as the Evening Star rises amidst other stars..., which is (literally stands as) the most beautiful star in the sky, thus a gleam came from Achilles' spear'. For similes introduced by οἷος cf. e.g. 4.75; 5.554, 864 (in total 15 x). Warriors and their armour are often compared to stars, but the present simile should be understood in connection with that of 25–32: the narrator chose to represent Priam's frightened focalisation there, but he now spotlights Achilles' victorious heroism. Perhaps the notion of the *Evening* Star also has a menacing tone. The *days* of Hector's glory, granted him in the context of the *Dios boulē*, have come to an end. See Moulton (1977) 26–7. ἀστήρ... ἀστράσι... | ... ἀστήρ: such repetition at close quarters is not uncommon in Homer (and later Greek).

εἶσι: see 27n. νυκτὸς ἀμολγῶι: see 28n. ἕσπερος: this is the only reference to the Evening Star in Homer, but cf. the Morning Star at 23.226 and *Od.* 13.93–4. The Greeks distinguished between an Evening and a Morning Star, until they acknowledged in Hellenistic times (as the Babylonians had done long before them) that the two are the same, i.e. the planet Venus. Venus is the brightest heavenly body in the night sky except for the moon. αἰχμῆς ἀπέλαμπ' εὐήκεος: literally 'it gleamed from his well-pointed spear', a unique impersonal use of this verb. Perhaps the narrator was inspired by ἡ δ' ἀστὴρ ὣς ἀπέλαμπεν . . . τρυφάλεια, 'his helmet gleamed like a star' (19.381–2), appearing in a passage which was in his mind anyway (see 315–16n.). The epithet εὐηκής appears only here and heightens the tension: soon the sharpness of the spear will be effectively employed to kill Hector.

320 For the threatening brandishing of a spear see 311n. φρονέων κακὸν Ἕκτορι δίωι: an effective collocation, which will be surpassed by the direct juxtaposition Ἕκτορα δῖον ἀεικέα μήδετο ἔργα at 395.

321–6 Although the narrator usually turns to a close-up at the moment of wounding (as he will at 327), here he uniquely inserts a close-up of Hector's armed body as Achilles scans it to find a place to wound him. The close-up is another retardation, adding to the build-up of suspense and grandeur at this climactic moment in the *Iliad*. For close-ups in Homer see de Jong-Nünlist (2004).

321 εἰσορόων: an instance of metrical diectasis (L 4): εἰσοράων (– ‿ ‿ –) > εἰσορῶν (– ‿ –) > εἰσορόων (– ‿ ‿ –). ὅπηι εἴξειε μάλιστα: lit. 'where it (Hector's body) would most give way', i.e. either 'where it would offer least resistance (to Achilles' spear)' or 'where it would offer most space (for his spear to wound)'. The first interpretation is suggested by 325 'the gullet, where loss of life is quickest' and 327 'through his soft neck', the second by 324 'but flesh showed'. In view of the parallel οὔ πηι χροὸς εἴσατο, πᾶς δ' ἄρα χαλκῶι . . . κεκάλυφθ', 'his body was nowhere visible, but it was entirely covered by his bronze armour' (13.191–2), the second interpretation is preferable. εἴξειε is an oblique optative depending on εἰσορόων ('looking and asking himself where . . . ').

322–5 'The rest of his body the bronze armour as good as completely covered . . . but flesh showed where the collar-bones separate the neck from the shoulders, the gullet, where loss of life is quickest'. τοῦ 'of him', sc. Hector (anaphoric pronoun: L 17), to be connected with χρόα. καὶ ἄλλο τόσον μέν . . . δ': lit. 'as for the rest so far . . . but'; cf. e.g. 'the horse was chestnut all over (τὸ μὲν ἄλλο τόσον), except that on his forehead (ἐν δὲ μετώπωι) was a white spot' (23.455). Adverbial καί emphasises ἄλλο τόσον μέν; cf. *GP* 319. φαίνετο δ': sc. χρώς, to be derived from χρόα. λαυκανίην: the accusative is puzzling, since one would expect a dative on a par with the ἧι-clause. A possible analysis in terms of oral syntax would be that the singer started with 'it (sc. the flesh) showed' and then, after the relative clause, wanted to reintroduce a subject but could not use the nominative λαυκανίη because the initial vowel of ἵνα would reduce the -η to a short syllable and, hence, distracted by αὐχένα, chose the accusative with its final -ν. Other solutions are to adopt the ancient variant readings φαῖνεν, 'but it (the armour) showed the gullet' or λαυκανίης, '(the flesh showed) in the part of the gullet where' (locative genitive) or 'as part of the gullet' (partitive genitive). The word recurs once at 24.642 (in the genitive, at the same position).

The place of Hector's fatal wounding much resembles that of Teucer at 8.325–7, who is, however, merely hit by a stone (thrown by Hector) and survives: 'him where collar-bone separates neck and chest, an especially dangerous spot, there Hector hit him'. The Homeric narrator displays great inventiveness in describing fatal injuries: a 'grim list' drawn by Morrison (1999) 143 contains no less than 24 different parts of the body which may be affected.

322 χάλκεα τεύχεα: it has been argued that Achilles' divine armour, given to his father Peleus on the occasion of his marriage to Thetis (133–4n.), lends invulnerability to its wearer. Though the Homeric narrator, avoiding as much as possible all references to magic, does not refer to such a quality explicitly, the circumstances that Patroclus first has to be stripped of the armour by Apollo before he can be killed (16.788–804) and that Achilles here carefully has to look for a place where the armour does not cover the body may be reflections of the folktale motif. Cf. the return to Achilles of his spear (275–7n.). See Kakridis (1961) and Burgess (2009) 16. At the same time, donning Achilles' armour brings death to its two substitute wearers, Patroclus and Hector; cf. Taplin (1992) 186. The well-known tradition that Achilles was invulnerable (except for his heel) because his mother Thetis dipped him into the Styx is post-Homeric; see Burgess (2009) 9–16.

323 This line is almost identical with 17.187, where Hector announces to his men that he will put on Achilles' armour. Here it represents Achilles' focalisation (while looking closely at Hector, he thinks back about this hero killing Patroclus and taking off his armour) and functions as an analepsis. Soon Achilles will also return to that moment in words: Πατροκλῆ' ἐξεναρίζων (331) ≈ τὰ Πατρόκλοιο βίην ἐνάριξε (323). Zeus and Thetis condemn Hector's donning of Patroclus' (= Achilles') divine armour (17.198–209, 450; 18.132–3); the narrator ominously connects this act with his imminent death (16.799–800); and Achilles considers the capture of the armour an important additional reason (next to the slaying of Patroclus) for wanting to take revenge on Hector (17.122, 472–3; 18.21, 82–5). **τὰ:** the anaphoric pronoun is used as a relative pronoun for metrical reasons (L 17). Πατρόκλοιο βίην 'mighty Patroclus'. A common type of expression in Homer; cf. e.g. Πριάμοιο βίην (3.105). ἐνάριξε: lit. 'take off the armour of a dead man', but also 'kill' (e.g. 331).

325 τε: epic τε, referring to an omnitemporal phenomenon (L 21). ψυχῆς . . . ὄλεθρος 'the loss of *psuche*'; a unique expression, but cf. ψυχὰς ὀλέσαντες at 13.763 = 24.168. Commentators understand it as either (1) 'the loss of life', with *psuche* for once being life itself rather than the principle of life, since the *psuchē* leaves the body upon death but is not destroyed (Jahn (1987) 30–1) or (2) 'the expiration of the last breath' (Clarke (1999) 135), with an unparalleled use of ὄλεθρος. For a discussion of the complex term *psuchē* in Homer see 362–3n.

326–66

The death of Hector is relayed in a much expanded version of the typical pattern of death scenes: (1) a warrior strikes his victim, (2) the victim is mortally wounded, (3) and dies. Here the second element is expanded with a dialogue between dying victim and victor, and the third with a final speech by the victor. These same two expansions are only found in the case of the death of Patroclus (16.820–63), while the death of Sarpedon (16.479–505) also has an expanded second element. Apart from these structural parallels, there are also many verbal and thematic echoes between the deaths of Patroclus and Hector, which encourage the narratees to connect the fates of these heroes (see Introduction 2d):

Patroclus	Hector
Hector thrusts his spear in Patroclus' belly (16.820-1)	Achilles hurls his spear and strikes Hector's gullet and neck, but does not sever the wind-pipe (22.326-9)
Patroclus crashes down (16.822) + simile (16.823-8)	Hector crashes in the dust (22.330a)
+ dialogue, consisting of two turns (16.829-54)	+ dialogue, consisting of four turns (22.330b-60)
victor: You thought (ἔφησθα) you would win, fool (νήπιε), now vultures will eat your body	*victor*: You thought (ἔφης) you could safely kill Patroclus, fool (νήπιε), now dogs and birds will maul you *victim*: Please give back my body *victor*: I will never give back your body
victim (ὀλιγοδρανέων): Now you win thanks to the gods, but death is near for you	*victim* (ὀλιγοδρανέων): I will never persuade you, but for you death is also near
death of Patroclus (16.855-7)	= death of Hector (22.361-3)
+ speech to dead Patroclus by Hector (16.858-61)	+ speech to dead Hector by Achilles (22.364-6)
Why prophesy my death? Perhaps I will kill Achilles	I will accept my fate when the gods fulfil it

For a general discussion of the typical structure of death scenes see Visser (1987) 46–8, 55–6 and Morrison (1999); for the specific similarities between the deaths of

Patroclus and Hector see Fenik (1968) 217–18, Rutherford (1982) 158, and Taplin (1992) 243; and for the parallelism of the speeches see Lohmann (1970) 159–61.

326 'there Achilles hit him (Hector) while he charged (μεμαῶτα) at him'. οἷ: personal pronoun of the third person, which, as the accent indicates, here is used reflexively (L 19). δῖος Ἀχιλλεύς: see 102n.

327 The same line is found at 17.49 (the death of Euphorbus) and *Od.* 22.16 (the death of Antinous). ἀντικρύ: related to ἀντί, but the precise etymology is unclear. It is found almost exclusively in battle contexts, of spear and arrows which fly 'straight' through the air and then through the body they hit. ἁπαλοῖο. . . αὐχένος: necks are called 'thick' (παχύς) or 'strong' (στιβαρός), but in the context of wounding they are 'tender' to explain why projectiles may enter the body here easily and the resulting death is quick.

328–9 'but the spear did not cut Hector's wind-pipe, *so as to make him* say something in answer to him'. This is a special use of ὄφρα, to express the natural consequences expected in the circumstances; cf. *Od.* 9.13; 11.94; 12.428, and see KG II 379–80, note 3. Scholars not recognising this special use and adhering to the normal, final force of ὄφρα, have difficulty explaining this passage. Aristarchus finds it 'ridiculous' that the spear would take care not to cut Hector's wind-pipe in order for him to be able to speak (ἵνα προσφωνήσηι), and athetises 329. The scholia, followed by Leaf, Ameis-Hentze, and Richardson, suggest that the gods or fate are arranging these events and adduce e.g. *Od.* 9.154–5 ('the Nymphs roused some goats, ἵνα my men could eat'), but no gods are mentioned in the present scene.

328 ἄρ': the particle (98n.) here has its original force, marking a surprising fact. μελίη. . . χαλκοβάρεια: only here is Achilles' Pelian spear (133–4n.) called 'heavy with bronze'; cf. 16.141 βριθὺ μέγα στιβαρόν, 'heavy, huge, massive'.

330 ἤριπε. . . ἐν κονίηις: intransitive aorist from ἐρείπω, 'to crash down to the ground from an upright position'. The verb is typically used of warriors being (mortally) hit and of trees being felled (cf. 13.389–92, where the two are combined). Warriors may crash down from their chariot, headfirst, in front of their opponent, or, as here (and cf. 5.75; 11.743), in the dust. ἐπεύξατο: this verb (8 x) introduces the customary vaunt after an opponent has been killed. δῖος Ἀχιλλεύς: see 102n.

331–6 Just as opponents exchange challenges *before* fighting, the victor often celebrates his triumph *afterwards* with a vaunt. Its regular nature becomes clear at 4.450 = 8.64, where the narrator says 'there was the groaning and boasting (εὐχωλή) of men killed and killing'. This chest-thumping often involves sarcastic mockery of the defeated enemy. The chief purpose is to hurt one's defeated enemy and demonstrate one's own superiority. For vaunts see Kyriakou (2001) and Stoevesandt (2004) 306–7, 424–7.

The structure of Achilles' vaunt – the last to be heard in the *Iliad* – closely resembles that of Hector spoken to Patroclus at 16.830–42, and we are dealing with the 'overarching' technique: when speeches spoken at different occasions (and often at different places, so that the speakers strictly speaking cannot know each other's words) nevertheless mirror, or react to, each other. This technique will later be employed to great effect, e.g. by Thucydides.

	Hector : Patroclus	Achilles : Hector
(*empty boast of opponent*)	You thought that you would destroy our city and rob the Trojan women of their freedom;	You thought that killing Patroclus you would stay scot free;
(*importance of speaker*)	Fool, the horses of Hector speed into battle and I am preeminent among the Trojans and ward off slavery.	Fool, I was left behind as his avenger, who killed you.
(*reality*)	Vultures will eat you.	You dogs and birds will maul, but him the Greeks will bury.
(*final dig*)	Achilles did not help you, who encouraged you to fight me.	

331–3 The motif 'You thought that . . . ; Fool' also occurs at 16.830–4 (Hector addressing Patroclus); 21.583–5 (Agenor challenging Achilles); and in a shorter form 5.473–4 (Sarpedon rebuking Hector). The thoughts ascribed to the addressee are hyperbolic: 'you thought that you could kill Patroclus without consequences for yourself'; (Hector: Patroclus, Agenor: Achilles) 'you thought that you would capture Troy'; (Sarpedon: Hector) 'you think that you can defend the city without allies'.

331 ἀτάρ που ἔφης: at the parallel places we find φῆς που (5.473), ἦ που ἔφησθα (16.830), and ἦ δή που μάλ' ἔολπας (21.583). This is the only place where the connective particle ἀτάρ (181n.) occurs at the opening of a speech, which may explain why one scholion has ἄφαρ. It 'indicates the contrast of what follows with the actual circumstances: he might have begun with κεῖσαι, but leaves it to be expressed by the grim reality' (Leaf and cf. *GP* 52). Modal που, 'probably', here conveys ironic certainty rather than hesitation. For ἔφης see 280n.

332 σῶς ἔσσεσθ': the combination σῶς (or uncontracted σόος) + a present tense of εἶναι occurs regularly (7 x *Il.* and *Od.*), e.g. 1.117 'I want my men to be safe (σόον εἶναι) rather than die'. Only here do we find the future, which expresses the idea of 'safely getting away with'. ἐμὲ δ' οὐδὲν ὀπίζεο 'and you did not at all reckon with me'. This is the only instance where the verb has a human rather than a divine object, which suggests that Achilles regards his wrathful revenge as equivalent to that of a god (Cairns (1993) 136–7). νόσφιν ἐόντα 'being far away'; νόσφιν is an adverb with fossilised -φιν ending. The Trojans had known about Achilles' absence from battle since 4.512–13, from Apollo.

333 νήπιε: νήπιος and the older form νηπύτιος, which is used as its metrical variant, are terms of abuse which opponents on the battlefield regularly hurl at each other (cf. e.g., 16.833; 21.99, 410, 441, 585). The word, originally referring to a child that cannot yet speak (νη + ἠπύω; cf. 484), indicates that a person is too optimistic about his own position and entertains false hopes. For the use of νήπιος by the narrator see 445–6n. **τοῖο δ' ἄνευθεν ἀοσσητὴρ μέγ' ἀμείνων** 'for as helper of him (I stayed behind) at a distance, much better (sc. than he)'. The anaphoric pronoun τοῖο is best taken with ἀοσσητήρ, the adverb ἄνευθεν being elaborated in νηυσὶν ἔπι γλαφυρῆισιν and μετόπισθε (*LfgrE* s.v. ἄνευθεν), rather than with ἄνευθεν as a repetition of νόσφιν ἐόντα (Ameis-Hentze, Leaf). ἀοσσητήρ is *nomen agentis* from the verb ἀοσσεῖν (first attested in the Hellenistic poet Moschus), which is derived from *ἄοσσος < *sm-sokʷyos (cf. Latin *socius*). Such helpers assist in situations of war or juridicial matters (when a man has killed somebody, *Od.* 4.165, or when an heir has to defend his patrimony in the absence of his father, *Od.* 23.119). The scholia and Ameis-Hentze understand μέγ' ἀμείνων as 'much better than *you*'.

334 μετόπισθε λελείμμην 'I was left = stayed behind'; cf. τίς τ' εὔχεται ἀνὴρ | γνωτὸν ἐνὶ μεγάροισιν ἀρῆς ἀλκτῆρα λιπέσθαι, 'a man prays that a brother be left at home as avenger of his death' (14.484–5).

335 τοι 'your knees'; a possessive dative (L 22). γούνατ' ἔλυσα: to 'loosen a person's limbs or knees' (so that s/he collapses to the ground) is a regular Homeric expression for describing the effects of a fatal wound or blow, hence effectively means 'to kill'; it may also, less dramatically, refer to the weakening effects of weariness, fear, or other emotions.

335–6 The threat to leave the body of one's opponent to be eaten by dogs and birds (once fish) is a regular item in challenges and vaunts (cf. 11.452–4; 13.831–2; 16.836; 21.122–7), but it has special resonance in connection with the body of Hector; see 337–54n. ἀϊκῶς 'in an ugly manner', i.e., in a way that will leave your body in a mutilated state which is ugly to see. The adverb occurs only here, instead of the regular (but unmetrical) ἀεικῶς. Chantraine has suggested reading ἀεικῶς with synizesis of ἀει-, West has conjectured ἀικέως with synizesis of -έως. κτεριοῦσιν 'they will give an honourable burial'; originally 'give a dead person's possessions (or other objects) as burial gifts (κτέρεα)'. For κτεριοῦσιν instead of κτεριοῦσιν see 256n.

337–54 The supplication of Hector somewhat deviates from the standard pattern (33–91n.): (1) – (2) the approach and gesture of the suppliant are lacking since Hector has fallen down on the ground; (3) supplication speech (338–43); (4) negative reaction of the *supplicandus* Achilles (344–54). Since Hector does not physically touch his *supplicandus*, this is a figurative supplication; cf. Odysseus' restraint from touching Nausicaa's knees while he is naked at *Od.* 6.141–85, and earlier in this book Priam and Hecuba gesticulating at Hector from the Trojan walls.

The *Iliad* contains four more supplications on the battlefield: 6.45–65; 11.130–48; 20.463–72; 21.64–119. Whereas supplications usually are effective since suppliants are under the protection of Zeus, those on the battlefield are never successful. This may be due to the *supplicandi* being Agamemnon, who is generally rather violent (the supplication of book 11; in book 6 the *supplicandus* is Menelaus but Agamemnon takes over and 'finishes the job'), and Achilles in his present revengeful mood (the supplications of books 20 and 21). In the past Achilles did spare people's lives (cf. 11.106; 21.40–1, 78–9, 100–2; 24.751–3). See Griffin (1980) 53–6 and Yamagata (1994) 41–5 (and the scholarship mentioned in 33–91n.). It may be no coincidence that only Trojans (Adrastus, Hippolochus and Pisander, Tros, Lycaon, Hector) are made to plead for their life; see Stoevesandt (2004) 149–56.

The dialogue between Hector and Achilles brings to the fore a theme that had appeared for the first time in the proem of the *Iliad* (1.4–5) and which will be central to the story until its very last line (24.804): the mutilation of Hector's corpse. The most common form of mutilation was leaving a person's corpse for the dogs and birds, sometimes cutting off the head or limbs (e.g. 11.146, 261; 17.39–40; 18.175–7, and see Friedrich (2003) 45–51). Mutilation is both practised and used as a threat, by individual opponents vis-à-vis each other and by generals exhorting their men (e.g. 2.391–3; 4.237; 18.271–2, 283). The theme plays a role in the two heroic deaths which are closest to that of Hector: Sarpedon (cf. 16.545–6, 559–61; his body is saved by the gods: 16.676–83) and Patroclus (16.836; 17.125–7, 240–1, 254–5, 272–3, 557–8; 18.175–7; his body is retrieved by the Greeks after fierce and prolonged battle: 18.231–8).

In the case of Hector this theme is referred to so often and by so many different characters that it becomes a leitmotif: Hector himself is preoccupied with the fate of corpses early on (7.76–86) and raises the topic of his own body right from the start of his duel with Achilles (258–9); after the death of Patroclus, Achilles announces more than once that he will mutilate Hector's body (18.334–5; 22.335–6, 346–54; 23.21, 182–3); and Hector's parents and wife fearfully foresee mistreatment (88–9, 508–10; 24.211–12, 408–9). The insistence on this theme by Achilles, whom we have also seen mistreat the bodies of Lycaon (21.120–7) and Asteropaeus (21.201–4), underlines the savage mood that characterises him after the death of Patroclus, in contrast with his earlier respectful treatment of dead opponents (notably Andromache's father, king Eetion: 6.417–20). But it also creates a highly effective instance of misdirection: as the narratees have been so often and so emphatically prepared for the non-burial of Hector and have seen Achilles' mistreatment of his body (395–404; 23.24–6; 24.14–18), the final release of his body by Achilles and his burial by the Trojans will come as a surprise (and impressive end of the *Iliad*). See Segal (1971a), Morrison (1992) 83–93, and Reichel (1994) 192–7.

337–43 Hector's supplication speech contains the usual reference to the speech-act of supplication (338), the request (339), the reason why the *supplicandus* should accept it, here a ransom (340–1), and a repetition of the request (342–3). Hector does not, like the other battlefield suppliants, plead for his life but for the return of his body and his burial; cf. Elpenor supplicating Odysseus to give him a proper burial (*Od.* 11.66–78). Bassett (1934b) notes that Hector's speech does not contain any vocative, which is rare in Homer and may be a sign of the urgency of the situation; Hector is using his last breath to speak. His last words (356–60) likewise will not contain a vocative.

337 The same line is used at 15.246, when Hector was knocked unconscious, and an almost identical one in the context of Patroclus' final speech (16.843). ὀλιγοδρανέων 'being able to do little', 'weakened'; this rare word is built from ὀλίγος and δράω. κορυθαίολος: see 232n.

338 λίσσομ' ὑπὲρ ψυχῆς καὶ γούνων σῶν τε τοκήων 'I beseech you by/in the name of your life, your knees, and your parents'. For this use of ὑπέρ, cf. 15.660; 24.466; *Od.* 15.261. For γούνων see 24n. Suppliants mainly invoke fathers, mothers, parents, wives, sons (15.662–5; 24.466–7; *Od.* 11.66; 13.324), or gods (*Od.* 2.68; 15.261). Hector here mentions parents, knees, and life (uniquely). The parents prepare for 341. The combination 'I beseech you by your knees' only occurs here and at 345, but cf. γούναθ' ἱκάνω/-ομαι (*Od.* 3.92; 4.322; 5.449, etc.). The closest parallel for ψυχή is *Od.* 15.261–2 (Theoclymenus: Telemachus) λίσσομ' ὑπὲρ . . . σῆς τ' αὐτοῦ κεφαλῆς καὶ ἑταίρων, where 'head' typifies 'life' (cf. 348n.). Clarke (1999) 58 suggests that 'Hector is asking Achilles to remember the things that bring a sense of moderation or self-restraint to Homeric man: his parents, his knees, and his mortality.'

339 'Do not let dogs devour me by the ships of the Greeks.' παρὰ νηυσὶ . . . Ἀχαιῶν: this location virtually means 'in the Greek camp' and hence has the connotation of 'on enemy ground'. Hector, like Hecuba at 89, anticipates that Achilles will take his corpse with him to the camp (as indeed he will do at 465), for his death takes place on the Trojan plain (cf. 404: ἐῆι ἐν πατρίδι γαίηι). κύνας: Hector employs the 'catchword'-technique (185n.): he picks up Achilles' σὲ . . . κύνες . . . ἑλκήσουσ' (335–6). καταδάψαι: cf. (Nestor about Aegisthus:) τόν γε κύνες τε καὶ οἰωνοὶ κατέδαψαν (*Od.* 3.259) and (Achilles) Ἕκτορα δ' οὔ τι | δώσω . . . πυρὶ δαπτέμεν, ἀλλὰ κύνεσσιν (23.182–3). The verb δάπτω is also used of wolves and lions devouring their prey.

340–3 To ransom captives was common practice in the Greco-Roman world; see Pritchett (1991) 284–8 and Naiden (2006) 82. In the Homeric epics, too, we regularly come across the phenomenon, often in the context of a 'supplication' scene, e.g. 1.12–32; 6.46–50, 427; 10.378–81; 11.106, 131–5; 22.49–51; see Wilson (2002) 13–39. Demanding ransom (normally precious metals like bronze, gold, and iron), together with the selling of captives as slaves, the raiding of cattle, and the plundering of cities, belonged to the regular benefits of warriors. It would seem that the ransom of a corpse was less common. Normally, the companions of a fallen warrior would fight until they have recovered his body (preferably with armour), as happens e.g. in the case of Patroclus' body, the fight over which fills book 17. Another possibility is to strike a truce so as to allow both parties to recover and bury their dead, as happens at 7.417–36.

340–1 δέδεξο: the verb δέχεσθαι is typical in contexts of accepting a ransom (cf. 1.20). Only here do we find the perfect tense, which seems to be used to fill the metrical slot (as at 20.377). There is a variant δέχεσθαι (imperative infinitive).

δῶρα τά τοι δώσουσι: the sentence is in apposition to χαλκόν... χρυσόν. τά is relative pronoun (L 17). πατὴρ καὶ πότνια μήτηρ: the expression is formulaic (9 x *Il.*), but here we may take it as a – belated – acknowledgement by Hector of the presence of his parents on the walls. πότνια is an honorific term of address of mortal or divine females. The word occurs in Linear B, and it originally may have designated a goddess. It is regularly combined with μήτηρ (1 x *Il.*, 13 x *Od.*): 'lady mother'.

342-3 δόμεναι = δοῦναι (L 11). According to Allan (2010), we find an imperatival infinitive when conventional social procedures are evoked. Here Hector, starting with two direct appeals in the form of imperatives (ἔα, δέδεξο), activated the 'script' of supplication and now presents the return of the body in the infinitive as the socially accepted action to perform. πυρός... λελάχωσι 'make (me) get the fire (cremation) to which I am entitled'; for the causative reduplicated aorist see 223n. Τρῶες καὶ Τρώων ἄλοχοι: Hector is envisioning a full and honourable public burial, as does Andromache at 512–14 (albeit without a corpse), and as will eventually take place at 24.785–804. Cf. 15.349–50, where Hector exhorts his men by threatening that whoever will not fight οὐδέ νυ τόν γε | γνωτοί τε γνωταί τε πυρὸς λελάχωσι θανόντα, 'him the men and women of his family will not give the cremation to which he is entitled after his death'.

344 See 260n.

345–54 Achilles' reply is one long and passionate rejection of Hector's supplication (containing no less than six negations), which mirrors his opponent's speech in its structure and wording (Lohmann (1970) 114–15): 'do not supplicate me by my knees and parents (*rejection of speech-act of supplication*; μή με... γούνων γουνάζεο μηδὲ τοκήων ≈ λίσσομ' ὑπὲρ... γούνων σῶν τε τοκήων). There is certainly not going to be someone to ward off the dogs from your head (*rejection of request*). Not even if they will offer me ten or twenty times a ransom or Priam himself would bring gold (*rejection of ransom*; Πρίαμος ≈ πατήρ), not even then will your mother lament you but dogs and birds will devour you (*once more rejection of request*; πότνια μήτηρ: 352, 341, κύνες... κατὰ... δάσονται ≈ κύνας καταδάψαι).' It is important for our evaluation of Achilles' behaviour here to take account of Naiden (2006) 129–47, who shows that rejection of supplication 'occurs in every genre and culture, regardless of the suppliant's choice of gesture, argument, or request' and that it does not 'offend the gods, who do not punish it'.

The nine lines which form the speech after the one-line opening are probably best analysed and hence punctuated, with Leaf and Richardson, as follows: (sentence one) αἲ γάρ... ἀνείη... ὡς οὐκ ἔσθ'... ἀπαλάλκοι. (sentence two) οὐδ' εἴ κεν..., οὐδ' εἴ κεν..., οὐδ' ὥς... δάσονται (cf. 9.379–87: οὐδ' εἴ μοι..., οὐδ' εἴ μοι..., οὐδέ κεν ὥς... πείσει). Others put a full stop after ἄλλα (Ameis-Hentze) or Πρίαμος (OCT and West).

345 κύον 'dog' (and cf. κυνῶπις 'dog-faced') is a common term of (self-)abuse in Homer with connotation of shamelessness; see Faust (1970) and for more literature *LfgrE* s.v. 2c. Hector is called 'dog' several times (8.299; 11.362; 20.449). με γούνων γουνάζεο: a unique instance of the *figura etymologica*, which is used derisively. For γουνάζομαι + accusative cf. 1.427 (καί μιν γουνάσομαι).

346–8 'If only my mind would somehow urge me, i.e. I could bring myself, to eat your flesh raw, just as there is no one who could ward off the dogs from your head.' The same combination of impossible wish and certain event appears at 8.538–41; 13.825–8; 18.464–7; *Od.* 9.523–5; 15.156–9; 17.251–3; 21.402–3. Usually wish and event are connected via correlatives (e.g. ὥς/οὕτω... ὡς); here and at *Od.* 9.523–5 and 17.251–3 the ὥς/οὕτω is lacking. The intensity of the wish may serve to affirm the certainty of the event (at least in the eyes of the speaker), as when Hector says, 'if only I could be deathless and ageless for all time, and honoured as Athena and Apollo are honoured, as surely as this coming day brings disaster to the Greeks'. Alternatively, the certainty of the event may affirm the intensity of the wish, as when Telemachus says 'if only I could talk thus having upon my return home to Ithaca found Odysseus, just as I go back having received all kindness from you', which amounts to 'I wish my chances of seeing my father were as real as your kindness'. See Leaf on 8.538, Edwards on 18.463–7, with more literature, and van Erp Taalman Kip (forthcoming). Here the clauses each seem to have equal force: Achilles conveys to Hector both his desire to eat his flesh raw and the certainty that dogs will devour him.

The idea of eating one's opponents raw is mentioned more than once in the *Iliad* (4.34–6: Zeus suggests that Hera could only assuage her anger by eating Priam and his children raw; 24.212–13: Hecuba wishes she could eat Achilles' liver). These statements are best taken as rhetorical, signifying extreme anger, rather than a reflection of actual practice. Only the beastly Cyclops Polyphemus eats human flesh (raw), to the abhorrence of Odysseus (*Od.* 9.291–5).

346 αἲ γάρ: this combination regularly introduces optatives expressing a wish (cf. Attic εἰ γάρ). αὐτόν με μένος καὶ θυμὸς ἀνείη: the combination of *menos* (96n.) and *thumos* (78n.) often occurs with verbs of inciting or ordering; cf. 24.198–9 μ' αὐτόν γε μένος καὶ θυμὸς ἄνωγε. αὐτόν με stands in contrast to the scavenger dogs of 348.

347 ὤμ': predicatively with κρέα, '(eat) your flesh raw'. This detail adds to the gruesomeness of the wish, in that, like an ὠμοφάγος wolf, jackal, or lion, Achilles wants to eat his opponent's flesh 'raw' rather than 'cooked'. For Achilles' animal-like state of mind at this stage of the story see 262–6n. ἔδμεναι: present infinitive (L 11). οἷά μ' ἔοργας 'the kinds of things you have done to me', i.e. *because* you have done me such wrong. For such syntactically loosely attached, explanatory οἷος-clauses cf. αἵματός εἰς ἀγαθοῖο, . . . , οἵ' ἀγορεύεις, 'you are from a good family, to judge from what you say' (*Od.* 4.611) and see *GH* II 238–9. The perfect has a totalising value, i.e. it implies that the state of affairs is the result of a series of occurrences. This value is often found with verbs of 'wrongdoing'; see Rijksbaron (2002) 37, note 3. οἷά μ' ἔοργας is the reading of the MSS, but some editors delete μ', so as to avoid the neglect of the digamma (ἔοργας < (ϝ)έ(ϝ)οργας).

348 οὐκ ἔσθ' ὅς 'there is no one who'; the same idiom e.g. 21.103. σῆς γε... κεφαλῆς: as often, the head metonymically stands for the whole person. Usually the connotation is solemnity, affection, or mortality (see Clarke (1999) 174); here Achilles focuses on (the mutilation of) his head because he wants to *hurt* Hector (cf. 74–5, where Priam talks about dogs mutilating his beard, head, and genitals, and 402–3, where we hear of Hector's head lying in the dust). ἀπαλάλκοι: the optative has potential force; cf. 17.640–1: εἴη δ' ὅς τις ἑταῖρος ἀπαγγείλειε τάχιστα.

349–54 'Not even if they will weigh out and bring here ten times or twenty times your ransom, and promise yet other things, not even if Priam would exhort me to weigh you yourself against gold.' This type of cumulative, expansive series is used twice more by Achilles (9.379–86, 401–9) and taken by Friedrich-Redfield (1978) 272–3 as typical of this speaker. For the '(not) even + hyperbole' motif see 220–1n.

349–50 εἰκοσινήριτ': the exact etymology and meaning of this *hapax* are unclear: εἰκοσιν-ήριτος ('twentyfold', cf. ἀριθμός) or εἰκοσι-νήριτος ('twenty times countless'). The unusual combination of an adverb (δεκάκις) and an object in the accusative (εἰκοσινήριτ' ἄποινα) seems due to Achilles' desire to coin an even stronger expression than the δεκάκις τε καὶ εἰκοσάκις τόσα which he employs at 9.379. κεν... στήσωσ' 'they will weigh out' (cf. 19.247; 24.232); the verb makes clear that Achilles is thinking of a ransom consisting of (unworked) precious metals. At 24.232 Priam will weigh out gold. The unexpressed subject 'they' most likely is Hector's father and mother (cf. 341).

351–4 Achilles' climactic parting shot is particularly harsh in that it rejects Hector's appeal to the sanctity of parents (cf. 338) and his offer of a ransom by his father and mother (cf. 341), and thus confirms Hecuba's forebodings (cf. 86–7). At this stage the narratees are not able to gauge whether this forceful prolepsis is reliable or not, and it seems likely that, lacking any signs to the contrary from the narrator, they will expect Achilles' words to come true (337–54n.).

351 σ' αὐτόν 'you yourself' > 'your body' (cf. 1.4; 9.547) > 'the weight of your body'. ἐρύσασθαι: from (ϝ)ἐρύω, 'draw', which here – uniquely – should mean 'weigh'; cf. Theognis 77–8 πιστὸς ἀνὴρ χρυσοῦ τε καὶ ἀργύρου ἀντερύσασθαι | ἄξιος, 'a reliable man is worth his weight in silver and gold'. Another interpretation is to connect it with (σ)ερύω (cf. Lat. *servo*): 'not even if Priam would exhort (the Trojans) to *save* you with gold' (*LfgrE* s.v.). ἀνώγοι: from the original perfect ἄνωγα a present ἀνώγω has been derived. Achilles changes from subjunctive to optative to indicate that he considers the act of Priam offering Hector's weight in gold as *merely* possible rather than *very* possible (the subjunctive); see Wakker (1994) 174–9.

352–4 οὐδ' ὥς σε... μήτηρ | ἐνθεμένη λεχέεσσι γοήσεται... | ἀλλὰ κύνες...: cf. Achilles to dead Lycaon: οὐδέ σε μήτηρ | ἐνθεμένη λεχέεσσι γοήσεται, ἀλλὰ Σκάμανδρος... (21.123–5). Unwittingly, Achilles also mirrors Hecuba's words at 86–7: οὔ σ'... κλαύσομαι ἐν λεχέεσσι... ὃν τέκον αὐτή.

352 πότνια μήτηρ: see 340–1n.

353 ἐνθεμένη λεχέεσσι 'having placed you on a bier', a reference to the *prothesis*, a standard part of the Greek burial ritual from Mycenaean times onwards and a familiar scene in archaic Greek vase painting. Despite Achilles' forceful denial here, Hector's prothesis will ensue, provisionally at 24.589 (αὐτὸς τόν γ' Ἀχιλεὺς λεχέων ἐπέθηκεν ἀείρας) and officially at 24.719–20 (τὸν μὲν ἔπειτα | τρητοῖς ἐν λεχέεσσι θέσαν).

354 κατὰ... δάσονται: the scholia suggest that the tmesis (L 20) gives expression to the tearing apart of the body. In view of the regularity of compound verbs in Homer still consisting of two elements, this seems fanciful and anachronistic. The verb means literally 'to divide' but it becomes 'tear apart', 'devour' with animals as subject. **πάντα:** predicatively with σε (352).

355 A unique speech-introduction, which, as the scholia note, well describes the progress from ὀλιγοδρανέων at 337. **κορυθαίολος:** see 232n.

356–60 To have dying persons speak impressive last words is a widespread literary phenomenon: at 16.844–54 Patroclus is given the same prerogative; at 24.744 Andromache regrets that Hector did not die in bed after 'speaking some weighty word (πυκινὸν ἔπος), which she could have remembered all her life'; and cf. further e.g. Hamlet's protracted dying speech (act v, scene ii). Many anthologies of famous last words spoken by real and fictional characters have been compiled, and the utterances tend to be prophetic. The idea is that a moment of clairvoyance comes at the moment of death; see e.g. Socrates in the *Apology*: 'I now wish to prophesy to you... : for I am now at the point where men are most wont to prophesy, when they are about to die' (39c); Virgil *Aeneid* 4.614–20; 10.739–41, *Genesis* 49. Saving his breath, Hector again does not employ any vocative; cf. 337–43n.

356–7 ἦ 'for sure' (40n.). **σ' εὖ γιγνώσκων προτιόσσομαι** 'I look at you in full understanding (of how things stand)' (Ameis-Hentze, *LfgrE* s.v. ὄσσομαι); cf. *Od.* 7.31 μηδέ τιν'... προτιόσσεο, 'do not look at anybody'. Hector is referring to Achilles' angry mien (344 and earlier 260) and the fury which speaks from his words. This interpretation better suits what follows (οὐδ' ἄρ' ἔμελλον) than 'knowing you well I foresee (my fate)' (Leaf, Richardson), for which cf. e.g. *Od.* 5.389 οἱ κραδίη προτιόσσετ' ὄλεθρον, 'his heart foresaw death'. **οὐδ' ἄρ' ἔμελλον | πείσειν** 'and I now realise (ἄρ') that I was not destined to persuade you'. For this use of μέλλω compare 5.205–6: 'I came trusting on my bow; but I now realise that it was not destined to be of any use to me (οὐκ ἄρ' ἔμελλον ὀνήσειν)', and see *LfgrE* 2bβ. The particle ἄρα is common in this context; see *GP* 36: 'the predestination of an event is realised *ex post facto*'. **σιδήρεος... θυμός:** iron is a ubiquitous and easily understandable metaphor for pitilessness; cf. 24.205, 521; *Od.* 4.293; 5.191; 12.280; 23.172.

358–60 This is the climax of a series of – increasingly concrete – prolepses announcing Achilles' death, which is not recounted in the *Iliad* (but does occur in one of the poems of the Epic Cycle: *Aethiopis*; see West (2003) 113). At first we merely hear that Achilles is destined to die young (1.352, 415–18); then Thetis tells him that he will die after killing Hector (18.95–6); the horse Xanthus is able to specify that he will be killed by a god and a man (19.416–17), while a prophecy of Thetis, which Achilles recalls when nearly drowning, speaks of arrows of Apollo (21.277–8); Hector, finally, discloses the names of Apollo and Paris and adds the exact location of his death (the Scaean gate, cf. also 'under the walls of Troy': 21.277; 23.81). See Duckworth (1933) 28–9, Taplin (1992) 245–7, Jones (1996) 115, and Introduction 2e. This technique of gradual revelation is also employed to great effect in the *Odyssey* in connection with Odysseus' revenge on the Suitors (de Jong on 13.372–439), or later on stage by Sophocles, famously in the *Oedipus Tyrannus*.

The death of Patroclus and Hector likewise are announced many times but never to the heroes themselves, who therefore march towards death unwittingly. In contrast, Achilles knows, chooses (9.410–16), and accepts (cf. 365–6n.) his fate. With Hector announcing Achilles' death we have come full circle in the lethal domino effect that determines the course of the last third of the *Iliad*: Patroclus kills Sarpedon – Hector, angry at Sarpedon's death, kills Patroclus, who foretells his death at the hands of Achilles – Achilles, angry at Patroclus' death, kills Hector but hears his own death prophesied. See Rutherford (1982) 152–8 and Introduction 2d.

The end of Achilles was portrayed by other texts and in art: he duels with the Aethiopian king Memnon (who dies, is removed from the battlefield through divine intervention, and buried) and then attacks Troy before Apollo and Paris kill him; see Burgess (2009). Apollo's motive is sometimes specified as anger at Achilles' killing of his son/priest Troilus.

358 τοι = σοι. θεῶν μήνιμα 'an object of the gods' wrath'; cf. *Od.* 11.73. In both cases the divine wrath concerns failure to give due burial. By introducing this term Hector adds a moral slant to Achilles' death, suggesting that it is the result of divine anger because of this hero's treatment of his corpse. Is this how the Homeric narrator wants us to look at the matter? Richardson suggests that he does: 'it looks as if Akhilleus' death may be seen as retribution for his behaviour towards Hektor's corpse'. The continuation of the story does not back up this idea, however. When Achilles continues to mistreat Hector, the pro-Trojan god Apollo criticises him severely and threatens that the gods' anger might strike him (μὴ . . . νεμεσσηθέωμεν: 24.53). But the point is not taken up by his interlocutor, Hera, who instead harps on Achilles' honour as the son of a goddess (*BK* on 24.56–63). When Zeus eventually decides that Achilles should give back Hector's body, he acts as upholder of the cosmic order (he wants to give both Apollo and Hera their due and to give in to his love for Hector while honouring Achilles: 24.65–76), not because he condemns the hero's behaviour. When he instructs

Thetis to tell Achilles that he is angry at his 'mad' behaviour (24.113–15), this seems like a rhetorical exaggeration in order to press his message (*BK* on 24.112–16). Finally, the way in which Achilles indeed releases the body cannot but absolve him from any divine wrath. The reference to a *mēnima* and Apollo's anger in 24 are perhaps to be seen as attempts to motivate Apollo's (future) killing of Achilles, which in the tradition was explained differently (see previous note). See also 395n. and Introduction 2e.

359–60 ἤματι τῶι, ὅτε 'on that (memorable) day when'. This type of temporal reference, which is an expressive variant of simple 'when', occurs 22 x (3 x narrator-text, 19 x speech). It usually refers to the past (e.g. 471–2, the narrator recalls the day when Andromache married Hector), but here and 8.475 it points to the future; see de Jong (2004) 234–6. ἐσθλὸν ἐόντ' 'though you are brave'. The word ἐσθλός in Homer is largely descriptive ('competent', 'valorous', 'useful') not moralistic ('good'); see Yamagata (1994) 192–9. ἐνὶ Σκαιῆισι πύληισιν: see 6n.

361–3 361 = 16.502 = 16.855; 362–3 = 16.856–7. The deliberate echoes link the deaths of Sarpedon, Patroclus, and Hector (see 326–66n.): 'the moment is recalled when Patroclus lay before Hector, as Hector now lies before Achilles. The poet often in this way links beginning and end and lets the contrast come out' (Schadewaldt (1959) 323, my translation).

361 μιν... τέλος θανάτοιο κάλυψεν: the moment of death of a Homeric warrior is only rarely described by the straightforward verb θνήισκω; instead, we find metaphorical or graphic expressions such as 'night' or 'death' 'covering' or 'being poured over the eyes', or 'limbs being loosened'. See Morrison (1999). Usually night/death covers the eyes (466) or a person... his eyes (whole-and-part construction: 16.503), but here and at 16.855 we find an abbreviated form: death covered *him*. The expression aptly describes the clouding of sight at the moment consciousness is lost. τέλος θανάτοιο is 'the fulfilment of death', hence death. τέλος originally means 'the accomplishment', and only later became 'end'; see Waanders (1983).

362–3 ψυχή... πταμένη: when a person dies both his *psuchē* and his *thumos* leave him, the narrator concentrating in one passage on *psuchē*, in another on *thumos*. Thus the present couplet is an expanded and memorable variant of ὦκα δὲ θυμὸς | ὤιχετ' ἀπὸ μελέων (13.671–2). The *thumos* upon death ceases to exist (*LfgrE* s.v. 1b). The concept of *psuchē* in Homer is complex. According to Jahn (1987) 27–38, the *psuchē* of a man knows three phases: when he lives, it is the principle of life (e.g.161); when he dies, it leaves him (here); and after his death, it is his representation in the underworld (e.g. 23.65). According to Clarke (1999) 53–60, 129–56, the basic meaning of *psuchē* is a gasp of breath, from which the other uses, the principle of life and the soul living in the underworld, are secondary or metonymical extensions. He analyses the present passage as: 'When the two great heroes breathe their last... the cold breath of death takes wing, emerging suddenly in a mythical shape out of the visible realities of the battlefield, and it flies off to become one of the wraiths that live out the shadowy afterlife in Hades' (148–9).

362 ῥεθέων 'limbs'; see 68n. Ἄϊδόσδε 'to (the house) of Hades'; cf. εἰν Ἄϊδαο δόμοισιν (52). βεβήκει: see 21n.

363 ὅν: possessive pronoun (L 18). πότμον: see 39n. γοόωσα: metrical diectasis (L 4): γοάουσα (◡ ◡ – ◡) > γοῶσα (◡ – ◡) > γοόωσα (◡◡ – ◡). ἀνδροτῆτα 'his manhood', i.e. his existence as a (living) man. The word is scanned with short first syllable because the original form was *anr-, with sonant r (> *anro > ἀνδρο-); see Wachter (2000) 70. The line is quoted by Plato and Plutarch with ἀδροτῆτα, 'vigour', which removes the metrical anomaly and, according to Latacz (1965) and *DELG*, is the correct form. ἥβην 'prime of life'. Despite Priam's earlier words about the beauty of a young man dying on the battlefield (71–3), to lose one's life before reaching old age, then as now, was seen as tragic.

364 = 16.858. καί 'even though' (adverbial). τεθνεῶτα: adaptation after quantitative metathesis: τεθνηῶτα (◡ – – ◡) > τεθνεῶτα (◡◡ – ◡) > τεθνειῶτα (◡ – – ◡). δῖος Ἀχιλλεύς: see 102n.

365–6 Only Hector and Achilles address their opponents even when they are dead; see 326–66n. The scholia explain this feature as expressive of Achilles' anger, but it seems more likely that in both cases the prophecy of the dying man calls for a reaction. The similarity of the scenes allows the narratees to savour the difference: whereas Hector rejected the prophecy of his death and still saw possibilities of victory over Achilles, Achilles accepts his fate although he quibbles over the exact moment ('I will die when Zeus decides'). It is an essential aspect of Achilles in the *Iliad* that he knows the circumstances of his early death with increasing precision (see 358–60n.) and, when Patroclus has died, accepts it: αὐτίκα τεθναίην, ἐπεὶ οὐκ ἄρ' ἔμελλον ἑταίρωι | κτεινομένωι ἐπαμῦναι, 'May I die directly, since I was not destined to help my friend at his killing' (18.98–9); cf. 19.421–3; 21.110–13. Indeed, at 18.115–16 Achilles used almost the same two lines when announcing to his mother Thetis that he would go after Hector, even if this, as she had just told him, would involve his death. The repetition of these lines at the moment when he *has* killed Hector is surely intentional and effective. At the same time they seem to have a slightly different tone here in that Achilles replaces Hector's 'ἤματι τῶι, ὅτε Paris and Apollo' by his own, more grandiloquent 'τότε... ὁππότε Zeus and the other gods', thus not allowing his opponent to have the last word but accepting his fate on his own terms.

Like Hector (337–43, 356–60nn.), Achilles uses no vocatives. Bassett (1934b) suggests that the absence is explained by the brevity of his speech (there are eighty-seven speeches of two verses, of which thirty-two, i.e. thirty-seven per cent, have no vocative). In view of the fact that Hector did use a vocative when he addressed the dead Patroclus (16.589), it may be preferable to take the absence as significant and expressive of Achilles' grim mood.

τέθναθι 'be dead'. The imperative standing alone is abrupt and dismissive. In this context we find an aorist (21.106: θάνε) or, more often, a perfect, cf. e.g. τεθνάτω (15.496) and τεθναίης (6.164). The perfect here expresses 'the satisfaction that the fate of his great enemy has been finally and fully fulfilled'(Ameis-Hentze, my translation). κῆρα: see 202n. τότε... ὁππότε: the correlative construction lends emphasis; cf. 9.702–3.

367–404

The death of Hector, the most important one in the *Iliad*, has a unique aftermath. The customary stripping of the armour is expanded with a scene featuring anonymous Greek soldiers (367–75) and followed by a speech by Achilles. In this hybrid speech he hovers between public triumph and private grief (376–94), and then abruptly announces the execution of his earlier threats that he would mutilate Hector's body, which takes an unexpected and for Iliadic warfare unprecedented form (395–404).

367–75 The act of despoiling a defeated enemy is mentioned often (e.g. 5.164; 6.28; 11.110, 246–7; 12.195; 13.201–2; 15.343, 524; 17.537; 21.183) and belongs to the status-seeking Homeric warrior culture: the armour serves as a trophy to prove martial success. Thus Idomeneus boasts that he has in his tent twenty spears, as well as shields, helmets, and corselets taken from Trojans as proof of his bravery (13.260–5); cf. also 6.480–1 (Hector prays for his son to bring home the – first? – bloody armour of a defeated enemy) and 7.82–3 (Hector says that he will dedicate captured armour in a temple, a habit probably taken over from the East that would become common practice in classical Greece and Rome). Thus the customary fight over a slain companion is aimed as much at saving his body for burial as at not allowing his armour to fall into enemy hands.

Usually the despoiling is described in one line or less, but here it is much longer. Firstly, there is the removal of the fatal weapon from the corpse. This was a preliminary to the despoiling (4.529–32; 5.620–2; 13.509–11) although it is not always explicitly recorded by the narrator. It occurs in the cases of Sarpedon's and Patroclus' deaths (16.503–5 and 862–3 respectively), and is one more connection between the deaths of these heroes; see Introduction 2d. Secondly, the narrator records the reaction of the Greek soldiers to Hector's body. As the tenses indicate, they watch *while* Achilles despoils Hector (368: imperfect ἐσύλα, followed at 376 by aorist ἐπεὶ ἐξενάριξε). Book 22 has a singularly theatrical nature, in that events are watched by a great number of (different) spectators; see 1–24n. The narrator here brings to the fore a set of viewers (cf. θηήσαντο), who had only played a minor role (cf. 3–4, 205) so far. The Greek soldiers are the first to react to Hector's death. Soon the camera will switch to Priam and Hecuba on the walls, the Trojans throughout the city, and finally Andromache inside the palace.

367–8 Cf. 21.200–201a, where Achilles pulls his 'bronze spear' out of the bank of the river Scamander. ἦ ῥα καί: see 273n. ἄνευθεν ἔθηχ' 'he put aside'. For the form of ἄνευθεν see 300n.

368–9 ὁ δ': δέ marks a new action rather than a new subject; see *GH* II 159. ἀπ' ὤμων: we regularly hear of armour being taken 'from the shoulders', both in the context of despoilings (e.g. 6.28; 11.579; 15.524, 544) and of the ordinary taking off of armour (7.122). This looks like a summary; cf. the fuller forms at 11.373–5 (the victor strips off the corselet from breast and the shield from shoulders) and 15.125–7 (Athena takes the helmet off Ares' head and the shield from his shoulders). τεύχε'... | αἱματόεντ': armour has twenty-one different epithets in Homer (see Dee (2002) 515–18), of which καλός, κλυτός, and ποικίλος are most frequent. Here we find the graphic and contextually relevant 'blood-stained' (cf. ἔντε'... αἱματόεντα at 13.640 and ἔναρα βροτόεντα at 245 and 7 x more in the *Il.*). περίδραμον 'ran up and stood around' (only here in Homer). υἷες Ἀχαιῶν: see 156n.

370 καί 'emphasises the fact that the relative clause contains an addition to the information contained in the main clause' (*GP* 294–5): the soldiers not only stand around Hector (which merely suggests interest) but admire him. Cf. Νέστωρ ἡδυεπὴς ἀνόρουσε... τοῦ καὶ ἀπὸ γλώσσης μέλιτος γλυκίων ῥέεν αὐδή, 'sweet-spoken Nestor stood up, from whose tongue (also) a voice streamed sweeter than honey' (1.247–9). θηήσαντο: this verb (derived from *θάϝα, Ion. θέη, Att. θέα, both the act of 'looking at' and 'sight') means 'watch', 'look at' a spectacle, in leisure and often in admiration. It was felt to be semantically related to θαῦμα (see *DELG* s.v.), and it is often found in conjunction with verbs of admiration, e.g. μαρμαρυγὰς θηεῖτο ποδῶν, θαύμαζε δὲ θυμῶι (*Od.* 8.265) and λαοὶ... θηεῦντό τε θάμβησάν τε (23.728). Here the admiration is suggested by ἀγητόν. φυὴν καὶ εἶδος ἀγητόν: cf. εἶδος ἀγητ- at 5.787; 8.228; 24.376; *Od.* 14.177, all in speech, which confirms that it represents the Greek soldiers' focalisation here. Next to the combination φυή and εἶδος (cf. *Od.* 5.212; 7.210), we also find εἶδος and δέμας combined (24.376; *Od.* 5.213; 8.116; 11.469 = 24.17; 14.177; 18.251; 19.124). In principle these three words, all of which roughly mean 'corporeal form/figure', have different nuances: φυή (from φύομαι) refers to muscular physique; εἶδος (from root -ιδ, cf. εἶδον) to overall appearance, often specifically beauty; and δέμας (from δέμω) to build. In practice, however, metrical factors may play a major role in their choice and combination.

Herodotus echoes this passage at *Histories* 9.25.1 (the Greeks admire the body of the Persian general Masistius): ὁ δὲ νεκρὸς ἦν θέης ἄξιος (≈ ἀγητόν) μεγάθεος εἵνεκα καὶ κάλλεος (≈ φυὴν καὶ εἶδος)... ἐκλιπόντες τὰς τάξις ἐφοίτων (≈ περίδραμον) θεησόμενοι (≈ θηήσαντο) Μασίστιον, 'the corpse was worth looking at because of its tallness and beauty... they broke their ranks in order to go and admire Masistius'.

371–5 An instance of an 'actual *tis*'-speech (as opposed to a 'potential *tis*'-speech:106–8n.): a speech voiced by an anonymous collective (in the nine Iliadic instances, the Greek or Trojan soldiers). They offer an interesting glimpse of the feelings and opinions of the masses, which are much less represented in the story than the individual leaders. Thus, we see them gloat at Thersites being forcefully disciplined by Odysseus and pray for the war to end (2.271–8). For a discussion of the Iliadic examples see de Jong (1987b).

The soldiers' speech is accompanied by a gesture: οὐδ'... ἀνουτητεί – οὐτήσασκε, they stab the corpse with their spear. This act, reported only here, may 'derive ultimately from the wish to ensure that the dead man is really and truly dead and that his ghost cannot harm his enemies after death' (Richardson). But it certainly is also relevant that those who are doing the stabbing are anonymous Greek warriors who probably would never have dared to face Hector while he was still alive but now want to 'share' in his downfall. Finally, as their words reveal, they intend to mock their once formidable opponent. The narratees will interpret their behaviour as increasing the pathos of the situation: the greatest warrior on the Trojan side suffers disgrace by unworthy opponents (Griffin (1980) 47). It is a preparation for what will happen at 395–404, when Hector's body is dragged through the dust by Achilles. The many wounds inflicted on Hector here will be recalled by Hermes at 24.420–1: 'since there were many who drove their bronze into him'.

371 οὐδ'... ἀνουτητεί 'not (one stood by) without stabbing'; for this type of expression and the ending -τεί see 304–5n. The adverb occurs only here (but cf. ἀνούτατος, 'not wounded', at 4.540). The litotic effect of this expression pertains not so much to the stabbing itself as to the number of people who were stabbing: there was no one who did not stab = everybody stabbed. οἵ: personal pronoun (L 19); the accent is due to enclitic τις following.

372 'Thus many a one said, looking at another man standing next to him.' This line introduces two other 'tis-speeches': 2.271; 4.81. For τις meaning 'many a one', cf. e.g. 19.71. The idea is that the one speech which is quoted represents many similar speeches. It is also possible to take πλησίον as substantival, while τις... ἄλλον almost is ἄλλος ἄλλον: 'each one said looking at his neighbour' (BK on 2.271). Looking at one another underscores the collectivity of the speech; the soldiers expect their own ideas to be shared by their neighbour.

373 ὢ πόποι: see 168n. ἦ μάλα δή: see 229n. μαλακώτερος ἀμφαφάασθαι 'softer to feel'. The verb is (probably) related to ἅπτω, and it usually refers to feeling or touching with the hand, e.g. of Eurycleia touching Odysseus' foot (Od. 19.475). Here feeling is a sarcastic understatement for the actual stabbing of Hector, who without his armour is 'soft', i.e. easy to wound (Ameis-Hentze and LfgrE ἀφάω 1, μαλακός 1a). The soldiers turn to the kind of sarcasm we typically find in vaunts (286n.), and Kyriakou (2001) 273 suggest that the 'tis-speech' could be considered as such. The continuation of the sentence also suggests a metaphorical undertone: now that he is dead Hector is easier to handle, i.e. deal with than when he set the Greek ships on fire. ἀμφαφάασθαι is a case of metrical diectasis (L 4): ἀμφαφάασθαι (– ⏑ ⏑ – ⏑) < ἀμφαφᾶσθαι (– ⏑ – ⏑) < ἀμφαφάεσθαι (– ⏑ ⏑ – ⏑).

374 ὅτε... ἐνέπρησεν: an analepsis of the climactic – and, for the Greeks, traumatic – moment when Hector set fire to one of the Greek ships (16.112–23). A Muse-invocation marked the importance of that moment, which saw both Hector's greatest military success and the beginning of his downfall, since Achilles at 9.650–3 had announced that he would return to battle when Hector set the ships on fire. The MSS hesitate between aorist and imperfect (ἐνέπρηθεν). Both tenses are found in subordinate ὅτε-clauses (cf. e.g. the aorist at 2.743 or imperfect at 2.351) and are equally possible in this place. πυρὶ κηλέωι 'with burning fire'. κήλεος is derived from καίω. πῦρ has ten epithets in Homer (see Dee (2002) 473–6), which mainly stress its destructive or glittering nature. The combination πυρὶ κηλέωι is consistently used in contexts where the actual burning of the fire is relevant: setting fire to ships (8.217, 235; 15.744), heating water (18.346; *Od.* 8.435), burning clothes (22.512), or hardening a wooden stake (*Od.* 9.328).

376 ποδάρκης δῖος Ἀχιλλεύς: this formula occurs 21 x in the *Iliad*. For δῖος see 102n. ποδάρκης is used only for Achilles, and it was clearly understood as similar to ποδώκης, 'swift-footed'; see 14n. Yet its original meaning may be 'defending himself (from ἀρκέω) with his feet', i.e. by running away or by kicking (see *LfgrE*).

377–95 The speech-introduction and capping do not inform us what kind of speech to expect (except that it is public) or in what mood it is spoken by Achilles. This is not surprising in that it actually is a unique, hybrid speech, which starts as a military *parainesis*, changes halfway through into a personal meditation, and ends as an embryonic paean. Its structure shows ring-composition (Lohmann (1970) 21–2):

A Friends, since the gods granted us to master this man, who has done so much harm (*victory*),

B let us continue fighting and see whether the Trojans leave their city or stay (*exhortation*).

C But why do I consider these things (*interruption formula*)? Patroclus is lying unburied, whom I will never forget.

B' Let us return to the ships (*exhortation*).

A' We killed Hector, to whom the Trojans prayed like a god (*victory*).

The deictic pronouns τόνδ' (379), τοῦδε (383), and τόνδε (392) strewn across the speech evoke the gestures which the narratees are to imagine Achilles making while he speaks: he repeatedly points at the corpse lying at his feet.

377 The line occurs almost identically at 23.535. The interpretation 'Taking up a position among the Greeks he spoke winged words (to them)', for which cf. e.g. στὰς ἐν μέσσοισι μετεφώνεεν (7.384), seems better than 'Standing up (after kneeling or stooping to strip Hector of his armour) he spoke winged words among the Greeks' (Ameis-Hentze). ἔπεα πτερόεντ': see 215n.

378–84 Achilles starts by suggesting that the Greeks exploit the momentum of the death of the most important fighter on the Trojan side and attack Troy.

This is one of a series of places where the Homeric narrator toys with the idea that Achilles might conquer Troy (cf. 18.261–5; 21.309–10, 516–17, 536, 544–6). Together these passages create an instance of misdirection: the narratees are led to believe that the traditional plot, in which Achilles does *not* capture Troy (cf. 16.707–9), might be abandoned. Similar examples relating to the theme of the fall of Troy are found e.g. at 3.281–7 (the duel between Paris and Menelaus might bring a peaceful solution) and 16.698–711 (Patroclus almost takes Troy). Although the narratees know that Troy *will* fall and Patroclus and Achilles will *die* before that moment, such deviations from the straight narrative course create suspense.

Scholars also look at this passage in neo-analytical terms (see Introduction 1c): Achilles' suggestion to attack Troy would then be modelled after his behaviour in the *Aithiopis*, where he kills Memnon and then immediately goes on to attack Troy. See West (2003) and Burgess (2009).

378 This whole-line vocative is found both in councils (e.g. 2.79) and on the battlefield (here and e.g. 11.276). Strictly speaking, it addresses only the military and political *leaders*, but it is used also in contexts where all Greeks are present (cf. 9.17; 23.457). Zenodotus' suggestion of Ἀτρεΐδη τε καὶ ἄλλοι ἀριστῆες Παναχαιῶν (found at 7.327; 23.236) as an alternative cannot be right, since Agamemnon is not present on the battlefield (he was wounded at 11.283; cf. 16.26 and 19.51–3). Some MSS have ὦ φίλοι ἥρωες Δαναοί, θεράποντες Ἄρηος, which always occurs when all Greeks are addressed (2.110; 6.67; 15.733; 19.78); this would be the best reading to adopt if it were not for the overwhelming manuscript evidence for the verse printed in the text. Ἀργείων: the Homeric epics have three ethnic indications for what we call Greeks (from Latin *Graeci*): Ἀχαιοί (inhabitants of the Achaean country = Northern Greece), Ἀργεῖοι (inhabitants of Argos = Argolis, the central part of the Peloponnese), and Δαναοί (descendants of Danaus). The term *Achaioi* is also found in linear B tablets (a-ka-wi-ja-de = Ἀχαιϝίανδε) and, like *Danaoi*, probably in Egyptian and Hittite documents. See *BK* on 1.2. Although originally dating from different times and referring to different parts of Greece, the three words are synchronically used as metrical variants.

379 ἐπεὶ δή: the first syllable has to be scanned long, as at 23.2 and 4 x *Od.*; see *GH* I 103. The particle δή indicates that what Achilles says is evident to both himself and his addressees: Hector is dead, for all to see; see 76n. τόνδ' ἄνδρα θεοὶ δαμάσασθαι ἔδωκαν 'the gods gave (it to me) to kill this man'. Homeric mortals tend to ascribe successes and failures to both the gods and themselves, according to the principle of 'double motivation' (the term derives from Lesky (1961)). Thus Achilles will refer to the mortal part of the action at the end of his speech: ἐπέφνομεν Ἕκτορα δῖον. The role of the gods often is merely *assumed* by the mortal agent, but here Achilles was explicitly informed by Athena of her support (216–23). For the gods 'giving' mortals things see 403–4n. The verb δάμνημι/δαμνάω, lit. 'tame', is used repeatedly in this book in connection with the death of Hector; cf. 176, 271, 446. It is an expressive variant for 'to kill' (253n.), with the connotation of vanquishing a particularly vigorous warrior. The active is much more common than the middle (it is used in three other instances in book 22), but the middle is used here to express that the subject (Achilles) benefits from the action in the sense that he exercises power over the object (Hector); cf. ἕλκεσθαι (398) and ἀεικίσσασθαι (404) and see Allan (2003) 113, note 199. Of course, it is also a convenient metrical variant.

380 A similar claim that Hector killed more Greeks than any other Trojan is made by Andromache at 24.737–8, and cf. Agamemnon at 10.47–52 (Hector killed the most Greeks in one day). This assertion proves accurate even within the four days of battle recounted in the *Iliad*. During this time, Hector kills twenty-seven Greeks; other Trojans kill two or three at the most. For an overview of all killings see Stoevesandt (2004) 388–412. **κακὰ πόλλ' ἔρρεξεν:** as almost always in Homer, κακός does not (yet) have a moralistic undertone but simply means 'did so much harm'; thus the same expression is used about a boar wreaking havoc at 9.540. The MSS hesitate between ἔρρεξεν and ἔρδεσκεν, and at 9.540, even between ἔρρεξεν, ἔρδεσκεν, ἔρρεζεν, and ἔοργε.

381–4 'Come, let us test (the Trojans) with arms all around the city, in order that we find out next what mood the Trojans presently have, whether they want x or y.'

381–2 εἰ δ' ἄγετ': for this formula of exhortation see 174n.; only here and at *Od.* 4.832 is it found in a main clause following a (temporal) subordinate clause. **σὺν τεύχεσι πειρηθέωμεν:** the verb is used absolutely, with Τρώων understood, cf. ἔπεσιν πειρήσομαι, 'I will test (the Greeks) with words' (2.73) and (with genitive) Τρώων πειρήσομαι . . . , αἵ κ' ἐθέλωσ', 'I will test the Trojans, to see whether they want' (19.70–1). πειρηθέωμεν is to be scanned with synizesis (-έω- counts as one long syllable). Some MSS have the younger, contracted form πειρηθῶμεν (cf. *Od.* 8.100). **ἔτι:** i.e. before we rest on our laurels or do something else. **κ' . . . γνῶμεν:** the final subjunctive in Homer may be found with κε/ἄν; see *GH* II 270–1. **Τρώων νόον, ὅν τιν' ἔχουσιν:** lit. 'the mind, i.e. mood, of the Trojans, whichever they have'; an instance of (grammatical) prolepsis (191–2n.).

383–4 ἢ καταλείψουσιν . . . ἦε μένειν μεμάασι: in dependent interrogative clauses the indicative is regularly found (next to the subjunctive and optative); see *GH* II 294. The idea that the Trojans might give up fighting and leave their city now that their general has died is also voiced by 'the Myrmidon'/Hermes vis-à-vis Priam at 24.383–5. Abandoning the city is one of several ways ancient sieges could end (besides victory, defeat, or a peaceful settlement). **πόλιν ἄκρην:** this combination means the 'acropolis' (cf. 172n.), and Achilles metonymically mentions the most important part of Troy. **τοῦδε πεσόντος . . . καὶ Ἕκτορος οὐκέτ' ἐόντος** 'now that this man has fallen . . . even though Hector no longer lives'. The genitive absolute is rare in Homer (see 47n.), but here we have two examples in quick succession.

385 This is the typical interruption formula used by speakers in monologues (see 122n.); its use here in a public speech is nevertheless apt in that it marks the transition to a more personal tone.

386-7 'There lies near the ships a corpse, unlamented, unburied, Patroclus.'
Much of the force of this sentence derives from its lack of connectives. πάρ =
παρά. In Homer prepositions may lose their final vowel, even if they are not
followed by another vowel; this is referred to as *apokopē* ('cutting off' the vowel).
ἄκλαυτος ἄθαπτος: the same combination is found at *Od.* 11.54, 72 (there of
Elpenor, Odysseus' companion, whose death had not been noted by the others),
and cf. the even more impressive ἀφρήτωρ ἀθέμιστος ἀνέστιός ἐστιν ἐκεῖνος | ὅς,
'without clan, law, and hearth is the man who' (9.63-4). Strictly speaking,
Patroclus has already been spontaneously lamented (19.282-339; cf. κλαίουσα:
286, 301, κλαίων: 338), but the official burial and lament will follow only at
23.8-257.

387-90 Achilles expresses the idea that he will never forget Patroclus in an
emphatic form: 'as long as I live, I will not forget Patroclus. And though people
in Hades tend to forget the dead, I will remember Patroclus even there.' Soon
Patroclus will reproach Achilles that he *has* forgotten him (23.69-70), but this is the
typical chiding found at the opening of dream speeches (cf. e.g. the dream/Athena
to Nausicaa at *Od.* 6.25: 'How did your mother come to have such a lazy child?').
Both underworld scenes in the *Odyssey* show us Achilles with Patroclus nearby
(11.467-8; 24.15-16).

Achilles' claim that the dead forget people is partly backed up in that the
dead in the underworld scenes cannot think or speak unless they have drunk the
blood of sacrificial victims (e.g. *Od.* 11.140-9, 153-4, 228-32, 390, and cf. their
qualification as ἀφραδέες, 'lacking *phrenes*': 11.476); elsewhere in these same scenes,
however, shades are fully in control of their thoughts and speech (e.g. 24.15-204).
As Clarke (1999) 193 notes: 'Just as Homer is ambivalent over whether the dead
in Hades are empty images or dead men of substance, so his conception of their
ability to think and speak like living men appears and disappears in different
contexts'.

The commonplace nature of 'I will never forget X' in the context of mourn-
ing should not make us fail to notice that Achilles' words are unparalleled in
Homer. They are expressive of his massive sorrow over Patroclus. The exact
nature of the friendship between these two men, most famously paralleled by
Gilgamesh and Enkidu (see e.g. West (1997) 337-8), has been much discussed:
are they friends or lovers (the second option was already defended in antiquity,
e.g. Aeschines *Prosecution of Timarchus* 133, 142)? The Homeric facts, briefly, are as
follows. Patroclus is Achilles' θεράπων, ἑταῖρος, ἡνίοχος , i.e. is a man of lower
rank. He is older than Achilles (11.786-7) and clearly functions as his foil, just
as Polydamas is Hector's foil (see 100-103n.): he is gentle (17.204; 19.300), while
Achilles is quick-tempered (11.653-4). Their close friendship is the result of their
having been raised together, when Patroclus had been taken up in Peleus' palace
as suppliant exile after he had inadvertently killed a man (23.84-90). Referring to
this shared youth Patroclus asks Achilles for his ashes to be kept together with his
(23.83-4, 91-2). There is no explicit reference to a homoerotic relationship, yet

the intensity of Achilles' feeling after Patroclus' death is unmatched in Homer. For discussions, see e.g. Dover (1978) 194–9, Clarke (1978), and more scholarship listed in *LfgrE* s.v. Πάτροκλος.

Another issue regarding Patroclus is whether he was invented by Homer or adapted from tradition in a more important role, perhaps based on that of Antilochus in the *Aethiopis*; for discussion see Janko 313–14.

387 ἐγώ γε: for this orthography see 86n.

388 The Homeric epics have many expressions for the idea of 'being alive': be among the living (here and cf. e.g. 23.47b), move one's limbs (here and cf. e.g. 9.610b), breathe (9.609–10a), and see the sunlight (e.g. 5.120). The present line is a combination of two of these expressions (23.47b + 9.610b), while a well attested ancient reading presents a unique variant: ζωὸς ἐν Ἀργείοισι φιλοπτολέμοισι μετείω. **μοι:** 'ethic' dative (38n.). **φίλα γούνατ'** 'my knees'. *Philos* originally means 'belonging to a social group of people bound by reciprocal obligations', from which an affective meaning, 'dear', 'beloved' developed. Often it merely has a weakened, possessive sense (scholia: φίλα = ἴδια), though something of the original force is still felt in that it is used mainly of inalienable possessions such as limbs or organs. See *DELG* and Robinson (1990).

389 εἰ . . . θανόντων περ: although placed after θανόντων, the particle περ should be taken together with εἰ. It concerns the whole clause (cf. later εἴπερ) and has concessive force; see *GP* 488–9 and Bakker (1988) 205–32. **καταλήθοντ':** this compound verb occurs only here. It was presumably chosen instead of ἐπιλήθομαι for metrical reasons (since περ has to scan long, it needs to be followed by a word starting with a consonant). **εἰν Ἀίδαο** 'in (the house) of Hades'; cf. 52.

390 αὐτάρ: here used apodotically; cf. 3.290 and see *GP* 55. It underlines the opposition between the behaviour of the 'they' of the subordinate clause and that of the ἐγώ, Achilles, in the main clause. **κεῖθι:** the suffix -θι indicates the place where. **φίλου . . . ἑταίρου:** Patroclus is regularly called Achilles' 'dear friend' (9 x *Il.*, of which 5 x speech, 2 x embedded focalisation), even his πολὺ φίλτα-τος . . . ἑταῖρος (17.411, 655). Although other characters may be 'dear friends' too (e.g. Automedon at 23.563), they usually are referred to as such only once or twice whereas Patroclus is the 'dear friend' *par excellence* of the *Iliad*. **μεμνήσομ':** future of μιμνήσκομαι, here with the meaning 'remember', see 268n.

391–4 Achilles suggests that he and his soldiers sing a paean. At 1.472–4 we also hear of a paean being sung, there to appease Apollo after he has sent the plague. The paean most likely started as a choral song-dance performance in honour of a deity called Paian/Paianon, a military god known from Linear B tablets from Knossos, while the Homeric epics feature the god Παιήων, healer of the gods (e.g. 5.401, 899, 900). Soon after Homer and Hesiod the god became identified with Apollo. The paean is sung on many occasions, including before and after battle. The victory paeans were performed in the course of the army's return to its camp right after battle, while setting up a trophy, and at a feast; cf. e.g. Thucydides *History of the Peloponnesian War* 2.91.2.; Xenophon *Hellenica*

7.2.15. See Käppel (1992) and Rutherford (2001). The scholia suggest that in lines 393–4 Achilles rehearses the content of the paean, as it were, or perhaps rather its refrain. Many have adopted this attractive suggestion: 'The asyndeton after 392 is in favour of this idea, as is the asyndetic simplicity, brevity and balance of the two separate hemistichs of 393' (Richardson). The paean is one of several non-epic genres which are referred to in the *Iliad*: cf. the *thrēnos* or lament (24.721), the *hymenaeus* or marriage song (18.493), and the harvest song (18.570); see Dalby (1998).

391 νῦν δ' ἄγ': see 174n. κοῦροι Ἀχαιῶν: *kouroi* refers to the age group of young (unmarried) men who perform tasks which suit their age: they hunt (17.726), dance (18.494; *Od*. 8.262–5), prepare ships (*Od*. 8.35), and serve at dinner (1.470). Here and elsewhere, however, the expression κοῦροι Ἀχαιῶν seems to be no more than a metrical variant of υἷες Ἀχαιῶν (156n.), which includes all adult men. In classical times the paean was sung by adult males, particularly those of military age (Rutherford (2001) 86).

392 ἄγωμεν: the use of this verb suggests that the Greeks will transport Hector's corpse on a chariot, which was commonly used as an 'ambulance' on the Homeric battlefield; cf. e.g. Νέστορα δ' ἐκ πολέμοιο φέρον Νηλήϊαι ἵπποι | ἱδρῶσαι, ἦγον δὲ Μαχάονα, 'Nestor the sweating horses of Neleus carried out of the battle, and transported Machaon too' (11.597–8). Soon it will turn out that Achilles has something else in mind.

393 Achilles uses 'we' when referring to the killing of Hector, which clearly was his doing alone. Three interpretations are possible. (1) We = I, as e.g. at 13.257 (τό νυ γὰρ κατεάξαμεν, ὃ πρὶν ἔχεσκον, 'for I broke the spear, which I had before'). (2) We = I together with you (so-called sociative plural): Achilles implies that the glory he has won makes *all* Greeks more glorious. This is the interpretation of the scholia (Ἑλληνικῶς κοινοποιεῖ τὴν νίκην, 'in typical Greek (democratic?) manner, he makes the victory a general one'), Wackernagel (1920) 98–100, and *GH* II 33. (3) We = we: since Hector was not only Achilles' personal enemy but also the common foe of all Greeks (cf. 373–4); Floyd (1969) 134–5. The second interpretation is the most attractive. In any case the plural fits the entire format of the speech, in which Achilles is talking about what 'we' should do now (cf. πειρηθέωμεν, γνῶμεν, νεώμεθα, ἄγωμεν), and corroborates the idea that 393–4 reflect the content of the choral paean. ἠράμεθα... ἐπέφνομεν: the asyndeton is expressive and adds weight to ἐπέφνομεν; see *GH* II 351. μέγα κῦδος: Athena had promised Achilles (and herself) *kudos* (217), but he graciously extends it to his men. We may also recall how at 57 Priam feared that Hector staying outside (and dying) would bring *kudos* to Achilles. For the meaning of *kudos* see 205–7n. ἐπέφνομεν 'we killed'. Reduplicated aorist ἐ-πέ-φν-ομεν, from IE root *ghʷen-,'hit'; cf. φόνος. The corresponding present is θείνω. Ἕκτορα δῖον: this generic epithet (102n.) is used 38 x of Hector, both by the narrator and by speaking characters. It here might therefore be a mere metrical automatism, but the next line suggests that it is used intentionally and expressively: 'godlike'

Hector, whom the Trojans prayed to as to a god. Achilles' laudatory appraisal of his opponent both ties in with his earlier suggestion that the Trojans might give up fighting after having lost such a general, and of course explains why the Greeks have won such great glory. Achilles also seems to have genuine respect for Hector, whom at 21.279–80 he had called 'the best' (ἄριστος) of the Trojans and a 'good' (ἀγαθός) fighter. Aristarchus, however, recalling 16.242–4, where Achilles claimed that Patroclus could be a match for Hector even on his own, thought Achilles' present praise a contradiction and athetised 393–4.

394 θεῶι ὧς εὐχετόωντο: people may 'look at' or 'greet' a person 'like a god' (e.g. 12.312; *Od.* 7.71; 8.173; 15.520), occasionally 'pray to' someone 'as to a god' (here and cf. *Od.* 8.467; 15.181). The reason for the veneration is martial valour (here), beauty, wisdom, or a gracious act. Hecuba will report the same about Hector at 434–5, where see n. εὐχετόωντο is an instance of metrical diectasis (L 4): εὐχετάοντο > εὐχετῶντο > εὐχετόωντο.

395 ἦ ῥα καί: see 273n. Ἕκτορα δῖον ἀεικέα μήδετο ἔργα: these words and the following scene come somewhat as a shock. Although Achilles had repeatedly talked about his desire to mutilate Hector's body, i.e. decapitate it or leave it unburied (see 337–54n.), his immediately preceding speech, especially the neutral ἄγωμεν and the deferential Ἕκτορα δῖον, had not suggested violence. It now turns out that he does carry out his threats, tying Hector's body to his chariot and dragging him through the dust.

Scholars have been divided about this act of Achilles, just as they have been divided about his whole figure (see Introduction 2e): is it excessive, just as his *mēnis* was, perhaps, excessive? Is the expression ἀεικέα μήδετο ἔργα to be seen as one of the rare narratorial comments in Homer, one which criticises Achilles? Scholars who take it as criticism are e.g. Bowra (1930) 21 and Segal (1971a) 12–17, esp. 13 ('repugnance and even some measure of moral outrage'). But many point out rightly that ἀεικέα... ἔργα means 'disfiguring deeds' and does not so much imply wrong deeds (for Achilles to commit) as shameful deeds (for Hector to suffer); thus Andromache envisions how Astyanax, after the fall of Troy, κεν ἔργα ἀεικέα ἐργάζοιο, 'would have to perform shaming work', i.e. the work of a slave (24.733). This is the position of, e.g. Bassett (1938) 203, Griffin (1980) 85, and van Wees (1992) 129. We should also realise that the ἀεικέα... ἔργα form part of the focalisation of Achilles (μήδετο), who earlier announced that he intended that dogs would maul his opponent ἀϊκῶς (335–6); cf. de Jong (2004) 138. As Vernant (1991) 70 puts it: 'By dirtying and disfiguring the corpse instead of purifying and mourning it, *aikia* seeks to destroy the individuality of a body that was the source of the charm of youth and life. Achilles wants Hector to look like Sarpedon... (16.637–40).' Achilles' act is even divinely 'authorised', as the narrator tells us at 403–4 that it is Zeus who allows his enemies to disfigure (ἀεικίσσασθαι) Hector. When Apollo criticises Achilles at 24.46–54, this seems to concern the fact that he continues the mistreatment *too long*; see also the discussion of μήνιμα at 358n. and *BK* on 24.22. All in all, this line is best taken as not implying moral criticism. It does convey pathos, however, through the juxtaposition of Ἕκτορα δῖον and ἀεικέα; see also 401–4n.

As for Achilles' actual act, here we may note that a Trojan, Hippothous, ties his shield-strap round the tendons at Patroclus' ankle and tries to drag his body away by the foot at 17.288–91. No other victorious warrior in the *Iliad* binds his victim behind his chariot, but according to Aristotle *Fr.* 166, this was an existing custom, which persisted to his times in Thessaly. In Sophocles' *Ajax* Hector is still alive when Achilles ties him to his chariot (1030–1). This could be this poet's own invention, but it more probably goes back to the Epic Cycle. It may even have been known to Homer but suppressed as being too horrible.

396–8 'He pierced the tendons of both feet at the back from heel to ankle, attached straps of ox-hide (to the pierced feet), bound (the straps) to his chariot, and let the head drag (over the ground).'

398 δίφροιο: δίφρος is the platform of a chariot on which the charioteer stood, a sense probably intended here, but it is often used as *pars pro toto* (and metrical variant) for the chariot as a whole, the ἅρμα, as in the next line. For Homeric chariots see Crouwel (1981). ἕλκεσθαι: for the middle cf. 24.15 and see 379n.

399 κλυτὰ τεύχεα: see 258n.

400 This is a formulaic verse (3 x *Il.*, 3 x *Od.*), which acquires a grim undertone in the present context: the horses perform their gruesome task 'not unwillingly'. μάστιξεν . . . ἐλάαν 'he whipped (the horses) so as to make them go'; for this loose, final-consecutive use of the infinitive see 5n. Achilles himself drives the chariot, both because the presence of the armour leaves no space for a second person and because he wants to perform the act of mutilation in person. τὼ . . . ἀέκοντε πετέσθην: dual forms (L 16, 17).

401–4 One of the most pathetic passages in the *Iliad*. To start with, it is a force-ful elaboration of the 'dust' motif. When warriors die it is regularly said that they fall in the dust (e.g. 5.75); a gruesome instance is found at 10.457, when Dolon's head mingles with the dust while it is still speaking; a playful one at 21.407, when Ares hit by a stone thrown by Athena sullies his hair in the dust. Pathos is increased when the *beauty* of man or armour falling in the dust is stressed (e.g. 15.537–8, where the plume of a helmet, shining with its crimson dye, falls in the dust). The motif links the fates of Sarpedon, Patroclus, and Hector (see Introduction 2d), in that Sarpedon's *body* is unrecognisable because it is completely covered by blood and dust (16.638–40), Patroclus' *helmet* is sullied in the dust (16.795–800), and Hector's *head* is intentionally and prolongedly dragged through the dust. In the case of Patroclus and Hector the narrator emphasises the difference between *former* beauty and *present* disfigurement: (Patroclus) πάρος γε μὲν οὐ θέμις ἦεν | ἱππόκομον πήληκα μιαίνεσθαι κονίηισιν | ἀλλ' ἀνδρὸς θείοιο κάρη χαρίεν τε μέτωπον | ῥύετ' Ἀχιλῆος. τότε δὲ Ζεὺς Ἕκτορι δῶκεν | ἧι κεφαλῆι φορέειν ≈ (Hector) κάρη δ' ἅπαν ἐν κονίηισιν | κεῖτο πάρος χαρίεν· τότε δὲ Ζεὺς δυσμενέεσσι | δῶκεν ἀεικίσσασθαι.

Another pathetic detail is the narrator's explicit comment that Hector was dis-
figured in *his own* fatherland (ἑῆι ἐν πατρίδι γαίηι), thus continuing the melan-
cholic tone of the description of the Trojan washing-places in the course of
Hector's deadly race (145–57n.): 'The bitterness of the ill-treatment of Hector's
head... is increased by his enemy having power to inflict it in his own father-
land, before the eyes of his own people' (Griffin (1980) 138). A similar emphatic –
but ironic rather than pathetic – use of the possessive pronoun is found e.g.
at *Od.* 19.209–10: κλαιούσης (Penelope) ἑὸν ἄνδρα παρήμενον... ἑὴν ἐλέαιρε
(Odysseus) γυναῖκα. Its use is even more marked here, since Hector is not the
grammatical subject in any of the proximate clauses; the narrator as it were looks
at the event through his eyes, as he does when speaking of 'his enemies' (δυσμενέες
occurs 16 x *Il.*, only here outside speech). At this peak of emotion the narrator
employs skewed verses (33–7n. and Introduction 4b).

401–2 τοῦ... ἦν ἑλκομένοιο κονίσαλος: lit. 'there was a cloud of dust of him
as he was dragged', i.e. 'a cloud of dust arose created by him being dragged';
cf. 3.13–14: τῶν... κονίσαλος ὄρνυτ'... | ἐρχομένων. ἀμφὶ δὲ χαῖται | κυάνεαι
πίτναντο 'on both sides (of his head) his dark hair streamed'; a unique expression.
While τρίχες refers to hair/manes in general and κόμη to hair which is dressed,
χαῖται is the word for loose hair/manes (which may stream when moving: 1.529;
6.509 = 15.266; 23.367, or which may be plaited: 14.175–6). There are two variant
readings, πίλναντο, πίμπλαντο, which will not do however, since both need a
complement. 'Dark' hair is κυάνεος rather than μέλας (cf. 1.528; 15.102; 17.209;
Od. 16.176 and the epithet κυανοχαίτης). Zooming in on the detail of the colour of
Hector's hair, never revealed before, the narrator leads up to the hero's handsome
face.

402–3 κάρη... ἅπαν ἐν κονίηισιν | κεῖτο: as 23.25 and 24.18 suggest, we must
imagine Hector's face to be turned face down to the ground. πάρος... τότε δέ:
the narrator's variant of πάρος... νῦν δέ in speech (cf. 233–5, 302–3).

403–4 Ζεὺς δυσμενέεσσιν | δῶκεν ἀεικίσσασθαι: it is difficult to decide
whether to analyse 'but then Zeus allowed his enemies to disfigure it (= Hector's
head)', with the infinitive as object (as at 379), or 'but then Zeus gave it to his
enemies, to disfigure', with a final infinitive loosely attached (cf. 5n.). For the
middle of ἀεικίζω (active at 256; 24.22) cf. 16.559 and see 379n.

The gods *give* mortals objects (e.g. a golden headdress: 470), special abilities
(archery, augury) or heroic qualities (courage, eloquence), temporary prosperity
and adversity (see especially 24.527–35 on Zeus's two jars, from which he gives,
δίδωσι, mortals good and evil), and failure or success (285, 379); see *LfgrE* s.v.
δίδωμι I 2 and van der Mije (1987). The mention of Zeus is important both in
that it elevates the death of Hector into a very special event once more (cf. the
divine scene at 166–87n.) and in that Achilles' treatment of Hector's corpse is
given divine authority (see 395n.). The gods now support Achilles, but when he
later leaves Hector's body for the dogs (23.182–3), they will protect it against them
and all other forms of mutilation and decay (23.184–91 and 24.418–23). In this

way they have their cake and eat it, too: they honour Achilles, granting him his revenge, while showing their respect for Hector at the same time.

405–36

When warriors die in the *Iliad*, the grief that their friends, relatives, or compatriots suffer may be briefly indicated. Only in the case of Patroclus (18.22–65; 19.282–302) and Hector do we get a more extended lamentation. That for Hector is the most elaborate: it starts with improvised laments on the walls of Troy (Priam: 416–28; Hecuba: 431–6; Andromache: 477–514), which will be followed by official ones at his home in book 24 after his body has been recovered and properly laid out (Andromache, Hecuba, Helen: 723–76); this is one of the connections between books 22 and 24 (see Introduction 2c). The speeches of Priam and Hecuba mirror those at the beginning of this book (38–76 and 82–9), as their fears have become reality. Likewise, Andromache's speech now should be compared to her earlier one at 6.407–39, when she was already full of foreboding and fear; see Lohmann (1988) 66–9.

405 The narrator effects a change of scene from Achilles in the plain to the Trojans on the walls, as often, via a μέν-clause that offers a recapitulation of what preceded and a δέ-clause (cf. 1–4n.). What is striking, however, is his use of the pluperfect κεκόνιτο in the μέν-clause instead of the customary imperfect that indicates that the activity at the one scene continues while we move to the other. From 464–5 it appears that Achilles does continue dragging the corpse behind his chariot towards the Greek camp, but rather than noting this *activity* the narrator has opted to stress the *state* Hector's head is in (it is completely covered with dust). τοῦ: anaphoric pronoun (L 17). νυ: see 9n. μήτηρ: throughout this final scene the narrator uses circumlocutions: μήτηρ, παῖδ' (407), πατήρ (408), γέροντα (412), ἄλοχος (437), and πόσις (439); cf. 33–91n. The effect is to turn this scene into a universal one: this is how family members behave when a loved one is killed.

406–7 τίλλε κόμην: for this gesture of mourning see 77n. ἀπό . . . λιπαρήν ἔρριψε καλύπτρην | τηλόσε: Hecuba flinging off her headdress is an anticipatory doublet of the much more expanded and emotionally charged scene of Andromache doing the same at 468–72. Women were expected to cover their hair, and throwing off their headdress (or even tearing it off: cf. *Homeric Hymn to Demeter* 40–1 or Aeschylus *Persae* 537–9) made for a conspicuous inversion of normality and thus a public display of grief; cf. Llewellyn-Jones (2003) 304. καλύπτρη is a head-scarf or shawl. The epithet λιπαρήν, 'glossy, shining' suggests that it was made of linen anointed with oil; cf. 154n. The addition τηλόσε is expressive of Hecuba's strong emotion.

407–9 κώκυσεν . . . ὤιμωξεν: both verbs mean 'cry out', but they are gender-specific: οἰμώζω, lit. 'cry οἴμοι', is used only to describe men in physical and/or mental distress, while κωκύω means crying out in lamentation and is used only for women. The verbs refer to the immediate and instinctive expression of grief, which may be followed by γοάω (cf. 430), a more formalised and individual form of lamentation (by both men and women) that is verbalised, which in its turn is followed by στενάχω, collective wailing (cf. 429, 515). The verb κλαίω, 'weep', finally, may refer to both inarticulate and articulate (cf. 429) lamenting. For a discussion of the various verbs of lamenting/grieving/mourning see Derderian (2001) 16–35. μάλα μέγα: this combination occurs only once more (15.321); cf. the unique μάλιστα μέγα (14.399). The narrator uses strong language at this moment of pitched emotion, cf. μάλιστα at 410. ἐλεεινά: internal accusative with ὤιμωξεν, to be translated adverbially. ἀμφί: adverbial (L 20). λαοί 'the people of Troy' (104n.). Cf. below πολῖται (429). κωκυτῶι τ' εἴχοντο καὶ οἰμωγῆι: the periphrasis with ἔχομαι indicates prolonged crying.

410–11 This comparison is unique in several aspects: it concerns a singular, specific event (the fall of Troy) rather than an omnitemporal one (e.g. waves crashing on a shore, a lion attacking a herd). The narrator does not just note the similarity between X and Y but the *close* similarity (the combination μάλιστ'... ἐναλίγκιον is found only here). Its primary function is to suggest the intensity and extent of the Trojan lamentation throughout the city. Its secondary function is to announce, once again (cf. 56–76n.), the fall of Troy: now that its main defender (cf. 506–7n.) is dead, the destruction of the city is imminent. Finally, this comparison also forms the climax of a series of similes dealing with the theme of a beleaguered city: cf. 18.219–21 and 21.522–5, and see Introduction 3b. To underscore the solemnity of the moment the narrator opts for vocabulary that is unique (ὀφρυοέσσα) or rare (σμύχοιτο).

410 τῶι... ἐναλίγκιον, ὡς εἰ 'it most resembled this, as if'; cf. τῶι ἰκέλη, ὡς εἰ ἐ βιώιατο... Τρῶες, '(Odysseus' voice) resembled this, as if the Trojans oppressed him' (11.467). For ὡς εἰ + finite verb cf. 11.389; *Od.* 10.416; 17.366; and see Ruijgh (1971) 619–20.

411 ὀφρυοέσσα 'beetling', lit. 'with brows, i.e. ridges', 'set on the brow of a hill'; for the brow, ὀφρύς, of a hill cf. 20.151.This epithet of Troy occurs only here; it is a metrical equivalent of the more common epithet ἠνεμόεσσα. Hesiod *fr.* 204, 48 has ὀφρυόεντα Κόρινθον. Since both cities indeed lie on a ridge, it is apt. Clarke (1997) 70–1 suggests taking it as 'eyebrowed' and connecting it with other metaphors such as the 'headdresses', *krēdemna*, and 'heads', *karēna*, of cities (16.100; 2.117). The many epithets of Troy/Ilion are discussed by Scully (1990) 69–80 and Visser (1997) 83–94. σμύχοιτο 'were burning'; the verb recurs only at 9.653, where Achilles talks about Hector who will 'burn down' (κατά... σμῦξαι) the Greek ships with fire. It seems related to 'smoke' (see *DELG* s.v.) and has the connotation of 'reduce to ashes'. κατ' ἄκρης: sc. πόλεως, 'from top to bottom', hence 'completely'; the same expression occurs thrice more, all in speeches by characters and in connection with the fall of Troy (13.772; 15.557; 24.728). This memorable passage was echoed in Virgil *Aeneid* 2.624–5: *Tum vero omne mihi visum considere in ignis* | *Ilium et ex imo verti Neptunia Troia*, 'then indeed all Ilium seemed to me to sink in flames and Neptunian Troy to be upturned from her base'.

412–28 Priam here impulsively announces what he will eventually do in book 24, there with the encouragement of Zeus and support of Hermes, i.e. go out to the Greek camp and supplicate Achilles; for the moment, however, he is restrained. Once more an action is presented as impossible or unthinkable only to occur later (cf. 351–4, where Achilles rejects the idea of accepting a ransom by Priam); this makes the *dénouement* of the *Iliad*, affected by the gods, all the more surprising and unexpected. For the many connections between books 22 and 24 see Introduction 2c.

412–15 Priam's lamentation culminates in a gesture of mourning (rolling in the dung). He is so worked up that the Trojans physically have to restrain him from leaving the city (and going to the Greek camp). The situation resembles that of Achilles' reaction to news of Patroclus' death, when the hero pours dust over his head, lies down on the ground, tears and defiles his hair, and Antilochus has to hold his hands for fear that Achilles might kill himself (18.22–35). See Parker (1983) 40–1 for these forms of self-defilement by mourners.

412 ἀσχαλόωντα: an instance of metrical diectasis (L 4): ἀσχαλάοντα (– ◡ ◡ – ◡) > ἀσχαλῶντα (– ◡ – ◡) > ἀσχαλόωντα (– ◡ ◡ – ◡). The verb is generally taken as derived from *ἄσχαλός (alpha privative and σχεῖν), 'not being able to control oneself'. In different contexts, it may acquire such nuances as 'being distressed/grieved/vexed'.

413 μεμαῶτα: see 35–6n. πυλάων Δαρδανιάων: see 194–5n.

414–15 A unique speech-introduction. κυλινδόμενος κατὰ κόπρον: the same gesture of mourning is made by Priam at 24.163–5 (and cf. 24.640). There he finds himself in the courtyard, where the dung of mules and cows was heaped (cf. *Od.* 17.297–9). We probably should not ask where the dung here, on the walls of Troy, comes from. ἐξ ὀνομακλήδην ὀνομάζων ἄνδρα ἕκαστον 'calling each man by his name'. This tautological expression is a combination of ἐξ ὀνομακλήδην (cf. *Od.* 12.250a: companions snatched by Scylla shout Odysseus' name for the last time) and ὀνομάζων ἄνδρα ἕκαστον (cf. 10.68b: Menelaus is to urge each Greek he encounters to stay awake calling him by his name). The ensuing speech is addressed to the Trojans as a collective (φίλοι) and does not contain names in the vocative. We must either assume that ὀνομάζων is here weakened to a mere 'addressed', as in the formula ἔπος τ' ἔφατ' ἔκ τ' ὀνόμαζε, or that the speech quoted is a summary of what in fact was a series of speeches addressed to indviduals (note the imperfect ἐλλιτάνευε). The second analysis seems preferable, and we may compare '*tis*-speeches', which are also quoted once but represent several speeches (see 372n.)

416–28 Priam's speech starts off as an appeal but changes halfway through into a lament. The change is reflected in the speech attributions: (introduction) ἐλλιτάνευε vs. (capping) ὣς ἔφατο κλαίων, ἐπὶ δὲ στενάχοντο πολῖται (the typical refrain to laments, see 429n.). It is a prime example of what Lohmann (1970) 45 calls free sequence (A-B-C), as against ring-composition (A-B-A') or parallel order

(A-B-A'-B'). This order is especially suited to speeches with mounting emotions, as here:

A (*appeal*) Friends, let me go to the Greek camp.
B I want to supplicate that man,
C to see whether he will respect and pity my age.
D For he has a father of like age, Peleus,
E who sired him to be an evil for the Trojans;
F (*transition*) me he gave most sorrows (of the Trojans), for so many sons of mine he killed.
G (*lament*) But I do not grieve over these so much
H as over this one: Hector.
I If only he had died in my arms and we could have mourned him.

The intense emotion also appears from the skewed verses at 419–22 and 424–6 (see 33–7n.), and the position of all vital elements in runover position: γῆρας, Πηλεύς, Τρωσί, ὡς ἑνός, Ἕκτορος.

The first part of his speech (416–20) elaborates what the narrator had indicated before: Priam wants to leave the city (ἐξελθόντα πόληος ≈ ἐξελθεῖν... πυλάων Δαρδανιάων) in order to supplicate Achilles. The second part (419–26) is, as it were, a rehearsal of the speech with which he will supplicate Achilles at 24.486–506: 'Think of your father, as old as I am. He is happy, but I am unhappy. Many of my sons have been killed. But you killed the single most important one, Hector. It is to release him that I have come. Respect the gods and pity myself.' As Griffin (1990) 367 notes, 'It is like the overture to a tragic opera, presenting the themes in short compass.'

416–17 'Let be and allow me to leave the city alone and arrive as a suppliant at the Greek ships.' σχέσθε: lit. '(put restraint on yourself =) stop', sc. holding me back (cf. 412: ἔχον). οἶον: Priam here introduces a leitmotif of book 24: at 148 Zeus instructs Iris that Priam should go to Achilles alone (these instructions are repeated to Priam at 177); at 203 Hecuba reacts in fearful disbelief to this idea; at 519 Achilles shows pity and admiration for Priam, who has dared to come to him alone. κηδόμενοί περ 'though caring much (for me)'; for the particle περ see 73n. For the variant reading κηδόμενόν περ, 'much grieving as I am', cf. *Od.* 7.215 ἀλλ' ἐμὲ μὲν δορπῆσαι ἐάσατε κηδόμενόν περ, 'but let me (Odysseus) eat, much grieving as I am'. It does not suit the present context as well because we would have two rather unequal participles with μ(ε). ἱκέσθ᾽ ἐπὶ νῆας Ἀχαιῶν: for the combination ἱκέσθαι and ἐπί + acc. cf. 2.17 = 2.168. For ἱκέσθαι see 123–4n.

418 λίσσωμ᾽: best analysed as an asyndetically added main clause. The subjunctive λίσσωμαι indicates that Priam has made a decision: 'I want to supplicate'; see *GH* II 207. ἀνέρα τοῦτον ἀτάσθαλον ὀβριμοεργόν: Achilles is not referred to by name but identified by a circumlocution (33–91, 38nn.); the effect here comes close to scolding. Likewise, the demonstrative pronoun τοῦτον may have a pejorative undertone. ἀτάσθαλον, 'outrageous', refers to behaviour which breaks social or religious rules; see 104n. ὀβριμοεργόν, 'who does mighty deeds', 'violent', is used once more, of Heracles as he shoots an arrow at the god Hades (5.403).

419 ἤν πως... αἰδέσσεται ἠδ' ἐλεήσηι 'to see if somehow he will show respect or pity'; for the final nuance of conditional clauses see 196n. αἰδέσσεται is an aorist subjunctive with a short vowel (L 15). For the appeal to respect and pity by suppliants see 82–3n. ἡλικίην 'my age'.

420 'for he (Achilles) too has such a father (as I am)', i.e. as old as I am. Cf. the fuller version which Priam employs vis-à-vis Achilles at 24.487: τηλίκου ὥς περ ἐγών, ὀλοῶι ἐπὶ γήραος οὐδῶι, 'as old as I am, on the miserable brink (of death) consisting of old age'. καὶ δέ: in this combination δέ is connector ('for'), καί adverb ('too'); GP 199–200. τῶι γε: anaphoric pronoun (L 17). There is a textual variant τῶιδε; ὅ γε and ὅδε are often variants in Homer. Here τῶιδε is less attractive, because Achilles has just been referred to with τοῦτον. τέτυκται: see 30n.

421–2 Πηλεύς: although Peleus does not play a role in the story of the *Iliad*, he acquires substance as a personage because he is mentioned often by characters: Nestor (7.124–8; 11.783–4), Odysseus (9.252–8), Phoenix (9.438–43), and above all Achilles himself (9.394–7; 16.15–16; 18.330–1; 19.321–3; 23.144–51). He is even quoted in direct speech once and 'comes alive' (9.254–8). After these preparations the narratees will be able to appreciate the impact of Priam's final emotional reference to Peleus at 24.486–512 on Achilles all the more. ὅς μιν ἔτικτε καὶ ἔτρεφε πῆμα γενέσθαι | Τρωσί: for this type of expression ('X was born/raised to be a disaster for others') cf. 6.282–3 (about Paris); *Od.* 12.125 (Scylla) and 287–8n. for a shorter version ('X is a πῆμα for others'). For the final-consecutive force of the infinitive γενέσθαι see 5n. μάλιστα... ἐμοὶ περὶ πάντων 'me most above all'; a unique, forceful combination of μάλιστα ἐμοί (6.493; 24.742; *Od.* 1.359 = 11.353; 14.138; 21.353; 23.61) and περὶ πάντων (20.304; *Od.* 11.216; 17.388). ἐμοὶ... ἄλγε' ἔθηκεν 'has inflicted woes upon me'. Some MSS read ἄλγεα θῆκεν.

423 For Priam's loss of many sons see 44–5n. μοι: either an 'ethic' dative (to be connected with ἀπέκτανε) or a possessive dative (with παῖδας). τηλεθάοντας 'in their bloom'; τηλ-εθά-ω derives from θάλλω, 'grow', with dissimilation of the aspiration (< *θηλεθάοντας). The metaphorical use of this verb in connection with young people is common and also found in θάλος (87n.).

424–8 The 'praise of the dead' and 'wish that the dead had died differently' motifs make clear that by now Priam's speech has changed into a lament; see 477–514n. The preponderance of words for weeping/mourning also 'advertises' the genre of his speech: ὀδύρομαι, ἀχνύμενος, ἄχος, κλαίοντε, μυρομένω.

424–6 A summary priamel: 'I do not grieve over those *all* so much as over *one*'; cf. *Od.* 4.104–5 and (a full priamel) 6.450–5: 'my grief will not be so much over *the Trojans, nor Hecuba, Priam*, or *my brothers*, as over *you*'. For priamels in Homer see 159–61n. At other places, too, Priam indicates that Hector was the most treasured and valued of his sons; cf. 24.255–9, 493–501.

425 'piercing grief over whom will lead me down to Hades'. ἄχος ὀξύ: ἄχος is grief (often mingled with anger) which suddenly and forcefully overtakes a person, as against πένθος, which refers to more enduring grief. Its typical epithets are αἰνόν (13 x) and ὀξύ (3 x). κατοίσεται: this compound occurs only here. Usually we hear about *achos* befalling/reaching/overwhelming a person, but here it uniquely (and with some degree of personification) *leads* Priam to Hades. Cf. the demons of death leading a warrior (to his death): κῆρες . . . ἄγον μέλανος θανάτοιο (2.834 = 11.332). The idea that grief can kill a person is also found at *Od*.11.197–203, where Anticlea explains to her son Odysseus in the underworld that longing for him caused her death. Ἄϊδος εἴσω: sc. δόμον.

426–8 'if only he had died in my arms: in that case we would have . . .': a combination of impossible wish and past counterfactual. Similar wishes for a different death at *Od*. 5.308–11 (ὡς δὴ ἐγώ γ᾽ ὄφελον θανέειν 'in battle at Troy rather than at sea: in that case I (Odysseus) would have won due burial rites'); 1.236–8; 14.274–5; Aeschylus *Choephoroi* 345–53 ('if only Agamemnon had died in Troy: then he would have been properly buried').

426 ὡς ὄφελεν: ὄφελεν is aorist of ὀφέλλω, Aeolic for ὀφείλω. It is used beside the imperfect ὄφελλεν/ὤφελλεν (see 481), a metrically convenient variant, with an infinitive to express an impossible wish concerning the past (as here) or present. θανέειν: metrical diectasis (L 4): θανέεν > θανεῖν > θανέειν. The form here is a poetic licence, by analogy to 15.289, where the -εν = -ειν is followed by a consonant and makes position.

427 τώ 'in that case'; the anaphoric pronoun (L 17) here has an old instrumental ending which is also found in ἄνω, πόρρω, etc. Most MSS have the accentuation τῶ, but West 1, xxii opts for τώ, which seems to have been the choice of the ancient grammarian Apollonius Dyscolus. κορεσσάμεθα κλαίοντέ τε μυρομένω τε 'we would have been sated with weeping and mourning', i.e. would have mourned as long as we wanted, until our desire to do so had been satisfied. Similar expressions occur at *Od*. 4.541 = 10.499; 20.59; and cf. κόρος κρυεροῖο γόοιο (*Od*. 4.103) and ἐπεί . . . ὀλοοῖο τεταρπώμεσθα γόοιο (23.10). κλαίοντε and μυρομένω have dual endings (L 16).

428 δυσάμμορος 'very unhappy one'; intensifying contamination of ἄμμορος, lit. 'without fate', 'unhappy', and δύσμορος, 'with bad/unhappy fate'. The artificial doubling -μμ- is for metrical reasons; it is modelled on cases where the doubling is historically correct (e.g. φιλομμειδής < -smei-; cf. 'smile'). Priam here touches upon the 'common fate of mourner and dead' motif, which will be worked out more fully by Andromache at 477–85 (cf. especially 485 σύ τ᾽ ἐγώ τε δυσάμμοροι).

429 This line is the typical capping of a lament, with the subject of στενάχοντο varying between πολῖται (as here), γυναῖκες (19.301; 22.515; 24.746), and γέροντες (19.338). The repetition 429 ≈ 515 is suggestive of the ritual nature of the laments, even if they are only improvised and spoken in the absence of Hector's body at this stage. See Tsagalis (2004) 64–5. ἐπί 'in response to', i.e. after, seems more apt than the scholiast's 'parallel to', i.e. simultaneously. Greek mourning typically involves a string of solos by the next of kin each followed by a refrain of keening; see Alexiou (1974) 12, 131 and next note. πολῖται: occurs only here as the subject of στενάχοντο, hence some MSS have the more common γυναῖκες (here impossible) or γέροντες. In view of λαοί at 408 and 412 πολῖται is to be preferred. The word occurs thrice more (15.558; *Od.* 7.131; 17.206) and should be understood as 'inhabitants of a *polis*', not as 'citizens': 'They are neither conscripted nor taxed, they are not governed by a constitution . . . Neither is it correct, however, to infer . . . that Homeric society is comprised of autonomous *oikoi*, with no higher unifying "entity" to define the relation between self and community. Such a position minimizes the importance of urbanization, of walled cities, and of residential concentration' (Scully (1990) 1).

430 Laments are addressed to same-sex audiences; thus while Priam addressed the male Trojans, Hecuba turns to the female ones. The same line occurs almost verbatim at 24.747. Τρωιῆισιν 'among the Trojan women' (locative dative). ἀδινοῦ ἐξῆρχε γόοιο 'she took the lead in a vehement lament'. The expression (ἐξ)ῆρχε γόοιο is found at 18.316; 23.17; 24.723, 747, 761; it is to be understood in combination with the capping formula ἐπὶ δὲ στενάχοντο: one individual leads a group of mourners, in that s/he voices a lament which is then followed by a collective wailing as refrain. The same verb ἐξάρχειν is found in the context of individuals leading a chorus of singers/dancers: 18.605 = *Od.* 4.19. The root ἀδιν- (or ἀδιν-) is perhaps to be related to ἅδην (13.315), 'to the full/satiety', and refers to thronging (of animals), throbbing (of the heart), or repeated and vehement bursts (of grief); see Silk (1983) 322–4. Used in connection with weeping (13 x), it perhaps was felt to be a synonym of πυκνός, 'dense', 'thick' (cf. e.g. ἀδινὰ στενάχοντα: 24.123 ≈ πυκνὰ μάλα στενάχοντα: 21.417).

431–6 Hecuba's lament does not have the regular tripartite structure (see 477–514n.), but instead consists of two parts: an address to the deceased and a narrative. It combines three typical mourning motifs: 'wish that the mourner had died too', 'praise of the dead', and 'contrast between past and present'. She speaks abruptly and informally, with skewed verses (33–7n.) evoking her emotion.

431–2 'To what purpose am I to go on living, having suffered terrible things, now that you are dead?' Hecuba does not, strictly speaking, wish to have died (as do Andromache at 481, 'I wish my father had never sired me', and Helen at 24.764, 'I wish I had died before Paris abducted me'), but her rhetorical question (202–4n.) indicates that life has become meaningless to her. ἐγὼ δειλή: mourners often also lament for themselves, since the death of the other means their own sorrow or even ruin; cf. Andromache (ἐγὼ δύστηνος: 477) and Thetis (ὤ μοι ἐγὼ δειλή: 18.54). βείομαι: a dubitative subjunctive with short vowel (L 15), from ζώω, aor. βιῶναι; *GH* I 452–3. -ει- is due to metrical lengthening (L 2), to avoid a sequence of three short elements. αἰνὰ παθοῦσα: a unique expression, the usual object of πάσχω being κακόν/κακά. Aristarchus read αἰνὰ τεκοῦσα, an expression which is used about Thetis at 1.414 and which means either 'unfortunate in my child-bearing' or 'having given birth to something terrible'. But there is no compelling reason to replace αἰνὰ παθοῦσα.

432–4 '(you) who day and night were a source of pride for me in the city and a benefit for all the Trojans throughout the city'. **ὅ:** the anaphoric pronoun functions as a relative for metrical reasons (L 17). The accent derives from the following enclitic μοι. **νύκτας τε καὶ ἦμαρ:** cf. e.g. 5.490; 24.73. This expression, with ἦμαρ functioning as a plural (cf. e.g. ἐννῆμαρ: 1.53), is an older variant of νύκτας τε καὶ ἤματα (24.745); see *BK* on 24.73. **εὐχωλή:** only here and 2.160 ≈ 176 predicatively of people. **κατὰ ἄστυ . . . κατὰ πτόλιν:** this passage illustrates that these two words are semantically indistinguishable in Homer and used as metrical variants; see *LfgrE* s.v. πόλις. **πελέσκεο:** this form does not have its normal iterative force (L 12) but is used as a metrical alternative to the imperfect. For πέλομαι see 116n. **ὄνειαρ** (from ὀνίνημι) means (concrete) 'refreshment', or (abstract) 'comfort', 'benefit'; the -ει- instead of -ε- is due to metrical lengthening. The word recurs in Andromache's lament (486). For Hector's role as (the most important) defender of the Trojans see 506–7n.

434–5 οἵ σε θεὸν ὥς | δειδέχατ':** for the Trojans venerating Hector like a god see 394n. The etymology of δειδέχατ(ο) is debated (see *LfgrE* s.v. for discussion and literature): from δείκνυμι, 'point at'? It is used in contexts of respectful or friendly greeting, by gesture and/or words, often of guests arriving or leaving, here and at *Od.* 7.71–2 (οἵ μίν (Arete) ῥα θεὸν ὥς εἰσορόωντες | δειδέχαται μύθοισιν) of citizens meeting a member of the royal family in the streets. For the third person plural form δειδέχατο see L 14.

435 ἦ γὰρ καί 'for indeed'; καί is adverbial and indicates that the content of the explanatory γάρ-clause is in accordance with what preceded. **μάλα μέγα κῦδος:** for κῦδος see 205–7n. For its use in connection with people ('source of glory') cf. the formulaic μέγα κῦδος Ἀχαιῶν, of Odysseus (e.g. 9.673) and Nestor (e.g. 11.511). The combination μάλα μέγα κῦδος recurs at 9.303 (but not of a person). **ἔησθα = ἦσθα.**

436 This same line occurs at 17.478 and 672 (said by Automedon of Patroclus). In his edition West removes the line here, which he calls weak and pointless. The contrast between present and past is a regular element of laments, however, and the line, which is present in all MSS, may stand. **νῦν αὖ** 'now however'. For the adversative force of αὖ see 119n. **θάνατος καὶ μοῖρα:** this combination occurs 10 x *Il.* Since μοῖρα almost always pregnantly means 'death-fate' (5n.), the expression is an instance of the typically Homeric synonymous doubling; see 203n. The device serves to create emphasis but is of course also expedient from the point of view of versification. Thus we find the shorter μοῖρα κιχάνει at 303. **κιχάνει** 'has overtaken you'. The present tense of certain verbs may indicate not so much a continuing state of affairs as the result; see *GH* II 190 and Rijksbaron (2002) 8.

437–515

The episode of Hector's death (which started at 25) and, on a smaller scale, the episode of the Trojan reaction to his death (which started at 405) is concluded by a scene totally devoted to Andromache, who comes as a climactic third after Priam and Hecuba. Her forebodings, amply expressed in book 6, have come true. There are many points of contact with book 6: her comparison to a maenad (460, cf. 6.389), her lament for Hector (477–514; cf. 6.500–2), and her visions of her own and Astyanax's fate after Hector's death (483–507; cf. 6.432). Together these ensure that the narratees have this book in the back of their minds. For discussions of this scene and its echoes of book 6 see Schadewaldt (1959) 328–32, Segal (1971b), Lohmann (1988) 63–9, and Grethlein (2006) 248–53. See also Introduction 2c.

437–46 The description of Andromache, who has not yet heard about Hector's death, innocently weaving and preparing a bath, is the longest and most moving of a series of 'not yet' scenes. Others include 11.497–501 (Hector did not yet know about the Trojan defeat); 13.521–5 (Ares had not yet heard about the death of his son Ascalaphus); and 17.377–80, 401–11 (Thrasymedes and Antilochus, Achilles have/had not yet heard about the death of Patroclus). The passages show us characters who do not know what has just happened, although they will be deeply affected by it and others already know. They function as prolepses: the 'not yet' suggests that the characters will find out at some stage. Thus Hector finds out about the defeat of the Trojans at 11.523–30; Ares about his son's death at 15.110–42; Antilochus about Patroclus' death at 17.684–96; and Achilles at 18.16–22. In most cases there is not only ignorance but also mistaken (positive) expectation: Thrasymedes and Antilochus 'thought Patroclus was still alive and fighting the Trojans in the clash of the frontlines'; and Achilles 'never expected that Patroclus was dead, but that, alive, he would press right up to the gates and then return again'. The scholia *ad* 17.401 have noted this effect: 'Homer regularly arouses sympathy in this way, when those who are suffering great disasters are unaware of their misfortunes and are carried towards tender hopes, as with Andromache in book 22.' Instead of directly giving us Andromache's thoughts the narrator indirectly reveals her hope through her domestic chores, weaving and preparing a bath; after her pessimism in book 6, this can be no more than hoping against hope. In the cases of Achilles and Andromache, the narrator heightens the effect of this type of scene by inserting a stage of foreboding between the 'not yet' of total ignorance and the moment of *anagnōrisis* (18.4–15 and 22.448–59). Only in the case of Andromache does the narrator explicitly comment on her ignorance and the contrast between her expectations and grim reality (445–6n.).

437–8 The formulaic ὣς ἔφατο κλαίουσ(α) creates the impression that the narrator will go on to recount the collective wailing of the Trojan women (cf. 429n.). Instead, the scene changes 'along a line of vision' (Richardson (1990) 111–14), here a negated one. οὐ πώ τι 'not yet at all' (τι is adverbial). ἄλοχος...

πέπυστο | Ἕκτορος: it seems best to connect the genitive Ἕκτορος with ἄλοχος rather than with πέπυστο. When πυνθάνομαι/πεύθομαι means 'hear about a person', we always find genitive + participle (cf. e.g. οὐδ᾽ ἄρα πώ τι πέπυστο . . . | υἱὸς ἑοῖο πεσόντος: 13.521–2). For the absolute use of πυνθάνομαι/πεύθομαι cf. οὐδέ πω Ἕκτωρ | πεύθετ᾽, ἐπεί . . . μάρνατο (11.497–8). ἄλοχος Ἕκτορος is a highly effective circumlocution. It makes the main issue of the scene to follow clear right from the start: Hector's death means the collapse not only of Andromache's personal life but also of her social identity. From book 6 we already know that she has lost her father, mother, brothers, and native city and hence is dependent on her husband Hector for her safety and existence even more than usual. Now this last bulwark in her life has been taken from her too, and the notion of wife has lost its meaning.

438–9 οὐ γάρ οἵ τις ἐτήτυμος ἄγγελος ἐλθών | ἤγγειλ᾽ 'for nobody came as a truth-telling messenger and told her'. οἵ is personal pronoun (L 19), the accent derives from following τις. ἄγγελος is used predicatively in Homer; cf. e.g. Τρωσὶν δ᾽ ἄγγελος ἦλθε . . . Ἶρις, 'for the Trojans came as messenger Iris' (2.786). The combination ἐτήτυμος ἄγγελος occurs only here in Homer, but cf. ψευδάγγελος (15.159). The negated event calls attention to what might have happened. Thus Helen in book 3 *is* told by a (divine) messenger that her two husbands, Paris and Menelaus, are about to fight a duel over her, and she watches it from the walls of Troy. That fight was the first in the *Iliad*; here Hector and Achilles have just fought the last. The narratees are clearly intended to connect the two scenes, as will become even more obvious when we hear about the weavings of both women (440–1n.); see Lohmann (1988) 60–2. ὅττι ῥά οἱ πόσις ἔκτοθι μίμνε πυλάων: the content of the hypothetical messenger's message is presented in indirect speech, with 'her husband' suggestive of how the speech may have sounded ('Andromache, your husband . . . '). οἱ is a personal pronoun functioning as possessive dative (L 22). ἔκτοθι μίμνε πυλάων indicates that the narrator goes back a little in time and describes Andromache's occupations from the moment of the start of the confrontation between Hector and Achilles (cf. 5–6: μεῖναι . . . προπάροιθε πυλάων; 92: μίμν᾽); he will rejoin the present, the wailing over Hector, only at 447. Such steps backward in time are extremely rare in Homer; see Rengakos (1995), Nünlist (1998), and de Jong (2007) 30–1. Its effect here is to increase the pathos: we hear not only what Andromache was doing in the moment when she found out about Hector's death but also what she had been doing *all throughout his fight for his life*. It seems that ἔκτοθι . . . πυλάων (instead of προπάροιθε πυλάων) was chosen with an eye on μυχῶι δόμου ὑψηλοῖο in the next line; it emphasises the contrast between Hector's fateful exposure outside with Andromache's sheltered world inside.

440–4 Whereas in book 6 Andromache was unexpectedly not found at home by Hector but had gone to the walls to watch the fighting, she now is at home while all the others are on the walls. She is doing exactly what Hector had instructed her to do the last time we saw them together: ἀλλ᾽ εἰς οἶκον ἰοῦσα τὰ σ' αὐτῆς ἔργα κόμιζε', | ἱστόν τ' ἠλακάτην τε, 'go home and see to your own work, the loom and the distaff' (6.490–1). Her mood is reversed: at 6.499–552 she was lamenting Hector although he was still alive, now she is weaving a colourful cloth and preparing a bath although we know that he is dead. Her hopefulness may seem slightly surprising and unmotivated, but it heightens the contrast with her total shock when she sees Hector dead. Moreover, it is only a thin veneer: the sound of wailing from the walls quickly makes her think the worst (455–7). We may compare Achilles, who is worried at the moment when Patroclus leaves for battle (16.247–8), is optimistic at an intermediary stage (17.404–7), but has an anxious foreboding shortly before hearing the sad truth (18.6–14).

440–1 Weaving is one of the main occupations of Homeric women and goddesses: Helen (3.125–8), Penelope (*Od.* 2.104 etc.), Calypso (*Od.* 5.62), and Circe (*Od.* 10.222–3) all weave; see Pantelia (1993). The narrator reveals the design of the webs only twice and the depictions are clearly intended to be connected and contrasted. Whereas Helen depicts the Trojan war, not as a scene of glory but – typically for this guilt-ridden character – of toils and suffering, Andromache weaves 'colourful flowery decorations', symbols of hope and life. Once more (156n.), we are reminded of how life used to be during more peaceful times – and how it should be. However, Andromache will soon have to conclude that the work of her hands will *not* benefit Hector (510–14); recalling Hector's pessimistic words at 6.456, we may realise that Andromache will be 'weaving at the loom at another woman's command' in future.

440 μυχῶι δόμου ὑψηλοῖο: the same formula is found at *Od.* 3.402 = 4.304 = 7.346, and cf. 9.663; 24.675 (Achilles' hut); *Od.* 5.226 (Calypso's cave). In all these passages the innermost part of the house is the place where couples sleep or make love. Thus the association of the setting where Andromache finds herself when the story turns to her is not only that of shelter (cf. 438–9n.) but also of marriage. At this secluded place the noise from the walls is, of course, also the hardest to hear.

441 δίπλακα πορφυρέην 'a purple double cloak', in apposition to ἱστόν. The adjective δίπλαξ, sc. χλαῖνα, is here used as a substantive. A double cloak actually was a blanket-like woollen cloth large enough to be wrapped around twice (cf. χλαῖναν... διπλῆν: 10.133–4; *Od.* 19.225–6), as opposed to 'single' cloaks (ἁπλοΐδας χλαίνας: 24.230; *Od.* 24.276). Griffin (1990) 368 suggests that purple, the colour of death (πορφύρεος θάνατος: 5.83 = 16.334 = 20.477), may carry an ominous undertone. This is attractive, but it should be noted that many pieces of clothing and mantles are purple. The connotation could just as well be that of royal and precious (Reinhold (1970) 16). ἐν δὲ θρόνα ποικίλ' ἔπασσεν 'and she wove colourful flowery decorations in it'. For the technique of weaving patterns into a cloth (rather than embroidering them on afterwards) see Lorimer (1950) 397–8. In antiquity θρόνα had already been taken to mean either 'decorations' or 'flowers' (cf. the D-scholia on our passage: ποικίλματα, ἄνθη; and a scholion on Theocritus 2.59: 'in Thessalian "decorations in the form of living beings", in Cypriot "clothes with flowers"'). The etymology is obscure. In Hellenistic times the word certainly means 'flowers', e.g. the magic herbs of the Theocritus passage. The verb ἐν . . . ἔπασσε is used both of sprinkling herbs on a wound (e.g. 4.219) and metaphorically of weaving in decorations (here and at 3.125–6). ποικίλος basically means 'multi-coloured' by nature (e.g. a spotted leopard-skin: 10.29) or, more often, as a result of an artistic process. By an easy extension it became 'artfully decorated', of a woven *peplos* (e.g. 5.734–5) but also of metal armour (e.g. 16.134).

442–4 Andromache's second domestic chore consists of preparing a warm bath for Hector. Homeric warriors regularly take a bath after returning from combat, cf. 5.905 (Ares); 10.574–9; and 14.5–7. The heating of bathing water, for a warrior or guest, is briefly referred to once (14.6–7) and described in detail twice (*Od.* 8.433–7 and 10.358–60). For an analysis of 'bath' scenes in the *Iliad* see Grethlein (2007). κέκλετο . . . | . . . στῆσαι: κέκλετο is a reduplicated aorist of κέλομαι. This formulaic expression has been interpreted as suggesting 'something of the peace and comfort conferred by the ministrations of these simple routines' by Segal (1971b) 41, but Grethlein (2007) 28–32 read it as ominous because it might also conjure up – for the narratees – the idea of a ritual washing of a corpse (cf. 18.343–5, where Achilles orders his companions to heat water to wash Patroclus). ἀμφιπόλοισιν ἐϋπλοκάμοις 'servants with beautiful plaited hair'. The epithet (27 x *Il.* and *Od.*) is used of gods and mortals, free women and servants. Cf. καλλιπλόκαμος (5 x), ἠΰκομος (21 x), and καλλίκομος (2 x). μάχης ἐκ νοστήσαντι: this clearly represents Andromache's focalisation; she hopes that Hector will come home safely. The verb νοστέω is related to νόστος, derived from νέομαι, which originally meant 'to come out of something safe and sound', i.e. to return alive (cf. 5.157; 17.406; 24.705, where it is coupled with the root ζω-), and then weakened to 'return'. It had been anticipated at 17.207–8 that Andromache would *not* see Hector come back safely: (Zeus gives Hector power, in recompense for the fact that) οὔ τι μάχης ἐκ νοστήσαντι | δέξεται Ἀνδρομάχη κλυτὰ τεύχεα Πηλεΐωνος, 'you will never return home from battle, for Andromache to take the famous armour of Achilles from you'. When Hector's corpse finally returns to Troy, Cassandra will recall the Trojans' joy at the occasions he had returned from battle while still alive: εἴ ποτε καὶ ζώοντι μάχης ἐκ νοστήσαντι | χαίρετ' (24.705–6).

445–6 At this dramatic point of his story the narrator, who is usually covert, steps forward and openly comments on the events he is recounting. νηπίη, οὐδ' ἐνόησεν ὁ: the same formulation 'Fool/poor (wo)man, (s)he did not know that', recurs at 2.38; 5.406; 20.264, 466; *Od.* 3.146; 22.32. This narratorial comment corrects – here sympathetically, often critically – characters' mistakenly optimistic thoughts. It forms a fitting conclusion to the whole passage describing Andromache's hopeful activities (437–46n.). See Griffin (1980) 126, de Jong (2004) 86–7, and Edmunds (1990) 60–97. For νηπί- see 333n. ὁ = ὅτι. μάλα τῆλε λοετρῶν:

adding this detail, the narrator both emphasises the contrast between Andromache's intention to bathe Hector and his actual state and coins a unique and poignant variant of the 'death far away' motif, which we find e.g. at 11.816–18 (Patroclus pities the Greek leaders who are fated to die 'far from your families and your homeland'); cf. Griffin (1980) 109–10. χερσὶν Ἀχιλλῆος δάμασε γλαυκῶπις Ἀθήνη: looking back on Hector's death, the narrator echoes Achilles' own words: Παλλὰς Ἀθήνη | ἔγχει ἐμῶι δαμάαι (270–1). For δάμασε + instrumental dative see 175–6n. Perhaps because of unfamiliarity with this construction, one papyrus reads χέρσ' ὕπ' Ἀχιλλῆος, 'under the hands of Achilles', for which cf. 5.564; 15.2; 20.94 (κε δάμην ὑπὸ χερσὶν Ἀχιλλῆος καὶ Ἀθήνης). The reading has been adopted by West.

447 κωκυτοῦ δ' ἤκουσε καὶ οἰμωγῆς: the echo from 407–9 (κώκυσεν... ὤιμωξεν... κωκυτῶι... οἰμωγῆι) signals that the narrator has regained the point of the story which he had left at 437; see 438–9n. ἀπὸ πύργου: Priam, Hecuba, and the Trojans are standing on the bulwark above the Scaean gate; see 97n.

448–59 For Andromache's fearful forebodings, which are wedged between her state of total ignorance and her *anagnōrisis*, see 437–46n. Even within her speech we see her fears gradually become focused from 'deeds' (450) to 'some disaster for the children of Priam' (453) to 'Achilles putting an end to Hector's courage' (455–7).

448 Andromache's physical reaction of shock forms an anticipatory doublet of her even stronger reaction at 466–72, where she faints. τῆς δ' ἐλελίχθη γυῖα 'her limbs quivered'. τῆς is an anaphoric pronoun. This expression occurs only here, but trembling (out of fear) is recorded often: 3.34 (ὑπό... τρόμος ἔλλαβε γυῖα); 10.95, 390; *Od.* 11.527. It would seem that ἐλελίχθη, used also e.g. of Zeus making Olympus shake (1.530), is a stronger or more expressive term than τρόμος ἔλλαβε. The Homeric epics display a wide spectrum of signs of fear: blanching, beating of the heart, chattering of teeth, and growing rigid; cf. esp. 13.279–83. Note that Andromache shortly afterwards will say – slightly contradictorily – that her 'limbs lock' (452–3). χαμαὶ δέ οἱ ἔκπεσε κερκίς: sc. χειρός; cf. e.g. τόξον δέ οἱ ἔκπεσε χειρός (8.329). Andromache dropping the shuttle can be compared to Eumaeus dropping the piece of leather he was cutting sandals from at the moment 'the beggar'/Odysseus approaches his abode and is attacked by his dogs (*Od.* 14.34). οἱ is personal pronoun (L 19), which may be labelled an 'ethic' dative (to be connected with ἔκπεσε) or a possessive dative (with κερκίς).

449 ≈ *Od.* 6.238. αὖτις: points back to 442 and marks that Andromache gives a different order: instead of heating water the servants are to accompany her to the walls.

450–9 Bassett (1934b) 146 notes that Andromache's speech exceptionally lacks a vocative, which indicates her feeling of urgency. We may also note the repeated use of of δή (76n.): 453, 455, 457.

450 δεῦτε: this originally is an imperative, 'come here' (cf. *Od.* 8.307: δεῦθ', ἵνα ἔργ' . . . ἴδησθε), but has weakened to a particle, 'come on', like ἄγε/ἄγετε. **δύω:** women leaving the house or their room are regularly accompanied by two servants; cf. e.g. Penelope at *Od.* 1.331. **ἕπεσθον, ἴδωμ':** the asyndetic combination of a second-person imperative and first-person exhortative subjunctive is also found at 6.340 (ἐπίμεινον, . . . δύω) and 23.71. The subjunctive in such combinations acquires a final nuance: 'follow me, I want to see' ≈ 'follow me, in order that I may see'; *GH* II 207. **ὅτιν' ἔργα τέτυκται:** lit. 'which deeds have been produced', i.e. what has happened. ὅτινα is the neuter plural of ὅτις, a metrically convenient (dialectal) variant of ὅς τις. The verb τεύχω can be used both for making concrete, material objects and for producing non-material actions or situations, as here; cf. ἐπ' αὐτῶι δ' ἔργον ἐτύχθη | ἀργαλέον Τρώων καὶ Ἀχαιῶν, 'and near him (a fallen warrior) a painful struggle between Trojans and Greeks was produced, i.e. took place' (4.470–1).

451 αἰδοίης ἑκυρῆς ὀπὸς ἔκλυον: once more (cf. previous note), a clause is asyndetically added, which is expressive of Andromache's agitation. Whereas the narrator noted that Andromache heard wailing and lamentation coming from the walls at 447, Andromache herself now specifies that she had heard the voice of her mother-in-law (Hecuba). The nominative of ὀπός does not occur and could be either ὄψ or ὤψ. This word specifically denotes the voice as it is heard, whereas φωνή and αὐδή refer to the voice in general. The reference to Hecuba with a circumlocution (33–91n.), αἰδοίης ἑκυρῆς, reveals Andromache's emotions and leads up to Πριάμοιο τέκεσσιν: if it is Hecuba who is wailing, one of her children must be involved. Her mother-in-law is αἰδοίη, 'worthy of reverence', like Helen's father-in-law Priam (3.172).

451–3 Skewed verses (see 33–7n. and Bakker (1997) 154) are expressive of Andromache's emotional state, which she herself describes explicitly and graphically. **ἐν δέ μοι αὐτῆι | στήθεσι** 'in my breast'; literally 'in myself, in my breast' (the 'whole-and-part' construction). αὐτός in Homeric Greek may be added to a personal pronoun in order to add emphasis, often in contrasts: 'Diomedes first hit Aphrodite and then he attacked *me* (αὐτῶι μοι)' (5.459). Here its force seems weakened, as e.g. at *Od.* 8.396; see *GH* II 157. **πάλλεται ἦτορ ἀνὰ στόμα:** literally 'my heart is leaping up to my mouth'; cf. κραδίη . . . μοι ἔξω στηθέων ἐκθρώισκει at 10.94. These two metaphorical expressions are an intense variant of the 'beating of the heart in the chest' (e.g. Ἕκτορι . . . θυμὸς ἐνὶ στήθεσσι πάτασσεν: 7.216). Modern languages have similar expressions: cf. Engl./Dutch 'his heart was beating in his mouth/throat'. Later Greek will display many variations on this theme, with hearts jumping, thumping or dancing out of fear. See also below 461n. πάλλω is (trans.) 'shake', e.g. of lots, (intrans.) 'leap'; cf. ὡς δ' ὅθ' . . . ἀναπάλλεται ἰχθύς, 'as when a fish jumps up' (23.692). **γοῦνα | πήγνυται** 'my knees are locked'; the verb is mainly used to describe how spears remain stuck in the earth after being thrown. Again a unique metaphorical expression adds relief to this scene of pitched emotion. Usually knees are *loosened* in situations of strong emotion (shock, grief, or joy), e.g., λύθεν δ' ὑπὸ γυῖα (16.805), but here Andromache refers to the well-known phenomenon that someone is 'paralysed' by fear.

454–9 Andromache describes what she fears has taken place, a hypothetical description which closely mirrors what has indeed happened (cf. esp. δίηται = δίηται: 189, ἀποτμήξας πόλιος ≈ ἀποτρέψασκε: 197, πεδίονδε ≈ πρὸς πεδίον: 198). However, she still does not spell out the idea of Hector's death but instead uses a euphemistic expression (Achilles has put an end to Hector's courage).

454 αἲ γὰρ ἀπ' οὔατος εἴη ἐμεῦ ἔπος: lit. 'may my word be away from my ear', i.e. 'may what I now say (by way of fearful suspicion) not become true'; cf. 18.272 αἲ γὰρ δή μοι ἀπ' οὔατος ὧδε γένοιτο, 'may something like that never happen'. The words are a kind of incantation and come close to the later Latin *absit omen*, 'may what I say not become an omen'; Andromache is afraid that she may bring about her worst fears by verbalising them. The sentiment underlying her fear is related to the *'nomen est omen'* principle, which we find throughout the Homeric epics, notably in connection with Odysseus' name (see de Jong on 1.48–62). αἲ γάρ is a common introduction to wishes in Homer.

455–6 δείδω μὴ δή μοι... δίηται: cf. Achilles' fearful anticipation of Patroclus' death: μὴ δή μοι τελέσωσι θεοὶ κακὰ κήδεα, '(I fear) that the gods will have brought to pass my misgivings' (18.8). μοι is 'ethic' dative (38n.). δίηται is aorist (subjunctive); see 189n. θρασὺν Ἕκτορα δῖος Ἀχιλλεύς: as so often a character uses epithets in his/her speech. While δῖος Ἀχιλλεύς is extremely common (102n.), Andromache's use of θρασὺν Ἕκτορα is significant. Hector is given this epithet six times, and the three instances preceding this one (12.60 = 210; 13.725) are all contextually significant: Polydamas warns 'bold Hector' to follow a more moderate military strategy. Its use here leads up to Andromache's ensuing complaint about Hector's excessive courage. When people still call him θρασύς after his death, this seems a sign of respect (24.72, 786, the latter passage perhaps focalised by the mourning Trojans). μοῦνον: Homeric Greek has two words for 'alone', μοῦνος and οἶος, of which the latter is older and already found in Mycenaean tablets. They are largely used indiscriminately (cf. 39, where Priam also refers to Hector alone facing Achilles, there with οἶος), occasionally as metrical variants (at 416 μοῦνον would have been impossible). For attempts to distinguish between the two see Biraud (1990), who claims that οἶος means that someone distinguishes himself from others, and Kahane (1997), who contends that οἶος, which is usually verse-terminal, refers to the hero of singular ability, while μοῦνος, which is usually verse-initial, describes the hero at his weakest.

457 καὶ δή μιν καταπαύσηι ἀγηνορίης ἀλεγεινῆς: lit. 'and made him cease from his grievous excess of courage', i.e. 'courage which causes me grief'; the same construction of παύω + acc. + gen., e.g. at 2.595; *Od.* 24.457. καὶ δή 'introduces something similar in kind to what has preceded, but stronger in degree, and marks a kind of climax' (*GP* 248). In her conversation with Hector Andromache had already indicated her fears that he would die because of his martial nature (φθίσει σε τὸ σὸν μένος, 'your drive will kill you': 6.407) and that his resulting death would ruin her life (408–13, 432). The idea that a warrior dies because of his courage may have been a commonplace (cf. 16.751–4, where we find it in connection with a lion = Patroclus: ἑή τέ μιν ὤλεσεν ἀλκή), but Andromache speaks of ἀγηνορίη (3 x *Il.*). Whereas its true etymology probably is a combination of ἄγω + ἀνήρ ('the leading of men'), the singers connected it to ἄγαν + ἀνήρ ('very manliness'); see *DELG* s.v. Graziosi and Haubold (2003) argue that ἀγηνορίη is always valued negatively in Homer ('excessive manliness'). As the comparison of Hector to a lion who dies because of his courage (ἀγηνορίη δέ μιν ἔκτα: 12.46) makes clear, it 'entails separation from other men, death, and, ultimately, negative consequences for the other men on the battlefield, as well as for one's family and community' (71). It is part of Hector's tragedy that his martial overconfidence is due to the support of Zeus and hence quite understandable (see Introduction 2b and d).

458–9 ἔχεσκ'... προθέεσκε: iteratives (L 12). Note that Andromache already speaks about Hector in the past tense. οὔ ποτ'... εἴκων: almost the same words are used by Odysseus at *Od.* 11.514–15 in connection with Neoptolemus. To fight in the front line is of course always a sign of courage, but all the more so in Homeric warfare with its continuous moving forward and backward (into the fray) of the *promachoi* (see 248–305n.). While Odysseus praises Neoptolemus (addressing his father Achilles), Andromache expresses a mixture of pride (cf. also 24.737–9) and fear (cf. 85, where Hecuba begged Hector not to take up the position of champion (*promos*) against Achilles. Of course her οὔ ποτ' is an exaggeration: as van Wees (2004) 156 writes, 'Most men retreat after only a short while at the front, or indeed run back immediately after launching their first missile or landing their first blow' and 'even this most energetic of fighters (Hector) from time to time falls back "towards the multitude" (11.359–60, and cf. 20.376–80).' τὸ ὂν μένος οὐδενὶ εἴκων 'in his fury retreating before no one' (*LfgrE* s.v. εἴκω 1b: *das Feld räumen*) seems better (because of the possessive ὂν) than 'yielding to, i.e. inferior to no-one in fury' (*LSJ* s.v. 5).

460 ὣς φαμένη: this speech-attribution may indicate that Andromache starts running both *while* still talking or *after* talking (247n.). μεγάροιο διέσσυτο 'she rushed through the palace'. διέσσυτο is middle aorist of διασεύομαι. μαινάδι ἴση: does *mainas* mean 'mad woman' in general or 'maenad', i.e. follower of Dionysus, specifically? Although we now know that Dionysus had belonged to the Greek pantheon since Mycenaean times, thanks to the appearance of his name on the Linear B tablets, and although he is referred to occasionally in the Homeric epics (notably at 6.132–4, where we hear how Lycurgus 'once chased the nurses of raving, μαινομένοιο, Dionysus down from the mountain Nysa'; and cf. 14.325; *Od.* 11.325; 24.74), most scholars opt for the first interpretation. This seems confirmed by the obviously and intentionally parallel expression μαινομένηι ἐϊκυῖα, used of Andromache at 6.389. The strong expression, which is used of no other character in the epics, suggests the intensity of her anxiety for her husband. If Andromache is compared to a maenad, the points of comparison would be that Dionysiac frenzy typically causes women to abandon their weaving and become warriors and hunters (Andromache does the former but not the latter) and that maenadism is a reversal of the marriage ritual (Andromache throws away the veil which she got at her marriage, and speaks a lament instead of hearing a *makarismos*). For discussion and literature see *LfgrE* s.v. μαινάς, to which add Seaford (1994) 332–8 (in favour of maenad) and Hershkowitz (1998) 135 (who concludes that the matter cannot be decided). The first certain reference to a maenad seems to be *Homeric Hymn to Demeter* 386.

461 παλλομένη κραδίην: this seems to refer to the same phenomenon as 452 ('with beating heart'). Others understand 'trembling all over, especially as regards her heart' (Ameis-Hentze and *LfgrE* s.v. κραδίη). κίον: this verb only has aorist forms.

462–5 This is perhaps the most moving instance of focalisation in the whole of the Homeric epics. It is emphatically prepared for by Andromache's taking up a position on the walls with a good view, and by the insertion of two verbs of seeing (παπτήνασ', νόησεν). She now sees what the other Trojans had seen already at 401–4, Hector being dragged behind Achilles' chariot: ἑλκόμενον . . . ἕλκον ≈ ἑλκομένοιο. Andromache's focalisation becomes very clear in ἀκηδέστως (465n.). The scholia noted the effect: 'Homer has done well to make her not hear about it (the dragging of Hector) from others; he wanted it to become the object of witnessing by a shaken soul.'

462 A papyrus has an alternative line which says that Andromache reached the bulwark *at the Scaean gate*. But the singular πύργον alone suffices to indicate this particular place (97n.), and the generally transmitted line which says that she reached the bulwark *and the other Trojans* seems preferable. ἀνδρῶν . . . ὅμιλον 'mass of people'; although ἄνδρες is generally more gender-specific than ἄνθρωποι, here it must refer to both the Trojan men and women who are present on the wall (for the women see 430, 476, 515).

463 παπτήνασ' . . . νόησεν: παπταίνομαι, which lacks a clear etymology, means 'to look around searchingly (and often anxiously)'; for the combination with νόησεν 'look around and then see what one is looking for' cf. 12.333–5. τὸν δέ: cf. 24.702 and Macleod's comment 'the lack of the name is expressive: "him" can mean only one person to Cassandra and the Trojans'.

464 ταχέες . . . ἵπποι: horses are often called quick, mainly ὠκέες, sometimes ταχέες (metrical variants); for the epithets of horses see 162n. But here the epithet may add to the horror of the scene: Andromache sees Hector being *rapidly* transported away to the enemy camp. Achilles' horses, Xanthus and Balius, are famous for their speed (cf. 19.415–16).

465 ἀκηδέστως: the root ἀκηδεσ- belongs to the character-language (10 x speech; only here in narrator-text), and its presence signals Andromache's focalisation. ἀκηδεσ- generally means 'taking/receiving no care' (e.g. *Od.* 20.130) but often has a specialised sense 'paying/receiving no funeral rites'. The scholia paraphrase with ὑβριστικῶς, and this has entered lexica (e.g. *LfgrE* s.v.: 'brutalement'). But this seems an unnecessary overinterpretation: her ensuing speech makes clear that Andromache *is* mainly concerned with the fact that Hector is not given a proper burial (508–14). Likewise, when the expression recurs at 24.417 in a speech of 'the Myrmidon'/Hermes, it is descriptive rather than moralistic. κοίλας ἐπὶ νῆας: ships are 'hollow' because they contain a hold, in which goods, men, or horses can be transported. The noun-epithet combination occurs 21 x *Il.*, 19 x *Od.*, and is mainly ornamental in the *Il.*, since the ships are drawn ashore and do not actually transport anything. It may have been chosen here, instead of the even more common θοὰς ἐπὶ νῆας, in order to avoid the combination 'swift horses . . . swift ships'. For a discussion of the epithets of ships in Homer see Kurt (1979) 32–75.

466–75 Homeric characters regularly swoon (warriors on the battlefield who are severely wounded: 5.310, 696–8; 14.438–9; or Laertes seeing Odysseus again after twenty years: *Od.* 24.345–9), but this is the longest instance. Swooning is described in terms closely resembling those of death: we have the darkness covering the eyes (466 = 5.659; 13.580), the falling to the ground (467a ≈ 5.47, 58; 11.743, etc.), and the leaving of the *psuchē* (467b, cf. 14.518–19). The one major difference is that the *thumos* does not leave the body when fainting, as it does when a person dies; see 362–3, 475nn.

466 κατ᾽ ὀφθαλμῶν 'over her eyes'; see *GH* II 113. ἐρεβεννὴ νύξ ἐκάλυψεν: νύξ is regularly used in the sense of 'darkness' (14 x); see *LfgrE* I 6 and cf. τὸν δὲ σκότος ὄσσε κάλυψεν (11 x *Il.*).

467–8 ἤριπε δ᾽ ἐξοπίσω: while other swooning people 'approach the earth' (14.438) or 'their knees are loosened' (*Od.* 24.345–8), in the case of Andromache we find the expressive verb ἐρείπω, which is used of dead warriors or trees 'crashing down'; see 330n. ἀπὸ δὲ ψυχὴν ἐκάπυσσεν: lit. 'and breathed out her *psuchē*', i.e. lost consciousness. The same idea is expressed at 5.696 with τὸν δὲ λίπε ψυχή, at *Od.* 24.348 with ἀποψύχοντα. The verb (ἀπο)καπύω occurs only here and probably is cognate with the noun καπνός, 'vapour', 'smoke'; the scholia gloss it with πνεύω. κεκαφηότα θυμόν at 5.698, *Od.* 5.468, paraphrased in the scholia with ἐκπεπνευκότα, is generally adduced as related, but that verb is intransitive, with θυμόν accusative of respect ('worn out as regards his *thumos*'), and Chantraine in *DELG* is sceptical of a connection. τῆλε δ᾽ ἀπὸ κρατὸς βάλε δέσματα σιγαλόεντα 'and threw off her shining headdress far from her head'. κρατός is the genitive of κάρη. For σιγαλόεντα see 154n. Scholars have been puzzled that Andromache could still throw off her veil after fainting. However, ἤριπε, ἐκάπυσσεν, and βάλε should be seen as more or less simultaneous; to bring this out, it is best to print a comma after ἐκάπυσσεν (instead of a full-stop, as all editors do). That she threw off the headdress 'far away' while fainting is slightly odd, but the narrator seems intent on stressing the parallel with Hecuba's gesture of grief at 406–7 (τήλοσε). Leaf and Richardson suggest that βάλε here means that Andromache throws it off involuntarily, i.e. drops it as a result of the violence of her fall. There is, however, no parallel for this meaning of the verb. The (too) radical solution of Aristarchus is to place 468–72 after 476. The vulgate reads χέε, which makes Andromache's gesture explicitly involuntary; cf. κατὰ δ' ἡνία χεῦεν ἔραζε of a fatally wounded charioteer crashing (ἤριπε) out of his chariot and letting go of the reins (17.619). There is no parallel, however, for the 'shedding' of a headdress. Moreover, τῆλε is even stranger with χέε than with βάλε.

468–72 In typical Homeric fashion, the narrator marks a climactic moment in his narrative with a retardation, a slowing down of the pace of his narration; cf. the extended digression on Odysseus' scar at the moment when Eurycleia recognises Odysseus and almost discloses his true identity. A cluster of *hapax legomena* also draws attention to this moment; see Richardson (1987) 172, 178. The retardation takes the form of the description of an object (*ekphrasis*); cf. the extended description of the Shield of Achilles in book 18, which marks the moment of his return to battle. The length of the description is also suggestive of the duration of time for which Andromache is unconscious.

The description of an object in Homer usually includes not only details about its outward appearance but also about its history (470–2n.); see Griffin (1980) 1–49, Richardson (1990) 61–9, Minchin (2001) 100–31, and Grethlein (2008). From antiquity onward, it has been noted that throwing off the headdress she received on the day of her marriage symbolises the extent of Andromache's loss. As she indicated at 6.410–13, it would be better for her to die when Hector dies because she will never have any joy anymore, only sorrow. But since a *krēdemnon* is a symbol of chastity (cf. e.g. *Od.* 1.334), Andromache's gesture may make the narratees also think of the sexual violation which awaits her now that Hector is dead and hence the fall of Troy close at hand; see Nagler (1974) 44–60.

469–70 The *ampux* is a metal strip or band possibly of beaten gold. The *kekruphalos* is a net-like cap or woven snood to keep the hair in order. The *plektē anadesmē* is a fillet, possibly twisted or plaited. The *krēdemnon*, lit. 'binding of the (hair of the) head', is a shawl that hangs from the back part of the head and covers the back and the shoulder of the wearer; cf. the synonymous *kaluptrē* at 406. In the present instance it covers all the other components of Andromache's elaborate headdress. See Llewellyn-Jones (2003) 215–58.

470–2 The history of Andromache's headdress takes the form of an external analepsis: we are transported back to the moment of her marriage to Hector, more specifically the moment he led her from the house of her father, King Eetion of Thebes, to his own palace. An impression of such a bridal procession is given in one of the scenes on the Shield of Achilles (18.492–7). Sappho later will elaborate this moment from the perspective of the Trojans welcoming back Hector and his new bride (fr. 44). The analepsis makes clear that Andromache's marriage to Hector was one of the high points in her life, with her happiness being symbolised by 'golden Aphrodite'. At the same time, mentioning Eetion prepares for Andromache's ensuing speech, which returns to this figure and his sad fate (477–84n.).

470 δῶκε χρυσῇ Ἀφροδίτη: for the gods giving mortals gifts see 403–4n., and compare the gods giving Peleus armour on the occasion of his marriage to Thetis (18.84–5). The name-epithet combination occurs 5 x *Il.*, 5 x *Od.* Whereas divine objects are typically golden (cf. e.g. 5.724, 727, 730; 8.19, 69 = 22.209; 24.20–1), Aphrodite is the only god to be called golden herself. The epithet refers to the beauty of her appearance and perhaps reflects her status as a dawn goddess (it is an appropriate description of the colour of a dawn cloud); at the *Homeric Hymn to Aphrodite* 65 and *Homeric Hymn* 6.7–12 we hear how she is adorned with golden ornaments. See Boedeker (1974) 22–3. In the formulaic combination χρυσῇ Ἀφροδίτη the MSS consistently give the contracted form -η instead of the older -εη (to be scanned with synizesis), and West 1, xxxvi–vii prefers this form (instead of changing to -εη, with Barnes).

471 ἤματι τῷι, ὅτε: for this expression see 359n. Since it is used mainly by characters, its use here by the narrator is a sign of emotional intensity. κορυθαίολος...Ἕκτωρ: for this epithet see 232n. It is a sign of the flexibility of the Homeric epithet that it can be separated from its noun by one or more intervening words. The effect may be a slight emphasis: we are reminded of Hector in his former glitter and glory, a picture which contrasts painfully with his present lack of a helmet (cf. 401–4). ἠγάγεθ᾿: the bringing home of a bride is typically expressed by the middle, which makes clear that the subject of the verb is the beneficiary of the action; see Allan (2003) 112–15.

472 Ἠετίωνος: for Thebes and its King Eetion see 477–84n. πόρε: this verb is found in aorist and perfect only. It usually concerns special (bridal, honorary, or guest) gifts, and thus seems to indicate a more festive, official kind of giving: 'bestow', 'present'. μυρία ἕδνα: a formulaic expression (3 x); cf. Andromache's epithet πολύδωρος (88n.). For the issue of dowry versus bride-price see 51n.

473 γαλόωι τε καὶ εἰνατέρες: two different words for sisters-in-law, i.e. the husband's sisters and his brothers' wives; these terms are not used any more after Homer, with the exception of occasional inscriptions in Asia Minor, which may be in imitation of Homer; see Gates (1971) 23–6, 34. For women like Helen and Andromache, who had entered the Trojan royal family from outside, these sisters-in-law were their natural companions (cf. 6.378, 383; 24.769). Their explicit mention here naturally follows the preceding analepsis of the wedding of Hector and Andromache. γαλόωι is an instance of metrical diectasis (L 4): γαλάοι> γαλῶι>γαλόωι. ἅλις 'en masse'. ἔσταν = ἔστησαν (L 14).

474 ἑ: personal pronoun (L 19). μετὰ σφίσιν εἶχον: a unique expression; her sisters-in-law 'held Andromache between them', i.e. they put their arms around her and made her sit up again, after she had fallen backwards. ἀτυζομένην ἀπολέσθαι 'shocked almost to death', a unique expression. An instance of the loose final-consecutive infinitive (5n.).

475 More or less the same line is found at *Od.* 24.349, when Laertes comes to after fainting, and 5.458, when shipwrecked Odysseus recovers from his exhausted breathlessness after finally reaching land. ἐπεὶ οὖν: the particle οὖν in Homer is usually combined with ἐπεί or ὡς, and is resumptive: πινέμεναι δὲ κέλευσεν . . . τὼ δ' ἐπεὶ οὖν πίνοντ', 'he ordered them to drink . . . After they had drunk' (11.641– 2). See *GP* 417. Here it is virtually untranslatable, but it signals the next logical step in the story: when a person faints it is reasonable to expect that he/she will regain consciousness again. ἄμπνυτο: this is the typical verb used (4 x *Il.*, 2 x *Od.*) when people regain consciousness after fainting or catch their breath. There does not seem to be a major semantic difference from the active, which is found once (222). Aristarchus wanted to change ἀμ- to ἐμ- both here and at 5.698, but this seems unnecessary and even misleading, since active ἐμπνέω means something different (a god breathing energy or courage into a person). ἐς φρένα θυμὸς ἀγέρθη: when a person faints the *psuchē* temporarily leaves the body (cf. 467), while the other vital element, the *thumos*, is weakened (through being dispersed?), cf. 14.439 (βέλος δ' ἔτι θυμὸν ἐδάμνα), but does not leave the body. Upon regaining consciousness, the *thumos* is collected again; cf. 15.240; *Od.* 5.458; 24.349; and (not in the context of fainting) 4.152; 21.417. For *psuchē* and *thumos* see 362–3n.

476 ἀμβλήδην γοόωσα: ἀμβλήδην (from ἀνά and βάλλομαι) is a *hapax* of uncertain meaning. Three interpretations have been proposed: (1) '(wailing) while raising her voice' (cf. ἀνεβάλλετο καλὸν ἀείδειν: *Od.* 1.155); (2) '(wailing) with deep sobs' (cf. λέβης ζεῖ . . . πάντοθεν ἀμβολάδην, '(the liquid content of) a kettle seethes, bubbling up everywhere': 21.362–4); and (3) 'starting (the wailing)' (cf. ἀνεβάλλετο καλὸν ἀείδειν: *Od.* 1.155 and τὸν δ' ἄρ' ὑποβλήδην ἠμείβετο, 'he interrupted and answered': 1.292); the expression would then be a variant of the common ἐξῆρχε γόοιο (cf. 430). The problem is that the meaning of the crucial parallel ἀνεβάλλετο καλὸν ἀείδειν is not clear either: 'he raised his voice to sing' or 'he began to sing'. The very first mention of Andromache has her 'wailing' (6.373), and we see her weeping repeatedly throughout the *Iliad* (6.405, 455, 496, 499; 24.723, 746), except for her famous brief 'smiling with tears in her eyes' (6.484) at the sight of Hector fondling Astyanax. γοόωσα is an instance of metrical diectasis (L 4): γοάουσα > γοῶσα > γοόωσα.

477–514 In the *Iliad* we find ten laments by family or close friends (usually explicitly marked as γόος: 18.51; 22.430, 476; 23.17; 24.723, 747, 761) for the dead: 18.52–64 (Thetis laments Achilles while he is still alive); 19.287–300, 315– 337; 22.416–28, 431–6, 477–514; 23.19–23; 24.725–45, 748–59, 762–75. Next to these individual laments, often voiced by women, there is the θρῆνος sung by a collective of professionals (24.720–2 and *Od.* 24.60–2). In both cases, *goos* (solo) or *thrēnos* (choral) are followed by a refrain of collective non-verbalised cries by others (see 429n.). Laments typically have a tripartite structure: address of deceased – narrative – renewed address. Within this structure recurrent motifs may be used, often in combination: the contrast between past and present, the contrast

between (or common fate of) mourner and dead, praise of the dead, the wish
that the mourner had died too, or had never been born, or that the dead had
died in another way. It is characteristic of Homer, who is interested as much in
the tragic as the glorious side of war, to devote so much space to lament in his
poem and thus to give women a chance to express themselves. In this respect,
too (cf. 296–305n.), Homer is the predecessor of Greek tragedy, which will bring
on stage many lamenting heroines and female choruses. Homeric laments are
discussed by Petersmann (1973), Alexiou (1974), Easterling (1991), Holst-Warhaft
(1992), Murnaghan (1999), Derderian (2001) 15–62, and Tsagalis (2004).

Andromache's lament has the following structure:

477–86	address of deceased
	Hector, poor me. We turn out to have been born for the same fate, *you* in Troy, *I* in Thebes, where Eetion raised me (*common fate of dead and mourner*). If only he had never fathered me (*wish that mourner had never been born*). *Now you* are dead and leave *me* a widow (*common fate of mourner and dead and contrast between past and present*). And our child is still very young. You will not benefit your son nor he you.
487–505	narrative
	For even if he survives the war, there will always be hardship for him afterwards. Being an orphan makes a child friendless. He is sneered at and excluded from dinner. *In the past* he sat on his father's knees and would sleep happily in his nurse's arms. But *now* there will be much suffering for Astyanax (*contrast between past and present*), whom the Trojans gave that name.
506–14	renewed address of deceased
	For you alone protected the city (*praise of the dead*). But *now* worms will feed on you, naked (*contrast between past and present*). But there are fine clothes for you, and I will burn them, not for your benefit but to bring you *kleos* among the Trojans.

Andromache's speech forms part of an overarching structure of three speeches
by her, in book 6, here, and in book 24; see 405–36n. and Introduction 2c.

477–84 Andromache's main train of thought is that she and Hector have a
similar fate, in that both were born in to wealthy and powerful families and cities,
but now he is dead and she is a widow. Mentioning her native city, Thebes, and
the city of Hector, Troy, in one breath is ominous. All throughout the *Iliad* the
fate of wealthy Thebes is evoked: at 1.366–9 Achilles first mentioned the sack
of Thebes as the occasion when he had taken Chryseïs captive (cf. also 2.691);
at 6.411–30 Andromache reminded Hector how Achilles once captured Thebes,
killed (but honorifically buried) her father, and sold her mother; and at 9.186–9;

16.152–3; and 23.826–9 we hear about spoils taken by Achilles on the occasion of the sack of Thebes. These repeated references cannot but make the narratees think of the sack of Troy itself: 'As dying cities, Troy and Thebes are sisters; the fate of the one announces the fate of the other' (Reinhardt (1963) 61, my translation, and see Zarker (1965) and Taplin (1992)). Once more that crucial event, even though it falls outside the boundaries of the *Iliad*, is evoked; see 56–76n.

477 ἐγὼ δύστηνος: see 431–2n. ἰῆι ... γεινόμεθ' αἴσηι: the etymology of ἴα is unclear (for suggestions see *LfgrE* s.v.), but the emphatic meaning 'one and the same' is relevant in most cases; cf. Hector and Polydamas who are born ἰῆι ... ἐν νυκτί (18.251). The dative expresses accompanying circumstances (comitative), as in κακῆι αἴσηι τέκον, 'I bore you for a bad fate' (1.418), which is virtually 'under an unlucky star'; *GH* II 75. γεινόμεθ' is γενόμεθ', with metrical lengthening (L 2). ἄρα 'apparently'; this particle, often hardly more than a stopgap in Homer (see 98n.), here expresses 'the surprise attendant upon disillusionment' (*GP* 35).

479 Θήβηισιν ὑπὸ Πλάκωι ὑληέσσηι: cf. 6.396–7. There we find Θήβηι, but such alternations between singular and plural are found in all three Homeric cities of Thebes (Boeotian, Hypoplakian, and Egyptian). Later historiographical sources mention 'the plain of Thebes' (Herodotus *Histories* 7.42; Xenophon *Anabasis* 7.8.7) in the south of the Troad at the spurs of the Ida, near Adramyttion (present day Edremit), but no further (historical or mythological) events are connected with this Hypoplakian Thebes.

480 ὅ: the anaphorical pronoun is used as a relative (L 17), for metrical reasons. ἔτρεφε τυτθὸν ἐοῦσαν: this expression is used of fathers raising their young children (8.283; 11.223; *Od.* 11.67), once a nurse (*Od.* 1.435). A child is τυτθός until he or she reaches adulthood (*hēbē*); the word is found in Homeric Greek more often than σμικρός, which is the common word for 'small' = 'young' in later Greek.

481 δύσμορος αἰνόμορον: an effective and pathetic juxtaposition; cf. θεὰ θεόν (*Od.* 5.97) and παρ' οὐκ ἐθέλων ἐθελούσηι (*Od.* 5.155). ὡς μὴ ὤφελλε τεκέσθαι 'how I wish he had never begotten me'; for this type of impossible wish see 426–8n. The aorist middle τεκέσθαι is used in Homer primarily, though not exclusively (cf. 48), of the father.

482 νῦν δέ: the typical 'but now, in reality' after impossible wishes or counterfactuals (16–20n.). Ἀΐδαο δόμους ὑπὸ κεύθεσι γαίης '(you go) to the house of Hades (*accusative of direction*), (which finds itself) down in the enveloping recesses of the earth'; ὑπὸ κεύθεσι γαίης is best taken as an apposition with Ἀ. δόμους. For Hades enveloping the dead cf. Achilles' words at 23.244: εἰς ὅ κεν αὐτὸς ἐγὼν Ἀΐδι κεύθωμαι, 'until I myself am hidden in the Hades'. Homer has three variants of the name of the god of the underworld: Ἀΐδης, *Ἄϊς, Ἀϊδωνεύς. It is probably to be etymologised as 'the one who is not visible' (*alpha privative* + ϝιδ-); for other explanations see *BK* on 3.322. Our present day 'Hades' goes back to the aspirated form found in Attic Ἅιδης (probably crasis of ὁ + Ἀΐδης).

483–507 From Hector Andromache turns to her own and Astyanax's fate as widow and orphan; cf. 6.407–9 and 432, where she, briefly, had broached the same combined theme. At that time she used the prospect of this dire situation as an emotional argument to convince Hector to stay inside Troy. By now her fears have come true, and the largest part of her lament is devoted to painting a bleak picture of Astyanax's life as an orphan in harsh colours, including a quotation of the kinds of taunts she imagines being hurled at him. In her lament in book 24 she will go even further and imagine her fate as a captive after the fall of Troy (cf. Hector at 6.450–65) and that of Astyanax also as a captive or, worse, being killed (24.731–5).

483–5 ≈ 24.725–7 (in Andromache's official lament). στυγερῶι ἐνὶ πένθεϊ: only here do we find the dative πένθεϊ + preposition (as against 3 x dative only: 9.3; 22.242; *Od.* 2.70), which makes the picture more graphic; the death of Hector leaves Andromache behind in the *megaron* as a widow *wrapped in* hateful mourning. Andromache clearly is the widow par excellence of the *Iliad*, and many scholars have connected her with the woman in an Odyssean simile who throws herself over the body of her dead husband and is then carried off into slavery (8.523–30). νήπιος αὔτως '(is) no more than an infant'. The same expression was used by the narrator of Astyanax at 6.400. δυσάμμοροι: surpassing her own earlier αἰνόμορον (481) Andromache turns to a word which twice (δυσ- and α-) expresses the idea of unhappiness; see 428n.

485–6 οὔτε σὺ τούτωι ... οὔτε σοὶ οὗτος: Andromache's οὗτος (cf. also 488) is anaphorical, referring to πάϊς in the previous line, rather than deictic. The child clearly does not accompany her this time, as he did in book 6 and perhaps will do again in book 24 (see 24.732–3, where she either addresses or apostrophises Astyanax). ὄνειαρ: see 432–4n. An idea of the mutual benefit of father and son is given by Telemachus and Odysseus in the *Odyssey*, who fight together against the suitors (and note the simile of birds weeping over their lost brood inserted at the moment of their reunion, suggesting they 'deplore the years of separation, during which Telemachus grew up virtually an orphan, and Odysseus was deprived of the joy of seeing his child grow up': de Jong on 16.216–19). A son will take care of his father (and mother) when he is old; cf. 17.301–2; 24.540–1. Later inscriptions will regularly refer to the ὄνησις τέκνων, 'benefit of their children' which people may have (e.g. *Tituli Asiae Minoris* V, 2 1148).

487–506 Andromache's picture of life as an orphan starts with Astyanax (487–9), merges into an omnitemporal picture of 'a child' (490–9, note the gnomic aorists ἐπέσχεν, δίηνεν, ἐστυφέλιξεν; epic τε (L 21) at 492, 495; the iterative optatives ἕλοι, παύσαιτο; iterative εὕδεσκ'; and the circumlocutions παῖδα, πάϊς, πατρός, πατήρ, μητέρα), and returns at the end to Astyanax (500–6). Critics have excised 487–99 (or even 487–505/507): the destitution described here would be unlikely to befall a royal prince like Astyanax while Priam or Hector's brothers are still alive, and the general nature of the description and abundance of *hapax legomena* (ἀπουρήσουσιν, παναφήλικα, ὑπεμνήμυκε, ἀμφιθαλής) are suspect; see A-scholia (Aristarchus), Leaf, and Ameis-Hentze. However, why would Andromache, overwhelmed by grief, not exaggerate and jump ahead to a situation where Astyanax, like the near-orphan Telemachus, would have to defend his property against rivals (such as, possibly, Aeneas: cf. 13.459–61; 20.178–83, 302–8) and be excluded from dinner with the leaders? Also, Homeric speakers do turn to generalising descriptions (cf. e.g. 1.80–3), and *hapax legomena* do occur in clusters, often in connection with aspects of everyday life (cf. 468–72n. and see Richardson (1987) 180–2).

487 ἤν περ γὰρ πόλεμόν γε φύγηι 'for even if he will escape at least from, i.e. survive, the war with the Greeks'. The particle περ turns the clause into a concessive conditional; see Wakker (1994) 315–19. πόλεμόν... πολύδακρυν: π(τ)όλεμος has 18 different epithets, which all stress its negative (destructive, grievous) nature; see de Jong (2004) 231–3.

488 τοι: 'ethic' dative.

489 'for others shall take away his fields'. οἱ: personal pronoun (L 19), used as possessive dative (L 22). ἀπουρήσουσιν: this verb occurs only here in extant Greek literature. It is to be connected with ἀπηύρα, ἀπούρας. Aristarchus read ἀπουρίσσουσιν, which should be connected with οὖρος, 'boundary', and hence mean something like 'remove the boundaries', i.e., 'appropriate' (for the presence of boundaries in fields see the simile at 12.421–4, where we hear about two men quarrelling over them). The wealth of Homeric princes consists among other things of estates (called *klēros* or *temenos*) with farms, arable land (ἀρούρας), gardens, and herds. This wealth is never secure: the prolonged absence of the owner and/or the youth of his successor may incite others to try to get hold of it. Thus Sarpedon anxiously refers to his 'many possessions, coveted by those who are in need' that he left behind in Lycia (5.478–81), and the suitors literally consume Telemachus' herds, so as to diminish his wealth and hence weaken his claim to royal status (*Od.* 2.55–9 and *passim*).

490 ἦμαρ... ὀρφανικόν: for this expressive type of periphrasis see 212n. παναφήλικα παῖδα τίθησιν 'makes a child entirely cut off from his contemporaries'. παναφήλικα occurs only here in Greek literature; for the intensive force of παν- cf. πανάποτμος, πανύστατος, πανδαμάτωρ. What Andromache is referring to is Astyanax's exclusion from the peer group of the *kouroi* to which he would normally (soon) belong; see 391n.

491 πάντα δ' ὑπεμνήμυκε 'he is downcast in everything/utterly'. The compound ὑπεμνήμυκε is another word that occurs only here in Greek literature. Its form was puzzling even to the scholiasts. It is most probably a perfect form of ὑπ-ημύω with a kind of Attic reduplication (ημ is repeated in εμ) and a *nu* being added *metri causa*. The simplex ἡμύω refers to bowing down one's head; e.g. 8.308; 19.405. δεδάκρυνται 'are covered with tears'.

492–9 In a passage marked off by ring-composition (δέ τ' ἄνεισι πάϊς ἐς: 492, 499), Andromache now turns to the exclusion of a young orphan from the dinners which Homeric princes regularly hold and which are a sign of their status (cf. 12.310–12) as well as an important means to forge social bonds (cf. *hetairous* at 492). Cf. Anticlea's (outdated) report on Telemachus to Odysseus in the underworld: he 'quietly enjoys your/his *temenea* and takes his share in the meals which are proper for a law-giving man, and all invite him' (*Od.* 11.184–7); see van Wees (1992) 44–8.

492 δευόμενος 'lacking', sc. (princely) food and drink. This verb is often used in connection with food; cf. e.g. 1.468 (οὐδέ τι θυμὸς ἐδεύετο δαιτὸς ἐΐσης). ἄνεισι... ἐς: the force of ἀν- here is not entirely clear. It seems best to take it as 'go up to', i.e. 'approach', but there are no parallels. At 499 the verb means 'return'; cf. e.g. *Od.* 1.259; 5.282; 8.568 (the verb there, however, is combined with ἐξ).

493 χλαίνης ἐρύων... χιτῶνος: for the gesture of pulling at someone's clothing so as to attract attention cf. the little girl in Achilles' simile, who εἰανοῦ ἁπτομένη wants to be picked up by her mother (16.9).

494 Homeric heroes normally drink out of a δέπας. Here both the κοτύλην, a small cup (at *Od.* 15.312; 17.12 the drinking cup of a beggar), and τυτθόν, 'for a little while', suggest that they give the orphan only very little to drink. This idea is worked out in the next line. τῶν δ᾽ ἐλεησάντων... τις: τῶν is an anaphoric pronoun (L 17) to which a participle is added, 'one of them, taking pity'.

495 ἐδίην᾽... οὐκ ἐδίηνεν: the repetition intensifies the picture of the boy only wetting his lips but not really quenching his thirst, a symbol of his not being fully accepted. ὑπερῷην 'palate'; this word occurs only here in poetry.

496 'but him a boy with both parents alive may also shove away (through a violent gesture) from the meal'. καί: adverbial. ἀμφιθαλής: a Homeric *hapax legomenon*. The status of the anonymous contemporary is carefully chosen so as to reinforce the contrast with Astyanax, who only has one parent. ἐκ δαιτύος ἐστυφέλιξεν: cf. 1.581; *Od.* 17.234. Here the violent gesture implied in στυφελίζω is specified in the ensuing χερσὶν πεπληγώς.

497 ὀνειδείοισιν: the adjective is used as substantive only here; the usual expression is ὀνειδείοις ἐπέεσσιν. Whereas the men have pity, the young boy's contemporary 'reproaches' him for wanting to take part in the meal to which he is not entitled since his father is not one of the diners.

498 When Homeric characters tell a story they may include direct speeches, often to make a crucial point or climax clear. When the embedded story is short, the quoted speech will be short, too: one line or half a line (e.g. 6.479; 8.149; 22.107). This device is taken over by many later authors, e.g. Pindar or the messenger in Attic drama. ἔρρ᾽ οὕτως 'get lost'. According to the scholia, this expression is coarse and colloquial. With one exception the verb only occurs in speech (13 x) and is frequently accompanied by terms of abuse (cf. e.g. 24.239: ἔρρετε, λωβητῆρες ἐλεγχέες). οὕτως is deictic, 'thus', accompanying the gesture of shoving away (Ameis-Hentze); cf. e.g. κεῖσ᾽ οὕτως (21.184), spoken by Achilles after he has jumped on the body of his defeated opponent.

499 ἄνεισι... ἐς: see 492n.

500–4 Andromache recalls Astyanax's protected childhood, which now irrevocably belongs to the past. The Homeric epics feature a number of such childhood vignettes: young Achilles sitting on the lap of Phoenix and soiling his chiton with wine (9.485–91), a little girl (in a simile) pulling at her mother's dress and crying until she is picked up (16.7–10), and Eurymachus sitting on the lap of Odysseus (*Od.* 16.442–4). All details of this vignette are aimed at evoking shelteredness, warmth, and affluence, so as to point out the contrast with the coldness and frugality of Astyanax's new life as an orphan: he sits on the knees of *his own* father, eats *marrow* and the *rich* fat of sheep, and, after he finishes *playing*, sleeps under *soft* covers, *in the arms* of his nurse, filled with *sumptuous food*.

500 πρίν: for this type of nostalgia see 156n. ἑοῦ: the possessive pronoun has expressive value; see 401–4n.

501 μυελόν: in many cultures, bone marrow is considered food or even a delicacy (think of Italian osso buco). The Homeric Greeks apparently already knew it was a source of energy because they figuratively called barley, which was taken on board ships as victuals, 'the marrow of men' (*Od.* 2.290).

502 νηπιαχεύων: the verb occurs only once more, in a late epitaph, but cf. νηπίαχος (3 x *Il.*, once of Astyanax: 6.408).

503–4 ἐν λέκτροισιν, ἐν ἀγκαλίδεσσι τιθήνης, | εὐνῆι ἔνι μαλακῆι: the repetition of ἐν clauses is expressive; cf. e.g. ἡμετέρωι ἐνὶ οἴκωι, ἐν Ἄργεϊ, τηλόθι πάτρης (1.30). The plural ἀγκαλίδες occurs only once more (18.555). The scholia suggest that it is a diminutive, which would suit the children of 18.555, and here, in connection with the nurse, might be expressive of Andromache's emotional and affective tone. We had met Astyanax's nurse at 6.399–400 and 467–8, where she was carrying him at her breast. θαλέων ἐμπλησάμενος κῆρ: neuter plural of the adjective θάλυς, used as a substantive, 'sumptuous things', i.e. the marrow and sheepsfat; cf. the scholia's τροφῶν καὶ ἐδεσμάτων. For filling one's heart with food cf. πλησάμενος... θυμὸν ἐδητύος ἠδὲ ποτῆτος (*Od.* 17.603). Others take θαλέων metaphorically ('good cheer'), but there are no parallels in Homer. There is no compelling reason to take the formulaic δαῖτα θάλειαν (7.475; *Od.* 3.420; 8.76, 99) as a 'cheerful' rather than a 'sumptuous banquet'.

505 ἄν... πάθησι 'he will suffer'; in Homer the futural subjunctive is also found in main clauses (119n.) πάθησι is a thematic subjunctive with an athematic ending (L 13). ἀπό... ἁμαρτών: tmesis (L 20). The verb ἁμαρτάνω means 'to miss' a target (cf. 279, 290); it is used only here and at 6.411 (again in the context of Andromache talking about Hector's death) of a person losing a loving one.

506–7 Cf. 6.402–3, where the narrator had given us more or less the same information. Ἀστυάναξ: the scholia point out the pathetic effect of the repetition of the name so soon after 500, especially since it recalls Hector and his role as protector of the city. ἐπίκλησιν καλέουσιν: cf. 29n.; the boy's real name is Σκαμάνδριος (6.402). For the phenomenon of double names in Homer see 115n. οἶος: see 455–6n. The idea that Hector is the 'sole' (= most important) protector of Troy is also voiced at 6.403 (narrator); 24.499 (Priam), 729–30 (Andromache); and implied at 12.10–11; 22.56–7, 382–4, 410–11; 24.728–30, where the question of his being alive or dead is directly related to Troy being saved or destroyed. σφιν: dative of interest.

The name Astyanax, 'chief of the city', is etymologised; for this widespread phenomenon in Homer see Higbie (1994) and Louden (1995). As often, a son is named after his father; cf. Telemachus ('far-fighter', with reference to Odysseus as archer). Neither Hector, whom Andromache addresses, nor (at this stage) the narratees need this explanation, and it sounds more like a mantra.

508–11 For the third time in her speech Andromache turns from the happy past to the miserable present (νῦν δέ). Unwittingly – but noticeably for the narratees – she echoes words that her mother-in-law Hecuba had spoken earlier: παρὰ νηυσὶ... νόσφι τοκήων... ἔδονται ≈ ἄνευθε... νῶϊν... παρὰ νηυσί... κατέδονται (88–9). With 'far away from your parents' Andromache voices a combination of the motifs of 'bereaved parents' (44–5n.) and 'death far away' (445–6n.). She also brings up the theme of the 'mutilation of Hector's corpse' again; see 337–54n. Whereas Hecuba talked about dogs devouring Hector's body, Andromache mentions both dogs and worms here. Achilles likewise had foreseen that worms would eat Patroclus' corpse (19.23–7). In both cases gods actually protect the corpses from dogs, worms, and flies (Patroclus: 19.29–31; 23.184–6; Hector: 24.414–15).

509 αἰόλαι εὐλαί 'wriggling worms', a unique combination, which, as Richardson suggests, being entirely composed of vowels and liquids is 'horribly appropriate'. More generally we may note that Andromache turns to an emphatic style of speech with many epithets as she reaches the finale of her lament; cf. τείχεα μακρά, νηυσὶ κορωνίσι, πυρὶ κηλέωι. ἔδονται: see 89n.

510 γυμνόν: warriors lacking (pieces of) armour are called 'naked' (e.g. 124; 17.711), and Hector was indeed stripped of his armour (cf. 368–9). However, Andromache is referring here to his not being covered by the clothes (shroud) in which corpses normally are dressed when they are laid out and cremated (cf. 18.352–3 and 24.588). κέονται: the athematic verb κεῖσθαι both has regular κείαται (24.527) and κέονται (with disappearance of iota between vowels and thematic ending).

511 Andromache lingers on the qualities of the fine and lovely clothes that should have covered the corpse of Hector. Although she speaks of them in general terms as 'made by the hands of women', the recent image of Andromache weaving (440–1) suggests that they are the work of *her* hands; cf. Penelope weaving a shroud for Laertes (*Od.* 2.94–102).

512–14 Andromache intends the burning of the clothes to be a kind of substitute funeral rite: lacking a body and thus the ability to arrange a proper cremation, she will burn Hector's clothes instead in order to honour him all the same. Griffin (1980) 2 suggests that the act also signals the end of her marriage and happiness: 'the garments which were the embodiment of her love have lost their meaning and can go into the fire'. Her words contribute to the misdirection around the treatment of Hector's body: we are still led to believe that it will not be given back and that he will never receive a fitting burial; see 337–54n.

512 ἤτοι: see 279–82n. πυρὶ κηλέωι 'in burning fire'; see 374n.

513–14 '(an act which is) no benefit to you (*apposition*), since you will not lie in them, but in order for there to be *kleos* (for you) on the part of the Trojan men and women (*final-consecutive infinitive*)'. κλέος: see 304–5n. His *kleos* had been uppermost in Hector's mind in the last moments of his life (see 110 and 304–5).

515 See 429n.

BIBLIOGRAPHY

Alden, M. 2000. *Homer Beside Himself. Para-Narratives in the Iliad*, Oxford

Alexiou, M. 1974. *The Ritual Lament in Greek Tradition*, Cambridge

Allan, R. 2003. *The Middle Voice in Ancient Greek. A Study of Polysemy*, Amsterdam

2010. 'The *infinitivus pro imperativo* in Ancient Greek. The Imperatival Infinitive as an Expression of Proper Procedural Action', *Mnemosyne* 63: 203–28

Allan, W. 2006. 'Divine Justice and Cosmic Order in Early Greek Epic', *Journal of Hellenic Studies* 126: 1–35

Amory Parry, A. 1973. *Blameless Aegisthus. A Study of AMYMⲰN and Other Homeric Epithets*, Leiden

Anderson, M. J. 1997. *The Fall of Troy in Early Greek Poetry and Art*, Oxford

Austin, J. N. H. 1975. *Archery at the Dark of the Moon. Poetic Problems in Homer's Odyssey*, Berkeley, Los Angeles, London

Bakker, E. J. 1988. *Linguistics and Formulas in Homer: Scalarity and the Description of the Particle* Per, Amsterdam

1997. *Poetry in Speech. Orality and Homeric Discourse*, Ithaca, NY, London

Bakker, E. J., Kahane, A. eds. 1997. *Written Voices, Spoken Signs: Tradition, Performance, and the Epic Text*, Cambridge, Mass.

Bannert, H. 1984. 'Die Lanze des Patroklos', *Wiener Studien* 97: 27–35

1988. *Formen des Wiederholens bei Homer*, Vienna

Bassett, S. E. 1921. 'The Function of the Homeric Simile', *Transactions and Proceedings of the American Philological Association* 52: 132–47

1923. 'Hector's Fault in Honor', *Transactions and Proceedings of the American Philological Association* 54: 117–27

1934a. 'The Ἁμαρτία of Achilles', *Transactions and Proceedings of the American Philological Association* 65: 47–69

1934b. 'The Omission of the Vocative in Homeric Speeches', *American Journal of Philology* 55: 140–52

1938. *The Poetry of Homer*, Berkeley

Biraud, M. 1990. 'Conceptions dynamiques de la totalité et de la restriction dans la langue Homérique. Étude semantique des couples de lexèmes ΟΥΛΟΣ et ΠΑΣ, ΟΙΟΣ et ΜΟΥΝΟΣ', in J. Granarolo, ed. *Hommage à René Braun I. De la préhistoire à Virgile: Philologie, littératures et histoires anciennes* (Paris, Nice) 83–94

Boedeker, D. 1974. *Aphrodite's Entry into Greek Epic*, Leiden

Bowra, C. M. 1930. *Tradition and Design in the Iliad*, Oxford

1952. *Heroic Poetry*, London

Bremer, J. M. 1987. 'The So-Called "Götterapparat" in Homer', in Bremer, de Jong, Kalff 1987: 31–46

Bremer, J. M., de Jong, I. J. F., Kalff, J. eds. 1987. *Homer: Beyond Oral Poetry. Recent Trends in Homeric Interpretation*, Amsterdam

Burgess, J. S. 2001. *The Tradition of the Trojan War in Homer and the Epic Cycle*, Baltimore

2009. *The Death and Afterlife of Achilles*, Baltimore

Burkert, W. 1985. *Greek Religion: Archaic and Classical*, transl. J. Raffan, Cambridge, Mass. (German original 1977)

1992. *The Orientalizing Revolution: Near Eastern Influence on Greek Culture in the Early Archaic Age*, Cambridge, Mass. (German original 1984)

Burnett, A. P. 1991. 'Signals from the Unconscious in Early Greek Poetry', *Classical Philology* 86: 275–300

Cairns, D. L. 1993. *Aidos. The Psychology and Ethics of Honour and Shame in Ancient Greek Literature*, Oxford

2003. 'Ethics, Ethology, Terminology: Iliadic Anger and the Cross-Cultural Study of Emotion', in G. W. Most, S. Braund, eds. *Ancient Anger. Perspectives from Homer to Galen* (Cambridge) 11–49

Clarke, M. J. 1995. 'Between Lions and Men. Images of the Hero in the *Iliad*', *Greek, Roman, and Byzantine Studies* 36: 137–59

1997. 'Gods and Mountains in Greek Myth and Poetry', in A.B. Lloyd, ed. *What Is a God? Studies in the Nature of Greek Divinity* (London) 65–80

1999. *Flesh and Spirit in the Songs of Homer. A Study of Words and Myths*, Oxford

Clarke, W. M. 1978. 'Achilles and Patroclus in Love', *Hermes* 106: 381–96

Clay, J. S. 1974. '*Demas* and *aude*. The Nature of Divine Transformation in Homer', *Hermes* 102: 129–36

Coffey, M. 1957. 'The Function of the Homeric Simile', *American Journal of Philology* 78: 113–132

Combellack, F. M. 1959. 'Milman Parry and Homeric Artistry', *Comparative Literature* 11: 193–208

Crielaard, J. P., ed. 1995. *Homeric Questions*, Amsterdam

Crielaard, J. P. 1995. 'Homer, History, and Archaeology: Some Remarks on the Date of the Homeric World', in Crielaard 1995: 201–88

Crotty, K. 1994. *The Poetics of Supplication: Homer's Iliad and Odyssey*, Ithaca, NY, London

Crouwel, J. H. 1981. *Chariots and Other Means of Land Transport in Bronze Age Greece.* Amsterdam

Dalby, A. 1998. '"Homer's Enemies". Lyric and Epic in the Seventh Century', in N. Fisher, H. van Wees, eds. *Archaic Greece. New Approaches and New Evidence* (London) 195–212

Danek, G. 1998. *Epos und Zitat. Studien zu den Quellen der Odyssee*, Vienna

2006. 'Die Gleichnisse der Ilias und der Dichter Homer', in F. Montanari, A. Rengakos, eds. *La poésie épique grecque: métamorphoses d'un genre littéraire* (Geneva) 41–71

Darcus Sullivan, S. 1995. *Psychological and Ethical Ideas: What Early Greeks Say*, Leiden

Dee, J. H. 2000. *Epitheta Hominum apud Homerum*, Hildesheim, Zurich, New York
　　2001. *Epitheta Deorum apud Homerum*, 2nd edn, Hildesheim, Zurich, New York
　　2002. *Epitheta Rerum et Locorum apud Homerum*, Hildesheim, Zurich, New York

Derderian, K. 2001. *Leaving Words to Remember. Greek Mourning and the Advent of Literacy*, Leiden

Dodds, E. R. 1951. *The Greeks and the Irrational*, Berkeley, Los Angeles, London
　　1954. 'Homer', in M. Platnauer, ed. *Fifty Years of Classical Scholarship* (Oxford) 1–7, 31–5

Dover, K. J. 1978. *Greek Homosexuality*, London

Duckworth, G. E. 1933. *Foreshadowing and Suspense in the Epics of Homer, Apollonius, and Vergil*, Princeton

Easterling, P. E. 1991. 'Men's *kleos* and Women's *goos*: Female Voices in the *Iliad*', *Journal of Modern Greek Studies* 9: 145–51

Eberhard, E. E. 1923. *Das Schicksal als poetische Idee bei Homer*, Paderborn

Edmunds, S. T. 1990. *Homeric Nēpios*, New York, London

Edwards, M. W. 1970. 'Homeric Speech Introductions', *Harvard Studies in Classical Philology* 74: 1–36
　　1980. 'Convention and Individuality in *Iliad* 1', *Harvard Studies in Classical Philology* 84: 1–28
　　1987. *Homer. Poet of the Iliad*, Baltimore, London
　　2002. *Sound, Sense, and Rhythm. Listening to Greek and Latin Poetry*, Princeton, Oxford

Effe, B. 1988. 'Der Homerische Achilleus. Zur gesellschaftlichen Funktion eines literarischen Helden', *Gymnasium* 95: 1–16

Eide, T. 1986. 'Poetical and Metrical Value of Homeric Epithets', *Symbolae Osloenses* 3: 5–18

Elliger, W. 1975. *Die Darstellung der Landschaft in der griechischen Dichtung*, Berlin

Erbse, H. 1978. 'Hektor in der Ilias', in H. G. Beck, A. Kambylis, P. Moraux, eds. *Kyklos. Griechisch und Byzantinisches. Festschrift Keydell* (Berlin, New York) 1–19
　　1986. *Untersuchungen zur Funktion der Götter im homerischen Epos*, Berlin, New York
　　2001. 'Achilleus' Erziehung', *Rheinisches Museum* 144: 240–50

van Erp Taalman Kip, A. M. 2000. 'The Gods of the *Iliad* and the Fate of Troy', *Mnemosyne* 53: 385–402
　　2011. 'On Defining a Homeric Idiom', *Mnemosyne*: forthcoming

Farron, S. 1978. 'The Character of Hector in the *Iliad*', *Acta Classica* 21: 39–57

Faust, M. 1970. 'Die künstlerische Verwendung von κύων "Hund" in den homerischen Epen', *Glotta* 48: 8–31

Feeney, D. 1991. *The Gods in Epic. Poets and Critics of the Classical Tradition*, Oxford, New York

Fehling, D. 1969. *Die Wiederholungsfiguren und ihr Gebrauch bei den Griechen vor Gorgias*, Berlin

Fenik, B. 1968. *Typical Battle Scenes in the Iliad: Studies in the Narrative Techniques of Homeric Battle Description*, Wiesbaden

1978. *Homer: Tradition and Invention*, Leiden

Finkelberg, M. 1990. 'A Creative Oral Poet and the Muse', *American Journal of Philology* 111: 293–303

Floyd, E. D. 1969. 'The Singular Uses of ἡμέτερος and ἡμεῖς in Homer', *Glotta* 47: 116–37

Ford, A. 1992. *Homer. The Poetry of the Past*, Ithaca, NY, London

Forssman, B. 2006. 'Epischer und chorischer Literaturdialekt: das Verbum ἐφέπω', *Incontri linguistici* 29: 111–17

Fournier, H. 1946. *Les verbes "dire" en grec ancien*, Paris

Fowler, R. 1987. *The Nature of Early Greek Lyric: Three Preliminary Studies*, Toronto

2004. 'The Homeric Question', in Fowler 2004: 220–32

Fowler, R., ed. 2004. *The Cambridge Companion to Homer*, Cambridge

Fränkel, H. 1921. *Die homerischen Gleichnisse*, Göttingen

Friedrich, P., Redfield, J. 1978. 'Speech as a Personality Symbol: the Case of Achilles', *Language* 54: 263–88

Friedrich, R. 2000. 'Homeric Enjambement and Orality', *Hermes* 128: 1–19

Friedrich, W. H. 2003. *Wounding and Death in the Iliad. Homeric Techniques of Description*, transl. P. Jones, G. Wright, London (German original 1956)

Führer, R., Schmidt, M. 2001. 'Homerus redivivus: Homerus Ilias, ed. Martin L. West', *Göttingische Gelehrten Anzeigen* 253: 1–32

Garner, R. 1990. *From Homer to Tragedy: The Art of Allusion in Greek Poetry*, London, New York

Garvie, A. F. 1994. *Homer, Odyssey Books VI-VIII*, Cambridge

Gaskin, R. 1990. 'Do Homeric Heroes Make Real Decisions?', *Classical Quarterly* 40: 1–15

Gates, P. 1971. *The Kinship Terminology of Homeric Greek*, Baltimore

Gill, C. 1996. *Personality in Greek Epic, Tragedy, and Philosophy: the Self in Dialogue*, New York

Goldhill, S. 1991. *The Poet's Voice. Essays on Poetics and Greek Literature*, Cambridge

Gould, J. 1973. 'Hiketeia', *Journal of Hellenic Studies* 93: 74–103

Grafton, A., Most, G. W., Zetzel, J. E. G. 1985. *F. A. Wolf: Prolegomena to Homer, 1795*. Translated with Introduction and Notes, Princeton

Graziosi, B. 2002. *Inventing Homer. The Early Reception of Epic*, Cambridge

Graziosi, B., Haubold, J. 2003. 'Homeric Masculinity: ΗΝΟΡΕΗ and ΑΓΗ-ΝΟΡΙΗ', *Journal of Hellenic Studies* 123: 61–76

Grethlein, J. 2006. *Das Geschichtsbild der Ilias. Eine Untersuchung aus phänomenologischer und narratologischer Perspektive*, Göttingen

2007. 'The Poetics of the Bath in the *Iliad*', *Harvard Studies in Classical Philology* 103: 25–50

2008. 'Memory and Material Objects in the *Iliad* and the *Odyssey*', *Journal of Hellenic Studies* 128: 27–51

Griffin, J. 1980. *Homer on Life and Death*, Oxford

　1986. 'Homeric Words and Speakers', *Journal of Hellenic Studies* 106: 36–57

　1987. 'Homer and Excess', in Bremer, de Jong, Kalff 1987: 85–104

　1990. 'Achilles kills Hector', *Lampas* 23: 353–69

Hall, E. 1989. *Inventing the Barbarian. Greek Self-Definition through Tragedy*, Oxford

Harris, W. 2009. *Dreams and Experience in Classical Antiquity*, Cambridge, Mass.,
　London

Haslam, M. 1997. 'Homeric Papyri and the Transmission of the Text', in Morris,
　Powell 1997: 55–100

Haubold, J. 2000. *Homer's People: Epic Poetry and Social Formation*, Cambridge

　2002. 'Greek Epic: a Near Eastern Genre?', *Proceedings of the Cambridge Philological
　Society* 48: 1–32

Heath, J. 2005. *The Talking Greeks: Speech, Animals, and the Other in Homer, Aeschylus,
　and Plato*, Cambridge

Hellmann, O. 2000. *Die Schlachtszenen der Ilias. Das Bild des Dichters vom Kampf der
　Heroenzeit*, Stuttgart

Hershkowitz, D. 1998. *The Madness of Epic. Reading Insanity from Homer to Statius*,
　Oxford

Heubeck, A. 1974. *Die Homerische Frage*, Darmstadt

　1987. 'Ἀμύμων', *Glotta* 65: 37–44

Higbie, C. 1990. *Measure and Music. Enjambement and Sentence Structure in the Iliad*,
　Oxford

　1994. *Heroes' Names, Homeric Identities*, London

Holoka, J. 1983. 'Looking Darkly (ΥΠΟΔΡΑ ΙΔⲰΝ): Reflections on Status and
　Decorum in the *Iliad*', *Transactions and Proceedings of the American Philological
　Association* 113: 1–16

Holst-Warhaft, G. 1992. *Dangerous Voices. Women's Lament and Greek Literature*,
　London

Horrocks, G. C. 1997. 'Homer's Dialect', in Morris, Powell 1997: 193–217

Jahn, T. 1987. *Zum Wortfeld 'Seele-Geist' in der Sprache Homers*, Munich

Janko, R. 1981. 'Equivalent Formulae in the Greek Epos', *Mnemosyne* 34: 251–64

　1982. *Homer, Hesiod, and the Hymns. Diachronic Development in Epic Diction*,
　Cambridge

　1998. 'The Homeric Epics as Oral Dictated Texts', *Classical Quarterly* 48: 1–13

Jensen, M. S. 1980. *The Homeric Question and the Oral-Formulaic Theory*, Copenhagen

Jensen, M. S., ed. 1999. 'Dividing Homer: When and How Were the Iliad and
　the Odyssey Divided into Songs?', *Symbolae Osloenses* 74: 5–91

Jones, P. V. 1996. 'The Independent Heroes of the *Iliad*', *Journal of Hellenic Studies*
　116: 108–18

de Jong, I. J. F. 1987a. 'Paris/Alexandros in the *Iliad*', *Mnemosyne* 40: 124–8

　1987b. 'The Voice of Anonymity: Tis-Speeches in the *Iliad*', *Eranos* 85: 69–84

　1988. 'Homeric Words and Speakers: an Addendum', *Journal of Hellenic Studies*
　108: 188–9

1992. 'The Subjective Style in Odysseus' Wanderings', *Classical Quarterly* 42: 1–11

1993. 'Studies in Homeric Denomination', *Mnemosyne* 46: 289–306

1998. 'Homeric Epithet and Narrative Situation', in M. Païsi-Apostolopoulou, ed. *Homerica. Proceedings of the 8th International Symposium on the Odyssey (1–5 September 1996)* (Ithaca) 121–35

2001. *A Narratological Commentary on the Odyssey*. Cambridge

2004. *Narrators and Focalizers. The Presentation of the Story in the Iliad*, 2nd edn, London (1st edn 1987)

2005. 'Convention Versus Realism in the Homeric Epics', *Mnemosyne* 58: 1–22

2006. 'The Homeric Narrator and His Own *kleos*', *Mnemosyne* 59: 188–207

2007. 'Homer', in de Jong, I. J. F., Nünlist, R., eds. *Time in Ancient Greek Literature*. Studies in Ancient Greek Narrative 2 (Leiden) 17–37

2009. '"Many tales go of that city's fall." Het thema van de val van Troje in de *Ilias*', *Lampas* 42: 279–98

de Jong, I. J. F., Nünlist, R. 2004. 'From Bird's Eye View to Close Up: the Standpoint of the Narrator in the Homeric Epics', in A. Bierl, A. Schmidt, A. Willi, eds. *Antike Literatur in neuer Deutung* (Leipzig) 63–83

Käppel, L. 1992. *Paian. Studien zur Geschichte einer Gattung*, Berlin, New York

Kahane, A. 1997. 'Hexameter Progression and the Homeric Hero's Solitary State', in Bakker, Kahane 1997: 110–37

Kakridis, P. J. 1961. 'Achilleus' Rüstung', *Hermes* 89: 288–97

Kearns, E. 2004. 'The Gods in the Homeric Epics', in Fowler 2004: 59–73

Kim, J. 2000. *The Pity of Achilles. Oral Style and the Unity of the Iliad*, Lanham

King, K. C. 1987. *Achilles. Paradigms of the War Hero from Homer to the Middle Ages*. Berkeley, London

Kirk, G. S. 1962. *The Songs of Homer*, Cambridge

Konstan, D. 2001. *Pity Transformed*, London

Kullmann, W. 1956. *Das Wirken der Götter in der Ilias. Untersuchungen zur Frage der Entstehung des homerischen 'Götterapparats'*, Berlin

1984. 'Oral Poetry Theory and Neoanalysis in Homeric Research', *Greek, Roman, and Byzantine Studies* 25: 307–23

Kurt, C. 1979. *Seemannische Fachausdrücke bei Homer, unter Berücksichtigung Hesiods und der Lyriker bis Bakchylides*, Göttingen

Kyriakou, P. 2001. 'Warrior Vaunts in the *Iliad*', *Rheinisches Museum* 144: 250–77

Lang, M. 1989. 'Unreal Conditions in Homeric Narrative', *Greek, Roman, and Byzantine Studies* 30: 5–26

Lardinois, A. M. P. H. 1997. 'Modern Paroemiology and the Use of Gnomai in Homer's *Iliad*', *Classical Philology* 92: 213–34

Latacz, J. 1965. 'ΑΝΔΡΟΤΗΤΑ', *Glotta* 43: 62–76

1966. *Zum Wortfeld 'Freude' in der Sprache Homers*, Heidelberg

1968. 'ἄπτερος μῦθος – ἄπτερος φάτις: ungeflügelte Worte?', *Glotta* 46: 27–47

1977. *Kampfparänese, Kampfdarstellung und Kampfwirklichkeit in der Ilias, bei Kallinos und Tyrtaios*, Munich

1995. *Achilleus. Wandlungen eines europäischen Heldenbildes*, Stuttgart

1996. *Homer. His Art and His World*, transl. J. Holoka, Ann Arbor (German original 1989)

2003. *Troy and Homer. Towards a Solution of an Old Mystery*, transl. K. Windle, R. Ireland, Oxford (German original 2001)

Lateiner, D. 1995. *Sardonic Smile. Nonverbal Behavior in Homeric Epic*, Ann Arbor

Lebessi, A. 1992. 'Zum Phalos des homerischen Helms', *Mitteilungen des Deutschen Archäologischen Instituts, Athenische Abteilung* 107: 1–10

Lee, D. J. N. 1964. *The Similes of the Iliad and the Odyssey Compared*, Melbourne

Leinieks, V. 1973. 'A Structural Pattern in the *Iliad*', *Classical Journal* 69: 102–7

Lesky, A. 1961. *Göttliche und menschliche Motivation im homerischen Epos*, Heidelberg

Létoublon, F. 1983. 'Défi et combat dans l'Iliade', *Revue des Études Grecques* 96: 27–48

Lilja, S. 1976. *Dogs in Ancient Greek Poetry*, Helsinki

Llewellyn-Jones, L. 2003. *Aphrodite's Tortoise. The Veiled Woman of Ancient Greece*, London

Lloyd, M. 1989. 'Paris/Alexandros in Homer and Euripides', *Mnemosyne* 42: 76–9

Lohmann, D. 1970. *Die Komposition der Reden in der Ilias*, Berlin

1988. *Die Andromache-Szenen in der Ilias. Ansätze und Methoden der Homer-Interpretation*, Hildesheim, Zurich, New York

Lonsdale, S. H. 1990. *Creatures of Speech. Lion, Herding, and Hunting Similes*, Stuttgart

Lord, A. B. 1960. *The Singer of Tales*, Cambridge, Mass.

1995. *The Singer Resumes the Tale*, Ithaca, NY, London

Lorimer, H. L. 1950. *Homer and the Monuments*, London

Louden, B. 1993. 'Pivotal Contrafactuals in Homeric Epic', *Classical Antiquity* 12, 181–98

1995. 'Categories of Homeric Wordplay', *Transactions and Proceedings of the American Philological Association* 125: 27–46

Luce, J. V. 1998. *Homer's Landscape. Troy and Ithaca Revisited*, New Haven

Maehler, H. 1963. *Die Auffassung des Dichterberufs im frühen Griechentum bis zur Zeit Pindars*, Göttingen

Mannsperger, B. 1993. 'Das dardanische Tor in der Ilias', *Studia Troica* 3: 193–9

Marinatos, S. 1967. *Kleidung*, Archaeologia Homerica A, Göttingen

Martin, R. P. 1989. *The Language of Heroes. Speech and Performance in the Iliad*, Ithaca, NY, London

1997. 'Similes and Performance', in Bakker, Kahane 1997: 138–66

Mastronarde, D. J. 1994, ed. Euripides *Phoenissae*, Cambridge

Metz, W. 1990. 'Hektor als der homerischste aller homerischen Helden', *Gymnasium* 97: 385–404

Van Der Mije, S. R. 1987. 'Achilles' God-Given Strength. *Iliad* A 178 and Gifts from the Gods in Homer', *Mnemosyne* 40: 241–67

2011a. 'Bad Herbs — the Snake Simile in *Iliad* 22', *Mnemosyne* 64: 359–82

2011b. 'πείθειν φρένα(ς), πείθειν θυμόν — A Note on Homeric Psychology', *Mnemosyne* 64: 447–54

Minchin, E. 2001. *Homer and the Resources of Memory. Some Applications of Cognitive Theory to the Iliad and the Odyssey*, Oxford

Monsacré, H. 1984. *Les larmes d'Achille. Le héros, la femme et la souffrance dans la poésie d'Homère*, Paris

Morris, I. 1986. 'The Use and Abuse of Homer', *Classical Antiquity* 5: 81–138

Morris, I., Powell, B. eds. 1997. *A New Companion to Homer*, Leiden

Morris, S. 1997. 'Homer and the Near East', in Morris, Powell 1997: 599–623

Morrison, A. D. 2007. *The Narrator in Archaic Greek and Hellenistic Poetry*, Cambridge

Morrison, J. V. 1991. 'The Function and Context of Homeric Prayers', *Hermes* 119: 145–57

1992. *Homeric Misdirection: False Predictions in the Iliad*, Ann Arbor

1997. 'Kerostasia. The Dictates of Fate and the Will of Zeus in the *Iliad*', *Arethusa* 30: 276–96

1999. 'Homeric Darkness: Patterns and Manipulations of Death Scenes in the *Iliad*', *Hermes* 127: 129–44

Most, G. W. 2003. 'Anger and Pity in the *Iliad*', in G. W. Most, S. Braund, eds. *Ancient Anger. Perspectives from Homer to Galen* (Cambridge) 50–75

Moulton, C. 1974. 'Similes in the *Iliad*', *Hermes* 102: 381–97

1977. *Similes in the Homeric Poems*, Göttingen

Müller, C.W. 1989. 'Der schöne Tod des Polisburgers oder "Ehrenvoll ist es, für das Vaterland zu sterben"', *Gymnasium* 96: 317–40

Mueller, M. 1978. 'Knowledge and Delusion in the *Iliad*', in J. Wright, ed. *Essays on the Iliad* (Bloomington) 105–23 (original from 1970)

1984. *The Iliad*, London

Murnaghan, S. 1992. 'Maternity and Mortality in Homeric Poetry', *Classical Antiquity* 11: 244–64

1999. 'The Poetics of Loss in Greek Epic', in J. Beissinger, J. Tylus, S. Wofford, eds. *Epic Traditions in the Contemporary World. The Poetics of Community* (Berkeley) 202–20

Murray, P. 1981. 'Poetic Inspiration in Early Greece', *Journal of Hellenic Studies* 101: 87–100

Nagler, M. N. 1974. *Spontaneity and Tradition. A Study in the Oral Art of Homer*, Berkeley

Nagy, G. 1996. *Homeric Questions*, Austin

2004. *Homer's Text and Language*, Champaign

Naiden, F. S. 2006. *Ancient Supplication*, Oxford, New York

Nesselrath, H.-G. 1992. *Ungeschehenes Geschehen. 'Beinahe-Episoden' im Griechischen und Römischen Epos*, Stuttgart

Nünlist, R. 1998. 'Der homerische Erzähler und das sogenannte Sukzessionsgesetz', *Museum Helveticum* 55: 2–8

2009. *The Ancient Critic at Work. Terms and Concepts of Literary Criticism in Greek Scholia*, Cambridge

Olson, S. D. 1995. *Blood and Iron. Stories and Storytelling in Homer's Odyssey*, Leiden

O'Nolan, K. 1978. 'Doublets in the *Odyssey*', *Classical Quarterly* 28: 23–37

Osborne, R. 2004. 'Homer's Society', in Fowler 2004: 206–19

Owen, E. T. 1947. *The Story of the Iliad*, New York

Pantelia, M. C. 1993. 'Spinning and Weaving: Ideas of Domestic Order in Homer', *American Journal of Philology* 114: 493–501

Parker, R. 1983. *Miasma. Pollution and Purification in Early Greek Religion*, Oxford

Parry, A., ed. 1971. *The Making of Homeric Verse. The Collected Papers of Milman Parry*, Oxford

Pedrick, V. 1982. 'Supplication in the *Iliad* and the *Odyssey*', *Transactions and Proceedings of the American Philological Association* 112: 125–40

Petersmann, G. 1973. 'Die monologische Totenklage der Ilias', *Rheinisches Museum für die Philologie* 116: 3–16

   1974. 'Die Entscheidungsmonologe in den homerischen Epen', *Gräzer Beiträge* 2: 147–69

Pritchett, W. K. 1991. *The Greek States at War, V*, Berkeley

Race, W. H. 1982. *The Classical Priamel from Homer to Boethius*, Leiden

Redfield, J. M. 1994. *Nature and Culture in the Iliad. The Tragedy of Hector*, 2nd edn, Durham, London (1st edn 1975)

Reece, S. 2005. 'Homer's *Iliad* and *Odyssey*: From Oral Performance to Written Text', in M. C. Amodio, ed., *New Directions in Oral Theory* (Tempe) 43–89

Reichel, M. 1990. 'Retardationstechniken in der *Ilias*', in W. Kullmann, M. Reichel, eds. *Der Übergang von der Mündlichkeit zur Literatur bei den Griechen* (Tübingen) 125–51

   1994. *Fernbeziehungen in der Ilias*, Tübingen

Reinhardt, K. 1961. *Die Ilias und ihr Dichter*, Göttingen

Reinhold, M. 1970. *History of Purple as a Status Symbol in Greece*. Brussels

Renehan, R. 1987. 'The *Heldentod* in Homer: One Heroic Ideal', *Classical Philology* 82: 99–116

Rengakos, A. 1995. 'Zeit und Gleichzeitigkeit in den homerischen Epen', *Antike und Abendland* 41: 1–33

Richardson, N. J. 1987. 'The Individuality of Homer's Language', in Bremer, de Jong, Kalff 1987: 165–84

Richardson, S. 1990. *The Homeric Narrator*, Nashville

Rijksbaron, A. 1997. 'Further Observations on Expressions of Sorrow and Related Expressions in Homer', in E. Banfi, ed. *Atti del secondo incontro internazionale di linguistica Greca* (Trento) 215–42

   2002. *The Syntax and Semantics of the Verb in Classical Greek*, 3rd edn, Amsterdam

   2006. 'The Meaning and Word-Class of πρότερον and τὸ πρότερον' in E. Crespo, J. de la Villa, A. R. Revuelta, eds. *Word Classes and Related Topics in Ancient Greek* (Louvain-la-Neuve) 441–53

Robinson, D. 1990. 'Homeric φίλος: Love of Life and Limbs, and Friendship with one's θυμός', in E. M. Craik, ed. *Owls to Athens. Essays on Classical Subjects Presented to Sir Kenneth Dover* (Oxford) 97–108

de Romilly, J. 1995. *Tragédies grecques au fil des ans*, Paris

1997. *Hector*, Paris

Rosner, J. 1976. 'The Speech of Phoenix. *Iliad* 9.434–605', *Phoenix* 30: 314–27

Ruijgh, C. J. 1971. *Autour de 'τε épique'. Études sur la syntaxe grecque*, Amsterdam

1981. 'L'emploi de HTOI chez Homère et Hésiode', *Mnemosyne* 34: 272–87

1995. 'D'Homère aux origines proto-mycéniennes de la tradition épique. Analyse dialectologique du langue homérique, avec un *excursus* sur la création de l'alphabet grec', in Crielaard 1995: 1–96

Rutherford, I. R. 2001. *Pindar's Paeans. A Reading of the Fragments and a Survey of the Genre*, Oxford

Rutherford, R. B. 1982. 'Tragic Form and Feeling in the *Iliad*', *Journal of Hellenic Studies* 102: 145–60

Sacks, R. 1987. *The Traditional Phrase in Homer: Two Studies in Form, Meaning, and Interpretation*, Leiden

Schadewaldt, W. 1959. *Von Homers Welt und Werk. Aufsätze und Auslegungen zur homerischen Frage*, 3rd edn, Stuttgart (1st edn 1944)

1966. *Iliasstudien*, 3rd edn, Leipzig (1st edn 1938)

1970. 'Hektor in der Ilias', in *Hellas und Hesperien. Gesammelte Schriften zur Antike und zur neueren Literatur* (2nd edn, Zürich-Stuttgart) 21–38 (1st edn 1956)

Schmidt, M. 1976. *Die Erklärungen zum Weltbild Homers und zur Kultur der Heroenzeit in den bT-Scholien zur Ilias*. Munich

Schmitt, A. 1990. *Selbständigkeit und Abhängigkeit menschlichen Handelns bei Homer*, Mainz

Schofield, M. 1986. 'Euboulia in the *Iliad*', *Classical Quarterly* 36: 6–31

Scodel, R. 2002. *Listening to Homer. Tradition, Narrative, and Audience*, Ann Arbor

Scott, W. C. 1974. *The Oral Nature of Homeric Similes*, Leiden

2009. *The Artistry of the Homeric Simile*, Hanover, London

Scully, S. 1990. *Homer and the Sacred City*, Ithaca, NY, London

Seaford, R. 1994. *Reciprocity and Ritual. Homer and Tragedy in the Developing City-State*, Oxford

Segal, C. 1971a. *The Theme of the Mutilation of the Body in the Iliad*, Leiden

1971b. 'Andromache's *Anagnorisis*. Formulaic Artistry in *Iliad* 22.437–476', *Harvard Studies in Classical Philology* 75: 33–57

Shipp, G. P. 1972. *Studies in the Language of Homer*, 2nd edn, Cambridge (1st edn 1953)

Shive, D. 1987. *Naming Achilles*, New York, Oxford

Sicking, C. M. J. 1993. *Griechische Verslehre*, Munich

Silk, M. S. 1983. 'LSJ and the Problem of Poetic Archaism: from Meanings to Iconyms', *Classical Quarterly* 33: 303–30

Slings, S. 2002. 'Oral Strategies and the Language of Herodotus', in E. J. Bakker, I. J. F. de Jong, H. van Wees, eds. *Brill's Companion to Herodotus* (Leiden) 53–78

Smith, W. 1988. 'Disguises of the Gods in the *Iliad*', *Numen* 35: 161–78

Stoevesandt, M. 2004. *Feinde-Gegner-Opfer. Zur Darstellung der Troianer in den Kampfszenen der Ilias*, Basle

Taplin, O. 1977. *The Stagecraft of Aeschylus. The Dramatic Use of Exits and Entrances in Greek Tragedy*, Oxford

   1992. *Homeric Soundings. The Shaping of the Iliad*, Oxford

Thornton, A. 1984. *Homer's Iliad: Its Composition and the Motif of Supplication*, Göttingen

Trachsel, A. 2007. *La Troade: un paysage et son héritage littéraire: les commentaires antiques sur la Troade, leur genèse et leur influence*, Basle

Tsagalis, C. S. 2004. *Epic Grief. Personal Laments in Homer's Iliad*, Berlin, New York

Vernant, J. P. 1991. 'A "Beautiful Death" and the Disfigured Corpse in Homeric Epic', in *Mortals and Immortals* (Princeton) 50–74

Visser, E. 1987. *Homerische Versifikationstechnik. Versuch einer Rekonstruktion*, Frankfurt, Bern, New York

   1988. 'Formulae or Single Words? Towards a New Theory of Homeric Verse-Making', *Würzburger Jahrbücher für die Altertumswissenschaft* 14: 21–37

   1997. *Homers Katalog der Schiffe*, Stuttgart, Leipzig

Vivante, P. 1982. *The Epithets in Homer: a Study in Poetic Value*, Bloomington

Waanders, F. M. J. 1983. *The History of Τέλος and Τελέω in Ancient Greek*, Amsterdam

   2000. 'Πέλομαι: To Be or . . . To Become?', *Živa Antika* 50: 257–72

Wachter, R. 2000. 'Grammatik der homerischen Sprache' in J. Latacz, ed. *Homers Ilias Gesamtkommentar. Prolegomena* (Berlin, New York) 61–108

Wackernagel, J. 1920. *Vorlesungen über Syntax, mit besonderer Berücksichtigung von Griechisch, Lateinisch, und Deutsch*, I, Basle

Wakker, G. C. 1994. *Conditions and Conditionals. An Investigation of Classical Greek*, Amsterdam

   1997a.'Modal Particles and Different Points of View in Herodotus and Thucydides' in E. J. Bakker, ed. *Grammar as Interpretation. Greek Literature in its Linguistic Context* (Leiden) 215–50

   1997b. 'Emphasis and Affirmation. Some Aspects of μήν in Tragedy', in A. Rijksbaron, ed. *New Approaches to Greek Particles* (Amsterdam) 209–31

van Wees, H. 1992. *Status Warriors. War, Violence, and Society in Homer and History*, Amsterdam

   1994. 'The Homeric Way of War: the *Iliad* and the Hoplite Phalanx (II)', *Greece & Rome* 41: 131–55

   1997. 'Homeric Warfare' in Morris, Powell 1997: 668–93

   1998. 'A Brief History of Tears. Gender Differentiation in Archaic Greece', in L. Foxhall, J. Salmon, eds. *When Men Were Men. Masculinity, Power and Identity in Classical Antiquity* (London, New York) 10–53

   2004. *Greek Warfare. Myth and Realities*, London

West, M. L. 1966. *Hesiod, Theogony*, Oxford

1978. *Hesiod, Works and Days*, Oxford

1982. *Greek Metre*, Oxford

1988. 'The Rise of the Greek Epic', *Journal of Hellenic Studies* 108: 151–72

1997. *The East Face of Helicon. West Asiatic Elements in Greek Poetry and Myth*, Oxford

1999. 'The Invention of Homer', *Classical Quarterly* 49: 346–82

2001. *Studies in the Text and Transmission of the Iliad*, Munich

2003. '*Iliad* and *Aethiopis*', *Classical Quarterly* 53: 1–14

2007. *Indo-European Poetry and Myth*, Oxford

Whallon, W. 1969. *Formula, Character, and Context: Studies in Homeric, Old English, and Old Testament Poetry*, Cambridge, Mass.

Whitman, C. H. 1958. *Homer and the Heroic Tradition*, Cambridge, Mass.

Willcock, M. M. 1970. 'Some Aspects of the Gods in the *Iliad*', *Bulletin of the Institute of Classical Studies* 17: 1–10

Williams, B. 1993. *Shame and Necessity*, Berkeley

Wilson, D. F. 2002. *Ransom, Revenge, and Heroic Identity in the Iliad*, Cambridge

Yamagata, N. 1991. 'Phoenix's Speech — Is Achilles Punished?', *Classical Quarterly* 41: 1–15

1994. *Homeric Morality*, Leiden

Zanker, G. 1994. *The Heart of Achilles. Characterization and Personal Ethics in the Iliad*, Michigan

Zarker, J. W. 1965. 'King Eëtion and Thebe as Symbols in the *Iliad*', *Classical Journal* 61: 110–14

INDEXES

I SUBJECTS

References in italics are to pages of the introduction

206

2 GREEK WORDS